D1607386

TWO SUNS OF THE SOUTHWEST

American Presidential Elections

MICHAEL NELSON

JOHN M. MCCARDELL, JR.

TWO SUNS OF THE SOUTHWEST

LYNDON JOHNSON, BARRY
GOLDWATER, AND THE 1964
BATTLE BETWEEN LIBERALISM
AND CONSERVATISM

NANCY BECK YOUNG

UNIVERSITY PRESS OF KANSAS

Published
by the
University
Press of Kansas
(Lawrence,
Kansas 66045),
which was
organized by the
Kansas Board of
Regents and is
operated and
funded by
Emporia State
University,
Fort Hays State
University,
Kansas State
University,
Pittsburg State
University,
the University
of Kansas, and
Wichita State
University

Library of Congress Cataloging-in-Publication Data

Names: Young, Nancy Beck, author.
Title: Two suns of the Southwest : Lyndon Johnson, Barry Goldwater,
and the 1964 battle between liberalism and conservatism / Nancy Beck
Young.
Description: Lawrence, Kansas : University Press of Kansas, 2019. |
Series: American presidential elections | Includes bibliographical
references and index.
Identifiers: LCCN 2018059049
    ISBN 9780700627950 (hardback)
    ISBN 9780700627967 (ebook)
Subjects: LCSH: Presidents—United States—Election—1964. |
Johnson, Lyndon B. (Lyndon Baines), 1908–1973. | Goldwater, Barry M.
(Barry Morris), 1909–1998. | Liberalism—United States—History—
20th century. | Conservatism—United States—History—20th century. |
BISAC: POLITICAL SCIENCE / Government / Executive Branch. |
POLITICAL SCIENCE / Political Process / Elections. | POLITICAL
SCIENCE / Political Ideologies / Conservatism & Liberalism.
Classification: LCC E850 .Y68 2019 | DDC 324.973/0904—dc23
LC record available at https://lccn.loc.gov/2018059049.

British Library Cataloguing-in-Publication Data is available.

Printed in the United States of America

10 9 8 7 6 5 4 3 2 1

The paper used in this publication is recycled and contains 30
percent postconsumer waste. It is acid free and meets the minimum
requirements of the American National Standard for Permanence of
Paper for Printed Library Materials Z39.48-1992.

CONTENTS

A remarkable cast of characters walked across the national political stage in 1964. Casting a long shadow over the events of the year was the late President John F. Kennedy, whose assassination on November 22, 1963, had such great effects on the following year's election, not least the elevation of Vice President Lyndon B. Johnson of Texas to the presidency. LBJ and others of the year's major figures loomed large not just in 1964, but in the near half-century that lasted from the 1950s to the 1990s.

Among Democrats, these figures included Hubert H. Humphrey, the senator from Minnesota whom Johnson chose as his running mate in 1964 and who emerged as the party's nominee for president four years later after Johnson withdrew as a candidate; Robert F. Kennedy, the slain president's brother who despised Johnson, left his cabinet position as attorney general to run a successful campaign for US Senate from New York in 1964, challenged LBJ and helped drive him from the race in 1968, and was himself killed by an assassin in June of that year; and Governor George C. Wallace of Alabama, who entered three northern primaries in 1964 and ran strongly enough against the president to lay the foundation for an independent campaign in 1968.

Leading Republicans also played a major role before, during, and after 1964. Senator Barry M. Goldwater of Arizona, the Republican nominee against Johnson, was an iconic figure in the budding conservative movement that in 1980 elected Ronald Reagan as president. Reagan made his own national political debut in 1964. A veteran screen actor, he delivered so compelling a televised speech for Goldwater that wealthy Californians decided to launch him into politics. Governor Nelson A. Rockefeller of New York was Goldwater's nemesis in 1964, the leading liberal Republican in the country. He was defeated for the nomination in 1964 and 1968 but reemerged as President Gerald R. Ford's appointed vice president in 1974. Richard Nixon, the vice president during President Dwight D. Eisenhower's two terms and then his party's presidential nominee in 1960, began the political comeback as the leading campaigner for Goldwater that led to his election in 1968. Meanwhile, in Texas, George Bush made his first appearance in politics as the defeated senatorial nominee of the rising Texas

GOP. He was elected to Congress two years later, served as Reagan's vice president, and then won the presidential election in 1988.

Those keeping score will note that all three of the future presidents who played leading roles in 1964 and later won the office were Republicans: Nixon, Reagan, and Bush. This record of future success for the GOP would have astonished anyone in the aftermath of LBJ's forty-four-state, 486 electoral vote, 61 percent national popular vote majority in the election—not to mention the congressional balloting in 1964 that gave his party more than two-thirds majorities in both the House of Representatives and the Senate during the Eighty-Ninth Congress.

Among those counting the Republican Party out were *New York Times* columnist James Reston, who described the GOP as "wrecked for a long time to come" and Republican congressman John Lindsay, who said his party lay "in ashes." Among those counting conservatism out were, well, just about everybody. For example, political journalist Robert Donovan confidently envisioned at least a quarter century of liberal Democratic presidents, starting with Johnson and lasting through Humphrey and one or both of the surviving Kennedy brothers, RFK and Senator Edward M. Kennedy of Massachusetts.

As Nancy Beck Young shows in this volume, rumors of Republican conservatism's demise were premature. A combination of congressional overreach in enacting Johnson's liberal Great Society domestic agenda and presidential excess in prosecuting the war in Vietnam, joined with careful Republican rebuilding at the grassroots level, led to a solid comeback for the GOP in the 1966 midterm contest. This set the stage for the election of the Republican nominee in five of the next six presidential contests, four of them by landslides. The victorious Republican candidates for president were all products of what soon would be called the Sun Belt—the South and Southwest: former California senator Nixon in 1968 and 1972, former California governor Reagan in 1980 and 1984, and former Texas Congress member Bush in 1988. The only Democratic presidents elected during the final third of the twentieth century were former governor Jimmy Carter of Georgia and Governor Bill Clinton of Arkansas.

Sun Belt only became a neologism when Kevin Phillips invented the term in his 1969 book *The Emerging Republican Majority*. But as Young suggests, the new word merely caught up with the reality of the election in 1964 that pitted a Texan against an Arizonan.

A close family friend asked about my work when I was finishing this book. I reminded her briefly what the book was about, and she replied in a horrified tone, "Why would you ever want to write a book about *that?*" I should note that she is in her eighties, is not terribly political, but did volunteer in one campaign for one candidate—Barry Goldwater in 1964. Her experience with that race is quite different from my own. Barely a year old when Lyndon Johnson was elected, I have no memory of the events I depict in this book, though at various times I still felt as if I lived through them. First, as a child I came to learn positive things about LBJ from my parents—both lifelong liberal Democrats. My mother even made a button just for me to wear during the election. Second, because I did most of the initial writing for this book during the election of 2016, I sometimes felt as if I were living through a dystopian mash-up of what 1964 might have looked like had the results been different.

Indeed, the 2016 contest provided intriguing comparisons with 1964. In both contests, it seemed like everyone not voting for the Republican nominee dismissed him as a lunatic unfit by disposition and preparation for the White House. Support for the Democrat ran the gamut from those who had long believed in that individual's brand of consensus liberalism to those who questioned the Democratic nominee's ethics but found the prospect of the Republican challenger too frightening to risk not voting Democratic. There were also stark differences between 2016 and 1964. The Republican nominee in 2016 had no political experience whatsoever prior to running for the presidency and no real appreciation for how the federal government worked, but in 1964 the GOP standard-bearer had a long political record and was well schooled in the ways of Washington, DC.

Surface similarities aside, there is far more that separates 1964 from 2016. Foremost, the two elections took place in very different political and social eras. In 1964, Johnson won the presidency in his own right at the seeming apex of midcentury liberalism. Americans by and large trusted the government to work for the best interest of the country. Access to the televised news was limited to three thirty-minute network broadcasts at 5:30 p.m. While some cities still had newspapers that published in the evening, most newspaper delivery occurred in the morning. The nuclear family remained as the primary unit of family organization. Immigration to the country was marginal, and Jim Crow segregation, though crumbling, was still a powerful social, political, and economic determinant for African Americans.

Above all, the 1964 election does not require the subsequent events of 2016 to appear important to historians. Long before any political pundit had ever considered the prospect of a Donald Trump presidency I had begun the research process for this book. Fred Woodward first discussed the possibility with me at a Policy History Conference before I finished *Why We Fight*, and I began research on this book in earnest in 2013. It did take other political developments after 1964, though, for the significance of the contest to come into focus. Johnson's landslide victory seemingly reified midcentury liberalism as the only legitimate governing posture for the nation. Conversely, Goldwater's brand of Far Right, outsider conservatism had been resoundingly dismissed. In 1964, an overwhelming majority of Americans had rejected a political movement built on the resentments of a narrow swath of the electorate. Democratic partisans boasted they had poured the cold water on Goldwater.

Until they had not. Sixteen years after Johnson's massive victory American voters sent the most conservative president in US history to the White House. That man, Ronald Reagan, had introduced himself as a political figure through his work for Goldwater in 1964. Indeed, the dawn of a conservative era in modern American politics caused scholars by the end of the twentieth century to look back at 1964 for the origins of that shift. Other than Johnson biographies, then, the earliest books to treat the 1964 contest in any detail focused on the loser, Barry Goldwater, and not the winner. A few more recent titles have explored 1964 from Johnson's perspective. No scholar has written a full-throated history of the campaign that treats both parties and all candidates equally. That was the purpose with which I began this project and it is also where I finished.

I could not have written this book without the help of countless individuals. Archivists and librarians across the country are at the top of the list. No historian could work successfully without the talent and dedication of these skilled professionals. Archivists at the Lyndon B. Johnson Presidential Library provided useful and important guidance on my many trips to Austin, Texas, to research this book. My deepest thanks go out to Claudia Anderson, Chris Banks, Allen Fisher, Liza Talbot, and everyone else in the library who has been so supportive of my work over the years. The staff of the Special Collections at Arizona State University were equally helpful during a two-week stay in Tempe, Arizona (in the middle of the summer, no less) when I conducted research in the Barry Goldwater papers. Monica Blank and the rest of the archivists at the Rockefeller Archive Center in Sleepy Hollow, New York, helped ensure that my research trip there was productive and successful as I worked my way through Nelson Rockefeller's papers. My thanks also go to the archivists at the Special Collections at Pennsylvania State University in State College, Pennsylvania. Without their assistance my work in William Scranton's papers would have been much less fruitful. I could never say enough about the wonderful archivists at the Manuscript Division of the Library of Congress in Washington, DC. The archivists there demonstrate every day the utmost of professionalism in their assistance for visiting researchers. Finally, I would like to thank Alex Simons, who is the history and government documents librarian at the M. D. Anderson Library at the University of Houston. Alex graciously helped me track down a number of hard-to-find items.

Just as important to the success of this book are the many, many scholars who have worked ahead of me on related topics. Because this book is as much a work of synthesis as it is driven by archival research, the monographs and biographies produced by other scholars were crucial to charting this story. The most important sources for my work appear in the notes and the bibliographic essay. I owe a large debt to these academics.

Current and former graduate students at the University of Houston have listened patiently as I worked through the ideas undergirding this project. I offer my thanks and appreciation for the penetrating insights each of these talented scholars brought to discussions about this manuscript. I would especially like to thank Anna Marie Anderson, Julie Cohn, Sandra Davidson, Lindsay Drane, John Goins, Chris Haight, John Huntington, Tatum Koval, and Allison Robinson. I am also grateful to the UH undergraduates I have taught in our required senior capstone courses who have offered critical commentary.

Friends and colleagues around the country helped in a multitude of ways by listening to my ideas as they took shape, by offering comments at conferences, by reading portions of the manuscript, and by providing opportunities to escape work on the book when I needed a break. My deepest thanks go to Josiah and Susan Daniel, Sarah Fishman, Mark Goldberg, Kelly Hopkins, Philip Howard, Betty Koed, Richard McCulley, Marty Melosi, Cathy

Patterson, Monica Perales, Michele and John Reilly, Todd Romero, Jimmy Schafer, Matt Sherman, Katherine A. S. Sibley, Mary Standifer, Landon Storrs, Philippa Strum, Matthew Wasniewski, and Leandra Zarnow.

I benefited from research support from the Small Grants program at the University of Houston. I also thank the university for providing a much-needed Faculty Development Leave for the spring 2016 semester, valuable time off from teaching that provided the space to write a first draft of the manuscript. Finally, I thank the UH College of Liberal Arts and Social Sciences for funding assistance with the illustrations, permissions fees, and indexing for this manuscript.

Multiple institutions graciously provided access to photographs and other illustrations within their holdings. I thank the Associated Press, the Dolph Briscoe Center for American History at the University of Texas at Austin, the Franklin D. Roosevelt Presidential Library and Museum, the John F. Kennedy Presidential Library and Museum, the LBJ Library, the Library of Congress, Penguin Random House, and the Ronald Reagan Library for providing images and granting permission for their usage here.

The University Press of Kansas has shepherded this project from its infancy to publication with great skill and grace. My thanks go to the series editors, Michael Nelson and John M. McCardell Jr., for inviting me to contribute this volume on the 1964 election to the American Presidential Elections series. I have worked with three very skilled and capable editors at Kansas: Fred Woodward, Chuck Myers, and David Congdon. There are not enough words to describe how helpful Fred has been to the development of my career over the years. I am forever in his debt. David also has been terrific in the final stages of work on this project. W. R. Rorabaugh provided a textbook example of how to write a reader's report. His review of the manuscript for the press was thoughtful and detailed. What appears between these covers is much better as a result of his meticulous criticism. I am indebted to Larisa Martin for guiding this book through the publication process. Many, many thanks go to Martha Whitt for skillfully copy-editing the manuscript, and to Grant Hackett for preparing the index. Finally, I would like to thank Michael Kehoe for work on marketing this book.

Finally, my thanks go to my family for their unyielding faith in me. My parents and my grandmother were the first people to teach me about the importance of American politics. I went to countless political meetings and speeches with my parents, and I have never lost my fascination with those mid-twentieth-century figures. My brother, John K. Beck Jr., has been an inspiration. Mark E. Young has done more than he will ever know to make this book possible. His love knows no bounds. Our son, Thomas, is a joy every day. It is my hope that he will always appreciate the importance of free and democratic elections. This book is dedicated to those professors who have taught me how to research and write American political history: Tommy Stringer, Dan Nesmith, Rufus Spain, Don E. Carleton, and Lewis L. Gould. Any errors of fact or interpretation that remain are mine alone.

INTRODUCTION

In *Two Suns of the Southwest: Lyndon Johnson, Barry Goldwater, and the Battle between Liberalism and Conservatism*, I explore the 1964 presidential election and its legacy for modern American politics. This election, which at the time seemed as unlike a generational shift as could possibly be true, has in the decades since come to be seen as exactly that, a definitional contest whereby Americans deliberated between two distinctly different visions for the future. To provide an additional twist, the losing candidate's vision has become much more central to American politics while the winning candidate's vision has grown stale.

The contest was simultaneously a showdown between liberalism and conservatism *and* between Lyndon B. Johnson and Barry Goldwater. This cleavage was new as ideology had not been terribly important in the political contests in the 1950s. Moreover, two more unlikely messengers could not be envisioned. Johnson's liberalism was suspect among East Coast liberals while Goldwater's conservatism was far to the right of what had been normal in previous decades. Region had much to do with explaining how Johnson and Goldwater practiced the politics of ideology. Both were sons of the Old West, where they had been shaped by the politics of the past, in Texas for Johnson and Arizona for Goldwater. Both also hoped they could be the sun around which American politics revolved, Johnson even more so than Goldwater. They advocated distinctly different versions of what the Southwest and thus the country could be if it but orbited their sun and their worldview. One looked nostalgically backward to the idealized past and the other boldly forward into an equally idealized future.

An important demographic shift helped shape this confrontation between two southwestern candidates, namely the rise of the Sunbelt. Not yet a named concept in 1964, the Sunbelt and its soaring population was nevertheless a factor in national politics. As late as 1940 the western population was so small that added to the South it was nowhere near a majority in the Electoral College. Only after 1960 did a Sunbelt strategy make sense. LBJ had put together western oil, gas, mining, and agriculture with southern coal, tobacco, and agriculture to create an effective majority in the Senate in the 1950s. That is really the beginning of the Sunbelt strategy, which looked very different depending on whether a liberal Democrat or a conservative Republican articulated it. Johnson's Sunbelt liberalism, then, was universalist, designed to create space for all Americans. In comparison, Goldwater's Sunbelt conservativism was restrained, at least with regard to what the federal government should do. That the Sunbelt political default some fifty years later reflected Goldwater's conservatism and not Johnson's liberalism is further proof that Goldwater's ideas won in the decades that followed even though Goldwater himself was trounced in 1964.

This book explores three intertwined stories of midcentury party building: the first by Dwight D. Eisenhower in the 1950s and the other two by Goldwater and Johnson in the 1960s. Whereas Goldwater crusaded to define the GOP as far right of center and fought unsuccessfully in the 1964 presidential election, both Eisenhower and Johnson had wanted to forge mainstream, moderate political movements that were not tainted with ideological extremes and that were widely popular across the political and geographic spectrums. Eisenhower's efforts paved the way for both Johnson and Goldwater. He championed modern Republicanism, a concept he insisted was liberated from the traditional conservative Republicanism of party leaders like Senator Robert A. Taft (R-OH). He believed Taft's conservatism was more often reactive against New Deal liberalism than proactive about its own agenda for the country. He presented modern Republicanism as a positive alternative that embraced internationalism, human rights, and fiscal conservatism. His motives were as much about governing as electing more Republicans. Just as important, he viewed American politics from the global perspective he gained as Supreme Allied Commander during World War II. As such, his goals for a modern Republican Party did not privilege one region over another but tried to address the whole of America.

Almost a decade after Eisenhower became president, tragedy brought

Johnson into the White House. Even more than Eisenhower, he needed a political movement that could become his own. Just a few weeks after Johnson became president *The New Republic* editorialized: "LBJ has no firm base of power. . . . He has just enough support from Negroes to alienate the South—and vice versa. Putting present evidence together, a case can be made that he is a liberal; also that he isn't." Johnson in 1964 was running as much against the memory of the martyred John F. Kennedy as he was his zealous Republican challenger. To prove himself worthy of the presidency Johnson also ran against himself, or at least the caricature drawn of him as a southwestern hick. Johnson told his aide George Reedy in early April 1964: "there's bigotry in the North against a southerner." He complained, "the Eastern press . . . always put a string bow tie on me because of where I was born. I never wore one in my life."[1]

In that way, he sought to eclipse his Texas roots in the buckle of the Sunbelt with a new iteration of liberalism, one that was comprehensive and unifying of all Americans and all regions of the country, and one that was more beneficent than Eisenhower's modern Republicanism. Indeed, Johnson's campaign, drawing on unfulfilled planks from the 1960 Democratic platform, was the most avowedly liberal in American political history, including calls for government-funded health care for the elderly, federal government funding for primary and secondary education, the elimination of poverty via federal spending, and federally funded urban renewal. He pitched his proposed Great Society as a frontlash initiative to unite Eisenhower's modern Republicans with independents and Democrats, except those whites from the South, and escape the backlash politics of resentment from Goldwater. Finally, Johnson sought to mix liberals with disaffected Republicans in ways that discomfited doctrinaire adherents of both political views. Indeed, his candidacy and his campaign challenged preconceived notions of what liberalism was.

Considering Johnson as a liberal involves his geographical identity but also his demeanor and grandiose ambition. To some who covered his career Johnson came across as "not a very likeable man" who took joy in shocking the well-heeled, who belittled subordinates, and who also could be both maudlin and overly generous. Johnson yearned to consolidate political power quickly. One White House correspondent said of Johnson, "He wants to carry all fifty states, Latin America, Greece and Turkey."[2] His most immediate legislative goal, though, speedy passage of the 1964 Civil Rights Act, threatened to divide his party and push white southern Democrats into the arms of the Republicans and risk his hoped-for landslide victory.

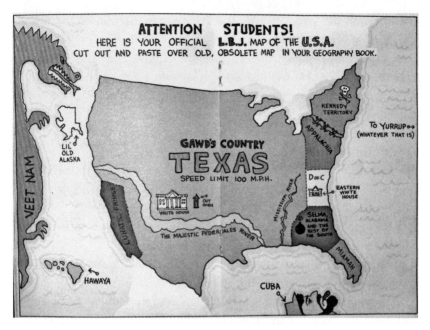

This map from a 1965 booklet, The Great Society Fun and Games Book *by Jack Hanrahan and Phil Hahn, depicts a satirical view of Johnson's map of the United States. Reprinted courtesy of Random House LLC.*

Johnson's remedy, the frontlash, was a nationalized version of what LBJ had learned years ago in one-party Texas: elide ideology and party, emphasize pragmatic goals and results, and turn campaigns into contests about personality. Eliot Janeway, who consulted on economic issues for the *New York Times*, first used the term "backlash" to describe white acrimony over increasing African American demands for equality. For Johnson, frontlash was not just a way to avoid talking about backlash but was—he thought—a way to realign the Democratic Party so that it could be both centrist and liberal and never overly partisan. Indeed, Johnson's consensus liberalism sounded a decidedly different tone than that to which Americans had grown accustomed with Franklin D. Roosevelt and John F. Kennedy, both East Coast patricians, or even that of Harry S. Truman with his Midwest twang and his roots in a haberdashery. Nor did Johnson's liberalism look like the identity liberalism that by the 1960s was displacing FDR's mid-century economic liberalism, something that marked him as old-fashioned within his party. Johnson's frontlash strategy was not initially the preferred choice of either party liberals, who wanted him to coordinate with congressional races and run a campaign based on a leftist policy agenda, or moderate Democrats, who wanted him to focus on keeping the diverse groups in the party united, including southerners who were threatening to abandon the party. By frontlash Johnson instead highlighted Goldwater's unfitness for office, his extremism, and made it difficult for GOP moderates and liberals to stay in the Republican Party. Johnson thought the tactics would prompt a realignment in the Democratic Party, further widen its base, and minimize the influence of the GOP in national affairs.

Goldwater unwittingly provided a partial assist for Johnson. So extreme was he in his views that Goldwater seemed more radical than Johnson's government-enforced racial equality. Goldwater's nomination and his extremist statements allowed Johnson to run as the respectable candidate without too much scrutiny of his own behavior. *New York Times* journalist Tom Wicker explained Johnson would not have enjoyed that luxury against any of the other Republican contenders. Instead, said Wicker, Johnson would have been deemed "the Western wild man, uninformed, undignified, provincial, above all radical, an untrustworthy and flamboyant political parvenu."[3]

Unlike Johnson, Goldwater embraced his southwestern identity; instead of overlooking American regionalism as did Eisenhower or attempting to transcend it as did Johnson, Goldwater located his political argument for the presidency within a conservative challenge to the liberal status quo. At an Eisenhower-Nixon dinner in 1960 Goldwater told the crowd that for the party to win it must adopt conservative principles. What was the source of Goldwater's conservatism? Conservative intellectuals were never a major factor in the Goldwater campaign. Scholars have argued Goldwater's conservatism was more pragmatic than intellectual, that his political ideology really came more from his gut and from his regional background. He externalized myths about the primacy of rugged individualism in the settlement of the Southwest. Goldwater relied most on instinct to define his politics. He forged several important core concepts into what became Sunbelt conservatism: he believed the growth of government and capitalism were antithetical, he practiced a new, harsh politics of morality, he opposed "monopoly unionism," and he exploited the politics of resentment by playing off the civil rights backlash. William Rusher, publisher of the *National Review*, called 1964 a "truly seminal year" for modern conservatism, arguing "it laid the foundation for everything that followed."[4]

Seminal or not, in 1964, Goldwater lost. Ronald Reagan's statement at the California victory party in June 1964 elucidates why Goldwater lost to Johnson later that November. Reagan understood aspects of the 1964 race that Goldwater did not. He, like Goldwater appreciated the anger on the right, but, unlike Goldwater, he realized Democratic converts would have to be won if the Republicans hoped to win in November. Reagan offered advice that Goldwater did not follow: "We are going to have to forget an awful lot of bitterness. We don't want to win a convention, we want to win an election. Let's start making love to Democrats."[5]

When did modern conservatism begin and who or what begat it? This question has inspired a tremendous debate among historians looking for the origins of the most important political development of the late twentieth century. Some scholars suggest it commenced with William F. Buckley Jr. and the founding of the *National Review* in 1955 and a direct line connected Buckley with Goldwater and Goldwater with Reagan. This view contends that prior to Buckley there was not a conservative movement per se, just a disparate array of conservative perspectives, including concerns about secularization and preservation of the cultural elite. These mixed with the Old Right, those who had fought the New Deal, been isolationist before World War II, and wanted a laissez faire economy and protection of individual property rights. Others have stressed the role of conservative intellectuals. George H. Nash, one leading scholar of conservatism, asserted, "The Arizona senator's campaign represented the first thrust of the postwar New Right into presidential politics." Nash expounded, "It is likely that without the patient spadework of the intellectual Right, the conservative political movement of the 1960s would have remained disorganized and defeated." Still others have linked modern conservatism to region, namely the Sunbelt.[6]

Where does Goldwater fit in the birthing of modern conservatism? Cliché though it might sound, the answer to that question depends on who one asks. *The New Republic* called Goldwater "the 'white hope' of America's thinning Neanderthal ranks." John S. Knight, a newspaper publisher, apologized on behalf of journalists for the "shabby" treatment meted out to Goldwater, and while noting the Arizonan "is not my candidate," he concluded there was more to the Goldwater movement than "kooks" and "Birchers," arguing it "represents a mass protest by conservatively minded people against foreign aid, excessive welfare, high taxes, foreign policy and the concentration of power in the federal government." Without saying it in so many words Knight explicated critical components of Goldwater's resentment politics. Similarly, newspaper publisher Gene Pulliam termed the Goldwater movement a "federation of the fed-up."[7]

The stereotypical Goldwater voter was part of the new middle class—beneficiaries of the military industrial complex—who either worked in defense industries as engineers, managers, or technicians or in the service sector, real estate, or construction. Also, they were young, recently married, and opposed to the establishment, meaning East Coast values and political priorities. One historian described them as "reactionary modernists for whom liberalism had become the new communism." There was also a certain amount of irony in their politics. They existed economically because of the federal government, and they voted against that same federal government advancing those same policies and programs that had secured their prosperity. Indeed, Goldwater's coalition was a motley bunch of former Taftites, anti–New Dealers, middle-class suburbanites in the Sunbelt, religious conservatives, and segregationists. Political observers believed he could win as long as he could unite his partisans with the regular Republican Party. He never achieved that feat because, as one historian put it, "When the soundness of the man became the issue, rather than the soundness of his ideas, it was over."[8]

Examination of leading Goldwater insiders—F. Clifton White, who organized the draft Goldwater movement; L. Brent Bozell, who was the ghostwriter for Goldwater's *The Conscience of a Conservative*; and Phyllis Schlafly, author of *A Choice, Not an Echo*—reveals all were connected to the Taft wing of the Republican Party, but they were also more conservative than their intellectual predecessors such as former president Herbert Hoover. This connection belies tendencies to see Goldwaterism as sui generis. Instead, the Goldwater movement is better understood as a stark generational shift and not as a new political movement. Put differently, the Goldwater conservatives did not "invent" their movement, but instead reconfigured what they had "learned" from the previous generation to apply to the conditions of the 1960s. One Goldwater loyalist observed that with his candidacy the word *conservative* shifted in meaning "from being a curse word" to instead reflect "a roaring challenge to the established power and the established aridities of the post-Roosevelt era."[9]

The 1964 election cannot be studied apart from the personalities and backgrounds of the two candidates. It was more than anything else a competition about two different views of the Sunbelt, Goldwater's backward-looking conservatism and Johnson's forward-looking liberalism. Both major party nominees were sons of the Sunbelt, and this contest reflects what other scholars have noted: there is no single archetype of the Sunbelt politician. Observed journalist Theodore H. White: "The gap between Johnson and Goldwater was total. Though as masculine Southwest types they used the same language, the same profanities, shared the same drinking style, indulged in the same homespun metaphors, these similarities were meaningless when compared to the philosophies that separated them." Ironically, Johnson's persona as a Texan, including the many photo ops at his Hill Country ranch, undercut Goldwater's efforts to claim the southwestern mantle.[10] Just as Johnson used his regional background to minimize Goldwater he also sought distance from it.

Johnson's shifting, ambiguous relationship with Sunbelt politics, which mixed embracing his natural folksy style with rejecting it to look presidential, helps explain why he demonstrated so many different personalities on the campaign trail. Said Theodore White: "One had been tempted, even before the campaign began, to make a catalogue of all the Lyndon Johnsons there were, for in the etymological sense of *persona* as mask, Johnson's *personae* were almost unlimited." They included his serious and somber television image as president, the "Kindly Lyndon" who could show great warmth and concern for other people, and "Imperial Lyndon" who used his physicality to show his dominance over others. When traveling in the country, many more personae became evident: "Fair-Shares Johnson" extolled equitable relations among social classes, "Preacher Johnson" stressed the golden rule, "Old Doc Johnson" intoned the importance of education, "Sheriff Johnson" differentiated right from wrong, "Uncle Lyndon" was a wizened and folksy political pro, and "Lonely-Acres Johnson" reminded voters of the national security burdens that were the president's alone.[11]

Goldwater's Sunbelt image was equally complicated. Journalist Richard Rovere contended: "Either someone is lying or there are two Goldwaters." He expounded that "the Senator on the hustings, the agreeable man with the easy, breezy Aw Shucks Western manner who speaks in rightist platitudes . . . has only a loose grip on ideology and not, apparently, much interest in it." The other Goldwater presented as a "dour authoritarian polemicist" most unlike "the Goldwater who can dispose of a large national problem by saying 'If we get back to readin', writin', and 'rithmetic and an occasional little whack where it will help, then I think our educational system will take care of itself.'" Rovere identified other aspects of the Goldwater identity: he was "a bit on the loose-lipped side, and he says it all straight out, and he is also a smiler, ready to be pardners with any straight-shooting, straight-talking man." Journalists Rowland Evans and Robert Novak agreed: "Goldwater, the voice of the renascent Republican right, was the antithesis of Lyndon Johnson: uninterested in power, inflexible, doctrinaire, essentially nonpolitical. He was, in short, everything a candidate for President of the United States should not be."[12]

Two more factors defined the contest as one rooted in Sunbelt identity: the politics of race and the differing views of what the federal government should be and do. The rise of the Sunbelt as a feature in American politics resulted because of the shared realities of the South and the Southwest: transcendence of their past histories as dependent, colonial economies; increased reliance on federal infrastructure development and deployment of defense contract spending in the region; and demographic growth as the older manufacturing economies of the northeastern and midwestern Rust Belt began to wane. The merging of these regions did not eliminate the ugly parts of southern history regarding racial bigotry; Sunbelt thus also becomes a sanitized term for southern. Individual rights versus collectivism, a term of opprobrium used by the right, became the key conflict between Goldwater conservatives and Great Society liberals. Not in 1964, but not long thereafter, conservatives convinced Americans that liberals no longer primarily worked to secure expanded individual liberties but instead for entitlements through social engineering and ever more heightened federal power over individual lives.[13]

Between 1961 and 1964 the percentage of southern African Americans who identified with the Democratic Party increased from 24 percent to 52 percent. Conversely, southern whites doubled their support for the Republican Party, from 9 percent to 18 percent. As Merle and Earl Black point out, the number of southern Republicans rose in the 1950s because of northern migrants, many of whom were middle-class plant managers. This was less a matter of southern Democratic converts than new residents. However, the Blacks also acknowledged that "the central political cleavage, as ancient as the South itself, involves race." Still, Goldwater denied that race and racism played a role in Republican ascendancy, contending "No analysis could be more absurd on its face. Republican influence in the South is growing in direct proportion to the South's moderation on the race issue." He overstated his case; race had much to do with the Goldwater ascendancy in the South and elsewhere as the chapters that follow will reveal. Goldwater's conservatism, though, did not have staying power, at least the part that centered on opposition to civil rights. Within a generation, conservatives rarely if ever spoke against civil rights, and instead they explained how Republicans voted for the Civil Rights Act of 1964 at a higher percentage than did Democrats.[14] These niceties shifted in the early twenty-first century as some conservative Republicans again relied on coded racial language and policy, namely efforts to roll back and eliminate Johnson's seminal Voting Rights Act of 1965.

Two Suns of the Southwest consists of seven chapters and a conclusion. The first two chapters set the stage for the political arguments waged in 1964, first by articulating the status of the Republicans on the eve of the election and second by studying not only the effects of the Kennedy assassination on Democratic Party identity but also the tensions within the party during the years of Camelot. To that purpose chapter 1 reaches back into the 1950s to assess the status of the GOP as a political party during the Dwight D. Eisenhower administration. It also looks at the growing conservative challenges, at least around the margins, to moderate Republicans who accepted the New Deal as political status quo. Chapter 2 explores Democratic Party politics during the Kennedy administration. Kennedy's domestic agenda met with reticence in Congress, but the opposition came as much from conservative Democrats as from the GOP. The chapter ends with consideration of the political ramifications of the Kennedy assassination.

Chapters 3 and 4 describe the Republican primaries and convention, showing how Goldwater won his party's nomination. Before the campaign began in earnest the favorites for the GOP nomination were former vice president Richard Nixon, Governor Nelson Rockefeller, and Henry Cabot Lodge II, the US ambassador to Vietnam. Right-wing grassroots organizations, including the John Birch Society, the Young Americans for Freedom, and the Young Republicans, fought to upset the East Coast establishment Republicans who had dominated the party for decades. The sixteen Republican primaries—only three of which were contested—devolved into a bloodbath over the question of war and peace. Goldwater had made clear he had no hesitancy to use nuclear weapons should the situation warrant it. In the three contested primaries, there were three different winners, Lodge in New Hampshire, Rockefeller in Oregon, and Goldwater in California. Still Goldwater appeared as the favorite for the nomination going into the convention because of his strength in the remaining thirty-four states that used caucuses and conventions to choose their delegates. He claimed the nomination on the first ballot.

Chapter 5 situates Democratic politics that year against the backdrop of the civil rights movement. Johnson faced no serious challengers, making the primary and the convention a pro forma series of events, save for one small issue that really was not so small. From the moment he became president Johnson made civil rights legislation his top priority, and in July 1964 he signed a meaningful Civil Rights Act into law. This major accomplishment did not assuage all concerns for activists seeking justice. Participants in Mississippi Freedom Summer challenged the white, racist leadership of the state's Democratic Party, and Johnson showed himself to be uninterested in doing very much to help change party dynamics there or elsewhere in the South. When the Mississippi Freedom Democratic Party demanded to be recognized and seated on the floor at the Democratic National Convention, they were turned away. This chapter looks at Democratic Party politics through the lens of civil rights, which was the most significant issue dividing the party.

Chapters 6 and 7 recount the campaign for and results of the general election that fall while also considering why so many (mostly liberal) Democrats were elected to Congress. These chapters will explore what these down ballot races meant for the national tug-of-war between liberalism and conservatism. From the moment Goldwater gained the nomination there was little doubt Johnson would win by an overwhelming margin, and he did. The most significant events of the campaign, then, had more to do with the various political methodologies employed by the two candidates and their supporters. The best-known aspect of the fall campaign was the infamous "Daisy Ad," which equated a Goldwater presidency with nuclear holocaust. The ad played as a campaign commercial only once, but it became the subject of significant discussion on the news. Just as important, but less well known, was Lady Bird Johnson's campaign swing through the Deep South aboard a train dubbed the Lady Bird Special. The Johnson team knew their candidate would lose some states in the South, but they still believed it important to campaign in the region in a respectful fashion. Indeed, Johnson and Goldwater split the former Confederate states with Goldwater taking the four Dixiecrat states from 1948—Louisiana, Mississippi, Alabama, and South Carolina—plus Georgia. Johnson prevailed in Texas, Florida, Virginia, North Carolina, Tennessee, and Arkansas. The final strategic campaign development of note was the use of direct mail marketing to grassroots conservatives by the Goldwater campaign. While the tactic did not work for the Republicans in 1964, it became a key method for conservatives in the decades that followed.

Finally, the conclusion explores the long-term significance of the 1964 election. Johnson's overwhelming victory suggested that liberal Democrats would hold power for another generation as had been true following Roosevelt's successes in the 1930s. Johnson had modeled himself after FDR, and he wanted a victory in 1964 bigger than any that Roosevelt had won. He also yearned for reforms grander than the New Deal, and a legacy more important than the president he emulated. Because the political trajectory

President Lyndon B. Johnson looking at a portrait of President Franklin D. Roosevelt in the White House, February 1965. LBJ Library, photo by Cecil Stoughton.

of the nation for the remainder of the century followed a crooked, but rightward path, the 1964 contest should be read as a cautionary tale that surface appearances are not necessarily reflective of the reality underneath. Put simply, the contest that placed the most liberal president in the White House also strengthened those conservative politicians who would for the next half century work to destroy the liberal legacy of 1964.

1

THE MYTH OF REPUBLICAN MODERATION IN THE 1950S

The story of the 1964 presidential election begins much earlier, with events that date back to the 1930s when both US political parties realigned, leaving Democrats triumphant and Republicans beleaguered. Franklin D. Roosevelt's four straight presidential election wins put the Republican Party into a tailspin. Efforts to run "me too" campaigns in the 1930s and 1940s failed miserably, and for two decades conservatives could not amass the support to earn the GOP nomination for the presidency. A despondent party regrouped for the 1952 race with an altogether different strategy, one that avoided the problem of ideology. It nominated General Dwight D. Eisenhower, a popular war hero who had not previously indicated his political preferences. Leaders of this initiative wanted a moderate who would appeal within the party, to independents, and even to Democrats.[1] Electorally successful, this approach nonetheless only led to a worsening of the Republican identity crisis during Eisenhower's presidency.

According to Gallup Poll data, the Democrats remained the majority party throughout the Ike decade. This point becomes obvious when polling data is examined for each presidential election year from 1952 through 1960. Indeed, the percentage of Americans who identified themselves as Democrats or leaning toward Democrats ranged from 50 to 54 percent while those who identified as Republican or leaning toward the Republicans ranged from 37 to 40 percent. Interestingly, though, the percentages by which Americans identified themselves as liberal or conservative did not match the party identification. Party and ideology were not synchronous. In 1955, just 30 percent of Americans identified as liberal and only slightly more, 31 percent, identified as conservative. Those with no opinion numbered almost 36 percent. Neither party had a clear ideological identity. Richard Nixon discussed this situation in his memoirs, noting that to win national elections Republicans needed votes from Democrats and independents, given the numerical superiority of Democrats. He believed the Cold War made it possible for Republicans to do this in most elections, since conservative Democrats were staunch anti-Communists.[2]

During the 1950s, the GOP never unified under one strategy. Indeed, the Republicans elected many moderate governors in the 1940s and 1950s. These individuals governed successfully and helped make Eisenhower president in 1952 by controlling their state delegations. A different, more negative, and generally mediocre in ability Republican Party dominated in Congress. More important, Eisenhower's two presidential wins masked a basic public acceptance of the New Deal welfare state, meaning programs like Social Security, regulation of banking and the stock market, and workers' right to unionize and strike. Conservatives still critiqued the federal government, and party moderates never captured the progressive mantle with the public.

In the late 1940s, both Republicans and Democrats concluded that Eisenhower would ensure a presidential victory for their party if he would but run. Eisenhower rejected all Democratic entreaties, but he entertained the Republican approaches. He pitched himself as a "modern" Republican, and he insisted for his party to be successful it must also be progressive. Eisenhower described in his diary his political philosophy in 1950, "I'm against the handout state but nevertheless a military liberal." He wanted a commitment to a strong US leadership role in world affairs, liberal programs for social justice and human welfare, and fiscal restraint on spending and government bureaucracy. He did embrace the New Deal, once telling his brother, "Should any political party attempt to abolish social security, unemployment insurance, and eliminate labor laws and farm programs, you would not hear of that party again in our political history." In all of his efforts to define a philosophy for the GOP, Eisenhower never used "liberal" as a modifier.[3]

Eisenhower's modern Republican strategy for permanent political realignment did not work. Large and small measures demonstrate Eisenhower's failure to transform his party to the party of progressivism. Doing so would have required a major realignment, syphoning moderate and even some liberal Democrats away from the party of Roosevelt and convincing them to vote for down ballot Republicans as well as the popular war hero. Memories of the Great Depression were too fresh for that to happen. An example from one small east Texas town shows the antipathy of the most dedicated New Deal Democrats there to the GOP. When an Eisenhower surrogate campaigned there in 1952, these Democrats—white and black—gathered armadillos and rabbits during the week prior to the event. They painted "Ike" on the sides of the animals, and they released them during the speech. One of the organizers yelled: "I lived through the Depression and armadillo was all we had to eat," the implication being a vote for Eisenhower meant more armadillo on the dinner plate.[4] The statewide vote for Eisenhower in Texas aside, this episode demonstrates the challenges of convincing devout New Dealers to abandon the Democratic Party.

Nationally, moderate leaders realized Eisenhower might be their only chance. Sherman Adams, the Republican governor of New Hampshire, worked to draft Eisenhower to run as a Republican. To do so he needed proof of Eisenhower's party identification. An associate of Adams wrote to the county clerk in Dickinson County, Kansas, where Eisenhower's home town was located, to learn whether the general had ever voted. The county clerk wrote back that Eisenhower had not voted and he also concluded, "I don't think he has any politics."[5]

Part of what convinced Eisenhower to run in 1952 was the proliferation of "IKE clubs" and other "outburst[s] of grass-roots volunteer action." Eisenhower recalled in his memoirs, "This phenomenon, representing strong sentiment on the part of substantial groups of citizens, provided one of the powerful arguments employed by friends in urging me to make myself available." Indeed, during the contest Eisenhower wanted the grass-roots Citizens for Eisenhower groups to have a bigger voice in party politics than the Old Guard Republicans who had long dominated party affairs. After working with Eisenhower for six years, first as campaign advisor and then as White House chief of staff, Adams concurred that the president was not a partisan, but was a "high-minded idealist." As such, he did not understand immediately "that many of the Old Guard Republican leaders were really using his prestige and popularity only to wrest political power from the Democrats."[6]

What then was Eisenhower's "modern" Republicanism? Such a term was politically charged. It became the rallying cry for Republicans intent on differentiating their party from New Deal Democrats *and* from Old Guard

Republicans. The term ultimately was as much about style as it was sub-stance. Jack Bell, a journalist working in Washington, DC, during the 1950s, observed the vicissitudes of Eisenhower's political ideology, noting how the "curve of progressivism in this man's public utterances arc high into the New Deal clouds" while also "descend[ing] again into a conservatism in which Taft would have been comfortably at home." The best example of such, said Bell, was "the Morningside Heights surrender" that occurred when Eisenhower met with Taft at his Columbia University presidential residence two months after Eisenhower won the nomination. Eisenhower thought he needed Taft's support to win in November. Critics avowed that Eisenhower had sold out, giving Taft and the Old Guard the upper hand in Congress. In reality, there was not that much difference between Taft and Eisenhower on domestic policy, and the concessions the general made—keeping the federal budget at $60 billion, reducing taxes, and preserving the Taft-Hartley labor law—did not restrict his agenda in Congress.[7]

In other aspects of his campaign Eisenhower revealed himself not to be a progressive. That fall he insisted on campaigning in the South against the advice of political professionals who argued campaigning there was a waste of time, money, and effort. The unstated aim was to capture white Demo-crats for the GOP. Ike explained, "the man in the White House, I believe, should think of himself as President of all the people." His tactics paid off; he won four states on the southern periphery, Florida, Tennessee, Texas, and Virginia. Florida and Tennessee had organized Republican Parties, but Ike's victory in Texas and Virginia came courtesy of disgruntled conserva-tive Democrats who bolted their party, Governor Allan Shivers of Texas and Senator Harry Byrd of Virginia, and led a sufficient number of voters to the GOP for Ike.[8]

Eisenhower entered the presidency hoping for bipartisanship. An im-mense challenge at any political moment, doing so in a time of flux proved nearly impossible. The new president headed a party dominated by iso-lationists, and, in the words of public opinion expert Samuel Lubell, had "instinctive yearnings [that] tug back to an age of simpler government." Shifts in the national and international political systems made relying on such old political dichotomies impossible. Still, early in his presidency Ei-senhower noted "Senator Taft has been the model of cheerful and effective cooperation." He also spoke positively about Styles Bridges (R-NH), Homer Capehart (R-IN), Everett McKinley Dirksen (R-IL), Joseph W. Martin Jr. (R-MA), Charles A. Halleck (R-IN), and John Taber (R-NY). On other occasions early in his term, Eisenhower criticized the "readiness of political legislators to fly into print at every possible opportunity." He attributed such behavior to Republicans having been "for so long a time . . . opposed to, and often a deadly enemy of, the individual in the White House." He refused to go after recalcitrant Republicans who objected to his policies. Eisenhower made clear, "So if I tell him off in public, what am I accomplishing? Just this much: I am yelling to the world, 'Please come and look, all of you, at the knucklehead I have representing me and my party and my program on Capitol Hill.'"[9]

On April 1, 1953, Eisenhower observed in his diary that the previous day an unnamed person had suggested he should work "quietly" to create "a new party" because congressional Republicans regularly voted against the White House agenda. Multiple examples of discord between the White House and Congress existed. Republicans could agree neither about tax policy nor budget priorities. Indeed, administration proposals passed in Congress fifty-eight times in 1953 because of Democratic Party votes. At the April 30, 1953, meeting of the Republican congressional leaders Taft yelled angrily at the president. Eisenhower had just told the assembly that he would not be able to balance the nation's budget during his first year in office, in part because of programs carrying over from the Truman administration and in part because of the work he was doing to radically reformulate the nation's defense strategies with more reliance on air power. Taft shouted, "With a program like this, we'll never elect a Republican Congress in 1954. . . . It's a repudiation of everything we promised in the campaign!" A deafening silence overtook the room before the president asserted his program was the only option for the nation. A chastened Taft returned to the next week's meeting apologetic for his behavior.[10]

Midway through 1953 Taft fell ill and later died on July 31. Senator William Knowland (R-CA) became Senate majority leader on August 4, 1953. Adams recalled of Knowland, "It would have been difficult to find anybody more disposed to do battle with much of the President's program in Congress." Eisenhower wooed Knowland with breakfast visits to the White House and public praise, but any positive results were fleeting. The predicament with Knowland resulted because the California Republican believed Congress should pursue its own agenda and not work only on presidential goals, because he had ambitions for higher office, and because he was obtuse about politics.[11]

Knowland was not the only problem person Eisenhower faced among the Republican congressional leadership. In the House, Speaker Martin and Majority Leader Halleck had a long-running "feud smoldering in the background," which Adams recalled, "made the weekly meetings of the party Congressional leaders in the White House an ordeal for Eisenhower." Moreover, Martin often seemed "uninspired and lackadaisical" when pursuing Eisenhower's agenda. Once when Eisenhower complained that the Republicans never agreed on anything, Martin explained, "Maybe that's the result of these last twenty years that we spent out in the wilderness." Indeed, between Martin and Halleck, Eisenhower spoke favorably of the latter, saying "this man is a different type," noting his Phi Beta Kappa membership, his "reputation as being a ruthless politician," and his demeanor as "a real team player" with "no patience" for lawmakers who "'stray off the reservation.'"[12]

Much of the squabbling between Eisenhower and the conservatives had to do with foreign policy. It galled Eisenhower not a little that many in his party did not trust his knowledge of foreign affairs, especially given his World War II background. The two major sources of opposition in the Republican Party came from Senators Joseph McCarthy (R-WI) and John Bricker (R-OH). Eisenhower observed theirs was a narrow perspective of the role the United States should play in the world.[13]

Such divisions in the party troubled Eisenhower and made his quest for progressive Republicans all that more elusive. At the end of his first year in office he told his childhood friend, Everett E. "Swede" Hazlett, "the mass of Republican and independent supporters have got to be behind the Administration—or else. . . . We have [also] got to have the support of reasonable and enlightened Democrats." The president could never understand why congressional Republicans would oppose aspects of his legislative agenda—spending for foreign policy was one example—simply out of apprehensiveness that voters would disapprove and kick them out of office. Despite such concerns, the record of the Eighty-Third Congress in 1953 had been positive.[14]

For Eisenhower part of building a modern, progressive Republican Party involved making lists of younger Republicans he believed were potential future candidates for the White House. Senator Barry M. Goldwater (R-AZ) was one person Ike named as a likely contender. That Eisenhower included Goldwater in one of his first lists of potential successors might seem odd given the ex-general's clear goals of building a moderate party and the senator's later association with a modern conservatism more radical, built on resentment, and more ideological than Old Guard Republicanism. In the early 1950s, though, Goldwater was a plain spoken westerner who possessed great personal integrity. As a junior member of the Senate he had

President Dwight D. Eisenhower standing with Lyndon B. Johnson (center)
*and other guests during a bipartisan luncheon at the White House,
Washington, DC, March 1955. Library of Congress, Prints & Photographs
Division, photograph by* U.S. News & World Report *Magazine Photograph
Collection.*

not yet thrown in with the new breed of conservatives. Before entering politics, he worked in his family's department store and developed a sense of
rugged southwestern individualism critical of federal government regulations. He once remarked, "I think the foundations of my political philosophy were rooted in my resentment against the New Deal." He preferred
the local and the private to the central and the public, believing the latter a
distortion of American values. Well liked in the community, Goldwater had
played a lead role in civic life in Phoenix.[15]

Eisenhower had better relations with the Democratic leadership, Senate majority leader Lyndon B. Johnson (D-TX) and Speaker of the House
Sam Rayburn (D-TX) than with the GOP congressional leaders. The Senate
Republican leadership situation remained bad until 1959 near the end of
his presidency when Dirksen became minority leader. Knowland had originally impressed Eisenhower, but he never coordinated congressional and
executive strategy for fear of the White House dictating policy to Congress.
Knowland did more damage when he voted against censuring McCarthy
in December 1954. An irate Eisenhower exploded, "What's the guy trying

to do? Here, he personally picked the committee to draw up the censure charges, he vouched for their honor and integrity and then he turns around and votes against them." White House press secretary James C. Hagerty explained this was "just another instance of Knowland being taken up on the mountaintop by the right wing and promised a lot of things." Knowland was not alone. All but one Senate Republican leader voted against censure. Moderate easterners in the party voted overwhelmingly for censure while former Taft supporters, meaning the Old Guard Republican Right, voted against.[16]

Eisenhower faced other partisan challenges in 1954, namely the midterm congressional elections. Uniting the regular Republican Party with the grassroots citizens groups that had worked for Eisenhower's 1952 election proved impossible in 1954; party leaders were obstinate and loathe to reform according to Eisenhower's plans. As such, Eisenhower was unwilling to help Old Guard Republicans, who he feared might "doublecross us." Party regulars "resented" citizen-driven organizations like the "Ike and Dick" clubs, arguing that "volunteer politicians" should be eliminated from Republican politics. Eisenhower told leading Republican officials that such groups had been useful in 1952 and could be again. He rejected the notion that they were displacing regular Republicans from patronage positions, asserting instead, "Most of the Citizens in the last campaign were intelligent independents and discerning Democrats who adhere to a moderate philosophy. We should try to make them one of our principal recruiting agencies. It would be sheer stupidity to fail to do so if we want to win more elections."[17]

The 1954 midterm congressional elections raised questions: How much should Ike campaign for his fellow Republicans? Would he draw the young and independents to vote for Republicans without his name on the ticket? He stated he would endorse all Republican candidates for the House and the Senate. Political commentators critiqued the electoral agenda as unwise, and White House insiders claimed the president needed a "ruthless s.o.b. to run its politics." Eisenhower got involved in the campaign, mostly on behalf of East Coast Republicans to try to prevent wins by the Old Guard. As it turned out, Eisenhower campaigned more than most presidents before him in the midterms, but without success. The Democrats regained control of both chambers with a 232–203 majority in the House and 48–47 in the Senate with one Independent, reflecting a pickup of nineteen House seats and one Senate seat. The biggest problem Republicans faced in 1954 were losses in Republican districts. In other words, the GOP held many of the new seats it gained in 1952, but lost, and lost big, in states and districts that had never gone Democratic during the New Deal and the war.[18]

Eisenhower told the congressional Republican leadership on December 13, 1954, that it would be necessary to "pick up the pieces and work on the Hill with the Democratic majority." More than anything else that meant maintaining a good working relationship with Rayburn and Johnson. Conversely, Eisenhower was much less interested in continuing to try to work with the radical right but instead would fight them. "I've had just enough from the McCarthys, the Welkers, the Malones, and people like that." This view was linked to Ike's indecision about whether he would seek a second term. He routinely said he did not want to, but he worried whether there was an electable moderate Republican prepared to run in 1956. The one thing he did not want was "a right-wing Old Guard Republican" candidate. Should that happen he promised "I'll go up and down this country, campaigning against them. I'll fight them right down the line."[19]

Following the midterms, pressure on Eisenhower intensified that he declare his plan to run for reelection in 1956. Getting Eisenhower to run became the paramount issue for the GOP. Retired four-star general and friend of the president Lucius Clay stressed he must run again if he hoped his reforms to the Republican Party would stick. Eisenhower ultimately agreed, noting this conversation in his diary, "The Republican Party must be known as a progressive organization or it is sunk." Conversely at least one GOP leader shied away from recruiting Eisenhower to run. In early January 1955, Knowland angered Eisenhower when he told the press he would not participate in a draft Eisenhower movement because a reluctant candidate was not good for the party. Eisenhower eviscerated Knowland in his diary on January 10, the day the story ran in the newspapers: "there seems to be no final answer to the question 'How stupid can you get?'"[20]

In the mid 1950s, though, Republican tacticians were divided over strategy regarding the black vote and also the white South. They realized going after one demographic would hinder chances with the other. Some Republicans argued the black vote should be disregarded as not winnable. Others hoped to capitalize on the fact that Chief Justice Earl Warren, the author of the *Brown v. Board of Education* decision, was a Republican. Even so, there was little hope in the 1950s for the GOP to crack the "Solid South" at the congressional level. Racial extremists believed preservation of Jim Crow relied on "maintaining a one-party system locally and a solid Democratic delegation in Congress."[21]

Those characteristics that most defined Republican safe seats had nothing in common with the race- and class-based voting among Democrats. Instead, Republican safe seats revolved around the issues of farm and foreign policy. The GOP needed to figure out how to retain rural midwesterners who preferred an isolationist foreign policy and agrarian subsidies and gain more southern, coastal, and mountain state voters using economic appeals. Making things trickier urban and industrial population shifts put seats in play for the Democrats that had long been safe for the GOP. Those Republicans hoping to remake the party looked to moderates as the potential source of additional GOP votes, but here the challenge was the increasing tendency of moderate voters to avoid party labels. Still, those congressional Republicans who recorded the strongest performances were moderate like Eisenhower. The most conservative Republicans in Congress ran behind the president in the 1952 election while moderates ran even with Ike.[22]

By the end of 1955 Eisenhower disdained all the most likely Democratic nominees and he was equally scathing about potential Republican candidates. He told Hagerty on December 13, he had hoped the party would use the occasion of his presidency "to build up men who could take my place and who could successfully keep out of that office the crackpot Democrats who were seeking it." Being considered the only viable GOP candidate discomfited Eisenhower, but so did the possible replacements. He lamented the prospect of running again, noting "I am not so sure I will not do it. We have developed no one on our side within our political ranks who can be elected or run this country. I am talking about the strictly political men like Knowland. He would be impossible."[23]

Eisenhower evaluated the GOP divisions in comparison with Democratic schisms. He contended that the latter were more significant but less well known to the public. In correspondence with his friend Hazlett he described the Democrats as a party too focused on labor union issues, pursuit of the "leftish vote," and support for "big paternalistic government and centralization of political power in Washington." He countered that "In the Republicans you find no extreme leftists. . . . We have what I like to call Progressive Moderates and the Conservative Rightists," groups that he noted typically compromised on "important matters." According to White House aide Emmet John Hughes, Eisenhower complained about the Republican National Committee's approach to the 1956 campaign: "All machinery and no imagination." Eisenhower knew that was not enough because he knew his party was still the minority party in the nation.[24]

Given these circumstances, party moderates convinced Eisenhower in

Delegates demonstrate for Eisenhower and Nixon at the Republican National Convention, August 1956. Library of Congress, Prints and Photographs Division, photograph by U.S. News & World Report *Magazine Photograph Collection.*

early 1956 that he had to seek a second White House term because no other Republican could be elected. Eisenhower held a press conference on February 29, 1956, where he announced he would run for a second term. He told the American people in a televised address that evening they would be justified in not wanting him to hold a second term because of his heart attack the previous year. Eisenhower indicated he would run on his record and not make a "barnstorming" campaign across the country. He knew as president he had more important work to do. Political insiders speculated on whether Eisenhower would retain Nixon on the ticket, a decision that spoke to the future of the party. There was no question about keeping Nixon on the ticket if that was his wish. However, Eisenhower did not think the matter to be that simple. He worried that two terms as vice president would not help Nixon win election as president in 1960, but ultimately Eisenhower retained Nixon as his vice-presidential running mate.[25]

Critics in the GOP made clear that the president needed to pay more attention to the Old Guard Republican Right. The "Taft Wing feel they have not been made as much a part of the team as their long service in the party warrants," declared Senate Minority Leader Knowland. The statement had

Republican election night party, President and Mrs. Eisenhower, November 6, 1956. Library of Congress, Prints and Photographs Division, photograph by U.S. News & World Report *Magazine Photograph Collection.*

less to do with the politics of 1956 and more to do with the future of the party after Eisenhower. One historian claimed Knowland's statement was the opening blast in the battle for control of the party in 1960.[26]

On the eve of his 1956 reelection victory Eisenhower told his friend Hazlett he did not want to win unless he garnered a large majority. He held that view despite characterizing the Democratic ticket of Adlai E. Stevenson and Estes Kefauver as "about the sorriest and weakest we have ever had run for the two top offices in the land." Eisenhower had several reasons for his statement. He took seriously his remaining "job of re-forming and re-vamping the Republican Party," the success of which would "be determined by [the Republican Party's] feeling as to how popular I am with the multitudes." Just as significant to Eisenhower's calculation was his understanding that the party division in Congress would "be very close. In almost every project some Democratic help will be absolutely necessary to get it accomplished. Again this strength can be marshaled, on both sides of the aisle, *only* if it is generally believed that I am in a position to go to the people over the heads of the Congressmen."[27]

Eisenhower won by a huge margin in the Electoral College, 457 to 73, and also in the popular vote, 57 percent to 42 percent. On election night he told the American people: "Modern Republicanism looks to the future," meaning younger voters. Eisenhower took hits from conservative Republicans in Congress. Goldwater complained of the president's talk of "modern" Republicanism, a term he charged meant nothing more than a "splintered concept of Republican philosophy."[28] Though he did not necessarily ally himself with the Old Guard, such statements by Goldwater suggest the Arizonan held political views in harmony with the conservatives who had bedeviled Eisenhower.

More than anything else the contest in 1956 had been about the middle class, marking just how different it was from the contests of the 1930s, which focused on economic want, or the contests of the 1940s, which focused on the war. Eisenhower's political success came from his ability to make the "middle class a nationalizing political force." So far, Eisenhower had made the GOP into a national party, a characteristic that had not been true of it for over a hundred years, but he stressed that the party still faced a major challenge, uniting those who had been in the middle class since the 1920s with voters whose middle-class identity came after the depression and who had been loyal to FDR.[29] An even greater challenge simmered beneath the surface of GOP politics, that being the brewing ideological schisms whereby conservative Republicans chafed at Eisenhower's moderation, and moderate Republicans bristled over the excesses of McCarthyism and other rightist behavior.

Eisenhower viewed the 1958 midterms through a highly partisan lens, and he was more eager to criticize liberal Democrats than conservative Republicans. During the 1958 elections Eisenhower fixated on one argument: "my conviction that the deficit-producing, inflation-inviting, irresponsible-spending proposals of self-described liberal Democrats in the Congress had to be combatted at every turn." He blamed unnecessary federal budget deficits as the main reason for the declining value of the dollar in the twentieth century, and he castigated Democrats for proposing "'unwarranted expenditures.'" Some, Eisenhower asserted, reflected "socialistic objectives" of the lawmakers while others came from members of Congress who "were trying to be politically clever, pushing preposterous money bills that would unquestionably bring on a presidential veto, but would give them a voting record to appease pressure groups in the next election." Eisenhower concluded, "not a few legislators of both parties seemed ready to mortgage not only the coming decade but the next century. Yet some had the effrontery to campaign not only on their own spending plans but, oddly, on an alleged 'support of the President.'" Eisenhower pushed hard his austerity message, but it was a tough sell even in his own party.[30]

Liberal Democrats were the biggest winners in the 1958 midterms, gaining advantages in Congress and among the nation's governors. Eisenhower identified several reasons why his party did so poorly: a dip in the economy, discontent over agrarian policy and labor policy, and the lack of an external GOP-leaning organization akin to the AFL-CIO, which heavily supported Democrats. For as much as Eisenhower talked about party building he had not changed the composition of the GOP. The Scripps-Howard newspaper chain took a harsher view: "But as a political leader, Ike has saved his zest for the golf course. Certainly he has not worked at building his party."[31] Despite the 1958 results Eisenhower kept working at remaking the GOP.

As the 1960 race for the presidency neared party leaders divided on what sort of candidate and what sort of ideology was needed to defeat the Democrats. There were four noteworthy factions in the GOP: progressives who included politicians like New York governor Nelson A. Rockefeller; Eisenhower moderates; the stalwart followers of Taft; and conservative adherents of the Goldwater philosophy as detailed in his 1960 book, *The Conscience of a Conservative.* Just one state committee chair on the Republican National Committee, Daniel E. McLean from Massachusetts, defended Eisenhower as the model of what the party needed in 1960. McLean declared, "I do not agree with these Republicans who are criticizing the President. I am proud of his leadership. I hope we can come up with another Eisenhower so that we can win again in 1960." For McLean, "another Eisenhower" meant New York governor Nelson Rockefeller, not Vice President Richard Nixon. Nixon had tried to avoid comment on Eisenhower's "modern" Republicanism, saying, "I don't wish to divide Republicans into groups. The President's program is the program of the Republican Party."[32]

The 1960 Republican nomination, though, did not proceed quite that easily for Nixon because Rockefeller never fully removed himself from consideration. The divisions within the party were not between the conservatives and the Eisenhower progressives, but instead within the latter. Despite a December 1959 statement that he would not seek the White House, Rockefeller continued to flirt with the idea of running. He made public statements critical of administration policy on foreign affairs, suggesting that the annual defense budget was low by about $3 billion. He also complained that Nixon had not fully made known his views on all pertinent matters of public policy, and he demanded that the vice president do so prior to the Republican National Convention. Specifically, he wanted Nixon and the party to make a stronger commitment to civil rights. Finally, in mid-June 1960 he told the press he would only run if he were drafted.

The internal divisions in the GOP became more apparent in 1960 as the party responded to the formation of the Democratic ticket, John F. Kennedy for president and Lyndon B. Johnson for vice president. Republican insiders suggested that the only way Nixon could win was by asking Nelson Rockefeller to be his running mate. There was one problem with the strategy; Rockefeller had no interest in seeking the number-two spot. Nixon met with Rockefeller in his New York home to discuss that and the Republican platform on July 22. Rockefeller refused the vice presidency, but he tried to influence the platform. While that process was under way Rockefeller released to the press the original platform language. The result: conservatives in the party, especially Barry Goldwater, accused Nixon of "surrender[ing]" to Rockefeller. Some even telegrammed Eisenhower asking that he endorse Goldwater. Eisenhower wanted a "sound" platform that would help the ticket, but he also expected it to affirm the accomplishments of his administration. Nixon told Eisenhower, "What I'm trying to do is to find some ground on which Nelson can be with us and not against us."[33]

At the convention Goldwater flirted briefly with challenging Nixon's nomination. He called the vice president's agreement with Rockefeller the "Munich of the Republican Party." Three separate pro-Goldwater groups attended the Republican National Convention: Americans for Goldwater, Goldwater for President, and Youth for Goldwater. Such support made some think Goldwater could claim the vice-presidential nomination, and the Arizona senator was not averse to the idea, remarking that only having "marijuana in my veins" would cause him to resist such an offer. Party conservatives nominated Goldwater at the convention, but he declined, telling the delegates they needed to unite behind Nixon in order to defeat the Democrats. He also alluded to a conservative future for his party: "Let's get to work if we want to take this party back—and I think we can."[34]

Election Day, November 8, 1960, was not a good one for the GOP. Nixon and his running mate, Henry Cabot Lodge, came close, but it was not enough. Kennedy and Johnson won a narrow victory. Some of what Nixon told Eisenhower is instructive of the problems the party had faced in the 1950s and would continue to face during the early 1960s. Said Nixon, "I ran 7 percent *ahead* of the other Republican candidates. Kennedy ran a little more than that behind other Democratic candidates." This meant Nixon was more popular than other candidates in his party and Kennedy less popular. Nixon and Lodge won more states than Kennedy and Johnson, twenty-six to twenty-three (Mississippi gave its delegates to Senator Harry Byrd of Virginia), explaining how the GOP was able to gain twenty House seats even when its standard-bearer ran ahead of the rest of the ticket.[35]

After eight years in office what should be said of Eisenhower's modern Republicanism? Presidential aide Emmet John Hughes argued, "Eight years of a Republican Administration did leave intact all such [New Deal] laws and measures. Yet it is hardly accurate to ascribe this to presidential statesmanship, liberalism, or even choice." Eisenhower led no purposeful challenge to these measures, instead "accept[ing] their immutability, as a matter of political necessity." Because Eisenhower felt only "antipathy toward TVA—and at least a tolerance toward right-to-work laws," Hughes deduced moderate Republicanism was more chimerical than real: "There was exceedingly little here, then, to suggest the labor of a President who was *trying* to be a farsighted consolidator of past social legislation. And it is not easy to assign historic credit to a man for achievements he never attempted."[36]

The "1950s essentially were a lost decade" for the Republican Party, at least from the perspective of intellectuals who shared Eisenhower's ambition for modern Republicanism. In terms of public policy, Eisenhower's administration was successful, but gauged from the perspective of party building at the grass roots it was not. The party had not grown sufficiently in popular vote. Nor had it coalesced around core principles. Going into the 1960s, then, there was no clear vision of what the GOP stood for. Hughes judged, "And Dwight David Eisenhower—by his own austere and negative prescription for the role of party leader—could not help it to make up its deeply divided mind." Moreover, Hughes assessed that Eisenhower, dubbed the father of modern Republicanism, was not suited to lead the party into a new era because "his economic and social views could not convincingly be described as 'modern.' And his political behavior could not, with rare exception, be described as militantly and passionately 'Republican.' The fact is that the President who was supposed to lead the Republican Party toward new, high ground—both 'liberal' and 'modern'—could not seriously be distinguished from a conservative Democrat." Some historians have gone further, arguing Eisenhower was just a conservative.[37]

Did the GOP learn anything from this history? Did it help congressional Republicans grapple with the Kennedy administration? Not really. Though Kennedy was not terribly successful getting his program through Congress, the fault lay as much with divisiveness in the Democratic Party and ineffectual presidential leadership as with GOP skill in rebuffing the administration. That is not to say the GOP was strong during the Kennedy administration. It was not. The party lacked a clear leader, and, while the search for a youthful moderate continued, no obvious choice appeared. This became even more true after Nixon lost his race for the California governorship in 1962. The GOP schism between Eisenhower's progressive Republicanism and Taftite conservatism became the defining factor in GOP party politics for the next two decades, with conservatives adopting the view they were the only legitimate spokespeople for the real America. Nor did the Republicans demonstrate a substantive and nuanced appreciation for the significant demographic and macroeconomic shifts under way in the United States. Too little notice was given to the rise of the Sunbelt and the decline of the Midwest and the Northeast, the two regions most critical to the past successes of the GOP.[38] Ike's failure in the 1950s to build a progressive Republican Party and Nixon's defeat in 1960 accounted for what made Goldwater possible in 1964. To get to that story, though, requires an examination of the affairs within the Democratic Party in the early 1960s.

A NEW FRONTIER FOR THE
DEMOCRATIC PARTY?

John F. Kennedy promised the American people a New Frontier when he sought the presidency in 1960, and he still mattered to party politics a year after his murder in Dallas. The reason JFK was important in 1964 was his death. Lyndon B. Johnson made the election into a referendum on JFK's unfulfilled agenda. Because Kennedy and Democratic Party politics during his administration are central to understanding the 1964 presidential election, a careful reading of the Democratic Party in the early 1960s, one that explains why the party endured turmoil, is necessary. Matters within the party were far from harmonious despite Democratic control of Congress and the White House. The fissures that ripped the party asunder at the end of the decade were already apparent by 1960 when Kennedy sought the presidency. Indeed, Democratic schisms—between liberals and conservatives and between southerners and the rest of the country—dominated Kennedy's presidency. Kennedy's work as head of his party while president is as important as the circumstances that prevented him from standing for reelection to any thorough analysis of the 1964 contest.

In the popular mind JFK is often remembered as a liberal lion who modernized the Democratic Party, which had struggled to regain its momentum during the 1950s. Kennedy did inspire young Americans and he did call for new reforms in education, health care, housing, the economy, and civil rights. His results were far less impressive than his promises. Liberals had high expectations after the 1960

President John F. Kennedy's birthday celebration on May 27, 1961, at the National Guard Armory. Left to right: Speaker Sam Rayburn; President Kennedy; Chairman of the Democratic National Committee (DNC) John M. Bailey. The fundraising dinner was given by the DNC and the Democratic Senatorial and Congressional Campaign Committees. Abbie Rowe. White House Photographs. John F. Kennedy Presidential Library and Museum, Boston.

election, but there was no liberal majority in either the House or Senate. Even though Democrats controlled both chambers of Congress, conservatives in that party worked with conservative Republicans to cripple Kennedy's New Frontier. A community of interests between conservative Democrats and conservative Republicans in Congress had brought this ideological faction known as the conservative coalition together in the late 1930s. Upon his death major legislation involving each of his reform goals remained at a stalemate. The party divisions that then Senate majority leader Lyndon Johnson (D-TX) and Speaker of the House Sam Rayburn (D-TX) had managed in the 1950s worsened in the early 1960s. Liberals had grown even more vexed with the ideological diversity in the party and what they believed was too much power for conservative southern Democrats. Senate majority leader Mike Mansfield (D-MT) and Speaker John

McCormack (D-MA) (Rayburn died of cancer in 1961) never satisfied the liberal Democratic expectations. Conservative resentment also threatened party harmony and widened party cleavages. This problem was most acute in the South where conservative Democrats dominated the local party structures. The story of the Democratic Party in the Kennedy years, then, is one of stasis and frustration, not of a new frontier. Kennedy developed a reelection campaign strategy based on this difficulty.

This party factionalism emerged from the diversity of views that had made possible the New Deal. By the 1950s that ideological heterogeneity degenerated into a skirmish for the future of the party. This breach had widened by the 1958 midterm congressional elections, which resulted in a triumph for liberal Democrats. Voters that year feared a GOP economic recession. Democrats picked up fifty new House seats and sixteen new Senate seats, leaving a margin of 282 Democrats and 153 Republicans in the House and 65 to 35 in the Senate. The mood of the new lawmakers included equal parts contempt for Republicans and for conservative Democrats, who they concluded cooperated too often with the GOP.[1]

In 1960, Democrats addressed this challenge by nominating a candidate—Kennedy—who claimed to represent a new generation, and by implication one who was not connected to the divides of the past. He beat back several influential and more seasoned Democrats, namely Senator Hubert H. Humphrey (D-MN), Johnson, and Adlai Stevenson, to claim the nomination. Kennedy ran against Republican Richard M. Nixon, from his same generation, who nonetheless was clearly linked to the politics of the past. The presidential campaign pitted these two moderates against one another. The campaign was not easy; Democratic difficulties abounded up and down the ballot. Observed one Kennedy staffer, "Kennedy liberalism was more a political strategy than a set of beliefs."[2]

For his running mate JFK selected LBJ, who was one of those ambitious and wizened Democrats senior to him in experience and accomplishments. Johnson balanced the ticket, regionally and attitudinally. Journalists and politicians in 1960 and historians since have opined at great length on the differences between the two Democratic running mates: Kennedy urbane and Johnson crude, Kennedy Harvard educated and Johnson degreed at a teacher's college, Kennedy liberal and Johnson conservative (the records of their two administrations suggest the inaccuracy of this point). Kennedy's brother, Robert F. Kennedy, helped draw these distinctions. He hated Johnson, and had bitterly opposed placing him on the ticket, still upset about statements Johnson and his partisans made in the primary campaign about

Johnson and Kennedy campaign together in September 1960 in Austin, Texas. The candidates are sitting in a convertible pulling away from the State Capitol building, greeting supporters on both sides of the car. LBJ Library, photo by Frank Muto.

Jack's health problems and about their father Joe Kennedy's sympathies for Nazi Germany in the 1930s.[3]

Bobby had good reason to dislike LBJ, but Jack was more forgiving. Earlier in the spring of 1960 Bobby had visited Lyndon at the LBJ Ranch to figure out whether Johnson would run, and if not, whether he would endorse Jack. A noncommittal LBJ took a naïve Bobby deer hunting, supplying him not with a deer rifle but with a ten-gauge shotgun. When Bobby fired, the recoil knocked him backward. Johnson told him, "Son, you've got to learn to handle a gun like a man." Journalist Rowland Evans noted Bobby Kennedy's recollection of his last conversation with his brother before JFK was assassinated. Bobby told Evans that Jack had said, "'Don't ever forget that

Lyndon Johnson is a congenital liar.'" Evans explained, Bobby "believed it. He thought Johnson was a bad man." Such mythology masked more important truths. JFK, according to cold warrior and journalist Joseph W. Alsop, viewed Johnson much more favorably, "He didn't have any contempt for Johnson. He greatly admired him. He told me over and over again during the campaign that if he couldn't get it, Johnson was the only man in the Democratic party who really deserved to be president of the United States."[4]

Why, though, was Johnson interested in being vice president? At the time of his nomination Johnson was the unequaled master of the Senate. Majority leader since 1955, Johnson had amassed an impressive record of working with liberals and moderates across party and regional lines, all the more notable given Republican control of the White House. He had ambitions beyond the Senate, making an ill-fated favorite son bid for the presidency in 1956 and a more serious but strategically flawed run in 1960. Johnson thought his knowledge of Senate politics prepared him for seeking the Democratic nomination, but it did not. A vastly different set of rules governed the national political parties, including required travel to all fifty states. Kennedy made a national campaign, visiting each state in 1959 before he announced in 1960. Johnson did not. Johnson mistakenly assumed if he held back the other contenders would do each other so much harm that he could claim the nomination at the convention. Rayburn observed of Kennedy, "Everywhere he goes he leaves behind an organization."[5]

Coming from one-party, factional Texas, Johnson did not fully appreciate the nuances of two-party politics or the increasing importance of primary elections in the presidential nomination process. Johnson, much to the frustration of those who wanted to see him elected president, did not announce his candidacy until July 5, 1960. He had presumed he would earn the nomination because of his Senate record, but he overlooked concerns about his crude manners and about his ethically questionable deal making. Johnson nevertheless was an attractive vice-presidential candidate because he brought geographic balance to the ticket. Johnson saw two advantages to being vice president: the office would provide him a pathway to the presidency and it would save him from the reduced circumstances of being majority leader with either a Democratic president or with the Republican Nixon, where in either case he would have much less power than he had had with Eisenhower.[6]

Lady Bird Johnson saw the matter somewhat differently. She ignored her husband's ambition, but instead said of his motivation for accepting the vice-presidential nomination: "Well, the real, I'm sure the compelling force behind Lyndon was . . . fifty-two years of party loyalty. You see, there's something a little bit old-fashioned about him. He came from an era when that was a strong thing in one's life, party loyalty, a discipline." Such loyalty did not cause him to behave in a "rancorous" manner toward Republicans, but it did cause him to believe he had to answer the call of his party: "if he were on the ticket as vice president, it was possible that he would help carry the south and the state of Texas, and the party might win by a narrow margin, and if he were not, that it would very likely lose."[7]

Senator Barry M. Goldwater (R-AZ) criticized the match between Johnson and Kennedy in 1960 as "an unholy wedding." Goldwater and Johnson had talked over drinks right before that year's convention, and the Texan had told Goldwater his only interest was in claiming the presidential nomination, saying "hell no" when Goldwater asked if he would accept the vice-presidential spot. Goldwater recounted the handwritten note he sent to Johnson right after the 1960 convention: "Sitting here trying to think of how I feel about your taking the nomination and all I can think of is 'nauseated.'" Goldwater told an interviewer, "every time he'd see me for a long time afterwards, he'd say, 'Barry, are you still nauseated?' And I'd say, 'Hell, yes.'"[8]

Careful parsing of Kennedy's campaign rhetoric reveals a centrist, not a liberal, Democrat. Certainly, he made the obligatory declarations that Democrats could not afford four more years of Republican government: "the American people . . . want a return to the dynamic and creative leadership of the Democratic Party." He chastised Nixon for having no core political values. He also used history to explain why electing a President Nixon in 1960 would be dangerous for the country: "Perhaps we could afford a Coolidge following Harding," Kennedy wondered. "But after Buchanan this nation needed a Lincoln—and after Taft we needed a Wilson—after Hoover we needed Franklin Roosevelt. . . . And after eight years of drugged and fitful sleep, this nation needs strong, creative Democratic leadership in the White House." Later in his first debate with Nixon, Kennedy declared his philosophy of the state, one that balanced individual and government responsibility. "I know that there are those who say we [Democrats] want to turn everything over to the Government. I don't at all. I want individuals to meet their responsibilities and I want the states to meet their responsibilities," Kennedy stressed. "But I think there is also a national responsibility" to solve problems individuals and states cannot.[9]

In the 1960 election, JFK argued that the decision by voters would determine not just the next four years but the entire decade. Among the

Texas float in the 1961 Inaugural Parade depicts both the southwestern past, with the oxen-driven covered wagon, and the Sunbelt future, with a representation of a global world. Johnson's portrait is positioned between the two poles. Robert Knudsen. White House Photographs. John F. Kennedy Presidential Library and Museum, Boston.

challenges Kennedy identified were the increasing number of children, upwards of 10 million, lacking a "decent education" and the 8 million new households needing "decent homes in decent neighborhoods." Moreover, he listed health care for the aged, an expanding population in need of jobs, insufficient water and power resources in the West, inadequate urban infrastructure, juvenile delinquency, racial tension, a nuclear arms race, and new nations rising from former colonized regions of the world. He concluded that since the 1960s would not be years of "status quo" but instead change, the GOP, a "party of the status quo," was ill-suited to govern.[10]

The results of the 1960 contest proved razor thin; Kennedy bested Nixon by a mere 112,803 votes even though Democrats nationally outnumbered Republicans by a three-to-two margin. Democrats enjoyed greater national loyalty than Republicans. This voter loyalty held together the party despite significant ideological differences between northern and southern party members. Democrats were about equally divided three ways among liberals, moderates, and conservatives, while the Republicans were mostly moderate and conservative with only a small percentage of liberals. In 1960, Democrats lost twenty-one House seats and two Senate seats. The defeated House Democrats were liberals to the left of Kennedy. Even so, Democratic National Committee chair John M. Bailey explicated the loss: "we had an awful good year in 1958," which created the "backlash" in 1960. Bailey avowed, "Some of them won in '58 who perhaps shouldn't have won."[11]

Kennedy knew going into the White House that he would face challenges with Congress given the dominance of the conservative coalition in the legislative branch. As soon as he won the presidency he began working on his congressional relations. Kennedy viewed Congress as "something very difficult and something that definitely had to be worked with all the time." One member of the Senate contended Kennedy was better than Eisenhower but not as good as Johnson in "keep[ing] a personal touch with the members of the Congress." He did enjoy the "enthusiastic support" of the legislative leadership. Finally, Kennedy relied on his aggressive congressional liaison office.[12]

Still, significant challenges remained with the Kennedy congressional liaison efforts. The president had little interest in domestic issues and did not want to do the work required for reform in Congress. Kennedy never made personal connections with lawmakers. Despite having been in Congress since 1947, Kennedy had few close friends on the Hill. He did not seek to make friends while in the White House, either. Not a backslapper, Kennedy "rarely asked" lawmakers to vote in a particular way. Because many members of Congress had run ahead of Kennedy in 1960, one lawmaker observed, "the people in Congress do not feel that they owe the president anything." Perhaps most significant of all Kennedy made no attempt to use what would have been his best asset with Congress: Vice President Johnson. Kennedy was happy for Johnson to chat up lawmakers, learn what they were thinking, but he did not want Johnson to lead efforts to get legislation passed. He was insecure about the older, more experienced Johnson taking a public leadership role in lawmaking.[13]

The southern Democrats proved to be the biggest problem for Kennedy and the Democratic Party. Senator Clinton Anderson (D-NM) said of the divisions in Congress during the Kennedy years: "I think the deep South and the moderate South were almost constantly opposed to him. I can't think of very many folks that really loyally rejoiced in his being elected. . . . But the deep South never gave him a chance." Nor did Kennedy try. White House aide Theodore Sorensen said of Kennedy's work with southern Democrats in the Senate: "I don't believe he ever met with a group of Southerners."[14]

The year 1961 proved dismal for Democratic reformers who had had great hope following the 1960 election. For the first time in eight years Democrats held the White House and both houses of Congress. Still they could not get much done. This failure—and reaction to it—showcased Democratic Party divides. Southern conservatives were quite happy that the Kennedy program stalled, but moderates and liberals regardless of region felt differently. Area redevelopment, a federal program of investment in private businesses in order to stimulate the economy in depressed urban and rural areas, was the only win from Kennedy's campaign platform. Other Kennedy bills failed in 1961: federal aid to education, college scholarships, and health care for the elderly.[15]

Nor did Kennedy fulfill civil rights promises solely within the purview of the executive branch. On the campaign trail Kennedy had castigated Eisenhower for not ending housing discrimination, which he argued the Republican president could have done "with one stroke of a pen." He failed to follow through with that implied promise, prompting civil rights groups to begin sending pens and ink to the White House. Kennedy justified his nonaction by saying this particular civil rights reform would harm both his overall legislative agenda and the party's chances in the 1962 midterm elections.[16]

Given the narrow margin in the 1960 election and the legislative failures in 1961, the midterm contests in 1962 were of paramount importance to the Democratic Party. Kennedy knew that a large Democratic sweep in 1962 could stimulate action on his moribund legislative agenda. More Democrats were required because, according to one insider, there were only 168 members of the House who would vote with the administration. Kennedy partisans believed the election of an additional fifty moderate and liberal Democrats would be necessary to impede the conservative coalition and produce legislative victories for the administration.[17]

Kennedy took a tentative approach. Initially, he avoided open campaigning but followed a behind-the-scenes strategy to help Democrats who were in trouble. An August 1962 poll showed twenty-four of thirty-five marginal Democratic seats in danger of defeat. Most of Kennedy's effort, though, focused on helping publicize his reform package and not speaking for particular candidates. Ultimately, Kennedy logged more miles on the campaign trail than Eisenhower had in 1954 and 1958 combined. He stressed that winning just five or ten more seats would make a huge difference, especially given the fact that wins and losses by three or four votes were common in the House. "So this is not an off-year," the president avowed, "it is an important year."[18]

Others focused on the Senate in 1962. Former member of Congress and labor union official Andrew Biemiller asserted: "We couldn't see any great gains or losses in the House. That was right. Our analysis was correct. But we did see a chance of gaining in the Senate and so we were over there working damn hard." Once the votes were in, Democrats lost four House seats and gained two Senate seats. Compared with all twentieth-century midterms through 1962, Kennedy fared well. For these years, the party that controlled the presidency typically lost seats: House losses averaged just over thirty-three and Senate losses almost four.[19]

The election, though, codified an untenable status quo. Could the Kennedys push civil rights and remain cordial with southern segregationists in Congress, individuals with whom Jack and Bobby had developed friendships in the 1950s? Could the Democratic Party weather such a storm? Joseph Alsop contended civil rights threatened "to make terrible trouble between the Kennedys and the people in the South." He explained, "You have to remember that the South was still very important to the Democratic party." Moreover, both Kennedy brothers liked the southern Democrats. Even so southern Democrats proved to be a substantial political challenge for the Kennedy administration. In a 1962 conversation with Senator George Smathers (D-FL), Kennedy groused about southern Democrats who did not want to get things done so the legislature could adjourn and go home. This schism within the Democratic Party harmed efforts to address civil rights legislation. Nevertheless, southern lawmakers panicked that motels and restaurants, for example, might be forced to integrate.[20]

Kennedy amassed a mixed civil rights record. He abetted conservative aims when he appointed five racists as federal judges in the South, and he intended a gradual program of reform. He rejected as unnecessary bills that would have hurried the progress of school desegregation. Civil rights leaders had limited faith in what Kennedy might do. Still he had taken incremental steps, issuing an executive order regarding equal employment opportunity, filing multiple voting-rights suits, supporting school desegregation initiatives, and announcing he would pursue the end of segregated travel facilities. Activists hoped to provoke the situation in the South and compel a more muscular response from Kennedy.[21] Following violently suppressed civil rights demonstrations in Birmingham, Alabama, in spring 1963, Kennedy called for a major civil rights bill.

Vice President Johnson was skeptical the administration had done enough to prepare for this step. He told Sorensen, "I don't know who drafted it. I've never seen it. Hell, if the vice president doesn't know what's in it, how do you expect others to know what's in it. I got it from the *New York Times*." Moreover, Johnson believed Kennedy must go to the South and talk to white voters: "If he goes down there and looks them in the eye, and states the moral issue and the Christian issue, and he does it face to face, these southerners at least respect his courage." Just as important, said Johnson, was meeting with African American civil rights leaders to convince them of the administration's sincerity.[22]

On June 19, a week after the murder of civil rights leader Medgar Evers, Kennedy introduced his bill. It guaranteed the right to vote to all with a minimum of a sixth-grade education, the elimination of discrimination in public accommodations and employment, and more authority to the attorney general to enforce school desegregation. Odds for passage in the Senate were not good because southerners were certain to filibuster the bill. Moreover, Kennedy feared that Martin Luther King Jr.'s planned August 1963 March on Washington would only make matters worse by goading the rabid segregationists without winning congressional votes for reform.[23]

Sorensen contended, "He [Kennedy] was neither optimistic nor pessimistic about the bill. He felt it was something which had to be done: that a national crisis required it; that the Congress had no other choice; that Republican support—which would be necessary in order to pass the bill in either house—would be forthcoming because the Republicans would not have any other real choice." Sorensen credited Johnson with playing "a major role in the formulation of the legislation." He also recounted Johnson "was at first concerned about what we were doing and what we were sending up. He felt that perhaps he had not been adequately consulted, that it was going to be politically harmful to the Administration in the Senate and in the South."[24]

The rest of the summer and into the fall liberals and conservatives fought a bitter battle over the bill with no real solution in sight. This legislative gridlock had the potential to harm the Democratic Party on the eve of the 1964 election. *New York Times* Washington Bureau Chief Tom Wicker held, the president "feared the power of Congress too much, and at the same time underrated the ways and means Congress had to thwart him."[25] As such, Kennedy was never able to exert his leadership over the legislative branch.

Vice President Johnson, at least with regard to civil rights, did not think

Kennedy expended enough personal capital. After the Birmingham riots LBJ stressed he and the president should travel the South together, speaking about the importance of civil rights reform. Doing so would "bring the authority and prestige of the President, the charm and force of President Kennedy's own personality and popularity and standing to this effort." Johnson insisted such was necessary for "paving the way for the successful passage of the bill."[26]

What then should be made of Johnson's relationship with Kennedy? Jack Valenti recalled, "I remember one incident at his ranch, in 1962, I guess, where there were a group of . . . very wealthy, conservative, Democrats and all of whom had a distaste for John Kennedy." At this gathering, according to Valenti, "a very close friend of Johnson's, longtime contributor, neighbor, close friend, began to inveigh against Kennedy. . . . Johnson fixed the fellow with that stony stare and finally he said to this man, called him by his first name, 'no one sits at my table and criticizes the president of the United States. You've got two choices, you shut up, or you leave.'" When Johnson finished, "the table fell silent, and the man said 'I'm sorry Lyndon, I'm sorry. Let's let it go at that.'" The vice president disagreed. Valenti avowed, Johnson "made clear that nobody criticized Kennedy in his presence."[27]

Even though Valenti tried to convey a mutual respect between LBJ and JFK, that respect was mixed with disdain. "He mentioned to me many times that, after he became president too, how President Kennedy was solicitous of him," said Valenti. "Always. He invited him, oftentimes, to second floor dinners where just the Kennedy social crowd" attended. At such gatherings Jackie Kennedy "was enormously affectionate to him. Always gentle to him. And I think he didn't feel comfortable at a lot of these social gatherings, these weren't his kind of folk. But the Kennedys never once diverged from this embrace of Johnson and Lady Bird. And he never forgot it." According to other sources, Kennedy did not enjoy socializing with Johnson. Johnson biographers noted the vice president and his wife were infrequent guests at second-floor White House social affairs. Moreover, guests made "brutal" comments regarding "the inside nasty stuff about Lyndon." Kennedy staff called the Johnsons "Mr. and Mrs. Cornpone." Such treatment along with the lack of meaningful work left Johnson morose and moody. He spent whole days in bed. "I cannot stand Johnson's damn long face," Kennedy once groused.[28]

Going into his reelection campaign Kennedy benefited from favorable public approval ratings, 59 percent in November 1963, which was down from 76 percent earlier in January. Aides attributed the popularity dip to

Kennedy's advocacy of civil rights. Moreover, Gallup polling suggested in the spring of 1963 that Kennedy would easily defeat any likely opponent, including Goldwater, Governor Nelson A. Rockefeller of New York, Governor George Romney of Michigan, or Nixon. Kennedy dismissed these optimistic projections because so much could happen in 1964 to change the dynamics of the contest. He knew passage of the tax cut and civil rights would help his cause but more dilatory tactics from Congress would hurt. He also knew there was little chance Congress would enact either bill before the election given Democratic divides in the legislative branch.[29]

Planning for the reelection campaign in 1964 had begun in earnest in 1963 and it unfolded on two tracks, one political and one legislative. Thinking about poverty influenced the latter; Kennedy read a review of Michael Harrington's book, *The Other America*, in the *New Yorker* and realized antipoverty legislation was necessary. The president also discussed the issue with Walter Heller, the chair of the Council of Economic Advisors. According to Sorensen, Kennedy wanted "a special anti-poverty program" to become "a major theme of his 1964 legislative program." Campaign strategy discussions that fall left him "a little shaken" about whether such an initiative was feasible. Census director Richard M. Scammon told Kennedy and his political team "most people did not consider themselves impoverished" and would not support a federal antipoverty initiative. Scammon also maintained, "these were not the people we were trying to reach." Instead, he argued Kennedy should seek votes of suburban residents. The president was intrigued and asked if research indicated at what income level such upwardly mobile people abandoned the Democratic Party and became Republicans. Scammon guessed perhaps not even $10,000 a year.[30]

By early fall 1963 Kennedy had begun his campaign. In September, the president visited the western states where he had fared poorly in 1960. Billed as a trip to discuss conservation issues, the journey offered Kennedy the opportunity to seek political favor. In his public outreach that fall he addressed issues where voters had questions, specifically the economy and civil rights. Kennedy stressed the "faster growth rates" in the United States as compared with Europe. Civil rights caused Kennedy to worry about the non-South as much as the South. Charles Roche, an official with the Democratic National Committee, advised that there was a long list of states Kennedy would likely not carry in 1964: Alabama, Arizona, Colorado, Idaho, Indiana, Iowa, Kansas, Kentucky, Maine, Mississippi, Nebraska, New Hampshire, North Dakota, Oklahoma, South Dakota, Utah, Vermont, Virginia, and Wyoming. The list of states Roche expected Kennedy to win was much shorter: Connecticut, District of Columbia, Georgia, Massachusetts, New York, Rhode Island, and West Virginia. Because his margin in New Jersey had been thin in 1960 Kennedy emphasized that state where there was a "weakening of the Democratic political machine, plus the frightening backlash flowing from the whole civil rights issue."[31]

Kennedy did not fret about right-wing influence on politics. Even though these fringe actors were well funded from foundation and corporate donors Kennedy hoped most Americans would reject their views on Social Security and unemployment insurance even if they supported the anti-Communist rhetoric. He even hoped Goldwater would get the GOP nomination because he thought defeating the Arizona Republican would be easy. He told aides, "Don't waste any chance to praise Barry. Build him up a little. Don't mention the others." In jest, he said, "Give me Barry, I won't even have to leave the Oval Office."[32]

Kennedy's biggest geographic concern, though, was with the South, the region where white voters were angriest with the administration's civil rights efforts and most susceptible to the politics of resentment. Kennedy told Walter Cronkite on September 2 that he knew he would lose some states in the South but he refused to give up the entire region. Kennedy had other considerations: with southern Democrats powerful in Congress a Kennedy loss in the region would render southern Democratic committee chairs even less cooperative. Pollster Louis Harris advised Kennedy not to agonize so much that "segregationist, states rights and right wing conservatism" dominated the region. Instead, he contended that a surging economy and moderate politics were dominant in the region. A critical component of the Kennedy reelection efforts included increasing African American voter registration, especially in the South. Kennedy advisors argued the key to carrying Texas in 1964 came from increasing registration of African Americans and Mexican Americans. One staff member in the Democratic National Committee recommended sending as much money as was required to the state to ensure the success of this registration effort. Moreover, in discussing plans for the convention in November 1963 Kennedy and his closest political advisors conferred on the challenges to writing a platform given southern Democratic hostility to civil rights. They questioned whether the platform could be limited to the president's extant statements on key policy issues to avoid multiple demands for inserting new topics in the document. Kennedy feared "having a lot of Negroes coming in and testifying about how they are being mistreated in Alabama."[33]

To keep at least part of the South, Kennedy decided to focus on Texas and Florida. His team thought he had the best chance of winning those southern states. Trips to both states were planned for November 1963. Given what happened in Dallas, the Florida trip has slipped from historical memory. He went to Tampa and Miami on November 18. There he talked about the economy and Latin American affairs. The president asserted, "complaining about Castro" and "blaming all problems on Communism" will not remedy turmoil in Latin America.[34]

Why Dallas? The trip, which had been planned for over a year, had two purposes: foremost fundraising and secondarily settlement of an instate political dispute between Texas governor John Connally and Senator Ralph Yarborough (D-TX). According to DNC officials, Texas Democrats had not given money to the national party since Kennedy's election. Conversely, Massachusetts Democrats had given $2.5 million in the same period. Kennedy had long wanted Connally to host fundraising dinners, but the Texan was not interested in appearing too close to Kennedy and his new civil rights agenda. Further complicating matters for Connally, the president's Texas backers were his political opponents. "To rally new support for him and to raise funds, therefore," Connally complained, "I would have to appeal to my supporters—literally, to spend my political capital—while knowing that in the election of 1964, in which I too had to run again, many of Kennedy's backers would be fighting me." Kennedy, Johnson, and Connally met in June 1963 about the trip. Kennedy believed the fundraising would help him improve his image in a state he feared he might lose.[35]

They traveled first to San Antonio on November 21 and then to Houston for a fundraising dinner that evening. They then flew to Fort Worth where they spent the night. On the morning of November 22, they traveled to Dallas where Kennedy was scheduled to give a speech. A second fundraising dinner was to follow in Austin that evening before the Johnsons were to host the Kennedys at the LBJ Ranch for the night. While Kennedy was in Houston the *Houston Chronicle* published a poll that showed Goldwater carrying Texas if the election was held then. *New York Times* reporter Tom Wicker recalled Governor Connally swore that by the time of the election a year later "Kennedy could carry Texas."[36]

Kennedy cast Johnson in the role of "peacemaker" in the Yarborough-Connally feud, which was more a sideshow than the main event of the trip. The vice president saw nothing to be gained from the trip because he believed no reconciliation to the fractured Texas Democratic Party could be had. Nor was he on good terms with either Connally—who disagreed with Johnson's strong civil rights views—or Yarborough—who did not like that presidential patronage for Texas went through Johnson and not him. Bailey recalled: "at first Connally didn't even want to invite Yarborough to the party at his house," meaning the Governor's Mansion. On the first day of the trip Yarborough had refused to ride in the same car with Johnson. White House staffer James T. Corcoran explained, "Well, it was a very brutal conflict. The conflict was brutal. . . . I don't think any one of them, they didn't like each other."[37]

According to Lady Bird, Lyndon had not urged Kennedy to go to Texas in November 1963: "Well, Lyndon wasn't, and this aggrieved him somewhat, he wasn't as much a part of the planning of that trip as he thought he should. I mean, it was just presented to him as something that was going to be done, is my recollection." She minimized the Connally-Yarborough split, noting "the odd thing from our standpoint was that Senator Yarborough had always been pretty good about voting with Lyndon's line of what he had wanted philosophically and legislation he had pushed." She added, "personally we were never close" with Yarborough, but "we were very close and devoted and had years of association with John. But it was just, perhaps just as simple as the fact that John was a good deal more conservative, and Yarborough was a good deal more liberal, and their chemistries just didn't mix."[38]

Jack Valenti made the arrangements for the Houston leg of the trip. He recalled that Johnson had phoned him and was "very upset" that they were even going to Texas. Valenti contended Connally had gone to Washington, DC, without telling Johnson and had "cut a deal with JFK" to make the journey. Nevertheless, said Valenti, "The trip had been dazzlingly successful," with large gatherings in San Antonio and Houston. "People were everywhere, we had not a hostile face in the crowd. Johnson was jubilant, absolutely jubilant."[39]

At the Houston dinner, Kennedy turned a verbal gaffe into a patronage argument for Democrats. Kennedy said, "'We are getting ready to send aloft a rocket with the greatest payroll in history!'" He intended to say payload, and when he corrected the mistake he asserted, laughing, "'Yes, and we've put a little bit of that payroll right here in Houston too.'" The crowd also laughed, and they gave money to Democrats.[40]

Kennedy awoke to rain in Fort Worth on November 22. The headline in the *Dallas Morning News* read "President's Visit Seen Widening State Democratic Split." Deeper in the first section of the paper on page fourteen ran a full-page advertisement funded by right-wing eccentric H. L. Hunt. It asked two questions of the president: "Why did you host, salute and enter-

President John F. Kennedy reaches out to the crowd gathered at the Hotel Texas parking lot rally in Fort Worth, Texas, on November 22, 1963. Also pictured: United Press International (UPI) reporter Merriman "Smitty" Smith and White House Secret Service agents Jack Ready, Stu Stout, Dick Johnsen, and Roy Kellerman. Cecil Stoughton. White House Photographs. John F. Kennedy Presidential Library and Museum, Boston.

tain Tito—Moscow's Trojan Horse?" and "Why has the foreign policy of the United States degenerated to the point that the CIA is arranging coups and having staunch Anti-Communist Allies of the US bloodily exterminated?"[41] Such rhetoric reinforced concerns that the right wing might cause problems during the trip. No one worried about the left-wing fringe.

Wicker recounted the details of the motorcade through Dallas: "They routed us right through the heart of town. The crowds were immense." He noted also that the people were enthusiastic to see Kennedy with just a few Goldwater signs. There was "no evidence whatever of hostility—very enthusiastic crowd, happy crowd, noontime crowd. Warm day, people in their shirt sleeves, pretty girls. A very happy crowd. The Kennedys had plenty of reason to be pleased with it." Until they did not. As the motorcade made its way through Dealey Plaza, lone assassin Lee Harvey Oswald fired three shots, killing Kennedy with his third bullet.[42]

The motorcade sped to Parkland Hospital where Kennedy was pronounced dead. Johnson wanted to return to Washington, DC, as quickly

*Swearing in of Lyndon B. Johnson as president aboard Air Force One, Love
Field, Dallas, Texas. Left to right: Mac Kilduff, Judge Sarah T. Hughes,
Jack Valenti, Albert Thomas, Marie Fehmer (behind Thomas), Lady Bird
Johnson, Chief Curry, President Lyndon B. Johnson, Evelyn Lincoln (eyeglasses
only visible above LBJ's shoulder), Homer Thornberry (in shadow, partially
obscured by LBJ), Roy Kellerman (partially obscured by Thornberry), Lem
Johns (partially obscured by Mrs. Kennedy), Jacqueline Kennedy, Pamela
Tunure (behind Brooks), Jack Brooks, Bill Moyers (mostly obscured by Brooks).
LBJ Library, photo by Cecil Stoughton.*

as possible and address the nation. Wicker described the swearing in of
Johnson aboard Air Force One in Dallas as containing "a little bit of contre-
temps" over the wording of the oath. Initially, the press worried that Judge
Sarah T. Hughes had not used the actual oath but she did. The process
by which she obtained the oath was tense. Johnson called the Justice Department in Washington, DC, to get the proper wording from the attorney
general, also the brother of the slain president. Still, because of the initial
reporting that Hughes and Johnson had not used the correct oath, Wicker

explained, "There was even a little . . . thing that Johnson wasn't really President because he had taken the wrong oath, you know. It was a lot of nonsense."[43]

The scene on Air Force One when it returned to Washington, DC, was one of "anxiety" and "stunning grief." Valenti described the Kennedy contingent as "traumatized human beings" suffering "disbelief, grief beyond all measure." According to Valenti, "The Kennedy people secreted themselves in the after part of the airplane. Mrs. Kennedy came out for the swearing in, there's that famous photograph over there, the only one extant." Upon landing at Andrews drama ensued when RFK boarded the plane. He "came aboard the forward part of the ship and raced down the cabin way . . . here was the new president and myself pinned against the wall and Bobby Kennedy came by without so much as a glance at either of us." Johnson, Valenti said, "expected to get off with the body of the president and Mrs. Kennedy, but the forklift took the entourage, so Johnson had to come off, you know, by himself. But his face remained passive, he never ever mentioned it, ever. I took note of it."[44]

Journalists observed soon after Johnson became president the intensifying tensions with RFK. Rowland Evans recalled an early December 1963 lunch he had with Bobby. The attorney general ruminated on what he might do next, "'I don't know whether I'll stay, or whether I want to go on the ticket in '64, or anything, until I know whether I think Johnson can be president of the United States and follow through with the Kennedy program.'" Kennedy declared it to be "'too early for me to even think about '64, because I don't know whether I want to have any part of these people.'" Evans reflected, "I knew that Bobby, the minute the president was assassinated—the Johnson-Kennedy thing could never work, you knew that. You knew it from 1960; you knew it from before that. You knew it from the personalities of the two men." Evans described Bobby as "head of the most powerful and able political aggregation inside the Democratic Party" while dismissing Johnson as "knowing nothing about national politics" and being "jealous of everything that Bobby did." Evans concluded that Bobby's real ambition was to become president himself, with the immediate question being "whether he wanted to be vice president in '64."[45]

Others in the Kennedy orbit were more favorable in their assessment of Johnson: White House advisor Arthur M. Schlesinger Jr. recorded in his diary for November 25, 1963, "My guess is that [Johnson] will be pretty good on issues, and that in some respects he will be more liberal than JFK." Schlesinger was not alone. Biemiller said of Kennedy and Johnson,

"Oh Johnson far out classed him on the thing. I mean what the hell, this was Johnson's life. I don't think Jack Kennedy ever really completely appreciated being a member of Congress. He had his eye on the presidency for a long, long time. And this was what he was working on." For Johnson at least this battle was one of the driving forces behind his ambition to win the presidency in 1964 by a margin greater than Franklin D. Roosevelt had in 1936 (the election in which he racked up the largest victory of his four presidential races). The Texan needed to prove himself to his critics in the party and the press as a legitimate leader. Several years later Johnson recalled to historian Doris Kearns, "I took the oath. I became President. But for millions of Americans I was still illegitimate, a naked man with no presidential covering, a pretender to the throne, an illegal usurper."[46] His challenge was not to prove his legitimacy but to unite a fractured Democratic Party, win the White House, enact massive new liberal reforms, and reveal himself as the new sun around which Democratic politics and national policy could revolve. Could he accomplish that?

A REPUBLICAN CIVIL WAR BEGINS

"[Dwight D.] Eisenhower won by virtue of being a trans-
partisan war hero, and not on the basis of any ideological
convictions or issues," so said *National Review* publisher
William Rusher. As one of the architects of modern conservatism, Rusher believed a conservative Republican could
win the presidency. He contended appealing to "liberal"
and "moderate" voters had only brought losses in 1940,
1944, 1948, and 1960. His conclusions about the possibility for victory appear bold and presumptuous given that,
in 1960, Republicans controlled just fifteen governorships.
Another conservative observer of mid-twentieth century
politics, Phyllis Schlafly, asserted "a small group of secret
kingmakers who are the most powerful opinion makers in
the world" had "dictated" who the GOP would nominate for
the presidency much in the same way that "Paris dressmak-
ers control the length of women's skirts."[1]

Winning, Rusher explained, required redrawing the party's geographical base to include the conservative regions of
the country: the Midwest, the mountain states, and the South.
Carrying all such states meant the GOP would win the White
House with only two more states, New Hampshire and Vermont, both of which he termed "conservative strongholds."
The party had carried all but two of the Midwest and mountain states in 1960. He deduced the chances were good that
the party would win in Dixie as long as it "would promise
to call off the national vendetta against the South, and take
the constitutional stand on states' rights." Rusher identified
suburbs as prime locations for finding GOP voters because
residents there were "middle-class, basically conservative."
He worried, though, about the lack of "troops" to do the

grassroots labor of a campaign. He indicated that young Americans were ready to do that work, but only for "a conservative candidate" and not "a 'me-too' candidate."[2]

Rusher's strategy for a conservative takeover of the GOP meant war with the eastern establishment. Through its donations, Wall Street had influenced the Republican Party since the 1870s. Since 1940, most of the GOP presidential nominees were New Yorkers or at least had lived for a period in New York, including Wendell Willkie, Thomas Dewey, and Eisenhower. Moreover, the election in 1958 had decimated congressional and gubernatorial Republicans. Two Republicans who prevailed that year were Senator Barry Goldwater of Arizona and Governor Nelson A. Rockefeller of New York, increasing their stature as possible presidential candidates. Rockefeller and Goldwater represented the two poles of the GOP debate during the 1964 presidential nomination fight. Rockefeller was a scion of the eastern establishment who had entered politics in 1958 as a liberal Republican, a stance that worked in New York politics. Conversely, Goldwater was a western conservative who rejected an activist government. Following Richard Nixon's defeat in 1960, a civil war ensued within the party between the eastern establishment and "the primitives," the term journalist Theodore H. White used for the heartland Republicans who controlled party affairs in Congress. By the early 1960s this faction found common ground with new right conservatives who gravitated toward Goldwater, the man they wanted to lead the ticket in 1964.[3]

A son of the Southwest, Arizona specifically, Goldwater embodied the mythology of rugged individualism. His father was Jewish and his mother Episcopalian. Young Barry was raised in his mother's faith, but as an adult he did not care much about religion. Most assumed he would follow in the family department store business. The store, Goldwaters, was a high-end retailer that catered to wealthy people who wintered in Phoenix. Goldwater became CEO of the company at age twenty-eight.[4]

Despite his rhetoric about individualism, Goldwater, like most westerners, enjoyed his social and economic status largely because of federal government programs to develop his native region: his family's first department store had been built with an army contract, federal reclamation projects caused the Phoenix population to boom (and consume), and the state spent far more federal dollars ($342 million in the New Deal era) than it paid in taxes during the same period ($16 million). In spinning his autobiography Goldwater avowed his wealth came from his own hard work. He ignored his vast inheritance, his wife Peggy's tremendous family fortune, and the federal government programs that made the Southwest habitable. He even said, "We didn't know the federal government. Everything that was done, we did it ourselves."[5]

Once World War II started he enlisted in the Army Air Corps, and after that war he became involved in local politics, assuming the persona of the "anti-politician." This anti-politician was elected to the Senate in 1952, and by the end of the decade he became chair of the Republican Senatorial Campaign Committee, a post that helped him meet party leaders around the country. His poor attendance record suggests he was not a force in Senate politics, though. In January 1960 Goldwater began writing a three-times a week column for the *Los Angeles Times*. His popularity with conservatives increased even more with the 1960 publication of his book, *The Conscience of a Conservative*. It secured the number-six spot on the *New York Times* bestseller list and proved especially popular with young Americans. They found in it arguments that allowed them to speak to voters who rejected New Deal liberalism, a spent force by 1960.

Goldwater's book included an initial print run of 10,000. Selling out quickly, the book went through many editions and within three years sold 3.5 million copies. Patrick Buchanan said of the book, "*The Conscience of a Conservative* was our new testament. It contained the core beliefs of our political faith, it told us why we had failed, what we must do. We read it, memorized it, quoted it. . . . For those of us wandering in the arid desert of Eisenhower Republicanism it hit like a rifle shot." *The Conscience of a Conservative* was at its core a work of political idealism. Goldwater explained what he assessed to be the key differences between liberals and conservatives. He argued conservatives cared about the "*whole* man," including economic and spiritual needs, but that liberals "look only at the material side of man's nature." He criticized liberals for being "in a hurry" to "*compel* 'progress.'"[6]

Goldwater and his aides drafted the Goldwater manifesto; the *Wall Street Journal* published excerpts from this document in January 1961. The manifesto laid out tactics for reaching "forgotten Americans," and it reflected an opening salvo by Goldwater to make himself his party's nominee in 1964. The manifesto contained four key ideas, all framed as negations of other strategies: it rejected Eisenhower's modern Republicanism, Nixon's attempt to merge conservatism and liberalism, efforts to reformulate New Deal liberalism for Republicans, and assertions Democrats would gravitate

Edmund S. Valtman cartoon, published in the Hartford Times, *December 12, 1962, shows the GOP elephant standing on the white line in the middle of the road, thumbing a ride in both directions. One lane is labeled "Goldwater Republicanism"; the other is labeled "Rockefeller Republicanism." It suggests that the Republicans are going to have to choose between the aims of the conservative wing of the party, identified with Senator Barry Goldwater of Arizona, and the liberal wing, identified with Governor Nelson Rockefeller of New York. Library of Congress, Prints and Photographs Division, drawing by Edmund S. Valtman.*

toward doctrinaire conservatism. Instead, the Goldwater manifesto promoted a less rigidly ideological conservatism, one that would attract "that dragooned and ignored individual, 'the Forgotten American.'" Goldwater, though, was unable to temper his conservatism for his own political advance. He abandoned the manifesto, which ultimately played no role in the 1964 race. Why then does it matter? It reveals Goldwater's style of political operation as instinctual, not as intellectual or necessarily even savvy about political strategy.[7] Indeed, Goldwater's improvisational sun promised much, but it also risked burning too hot, too fast.

Goldwater wore the badge of anti-politician with pride. He later recalled in his memoirs, "the double standards and selfishness of the Eastern establishment excluded most of the nation. These had to go if conservatives were to rebuild the GOP from the grassroots up and broaden our base into mainstream America." He feared no existing shibboleths, making it easy for him to forge a new, much more radical form of conservatism, one that attracted interest from disaffected Americans unhappy with the liberal status-quo. Both *Time* and *Newsweek* ran cover stories in 1961 featuring Goldwater as leader of the conservatives, and he earned the title of "Mister Conservative."[8]

Barry Goldwater championed one view of the Republican Party: antistatist, oriented to the Sunbelt, and brimming with moral resentment of liberalism. It projected what dominated by the 1980s, but in the early 1960s it was not something a majority of Republicans were ready to embrace. Another view of the party was reflected in the potential campaigns of several moderates: namely Governor Rockefeller, Ambassador to South Vietnam Henry Cabot Lodge, Vice President Richard M. Nixon, Pennsylvania governor William Scranton, Michigan governor George Romney, and Maine senator Margaret Chase Smith. Arrogant in demeanor, Rockefeller spooked all the other moderates to move cautiously if at all. The other moderate politicians resented Rockefeller's wealth and its potential impact on the race. Romney declared he was out and meant it. Scranton said similar things but flirted several times with getting in. An asymmetrical intraparty civil war for the nomination resulted because establishment Republicans disliked Rockefeller, the leading candidate for the moderate GOP voters. Conservatives remained angry at Rockefeller and Nixon for replacing the more conservative platform with a moderate to liberal document in 1960.[9]

Conservatives began working on behalf of Goldwater as early as Kennedy's election. Goldwater himself was much less clear about his intentions, thinking it too early to begin a White House race. He vacillated whether he even wanted to or should run in 1964. He was up for reelection to his Senate seat in 1964. Arizona law would not permit him to run for both the presidency and the Senate. Goldwater liked the Senate, and he was unsure he wanted to leave it.[10]

Goldwater's position proved slippery. At times he argued that decisions about the nominee in 1964 should be left to the convention, but he had made a name for himself as chair of the Republican Senate Campaign Committee. Goldwater traveled the country more than any of his predecessors in doing this work. He delivered almost 800 speeches around the country between January 1960 and November 1963. Goldwater later attributed the work he did for his party in 1960 as integral to his getting his party's presidential nomination in 1964. His speeches raised as many questions about the status quo within the GOP as with the Democratic Party. Nor did he distribute funds equally to all GOP Senate candidates. In 1960, Senator Jacob Javits (R-NY) tried to use this against Goldwater, with whom he differed politically. The next year, an aide to Nelson Rockefeller, George L. Hinman, shared these concerns, and recklessly complained that "Goldwater's man, Stephen Shadegg" was a "neo-fascist."[11]

Goldwater was not the only national Republican seeking to shape the future of the party. The last Republican president, Dwight D. Eisenhower, wanted to help his party prosper in the 1962 midterm contests much in the same way he had won the White House—through the formation of a moderate Republican citizens organization that would function independently of the Republican National Committee. To boost the new organization Eisenhower lobbied his friends and associates from the military and from corporate America. Eisenhower did not include Nixon in this outreach, and party leaders in Congress and around the country appeared hostile to Eisenhower's plans. Eisenhower instructed one business leader, "what we're trying to do is build a bridge between the Republican Party on the one hand and the Independents and the dissatisfied Democrats on the other so that these latter people may eventually find themselves more comfortable living with Republican policies and personalities." Goldwater complained to William E. Miller, the chair of the Republican National Committee, such efforts would "lead us down the path to political destruction."[12]

Goldwater advocates had clear goals for 1962. The Arizona senator had gained the loyalty of angry white Christians who believed the Communist threat remained real, who worried about godless secularism in the public schools, and who disliked integration. They were upset with the 1962 Supreme Court decision outlawing prayer in schools. A grassroots movement for Goldwater included these conservatives as well as a range of Far Right fringe groups such as the John Birch Society. Goldwater himself had remarked in 1961 of the Birchers: "I am impressed by the type of people in it. They are the kind we need in politics."[13]

While the activists might have been sure of their course, the prospective candidates were not. They remained divided on how they should respond to political issues in the early 1960s. The reactions of Rockefeller and Goldwater to the Republican loss in 1960 help illuminate the major issue in the civil war of 1964, race and civil rights. Rockefeller blamed Nixon's defeat on the candidate's unwillingness to court urban and African American voters outside the South while spending too much time seeking southern white votes; Goldwater drew the exact opposite conclusion, arguing Nixon should have spent more time courting white southerners. Goldwater's interpretation of Nixon's loss, though, does not necessarily mean he thought a racial strategy should have been deployed in 1960. When Goldwater spoke in the South in 1961 and 1962 he addressed business groups and stressed low taxes. The southern Republican Party in the early 1960s consisted mostly of northern transplants, not converted southern Democrats. Race was less important than low taxes and business regulations. Still, political scientists Earl and Merle Black professed, "At the time of federal intervention in southern race relations most Republican candidates followed the lead of Arizona senator Barry Goldwater, the 1964 presidential nominee of the Republican party, in disregarding potential black support and attempting to unify whites behind a program of racial and economic conservatism."[14]

In November 1961 Goldwater participated in a discussion in Atlanta with southern Republicans about how the GOP might win votes in the region. He rejected arguments the party should seek African American votes and urban votes. "We ought to forget the big cities," Goldwater argued, noting his party could not best Democratic promises to ethnic voter groups. Instead, he contended the GOP should seek votes in the "hinterland." He insisted the federal government should not play a role in school desegregation, and he bragged that Arizona had been "Confederate" territory during the Civil War. Such statements were part of his gradual shift to a southern strategy that incorporated race. Still speaking at the November 1961 meeting, Goldwater observed, "We're not going to get the Negro vote as a bloc in 1964 and 1968." He concluded, "so we ought to go hunting where the ducks are."[15]

Goldwater movement workers wanted to identify for each state a contact person who would be responsible for selecting convention delegates. Additionally, they wanted movement leaders for each state to fill the following state level offices: chair, a finance chair, and a women's leader. Those individuals would build Goldwater networks at the congressional district level and the county level. Finally, Goldwater movement workers recognized the importance of coordinating with Young Republican leaders, especially since the Young Republican National Convention was being held in 1963.[16]

Young Republicans under the guidance of F. Clifton White, a bookish individual from New York who had extensive experience as a political organizer, had become a vital force in the GOP. White detested the sway moderate Republicans held over the party, and he brought together multiple conservative groups to advance Goldwater. They were working in secret as early as 1961 to disrupt the Republican Party presidential nominating process in favor of Barry Goldwater. Conservatives affirmed "that by taking over the YR's they will have achieved a major objective in promoting Barry and blowing out NAR."[17]

Planning for youth involvement made sense given Goldwater's popularity with college students and young adults. Members of the Young Americans for Freedom (YAF), an organization created in 1960, idolized Goldwater. YAF had 20,000 members when the New Left organization Students for a Democratic Society had less than 1,000. In 1962, the YAF filled Madison Square Garden with 18,000 conservative youth. It was the only student activist group with a conservative bent. YAF drew on Young Republicans, the party organization for young voters, for leadership. Yet the organization also avoided being identified as an entity intended to promote the GOP, stressing its loyalty was to conservatism, not a political party. In the early 1960s, conservative journalist M. Stanton Evans reflected on the inability of liberals to understand the fervent conservatism of youth: "When categories" of liberals as young and conservatives as old "no longer hold, the universe loses its certainty. Uncertainty breeds fear."[18]

White had begun organizing the Goldwater movement in 1961 with a secretive meeting on October 8, 1961, in Chicago. Twenty-two people, mainly business figures and a smattering of politicians, joined with him to plot how they might take over the GOP, impose a conservative agenda on the party, and win the nomination in 1964 for Goldwater. Several southerners took leadership roles. Though they knew the presidential primaries would matter, Goldwater partisans realized that most Republican convention delegates, 769 out of the total of 1,309, would be selected through the traditional mechanisms of state party governance. As such the draft Goldwater movement spent considerable energy working to capture these state organizations. Despite eastern liberal and moderate control of the national Republican Party, most grassroots workers had long been conservative. White traveled the country in an almost evangelical manner meeting with governors, mid-tier Republican leaders, and fervent volunteers to spread the conservative gospel. White briefed Goldwater in November regarding the conservative initiative to take over the party. Goldwater replied, "this is the best thing I've ever heard of since I became active in the Republican Party." At their December meeting, White's group divided the country into nine regions and established fund-raising goals. He acknowledged that established party leaders "would fight us tooth and nail every inch of the way once they discovered what we were up to."[19]

This mobilization was obvious to even casual political observers, and certainly to Goldwater. Though Goldwater denied awareness of White's work on his behalf, such statements defy credibility because White regularly sent Goldwater progress reports. Moreover, Goldwater received 800 letters a day and 100 speaking invitations each week. His book was on its twelfth printing, and conservative magazines sold Goldwater for president sweatshirts, bumper stickers, and buttons. Goldwater's policy statements expanded his popularity.[20]

Goldwater still had to fight for the nomination because mainstream Republicans had no intention of anointing him. The moderates, though, lacked the grassroots enthusiasm. Governor Rockefeller struggled with how to position himself for 1964. *New York Times* journalist Arthur Krock described the New York governor as a "Liberal (he is that on alternate Tuesdays)." Rockefeller aides stressed the importance of not identifying their candidate as a "New York Republican" for two reasons: one, the term was viewed as a synonym for liberal, and, two, New Yorkers did not have the best reputation in the country. Rockefeller's policy agenda had evolved from 1958 when he was first elected governor. He realized quickly his liberal views would not work nationally, so to compensate he advocated fiscal conservatism. In so doing, he never abandoned support for government welfare programs. Instead, he averred such initiatives must be paid for with current dollars. He remained a liberal on human rights issues. His record for social liberalism came from his civil rights work, including substantial financial donations, payment of a hospital bill for Martin Luther King Jr., and coverage of the bail for protesters in the 1963 marches in Birmingham, Alabama. During his governorship he enacted civil rights measures reducing housing discrimination, tightening anti–job discrimination, and endorsing bans on public discrimination. He hosted a King visit to Albany.

Part of Nelson Rockefeller's problem within his party was his familiarity with Democrats, as depicted in this photograph picturing Rockefeller, Eleanor Roosevelt, John F. Kennedy, and David Dubinsky at the dedication of the Penn Station South Cooperative Houses, a cooperative housing project of the International Ladies' Garment Workers Union in New York City, May 1962. Courtesy Franklin D. Roosevelt Presidential Library & Museum.

When aides told him doing so was politically unwise, Rockefeller retorted: "If it's morally the right thing, it's the politically right thing."[21]

While Rockefeller shifted his ideological views, Goldwater did not. Goldwater addressed a July 1962 Young Republicans breakfast where the attendees were "very conservative." He argued Republicans could do quite well in the 1962 midterm elections, with estimates of a net gain of about fifty seats in the House of Representatives and also gains in the Senate. Goldwater believed "all Republicans should get out and work for the party ticket" regardless of whether party nominees were conservative, moderate, or liberal. He also commented about the GOP field for 1964, noting that if the only names discussed were Nixon, Goldwater, and Rockefeller, the party would be "in damn bad shape." Goldwater said a "brand new face" was needed. He said, "God knows I'm not the least bit interested [in running], never have been." He eclipsed his own sun when he remarked to a journalist, "I haven't got a really first-class brain."[22]

Rockefeller regularly reached out to Goldwater during this period, in part to stop Goldwater from entering the 1964 race and in part because the two developed a friendship of sorts that left other politicians "aghast." The two agreed about several important things: they did not like Eisenhower or his approach to foreign policy, nor did they like Nixon, and they also were anti-Communist backers of free enterprise. In their discussions Rockefeller persuaded Goldwater that he, meaning the New York governor, had already secured the nomination, and Goldwater did not disapprove the idea of a Rockefeller presidency. For example, Rockefeller wrote to Goldwater in November 1962 about his political plans moving forward. He thanked Goldwater for "the kind things you recently said in California. I hope we can keep in close touch in the days ahead. . . . We are not authorizing any activity looking to '64." Still, said one Rockefeller surrogate, the New York governor concluded it most important to develop a "positive program" on which his party could run in 1964.[23]

Rockefeller's entreaties had little effect on Goldwater and his adoption of a southern strategy. For Goldwater this tactic evolved after the 1960 elections, and it proved integral to the approach in 1964. Peter O'Donnell, a young Texan and chair of that state's GOP, helped develop and implement it. He succeeded in large part because the Republican Party was unsure what to do regarding civil rights in the early 1960s. One historian compared Goldwater's southern strategy with the worldview of slaveowners, arguing both preferred a society where white privilege was accepted without question, where the monied elite were protected, and where employers dominated workers at will. Moreover, according to this argument, Goldwater fought against all attempts at social and economic leveling in society. For O'Donnell and for Goldwater the southern strategy meant winning the votes of racist white southerners, a plan that Goldwater and his partisans began developing as early as 1960. They minimized the methods of the Ku Klux Klan, replacing that brand of racial demagoguery with a subtle pursuit of middle-class southerners and suburbanites based on antiunion, anti-Communist, and antiwelfare arguments. Goldwater equated civil rights and civil disorder, using coded language that blamed blacks for increased crime rates. He did not stress his earlier work to integrate the Arizona Air National Guard and the Phoenix Sky Harbor Airport. Instead, he argued that GOP gains in the South came from new migrants to the region voting on economic issues. O'Donnell had the math to back his tactics. He explained in May 1963: Goldwater needed to keep the Nixon states from 1960 and add most of the South to have 320 Electoral College votes, "more than enough to win" and to ensure "the South will take the lead in making Kennedy a one-term president."[24]

J. D. Stetson Coleman, a Goldwater supporter and GOP pollster, noted in November 1962: "You will definitely carry the South if you campaign down there properly." Winning the South, Coleman understood, was crucial to breaking the Democratic Party hold on the presidency. Ultimately, by 1964, the manner in which Goldwater went about claiming southern votes put the GOP in opposition to civil rights reform. Because the region did not enjoy a two-party system, Goldwater strategists had earlier argued, Democrats acquired southern electoral votes without working for them. Conservatives discerned they had a message that would win in the region, and would force Democrats to campaign there and to assume less liberal positions nationally. Moreover, Coleman asserted in 1962, "Rockefeller couldn't carry the South. I have polled this question in all of the southern states and I can assure you that if he is the candidate against Kennedy, the South will go solidly for Kennedy."[25]

Rockefeller and his aides saw the matter very differently. George Hinman argued, "The 'Southern Strategy' so-called, is indefensible morally and suicidal politically. While in the short run it offers a hope and even the possibility of success, in the long run it would destroy the Party." He insisted Rockefeller was "the only person who can hold the Party in line against 'going South,' and still not foreclose the always important and possibly decisive possibility of picking up some or all of the Southern States in the 1964 election." A year later, Rockefeller made an even stronger condemnation of the strategy: "The transparent purpose behind this plan is to erect political power on the outlawed and immoral base of segregation and to transform the Republican Party . . . to a sectional party for some of the people." Rockefeller presumed all regions of the country would reject the plan. He concluded the party of Lincoln must never "turn its back on its heritage" by committing "an act of political immorality rarely equaled in human history."[26]

The 1962 midterms did not end in the manner Goldwater predicted with large GOP victories. Instead, Democrats gained two Senate seats, increasing their margin, and lost only four House seats. Even so, conservatives still controlled Congress. The previous year Texas Republican John Tower had taken Lyndon Johnson's Senate seat in a special election that conservatives hoped was a harbinger of southern realignment. Some Republican losses were close in 1962. In the Alabama Senate race, the Republican candidate, James Martin, an obscure business leader who enjoyed the support of racist elements, came within 6,800 votes of victory over Senate veteran Lister Hill, who had brought a tremendous amount of federal aid to Alabama. Conservatives saw the closeness of these losses as a sign the southern tactics would work. Republican House candidates collectively nearly doubled their vote totals from 16.3 percent in 1958 to 31 percent in 1962, and Republican contenders gained four new House seats in the South. The southern political director for the GOP observed, "I like to fish when the tide's coming in. . . . And the tide's coming in now in the South." Goldwater agreed, "Republicans in the South are no longer made to feel like skunks at a church social."[27]

Gubernatorial elections in 1962 also had an impact on presidential politics in 1964. California voters rejected Nixon's bid for the governorship, "adding to his odor of a loser." His next step—announcing he would leave politics forever and move to New York City to practice law on Wall Street—seemed to indicate he would not be a candidate in 1964. Several other Republicans did well in their gubernatorial races: Rockefeller won reelection in New York, Romney won his first race for the Michigan governorship; and Scranton, described as having "the quality of a Kennedy," won a "brawling, venomous" race for governor of Pennsylvania.[28]

Republicans of all ideological stripes hoped for an opening for 1964. Even though Kennedy's approval rating remained in a range where presidents typically do not lose, 55 percent, it had fallen from 70 percent after he came out publicly for civil rights legislation in June 1963. The big question for all potential candidates was when to declare their intentions. Historically races did not emerge publicly until the election year. What then if anything should prospective campaigns do in 1963? The question was particularly charged for the conservatives who wished a revolution in their party. Goldwater partisans feared that doing nothing between December 1962 and the convention would result in a Rockefeller nomination. They made their case to Goldwater: "An emotional surge in your behalf at that time will be no more capable of denying him the nomination in 1964 than it was of denying it to Nixon in 1960." Moreover, Goldwater partisans feared that a triumph by Rockefeller would be a victory for modern Republicanism, thwarting for a generation the conservative effort to take control of the party.[29]

Leaders of the GOP establishment also fretted. They did not like Rockefeller, and they dismissed Goldwater as a radical. Little time remained as of the fall of 1963 to develop another candidate. Rockefeller's negatives—as far as GOP insiders were concerned—included his recent divorce and remarriage to Margaretta "Happy" Murphy, a much younger woman who abandoned her children and their father; his arrogance; and his aloofness. Indeed, Rockefeller had never curried favor for his liberal views, but for his power as a vote getter. The remarriage ruined that. Prior to the candidate's second marriage, Rockefeller forces thought their candidate had secured much of the country in the GOP nomination race. New England appeared solid as did the mid-Atlantic, most of the Midwest, California, Washington, Oregon, Idaho, and even parts of the South. Rockefeller and his team had made strategic alliances with important local Republican leaders. His advisors were cocky with the only question they asked being could he defeat Kennedy. Rockefeller had led Goldwater in the polls, 43 to 26 percent, but after the remarriage the poll numbers flipped and Goldwater led Rockefeller. Rockefeller, given over to immense hubris, did not see the opposition to his divorce and he did not leave the race to make room for another moderate. Religious fundamentalists on the right responded in an unprecedented manner. A writer in one religious tract beseeched voters, "How can the decent, respectable people of the United States possibly place in the White House a man whose conduct is so obviously contrary to the moral standards of the Holy Scriptures as they pertain to holy matrimony[?]" Even Soviet premier Nikita Khrushchev attacked Rockefeller as among the "parasitic capitalists who live a life of luxury, drinking, carousing, and changing wives."[30]

Goldwater followed the traditional political calendar, though, and resisted a public declaration of intent even after Rockefeller fell in the polls on news of his remarriage. Rusher told Goldwater he agreed with his decision to withhold announcing his candidacy because "it is strategically too early . . . and certainly tactically far too early to announce it." Rusher balanced that assessment with concern that the work done over the last fifteen months to draft Goldwater might go for naught should the national grassroots movement not be made public. Goldwater replied that he did not know of the efforts on his behalf, thinking instead that the operation was working more generally for conservative principles in 1964. He indicated he had made no commitment to seek the nomination or be drafted. Nor did Goldwater understand the logic of political organizing; said one observer, "Goldwater's favorite style in politics is exhortation; he is a moralist, not an organizer." Rusher then clarified that the original intent had been more generic, but as 1964 drew near it became necessary to identify a candidate. "It was the unanimous consensus," Rusher stressed, "that you are the obvious and probably the only possible conservative standard-bearer." Despite these enthusiastic supporters Goldwater was hesitant even after learning White's group had secured 400 delegates for him.[31]

Following this exchange, White explained to Goldwater what had already been done. The working group had laid plans to ensure delegates to the 1964 Republican National Convention shared their conservative philosophy. They procured Nixon's preconvention delegate files from 1960, and also the same material for Robert A. Taft from 1948 and 1952 along with the 1952 and 1956 delegate lists. The conservative activists also networked with the Young Republicans, the Women's Federation, the Young Americans for Freedom, and the American Medical Association. Moreover, Goldwater had the advantage of large numbers of conservative Republicans from the South and the West who were disgusted with the eastern establishment. Elly Peterson, a liberal Republican who was appointed assistant chair of the Republican National Committee in 1963, observed, "everyone on the Committee was working openly for Barry Goldwater."[32]

The Goldwater takeover of the RNC had unsavory characteristics as well, which showed the dark side of the Arizona senator's sun. At a June 1963 meeting of the Republican National Committee in Denver, Colorado, southern party conservatives behaved in a racist fashion toward African Americans. At a luncheon where the wait staff was black the southerners regularly and loudly spoke of "niggers" and "nigger-lovers." An East Coast Republican at the event noted no one complained and "only a few of us were uncomfortable." Another observer was convinced the southerners wanted to turn "the Republican Party into the White Man's Party."[33]

The White coterie continued meeting, but no longer in secret. In December 1962, Walter Cronkite reported on the *CBS Evening News* that conservatives were conspiring to prevent Rockefeller from being nominated. The news broadcast embarrassed Goldwater, but his advocates did not quit. Instead, on February 17, 1963, they formed the National Draft Goldwater Committee. Goldwater rejected the efforts, saying he would not run. He told White, "You guys are just a bunch of amateurs. I haven't seen one Senator, one Congressman, or one state chairman come out for me yet and I don't see how you can expect me to take this thing seriously." The group continued unabashed. They decided they would "draft the son of a bitch," meaning Goldwater, whether he wished to run for the presidency or not.[34]

In April 1963, Citizens for Goldwater circulated petitions calling for Goldwater's nomination. This citizens group was different from the draft movement in that it was strictly a volunteer, grassroots initiative without political operatives in leadership positions. Both shared right-of-center political values, though. In addition to getting signatures for petitions these volunteers raised money, researched GOP delegates, canvassed neighborhoods, and were enthusiastic volunteers willing to do whatever was necessary to advance Goldwater's candidacy. Most people involved with the citizens' groups had no previous political experience, and Goldwater never fully trusted them. Letters were sent to all elected Republican officeholders in the United States as well as volunteers. This correspondence stressed the importance of the work: "we all have a BIG JOB to do, but we are working for a BIG MAN and a BIG CAUSE. The job—getting hundreds of thousands of petitions signed. The man—Senator Barry Goldwater. The cause—conservatism."[35]

This spirit shaped the July 4, 1963, draft Goldwater rally held in Washington, DC, at the National Guard Armory. Almost 9,000 people from around the nation came in by the busload, forty-three buses from New York alone. Observers said this rally was the fourth-largest event ever staged at the armory (behind the inaugurations of John F. Kennedy and Eisenhower and a revival that Billy Graham preached). A Goldwater biographer described the crowd as containing "little old ladies in tennis shoes," tattooed truck drivers, libertarian-leaning professors, "right-wingers convinced that Wall Street and the Kremlin were conspiring to run the world," southern whites, retirees, "Westerners tired of catering to Easterners," anti-Communists, small businessmen, those who read *The Conscience of a Conservative*, and "high school and college rebels looking for a cause." Given Goldwater's lack of participation, one *New York Times* writer declared, "Goldwater's not running the conservatives, the conservatives are running him."[36]

Goldwater was not the only candidate testing the waters. As early as spring 1963 Scranton commissioned polls to determine the mood of the presidential electorate, belying his claim that he was not interested in the presidency. He wanted data to show which candidate would most help down ballot Republicans and to prove Rockefeller was "a weak candidate." Scranton had advantages. He was more conservative than Rockefeller, but not so much so that establishment Republicans would shun him. He believed he could unite the heartland Republicans and the new conservatives who followed Goldwater while also attracting moderate Republicans. Moreover, he had quickly built an impressive record in Harrisburg: civil service reform, increases in public education spending, a sales tax increase, and measures to increase industrialization in the state. Eisenhower boosted Scranton's chances when he stopped to visit with the Pennsylvania governor in December 1963, but he did not offer an endorsement. Ironically,

Scranton never made clear his intentions, asking his visitors, "All right—can you tell me one good reason why I should *want* to be President of the United States?"[37]

Rockefeller did want to be president. After his fall in the polls he hired a political strategist to depict Goldwater as an extremist. In a July 14, 1963, address, Rockefeller, according to one historian, "declared war on Goldwater." He continued his attack against Goldwater and the extremists later that summer, dismissing the radical right as either "escapist" or "completely unrealistic" for advocating muscular anti-communism and abolishing the income tax. Rockefeller maintained doing the latter would cut federal revenue by 80 percent, leaving no money to fund the military and "our nuclear program." Should "the lunatic fringe" take over the GOP, Rockefeller insisted, "I don't think that our party would be able to offer an effective alternative in a two-party system, which is essential to democracy."[38]

Rockefeller's civil rights supporters refused to give in to the southern strategy. "It may appear that a 'White party' is in the best interest of the Republican party on a National scale, but it is going to hurt a great deal more in large metropolitan areas than it does on the National scene," baseball hero and registered Republican Jackie Robinson told Rockefeller. "If it were not for men like yourself I would just devote my time to the getting out the Negro vote and pile up as big a margin in the Negro area as possible for the Democrats," Robinson controverted. Robinson wrote an article for the *Saturday Evening Post* in which he suggested the extreme right was turning the GOP into a white man's party. If it did, and if it nominated a segregationist, though he did not offer any objectionable names, Robinson promised he would work tremendously hard for John F. Kennedy's reelection. "We would refute the evil proposition that one group of Americans may legitimately gain by barring other Americans from their rights," Robinson avowed.[39]

Goldwater's acceptance of the politics of resentment drew Far Right conservatives to his campaign. In August 1963 the John Birch Society attacked Rockefeller while insisting they were a nonpartisan group with half their membership Democrats and half Republicans. Since the organization enjoyed popular support in the South, this claim is valid. Robert Welch, the leader of the JBS, alleged that Rockefeller wanted "a one-world international socialist government." Goldwater, for pragmatic and personal reasons, opted not to condemn the Birchers. He realized Birchers would make good campaign workers, and also he had friends in the Phoenix, Arizona, chapter.[40]

Conservatives elsewhere in the polity flocked to Goldwater. Part of that process played out at the Young Republican convention in August 1963. Goldwater was the only potential candidate to address the convention. He warned of the "corrupt big-city machines" and warned liberalism was but "a form of rigor mortis." Four different groups strived for control of the convention. One group sought Republican unity for 1964. These Young Republicans did not support Goldwater, but they argued the Young Republicans should wait and work for whomever the Republican National Convention nominated the following year. A second group was affiliated with the draft Goldwater movement. A third group of radical extremists mostly from California advocated abolishing the income tax, impeaching Earl Warren, and adopting isolationism in foreign affairs. The last group used the occasion to create conflict and confusion by "infiltrating delegations" and deploying "rough tactics." Their goal was to prevent Republican unity behind a moderate candidate the following year. A Goldwater supporter was elected president of the organization, suggesting conservatives were winning the civil war for control of the party. Even though the YAF and Goldwater partisans controlled the convention, they never won over moderate Republicans. The most important legacy of this convention was the ideological turmoil it bequeathed to the party. Moderate Republicans termed the convention "a rightist putsch."[41]

Goldwater exacerbated his right-wing problem when he talked to the press. He told an interviewer in 1963 there was nothing wrong with secret organizations like the JBS. He tried to equate the Americans for Democratic Action with the JBS, noting that the former had paid someone to spy on and "double cross" former Senator Joseph McCarthy (R-WI). Goldwater denied that Birchers even held political views other than opposition to the income tax and anti-communism. Regarding the latter Goldwater insisted: "So I think this whole Birch thing should be cleared up. I can't comment intelligently on it because I don't know what people are really opposed to it for. If it's because they're anti-communist, then the people who oppose it have no right opposing them because all Americans should be anti-communist." He blamed the "radical press, the radical left" for tagging the Birchers as "conservative," arguing for the normalization of conservatism. Goldwater asserted, "Conservatism to [liberals] is still a dirty word. It means reactionary to them, when they, through their own ignorance, and I say this charitably, are actually advocating a reactionary movement, back to bureaucracy, which our forefathers came to this country to get away from."[42]

On September 13, 1963, Walter Cronkite declared on the evening news that Goldwater would likely be the Republican nominee in 1964: "Not only is President Kennedy cognizant of the possibility that Senator Goldwater will be the Republican candidate, but recent surveys, one as late as of today, indicate that he is at this moment the frontrunner." At this date Goldwater had yet to declare his candidacy. Cronkite had interviewed Goldwater for this broadcast, and the news anchor asked Goldwater what would influence his decision. Goldwater replied, "I think a major factor would be: what effect would a defeat have on the conservative movement?" Goldwater dismissed Cronkite's skepticism that he could gain the support of eastern financial interests, a group that all prospective Republican nominees needed to claim their party's nomination. Goldwater explained that his background with his family's department store left him well equipped to work with the country's business leaders. Cronkite then asked Goldwater why he was so popular in the South given his past NAACP and Urban League membership. Goldwater replied that "integration—segregation, whatever you want to call it—is not the overriding issue in the South." He acknowledged such had not always been true, but the postwar emergence of a southern middle class changed the political calculus in the region. "Now today you have a growing group of young people—I'd say from college age up to, possibly, fifty," Goldwater estimated, suburban, middle class white southerners "with comfortable incomes . . . are oriented towards a conservative economic philosophy." That, Goldwater postulated, was not valued in the Democratic Party.[43]

Part of the story that has been missed in the northern middle-class urban migration to the South is the failure of southern Democrats to cultivate these outsiders. Southern Democrats operated effective local parties based on family ties and traditional white patron arrangements, which included recruitment of white youths into the party. But there was no outreach to outsiders. The South had not had much immigration in the late nineteenth and early twentieth centuries, so southern Democrats did not know how to approach outsiders in the same way big city machines in the north did. Based on these realities, Goldwater had calculated that he could win southern and western votes against JFK, but running against LBJ was a different matter.[44]

The Kennedy assassination also threatened the Goldwater campaign. Goldwater had expected to run a close race against Kennedy, and indeed Goldwater likely would have done better in that matchup then he ultimately did against Lyndon B. Johnson. Gerald Ford, then a GOP House leader recalled, "Although we as Republicans thought Kennedy's popularity following the election of '60 would make him automatically reelected in '64, by '63 there was a growing anti-Kennedy political view." Immediately after the assassination Goldwater wavered whether he should run. Until lone assassin Lee Harvey Oswald's Marxism was widely reported in the press, Goldwater suffered from countless media stories questioning whether his brand of right-wing extremism had made possible the atmosphere in which Kennedy was murdered. Advisors close to Goldwater contend that the Kennedy assassination changed him. Stephen Shadegg wrote, "He was never quite the same. The Senator's heretofore unfailing good humor vanished." The assassination did not hinder the organizations working on Goldwater's behalf. The National Draft Goldwater Committee announced it would "observe a moratorium on public activity for a period of 30 days" out of respect for the Kennedy family following JFK's assassination, but it also declared it "*will* continue to work toward its goal—to persuade Senator Barry Goldwater of Arizona to announce his candidacy for the Republican Nomination for President. *The principle which motivated the formation of this committee was and is to provide a clear-cut choice of candidates for the American electorate.*"[45]

Earlier in August 1963 Goldwater took steps to gain control of the volunteer movement that demanded his nomination. He brought Denison Kitchel, a close friend from Phoenix and a Harvard-trained lawyer, to Washington, DC, to coordinate volunteer efforts. Kitchel made screening the volunteers for "kooks" a priority. He worked with another Goldwater loyalist, Shadegg, also from Phoenix, and they were dubbed the Arizona mafia. These changes meant the demotion of White, who had masterminded the Draft Goldwater movement.[46]

Still Goldwater was not decided. He told one observer, "I'm doing all right just pooping around" without a formal declaration. By December 1963 party leaders backing Goldwater pushed for a decision. They needed to know whether to mount a campaign in early primary states, especially New Hampshire. Also, if he was not running then they wanted to line up with other candidates. Goldwater hesitated to announce because he wanted no part of a race against Johnson, whom he viewed as a "dirty fighter" who would use "a lot of innuendo and lies." He noted, "The country doesn't want three presidents in a year's time. I can't win. In the process, we could harm the conservative cause."[47]

By the end of 1963, Goldwater was ready to commit. He discussed the matter with his wife, who told him: "Well, if that's what you want to do, you go ahead and do it. I don't particularly want you to, but I'm not going to

Senator Barry Goldwater announced he would seek the Republican presidential nomination on the patio of his plush home in Paradise Valley, a suburb of Phoenix, Arizona, on January 3, 1964. Courtesy the Associated Press.

stand in your way." In a January 3, 1964, press conference at his Arizona home, Goldwater, standing on crutches because he was recovering from a minor surgery, announced his candidacy. He declared: "I have not heard from any announced Republican candidate a declaration of conscience or of political position that could possibly offer to the American people a clear choice in the next presidential election." He promised Americans, "I will not change my beliefs to win votes. I will offer a choice, not an echo." Upon Goldwater's entry into the race, O'Donnell declared, "We are delighted that the objective of the National Draft Goldwater Committee has been achieved: Senator Barry Goldwater is a candidate for the Republican presidential nomination. We are proud of our part in the first authentic nationwide draft movement in modern political history."[48]

Once he was in the race, Goldwater relied on the conservative American Enterprise Association for Public Policy Research (AEA) for policy guidance, working closely with two AEA officials, Karl Hess and William Baroody, despite the fact that neither of them had yet published anything substantive. He did not rely on the much more accomplished conservative economists and cold warriors who had endorsed his campaign, Milton Friedman and Gerhart Niemeyer. Still, Ayn Rand concluded Goldwater was the only acceptable Republican running, and she encouraged conservatives to support him. Rand and Goldwater shared libertarian values. He also praised the writings of conservative intellectuals as found in the *National Review*, remarking such thinkers "burst on us like a spring shower, proclaiming that the liberals were all wet." One young libertarian compared Goldwater to John Galt, the fictional hero of Ayn Rand's 1957 novel *Atlas Shrugged*, "More important than his message was the fact that Goldwater managed to look the part as though he had been made for it. . . . One look at him and you knew he belonged in Galt's Gulch, surrounded by striking heroes with blazing eyes and lean, dynamic heroines with swirling capes."[49]

The Goldwater campaign provided an opportunity for other conservatives to build their public platforms. Schlafly wrote *A Choice, Not an Echo* to win votes for Goldwater. She self-published the book because other far-right titles—namely John Stormer's *None Dare Call It Treason* and Goldwater's *The Conscience of a Conservative*—had achieved tremendous success with that method. Schlafly ordered a first printing of 25,000 copies, and she sent 100 complimentary copies to friends and associates she had met in her political work. She arranged for wealthy conservatives to purchase and distribute the book to as many disgruntled conservatives as possible. Demand was immediate and intense. Schlafly's book reflected the views of the John Birch Society as well as past right-wing conspiracy theorists. Robert Welch called Schlafly "one of our most loyal members." Schlafly denied such assertions, but previous scholars have noted she never criticized the Birchers. The book benefited Goldwater as well as Schlafly. "[Barry] Goldwater['s] people" used *A Choice, Not an Echo* "as a bible." It was their "example of how the 'big eastern money interests' are out to land the nomination" for a moderate Republican.[50]

During his campaign, Goldwater performed a delicate balancing act between courting the likes of John Birch Society members and more mainstream Republicans. At a January 18, 1964, press conference, he declared of the John Birch Society, "as long as they don't advocate the violent overthrow of the government who can object to them." Still, his opponents for the nomination watched this carefully. One Rockefeller supporter highlighted what Goldwater said when speaking at the University of Nevada in February 1964: "if you could read the purposes of the John Birch Society, it would be very difficult for any American to disagree with them. It's sort of like free beer and mother love. You got to go along with them." Rockefeller strategists suggested such rhetoric should be used to "bait" the Arizona Republican into a discussion about exactly what right-wing issues he endorsed.[51]

Because there was no consensus candidate by early 1964 other Republicans considered entering the race. Maine senator Margaret Chase Smith, perhaps best known for standing up to Senator Joseph McCarthy in the 1950s, jumped in the contest. Not all in the country were eager to support a woman. A Democratic insider said Smith "was a great lady but in the wrong party." In addition to Smith, Scranton also remained a question mark. Said Goldwater, "Frankly, I don't think Scranton is going to run as I am convinced that he won't do it unless it is handed to him on a silver platter, and as of now, that can't be done." The final possible contender was Nixon. He had been giving speeches and suggesting his availability as a centrist.[52]

The extended, public battle in the GOP civil war commenced in the New Hampshire primary, the first of the three contested primaries. Only sixteen states held primaries and most of these were not contested, meaning that only one candidate was actively campaigning in these uncontested states. Often an esteemed state politician ran as a stand-in, or "favorite-son," either to benefit one of the actual contenders or to keep the state delegations unified for bargaining purposes at the convention. Participating in primaries was relatively new, so candidates did not automatically enter. The primaries mattered more for those challenging Goldwater given his massive lead in the delegate count. Only with substantial victories could they convince delegates from states relying on caucuses and conventions to switch loyalties. Earlier an October 7, 1963, *Newsweek* survey revealed Goldwater to have 500 "solidly committed convention votes . . . and another 82 leaning to his side. All this in advance of a definite statement by Goldwater that he is running!" Schlafly told Goldwater: "Please, please do not enter the New Hampshire primary. . . . This step would be as fatal to you as it was to Bob Taft in 1952. It is too easy for the 'big boys' to buy up a little state like New Hampshire." Goldwater viewed these contests as "political booby traps" and tried to avoid all but the California contest. He entered the New Hampshire contest, though, in response to arguments he could win there.[53]

Knowing New Hampshire mattered. In the early 1960s the New England state in reality had little in common with the stereotype of "twangy, skinflint Uncle Ephs or Uncle Calebs who make their living by whittling antiques, milking cows and squeezing tourists." Instead, the state enjoyed a newfound prosperity derived from new industries in electronics and scientific production, a diversification away from older textile and leather goods manufacturing. It was just one of three states so prosperous that it did not qualify for federal redevelopment funding. State voters had embraced some

Democratic policies. Because New Hampshireites tended to be older than the typical American, support for Social Security was high. State residents enjoyed a deep commitment to the United Nations. As candidates criss-crossed the state the bulk of the questions they fielded dealt with foreign policy challenges: the Soviet presence in Cuba, mainland China's interest in joining the UN, and the future of Berlin. Domestic questions pertained to Social Security, race relations and civil rights, income taxation, and fed-eral budget priorities.[54]

A big challenge for party moderates came from the powerful *Manches-ter Union-Leader*, a conservative paper with a conservative editor, William Loeb. Loeb's family had deep roots in conservative Republican politics. To counter this problem, Rockefeller campaign staff members visited with each newspaper in New Hampshire. They hoped the papers would run a series of columns Rockefeller was writing. An editor for the *Hanover Gazette*, a weekly paper with a circulation of just over 1,000, advised that Rockefeller criticize Goldwater's current statements, "not what he wrote or said six months or year ago." The editor of the *Claremont Eagle* "urge[d] that all possible use be made of Boston papers—*Traveler* and *Globe*—to offset statewide *Union-Leader* circulation." Reported one Rockefeller campaign worker, Goldwater "is prime beneficiary of a virtual newspaper monopoly. He is the loud, clear choice of the czar of New Hampshire newspapers, dyspeptic, Cro-Magnon Republican William Loeb, publisher of the *Man-chester Union-Leader*." No other paper in the state "has the power, the staff, the money, and—perhaps—the moxie to talk back."[55]

Goldwater performed poorly in New Hampshire. He had flubbed an NBC News *Meet the Press* interview after announcing his candidacy, mak-ing naïve statements and careless comments such as saying he would break the Test Ban Treaty to test nuclear weapons in the atmosphere and that the Soviets would abandon Cuba if the United States told Cuba they had to foreswear all Soviet munitions. These comments paralleled more egre-gious statements he made in less guarded circumstances. Voters learned through his unfiltered habits of saying exactly what he meant that he was not a typical conservative. Since October he had called for the usage of nu-clear weapons by NATO troops, advocated selling the TVA, and endorsed elimination of the income tax. He also described US missile systems as "undependable," the unemployed as having "low intelligence or ambition," and he was famous for using pithy, unpolitic phrases such as his advocacy for "saw[ing] off the Eastern Seaboard and let[ting] it float out to sea" and for "lob[bing] one into the men's room of the Kremlin." Such inflated rhetoric did not impress proper New Englanders. Because he continued making such statements in extemporaneous remarks reporters covered those events more closely than his prepared speeches. Goldwater fumed at press coverage and analysis, but blame rested only with the candidate and the candidate's staff.[56]

Voters termed his statements "silly," "ambiguous," and "crazy." A Concord businessman who had initially supported Goldwater told a journalist, "If he doesn't mean what he says, then he's just trying to get votes; and if he does mean what he says—then the man is dangerous. So I quit." O'Donnell counseled Goldwater: "'Shooting from the hip' will be fatal to your candidacy." He instructed Goldwater to retain "the witty and spontaneous way in which you answer questions," but to "control the issues by only discussing those things which you have considered in advance." O'Donnell warned Kitchel that "there are serious weaknesses in organization, finance, public relations and advertising, and in my opinion, we stand a great chance of being clobbered" in New Hampshire.[57]

The more Goldwater spoke the less people in New Hampshire liked him. Instead his handlers had him pressing the flesh. He campaigned eighteen hours a day with one foot still in a cast from his recent surgery, experiencing tremendous pain as a result. His mode of travel in the state, a shiny black Cadillac, annoyed frugal New Englanders, as did Peggy Goldwater's full-length mink coat.

Goldwater self-destructed in a state he should have won handily. Popular culture played a role in Goldwater's downfall. Showings in New Hampshire movie theaters harmed Goldwater during the primary there. Viewers could see *Point of Order*, a documentary about the downfall of Senator Joseph McCarthy (whom Goldwater had supported throughout); *Seven Days in May*, a feature film about a failed military takeover of the United States that had been triggered by a disarmament treaty; and *Dr. Strangelove, Or: How I Learned to Stop Worrying and Love the Bomb*, which was a comedic parody of nuclear war.[58] Each film hinted at negative aspects of Goldwater's record.

New Hampshireites sought an alternative, and they first turned to Rockefeller. They did not love him but they admired his steadiness. He also benefited from having a good number of his friends from Dartmouth College, his undergraduate institution, living in New Hampshire and working on his behalf. Said Theodore White, "One of Rockefeller's staff members had observed that in the priesthood of government Nelson Rockefeller would end as a Cardinal, not as a Pope—for he could not jump the bridge

The biggest argument for Henry Cabot Lodge's presidential candidacy was his work as US ambassador to South Vietnam. Here he is pictured in the Oval Office in August 1963 meeting with President Kennedy after his appointment as ambassador. Abbie Rowe. White House Photographs. John F. Kennedy Presidential Library and Museum, Boston.

from the administrative to the spiritual." Still Rockefeller had improved in New Hampshire polls by January 1964 when he seemed to be tied with Goldwater, reversing Goldwater's three-to-one lead as of the end of 1963. As part of his New Hampshire campaign Rockefeller excoriated an overly activist federal government. He avowed, "This big government philosophy is a continuing threat to our federal system." Rockefeller also chastised Barry Goldwater, specifically his calls to make Social Security voluntary. Said Rockefeller, "if Senator Goldwater's radical plan ever won adoption, it wouldn't merely change our Social Security set up. IT WOULD WRECK IT."[59]

Rockefeller was not without challenges of his own in New Hampshire, namely the disconnect between his political values—liberalism and government spending—and those of the average New Hampshire Republican. Reasoned one reporter, "a New Hampshire liberal is several degrees to the right of a New York conservative." Perhaps his biggest problem, though, was Ambassador Lodge, a distant candidate for the presidency. Lodge remained in Southeast Asia, and had little to do with the politicking on his behalf. Still, he enjoyed a geographical advantage as a fellow New Englander. Happy with Lodge's decision to not campaign, Rockefeller told Lodge, "I think that it is terribly important that the moderate cause prevail in the New Hampshire primary. As you know, the matter is touch and go and any fragmentation of the moderate effort could be dangerous." Goldwater people realized this, explaining "The Rockefeller campaign strategy of late is to shout at every opportunity that this is 'strictly a two-man race,' obviously indicating to those who might vote for Nixon, Lodge, [Harold] Stassen or Mrs. Smith that they will be wasting their votes."[60]

Lodge's campaign prospered because amateurs who believed in his qualifications for the White House worked ceaselessly on his behalf. A shoestring staff of Washington, DC, professionals joined them. Robert R. Mullen, a publicist who had worked on Eisenhower's campaigns, was the key figure. They predicted Lodge would pull votes from Rockefeller and not the Arizona senator. Lodge volunteers used the newly emerging technique of direct mail to reach New Hampshire GOP voters and educate them on how they might vote Lodge in the March primary. Lodge had not filed and his name was not on the ballot. Multiple mailings instructed how to write Lodge's name in. His volunteers also produced a television program to introduce Lodge to voters.

By late February 1964 the situation in New Hampshire had changed. Lodge partisans noted that Rockefeller had called the ambassador twice in Saigon about the race. Private candidate polling suggested Lodge led the race. Moreover, newspaper columnists observed that Lodge took more voters from Rockefeller than from Goldwater. Mullen explained, "our own soundings confirmed the widely held impression that neither Rockefeller nor Goldwater really appealed to a majority of the Republicans. The need for an alternative was clear and it was on that basis that we offered Lodge." Because Lodge was not yet a declared candidate, he did and said nothing about domestic politics, focusing all his energy on his ambassadorial duties. This tactic was not unlike Eisenhower's New Hampshire campaign in 1952. Mullen declared, "If we give him a clear indication that he is a serious contender, he will come back and put on the most spirited and effective campaign ever seen in the US history." There were Lodge clubs in thirty-one of the fifty states, and the Draft Lodge movement designated Oregon as the next battleground state. Mullen explained their post–New Hampshire plans: "We will go into those primaries where there is a clean chance to demonstrate Cabot's true support from the voters, where the situation is not loaded, and where there are delegates to be gained. At this time we are exploring Oregon and California." They opted not to enter primaries in states where the Republican leaders wanted to send a favorite son candidate.[61]

Days before the election, Goldwater staffers predicted, "The amateurs running the Lodge write-in may surprise the nation. They have sharp organization in some spots, and the Lodge name is hot." Election day brought half a foot of snow, but voters were not deterred. The day saw a record turnout and another half-foot of snow. Lodge pulled off an upset win against two highly organized, professionally run campaigns, claiming 33,007 votes to 20,692 for Goldwater, and 19,504 for Rockefeller. Nixon, also a write-in, claimed 15,587 votes. Lackluster performances by Goldwater and Rockefeller in New Hampshire created "an upsurge of interest in Nixon." A Draft Nixon for President Committee was formed in the Pacific Northwest where Nixon "always has been well received." Despite his loss, Rockefeller found some good news in the New Hampshire results, namely his rise from "political 'corpse'" following news of his remarriage six months earlier to "prime contender."[62]

Rockefeller blamed Lodge for ruining his chance. A conversation he had with Paul Grindle, a Lodge promoter in New Hampshire, reveals much about Rockefeller's thinking. Rockefeller asked Grindle what it would have taken to get Lodge out of the New Hampshire race. Grindle replied, "a bribe." Rockefeller asked, "how much?" According to Rockefeller's biographer, an impassive Grindle responded, "for ten thousand dollars, you would have seen the back of me." A stunned Rockefeller replied, "Oh, my Christ. And I spent three million."[63]

Why, though, did Goldwater falter in New Hampshire? A Goldwater staffer observed, "when Barry Goldwater said he must have 'goofed somewhere' he was making the understatement of the campaign." The campaign acknowledged that "the dissension in the ranks . . . was even worse than suspected." Local volunteers did not get along with Goldwater's out-of-state campaign staff. Little effort was given to day-to-day strategy. A local man observed "'they didn't talk to us, Goldwater didn't talk much to them, and

Goldwater on election night, March 10, 1964, after the New Hampshire GOP primary. Library of Congress, Prints and Photographs Division, photograph by U.S. News & World Report *Magazine Photograph Collection.*

hardly at all to us.'" Instead, observed a campaign staff worker, "Goldwater would finish his hand-shaking—which never did come naturally to him—and head for his room for the night." Goldwater staffers concluded "the New Hampshire results may have hurt Goldwater's standing among man-on-the-street," but they also reasoned, "it has little affected his stock among the working party activists—the sort who attend precinct caucuses."[64]

When asked why he voted for Lodge, a New Hampshireite joked, "Dunno, mebbe 'cause he din't bother us none." Still, the Lodge boomlet was important. The ambassador to South Vietnam enjoyed a 42 percent favorability rating among GOP voters, and volunteers hoped a win in Oregon in May would make Lodge a contender at the convention. Rockefeller also gambled heavily on Oregon, traveling there the day after New Hampshire voting ended. Goldwater did not. Chastened by his loss in a primary system he did not fully understand, Goldwater announced he would sit out Oregon, contending "why get bloodied by Rockefeller again for eighteen delegates; I can get that many out of Nebraska in one speech." After Goldwater lost New Hampshire, William F. Buckley Jr. wrote a memorandum to

National Review staff: "It is a grave wrong, moral and strategic, to let Gold-water down in any way." But he also advised that the magazine needed to be pragmatic, declaring it "a grave, perhaps graver wrong, strategically and morally, not to leave ourselves room to say" years later that Goldwater "did not really have his heart in the campaign, and was not as well qualified to run or serve as (fill in the New Hero)."[65]

Despite losing in New Hampshire, Goldwater had accomplished what would have been unthinkable four years earlier. He seemed likely to win the GOP civil war, remaking his party into a Sunbelt-focused organization. The New Hampshire results exaggerated the southwestern emphasis of Goldwater's conservatism, an ideology that emphasized the politics of morality and resentment. Goldwater stood on the precipice of winning his party's nomination if he could continue claiming delegates in the caucuses, uncontested primaries, and at least one competitive primary. He changed the way people thought about the word *conservative*. Said one follower of the Arizona senator, conservative ceased "being a curse word, a designation from which all but the most intrepid fled" and instead became "a roaring challenge to the established power . . . of the post-Roosevelt era."[66]

4 PYRRHIC TRIUMPH OR EXTREMIST VICTORY?

He almost lost in California. Such a sentence rarely leads a discussion of the 1964 GOP primary and Barry Goldwater's capture of his party's nomination. Goldwater's near defeat in his neighboring Sunbelt state came even as he preached the emerging Sunbelt politics of resentment. Under this narrative Goldwater radiated a miserly sun that begrudged equal rights for society's dispossessed and encouraged discordant feelings among different social and racial groups. By winning California, he crystallized the fragile, narrow victory for extremists over mainstream Republicans. A divided party did not universally welcome the prospects of a Barry Goldwater nomination, so even after the primary season ended, moderate and mainstream Republicans tried to deny Goldwater his victory. This battle deepened the schisms in the party and made conservatives all the more insistent on their mission to take over the party, raising the question of whether Goldwater's victory gained anything for the party or whether it endorsed the unhelpful politics of white resentment. Goldwater partisans saw themselves as defenders of individualism who did not need a strong federal government. I. F. Stone asserted that the Goldwater voter "likes to think of itself as rugged and frontier. . . . But the covered wagons in which it travels are Cadillacs and its wide open spaces have been air-conditioned."[1]

Goldwater tried to skip as many of the primaries as possible. He had a different plan for amassing delegates, one that removed him from the competitive fray as often as possible: in addition to winning many of the uncontested primaries Goldwater also captured delegates through multiple state conventions. These victories gave Goldwater over 290 delegates. He also commanded an unknown number of "sleeper" delegates, individuals whose true loyalty was to Goldwater and would switch from their official designation to the Arizonan.[2]

Rockefeller conversely found himself playing catch-up after New Hampshire because he did not enjoy the same delegate advantage as Goldwater. Following Rockefeller's loss in New Hampshire, a supporter gave a very negative report about the New York governor's chances in New Jersey. "I cannot find the remotest grass root movement for Rockefeller. In fact, I cannot find a single supporter. I am not exaggerating. People may have differences of opinion as to the various candidates but they are unanimous in being against Rockefeller." Among the reasons given were "his irresponsible campaign," "how he let Nixon down" in 1960, and his divorce and remarriage. There were other reasons for conservatives and liberals to disdain Rockefeller, namely his willingness to use his powers as governor to benefit his family fortune through advocacy of favorable banking and insurance laws. Indeed, Rockefeller placed last among the various contenders for the nomination with just 3.2 percent of the primary vote in New Jersey.[3]

Perhaps some of the most significant developments in noncompetitive primary states occurred in the South, where GOP strength was increasing. Even though these elections were not contested they nonetheless helped congeal Goldwater's brand of conservatism. In Texas the beneficiaries were to the far right with Goldwater enjoying more popularity than Rockefeller or any of the other challengers. Rockefeller officials charged Goldwater leader Peter O'Donnell with unfairly manipulating the contest in Texas to benefit Goldwater. They claimed Rockefeller had all but "renounce[d] his American citizenship" to avoid running in the Texas primary but O'Donnell refused to let him "off the hook."[4]

Florida presented challenges similar to the rest of the South. One observer of Florida politics noted the state's heightened conservatism: "This conservatism is no fluke, nor is it a narrow philosophy tied to racial issues." Voters in the state also opposed unions, federal urban renewal initiatives, and Democratic presidential candidates. Goldwater officials understood, though, that conservatism did not equal Republicanism: "No Republican presidential candidate can win Florida by dealing only with Republican officials. Simple arithmetic shows that any Republican candidate must get more votes from registered Democrats than there ARE registered Republicans in order to win our state."[5]

The GOP was advancing rapidly in Alabama where it fielded a full slate of candidates for Congress as well as statewide and county offices. They had an advantage because the legislature had not redistricted, meaning that congressional candidates had to run statewide. This gave Republicans operating in concert with former Dixiecrats and Independents "a good chance to defeat some of the state's Democratic congressmen," said one Goldwater partisan. Moreover, Governor George C. Wallace, elected as a Democrat, waged a "favorite son" campaign for the presidency, which benefited Goldwater by encouraging racial conservatives to participate. Finally, John Synon, a White Citizens' Council activist, developed the independent elector movement for the general election that fall. He did so to protect his native South from the reelection of Kennedy or the election of a liberal Republican like Rockefeller. Each southern state would name a segregationist to lead slates of independent third-party electors. Synon believed that if all such slates were elected then the South could deadlock the Electoral College and make demands on the person selected for the White House. He also wanted the Democratic electors on the fall ballot to be unpledged to Lyndon Johnson.[6]

Indeed, moving into the South presented Goldwater with very different challenges than he found in other regions. For better or for worse he crafted much of his rhetoric to fit southern conditions and resentments, especially regarding civil rights. In the South, unlike the rest of the country, there was no effective GOP, so Goldwater Republicans were building new party structures. Elsewhere in the country, though, movement leaders sought to overthrow the establishment Republican Party. Any alliances with Democrats, then, were of negligible long-term value and not encouraged. For example, in Virginia a Goldwater loyalist warned against using "Byrd Republicans," meaning otherwise Democratic voters who supported Senator Harry F. Byrd (D-VA) and would remain with the Democratic Party, to seek support in Virginia. GOP delegates to the RNC, "especially younger ones," wanted the state to "become two-party overnight."[7]

Goldwater's efforts in the states without competitive primaries did not relieve him of running in the remaining contested primaries: Oregon and California. The May 15 Oregon primary proved strange. Lodge, Goldwater, and Rockefeller were all put on the ballot by the secretary of state, along with Richard Nixon as a write-in candidate, but only Rockefeller campaigned in the state, or as it was expressed to voters there, "he cares enough to come." Goldwater was focused on California, where Republicans voted in a June 2 primary, which most political prognosticators avowed would decide the race. Lodge's effort proved chimerical. He overestimated the value of his high popularity ratings with average voters going into the race, thinking a win in Oregon would "outweigh the result of the California" contest where only Rockefeller and Goldwater were on the ballot.[8] Moreover Lodge had deceived himself that his New Hampshire strategy of a noncampaign directed by grassroots volunteers would carry over throughout the country.

Robert R. Mullen, who had done public relations work for Dwight Eisenhower's campaign in 1952 and managed the Draft Lodge 1964 movement, found that his biggest obstacle resulted from Lodge's popularity, or more specifically, the source of it. Lodge benefited from a "vacuum" in the Republican Party. The three frontrunners—Goldwater, Rockefeller, and Nixon—all had high negatives. The argument against Goldwater was, according to Mullen, his "'far out, belligerent views,'" while voters still disliked the idea of Rockefeller's divorce and remarriage. Finally, they discounted Nixon because he lost in 1960. Lodge had several things in his favor: familiarity, work as ambassador to the United Nations in the 1950s, and ambassador to South Vietnam in the 1960s. His diplomatic accomplishments included negotiations with the Soviet Union to ensure that outer space was not weaponized and work to bring about a cessation of hostilities following the 1956 tripartite invasion of Egypt by Britain, France, and Israel. Finally, according to Mullen, "A strange feeling of absence and longing for John Kennedy transfers to Lodge, because he has somewhat the same voice and manner." Mullen hoped victory in Oregon would cause the "king makers of the GOP—who up to now have been fence sitting" to endorse Lodge.[9]

Rockefeller arrived in Oregon exhausted from the New Hampshire campaign, but he also was engaged with his pursuit, something voters noticed and appreciated when he stumped the state. Each weekend, though, Rockefeller flew back to New York to be with his pregnant wife, who was due to deliver about the same time as the California primary. As Rockefeller settled in to his grueling schedule he developed a resolve to continue, telling the journalists who traveled with him: "I don't care any longer if I win—but I feel strongly about" stopping Goldwater and stopping the Sunbelt takeover of the GOP. During this phase of the campaign Rockefeller introduced the term "mainstream" to describe and distinguish his views from Goldwater, whom he called an extremist. The word play annoyed Goldwater, but it became a central component of the political lexicon.[10]

In Oregon, the Rockefeller forces deployed the same tactics Lodge volunteers had used in New Hampshire: grassroots mobilization and direct mailing. The Rockefeller campaign borrowed a political expert from Representative John Lindsay (R-NY) to oversee this effort. New York attorney Robert Price presented his critical analysis of the situation in Oregon to Rockefeller on April 11. He complained the campaign there was a story of neglect and ineptitude. Phone calls were not being returned, and political leaders in Oregon were treated poorly by easterners. Once Price agreed to work for Rockefeller, the New York governor asked what he wanted for payment. Price replied, "I don't want to get paid because I want to be able to say to you, 'Governor, fuck off, I'm quitting.'" He performed great work for the New York governor, and his initiatives enhanced a massive Rockefeller media budget. They combined newspaper advertisements with television—so much so that one student of the campaign said, Rockefeller "totally dominated the Oregon home screens for the forty-eight hours before voting."[11]

Rockefeller opted to "go all out on exposure to voters," spending most of his time in Oregon the week before the May 15 primary. His campaign's get-out-the-vote efforts included mass mailings to registered Republicans, telephone calls, and television telethons. Just as important were personal visits. The Rockefeller campaign ran newspaper announcements in each Oregon town Rockefeller visited prior to the primary saying, "Rockefeller cared enough to come to _____," with the blank filled in with that town's name. Nixon also courted Oregon voters by telling the press he was available to run should his party wish to nominate him, but Lodge and Goldwater did not. In so doing, Nixon was practicing a then traditional mode of seeking the presidential nomination. Noted one observer, "Goldwater is not likely to show as gaining when the next poll comes out. He is more likely to be down. Speech cancelations not only miffed prospective voters, but had a demoralizing effect on his most enthusiastic workers." Goldwater justified his Oregon event cancelations because of the civil rights debate in the Senate, but such legislative business did not stop him from campaigning in California.[12]

Knowing he was the underdog, Rockefeller worked all that much harder in Oregon. Crowd size was good for Rockefeller, but most of the applause came at the introduction and conclusion and not for anything he said in his speeches. An observer remarked, "Rockefeller, of course, is trying to create an image of competence and knowledgeability that will blanket or overshadow the divorce and remarriage issue. He does a good job of lambasting both Johnson and Goldwater, and setting forth his views on foreign and domestic matters." Goldwater backers in Oregon fixated on how Rockefeller handled his "family situation." They pronounced he connected with voters, showing his "great respect" for them and his belief they would "weigh this fact (the divorce and remarriage) *and others.*" The campaign concluded, "It seems that the way he is handling himself would tip the scales a little more in his favor . . . , but it is extremely difficult now to tell how much."[13]

Rockefeller's massive effort paid off. He won the Oregon primary with 33 percent of the vote, but the question remained: did it matter? Goldwater aide Stephen Shadegg assessed the Oregon race, taking pleasure in Lodge's fourth-place finish and arguing the Rockefeller win did not establish the New Yorker as a frontrunner. Instead, said Shadegg, Rockefeller's lavish spending suggested his weakness as a candidate. He intimated that Rockefeller, according to "local gossips," had "paid handsome fees" to "top lieutenants in Oregon." He deduced that the only reason Rockefeller did well in the state was because Lodge remained in Saigon, Goldwater in Washington, and Nixon "diffident and aloof." Rockefeller's victory in Oregon did little to change the GOP field. Lodge dropped out, but Goldwater contended the win meant little, dismissing it as "a victory for the radical left" and stressing "if I drop dead today, he [Rockefeller] still couldn't get the nomination."[14]

Once the Oregon primary was complete all eyes shifted to California where the final contested primary was scheduled for June 2. Barry Goldwater's Sunbelt extremists had long been working to take over the state's GOP. "Rockefeller people are frightened by Goldwater strength," claimed a Goldwater backer. "They are building an organization, but their main strength seems to be anti-Goldwater, not pro-Rockefeller. Nixon supporters are not showing any activity. Too many people here still remember his gubernatorial race with distaste." Rockefeller, conversely, did not apply the lessons from Oregon. In California he did not build a grassroots following, he did not spend sufficient time in the state, and he did not use his financial resources wisely to extend his media reach. Said one Goldwater partisan: Rockefeller's crowds resulted more because people "want to see what a Rockefeller looks like."[15]

Another problem Rockefeller faced in both Oregon and California was that only registered Republicans could vote in the GOP primary. Registered Independents gave Rockefeller substantial support but they could not vote in the primaries, rendering their support meaningless. Moreover, California had many conservative registered Democrats who often voted Republican in November. In most of California, Democratic primaries were far more contested than GOP primaries, so it was better to register as a Democrat. Reregistering to change parties was hard in both states. Whereas this challenge did not hurt Rockefeller in Oregon, which was less competitive than California, it did in the Golden State.

Just as Goldwater delivered a fracturing message, one that ruptured the GOP, so also did his campaign. The tactics it deployed in California matched perfectly with Goldwater's rhetoric of resentment. There were three separate entities to the Goldwater camp. Conservative former US senator William Knowland ran the main headquarters, where volunteers, many female, streamed in and out. The Goldwater campaign credited Knowland for aiding Goldwater's California delegate drive. Goldwater's closest advisors, though, worked out of an apartment about a mile away where Greta Garbo once lived. Denison Kitchel, F. Clifton White, Richard Kleindienst, and Dean Burch plotted strategy from this location. The third group of Goldwater backers—the Young Republicans, the John Birch Society, and other Far Right types—supported the Arizona senator, but viewed him as too moderate. Goldwater preferred that these volunteers not advertise their far-right affiliations. Their activities caused the main Goldwater campaign untold amounts of grief with one individual saying, "We've got super patriots running through the woods like a collection of firebugs, and I keep running after them, like Smokey Bear, putting out fires. We just don't need any more enemies." Another observed, "The senator is too busy to run a security check. Anybody who wants to carry a leaflet can carry a leaflet. We'll take the money of anybody who isn't on the Attorney General's list. They're not going to stop each check and ask, 'Does this guy think right?' All they're going to do is deposit the checks as fast as they can and hope to God they don't bounce."[16]

According to a memorandum in *National Review* publisher William Rusher's papers, Goldwater supporters analyzed California in March 1964. They began with the premise that it would take more than just the "overwhelming support of regular party workers" to win. Grassroots county organizations would be of paramount importance. Battle plans needed to be less "ad hoc" and more rigorously planned. Campaign financing presented a large challenge as Rockefeller had more available resources for television advertising. They advised using polling to determine Goldwater's schedule, sending him to areas where he was most likely to swing voters and not to areas where support for him was already strong. Such work would also maximize "the anxieties of the voters in a given area." They increased efforts to mobilize women. Finally, they discussed the "substantial" role that John Birch Society members were playing in the contest as "workers" and as "leaders" of the Goldwater campaign. This situation left the campaign with a challenge: how to retain an important grassroots constituency of voters and volunteers without losing other voters who viewed the Birchers as extremists.[17]

Extremism was the central issue in the California primary. Could Goldwater seek and win the votes of moderate as well as conservative Republicans? He faced a newly invigorated Rockefeller, the victor in the Oregon primary from two weeks previous. According to campaign public relations director Stuart Spencer, Rockefeller stated as his California goal to "destroy Barry Goldwater as a member of the human race." As such, questions remained for Goldwater. What would he do about the John Birch Society? He ignored opportunities to condemn the radical right group and instead courted conservative and popular Hollywood actors, including Rock Hudson, Raymond Massey, Ronald Reagan, Robert Stack, and John Wayne, all of whom campaigned for Barry.[18]

The mainstream opposition to Goldwater saw California as the last opportunity to stop him from being nominated, but Rockefeller never made a consistent, firm push to win. For example, Rockefeller's advisors prepped anti-Goldwater literature and even a thirty-minute television program that stressed the Arizona senator's extremism. Rockefeller rejected the latter as unfair to Goldwater. He described such tactics as "McCarthyism-in-reverse." His principled decision reflected naiveté about presidential politics. He repeated this mistake with his requirements for the workers hired to run his phone bank operation. He insisted on a racially blind hiring policy, so his campaign wound up with mostly African Americans. Many were from the South, had southern accents, and were loyal to the Democratic Party. Their job was to call Republican-leaning voters in Southern California who typically opposed civil rights legislation. Nor did Rockefeller make wise decisions about how to spend his money. To avoid looking like the millionaire he was, he deployed a minimal advertising campaign, spending his money instead on these paid campaign workers. Indeed, Rockefeller ran just one page in the Los Angeles Times the weekend before the primary whereas Goldwater had purchased four and a half pages in the same paper.[19]

Rockefeller had a more streamlined campaign, but he did not benefit from the efficiency. George Hinman, Rockefeller's campaign chief, found California a baffling place, so he concentrated on delegate selection. Primary voters would vote for named delegates by precinct associated with each candidate. Hinman wanted to use the most well known and accomplished moderate and liberal Republicans in California. There was just one problem: mainstream party leaders were "not doorbell-ringers, not troops." Rockefeller's big challenge was mobilizing a voter base—moderates that typically did not vote. Instead of relying on grassroots efforts, as the Goldwater campaign did, Rockefeller hired a professional firm, Spen-

cer-Roberts, to handle this work. Spencer-Roberts opened over fifty different Rockefeller campaign offices in California. This agency had managed
the successful campaign of a John Bircher for Congress in 1960. In 1964,
it paid people to seek Rockefeller voters. Rockefeller's campaign staff was
willing to "buy the people necessary to get this done." Said one political
insider, "Moderates are moderates. Raising the sword of moderation and
marching down a street is a contradiction in terms." Officials with the
Rockefeller campaign estimated that the candidate spent somewhere
between $2 and $3.5 million on the California primary. Clif White said
Rockefeller was spending so much money in California he was "making
Kennedy look like a piker."[20]

Rockefeller had the support of labor and the media. The *Los Angeles Times*
endorsed Rockefeller in California, but the words it offered were tepid and
unenthusiastic: "We tend to agree with Goldwater's broad objectives for
the United States, but we cannot support a great many of the senator's
solutions." The *Times* did state that it would support Goldwater in the fall
should he win the Republican nomination.[21]

Moreover, Rockefeller hoped he would benefit from Eisenhower's May
24, 1964, statement to the *New York Herald Tribune* on the ideal presidential candidate. Eisenhower called for more of the "responsible, forward-looking Republicanism I tried to espouse as President" and that had
been defined in the 1956 and 1960 Republican platforms. Rockefeller's
campaign staff prepared a detailed comparison of how the two GOP frontrunners aligned with Eisenhower's stated qualifications. They noted that
Goldwater had rejected the 1960 platform and that his political sun had
nothing in common with the light Eisenhower had shined for eight years
in the White House. Though Eisenhower did not name Rockefeller, most
readers identified the New York governor in the former president's words.
The statement initially hurt Goldwater, but when other Republicans complained to Eisenhower he modified his views saying he had not intended
an endorsement of Rockefeller but just an observation in the most general
fashion about what it took to be a good president. Other Republicans who
hoped to claim the nomination should Goldwater and Rockefeller destroy
each other remained neutral, though in the case of Scranton, one of his
allies assured him that he, not Rockefeller or Goldwater, was the person
best in sync with what the last Republican president advocated. Rockefeller observed, "It's understandable. All of them are available for the nomination and hoping that lightning will strike. What other position could
they take?"[22]

Goldwater found the best response. He changed the subject by appearing on Steve Allen's television show on May 29. Allen was a liberal talk show host who intended to make Goldwater look bad. He set up a gag where he received a call on the far-right hotline. The caller provided an extremist's perspective on the events of 1964 as well as the recent past. The panicked voice exhorted "an almost total blackout in the nation's mass communications news media" was a precursor to "an internal takeover of the United States by the Communist conspiracy later during the year." The caller reported "large-scale recruiting on college campuses is going to secure student participation in racial agitation this summer." The current pattern of events, the caller warned, matched "the internal takeover of Czechoslovakia in 1946." The caller admonished all listeners: "Do not trust the newspapers, radio, TV, and newsmagazines for your information. These are the main weapons the enemy has to use against us."[23]

Goldwater avoided the trap. He told Allen's audience he would not "laugh . . . these people off" because he "recognize[d] them as people who are concerned, people who recognize that some things in this government are not going the way they like." This declaration drew applause from an audience that had intended to join Allen in laughing at Goldwater. The Arizonan went on to state he did not believe there were Communists in the country, stressing that instead he worried about demands for a "centrally controlled economy run by the government." By the time the program was over Goldwater owned the audience. To great applause he concluded, "these people like the gentleman on the phone are merely expressing their frustration and their concern—you might say, like a man standing outside the tent throwing rocks while the other bunch are inside breaking up the furniture."[24]

A different Goldwater—more raucous, less sensible, and more inclined to the politics of resentment—reached to his base. Campaigning in Riverside, California, in the GOP primary, Goldwater sneered with disdain when he mimicked liberal government bureaucrats and blamed them for the decline of family values: "Don't worry about Mom and Pop, don't lay aside any money, enjoy yourself, the Federal Government will take care of Mom and Pop." Goldwater avowed, "*this* is the ultimate destruction of the American family. When this happens, Communism will have won."[25]

The rhetoric and the passions boiled over in California. Hecklers pestered both Goldwater and Rockefeller, with signs such as the following: "Goldwater: The Fascist Gun in the West" and "Do you want a leader, or a lover in the White House?" Words merged with physical threats; both campaigns received bomb threats. For as energetic as were his crowds, Goldwater did not always deliver equally enthusiastic speeches. His content was provocative, but his delivery did not match the vitriole of his words. One scholar described Goldwater events in California as "festivals," but his speeches rarely contained the "red meat" his audiences wanted, instead seeming more like "overcooked broccoli."[26]

An Orange County Goldwater leader reasoned the importance of right-wing publications in Goldwater's campaign, "there was literature coming out in every way. Hard-cover books to soft-cover books, tracts, one-page sheets. You couldn't imagine the stack. . . . It was incredible." Goldwater followers in California explained that the media bias against Barry made it difficult to understand his candidacy from national newspapers and television news broadcasts: "Goldwater was a mystery to us. Because the press, what did the press say about him? 'Well he's against Social Security, he's a war-monger,' that's what we heard. She [Phyllis Schlafly] wrote a book, *A Choice, Not an Echo* and she . . . made us familiar with this person and what he was about. . . . Then we identified with him." Schlafly's book, published in April 1964, sold 3 million copies in its first year of publication. Goldwater partisans distributed the book in California precincts where Rockefeller enjoyed a lead in the polls. Voter research suggested that in precincts where *A Choice, Not an Echo* had been disseminated, Goldwater enjoyed a 20 percent higher vote than in precincts where the book had not been delivered.[27]

Political pundits judged the race as even or maybe a Rockefeller lead. Rockefeller had the votes in northern California while Goldwater enjoyed the support of the more populous southern part of the state. The Oregon effect was tremendous for Rockefeller, at least initially. Before voting in Oregon, Goldwater led Rockefeller 48 percent to 39 percent, but five days after the Oregon primary the numbers were reversed, Rockefeller with 47 percent and Goldwater with 36 percent. Even so, Goldwater enjoyed a volunteer advantage and an enthusiasm advantage in California. Just in Los Angeles County campaign volunteers talked to 300,000 voters. In all, 40,000 volunteers worked throughout the state.[28]

As the June 2 election day drew nearer Goldwater closed the gap as the Louis Harris poll showed. Five days before the election Goldwater was at 40 percent and Rockefeller at 49 percent, but on Sunday before the Tuesday primary Rockefeller was down to 42 percent and Goldwater held steady at 40 percent. The undecided vote had increased from 11 percent to 18 percent. The reason: the birth of Rockefeller's baby reminded voters of his affair and divorce and his new wife's decision to abandon her children by her first husband to be with Rockefeller. In the last month of the California campaign—also the last month of Happy Rockefeller's pregnancy—Rockefeller returned to New York every weekend to be with her despite objections from his staff: "I have a show opening on both sides of the continent the same weekend," he declared.[29]

Goldwater beat Rockefeller in California by just 68,000 votes or 51.6 percent. His victory resulted because of his dedicated volunteers. The afternoon before the primary Goldwater volunteers met in churches for prayer meetings. Julius A. Leetham, the Los Angeles County Republican Party chair, neutral in the Goldwater-Rockefeller contest, made astute observations about voters in his state. Noting the "transitory quality" of California voters, Leetham contended "it's a very odd person who's lived in the same house for long." He said, "the bumbling, disoriented, inept amateurs who are out stumping around" for Goldwater "make people feel that someone is interested in *them*." Many of the new residents were army veterans. They disliked "brainwash[ing] by indoctrination," and they objected to the *Los Angeles Times* editorializing in favor of Rockefeller. They "resent[ed] being called an extremist" for wanting Goldwater to win. Housewives responded favorably to the female "Goldwater doorbell-ringer[s]." Leetham affirmed these individual interactions would have more importance than the *Los Angeles Times* editorial, or, put differently, "Mr. Goldwater is going to win at the doorstep."[30]

Republican businessman and future president George H. W. Bush told the *Houston Chronicle* that Goldwater's California win was "great news for Texas and all America. It indicates what hard work at the grass roots level will do to bring out a response to the Goldwater principles for real conservatism. It is a tremendous step toward his nomination." California conservatives enjoyed a "more emotional, crusading spirit" than the moderates, helping explain Goldwater's defeat of Rockefeller. Population demographics also benefited Goldwater. Almost 40 percent of the state's population lived in Los Angeles County according to the 1960 census, where the Goldwater precinct workers "outmanned the Rockefellers and did a better job on the earlier 'uncommitted' voters."[31]

Conservative understandings of morality played a huge role in the California contest. The right wing in California took great pleasure in demonizing Rockefeller, calling him "a *licentious* person politically and economically—*not fit for any political office*." They also exerted tremendous effort to carry the day for their candidate. Even a Rockefeller partisan observed, "I think that the baby's birth served to bring out again, to the women's attention especially, the problem that we dealt with during the whole campaign—that he was a wife-stealer and that she was a home-wrecker." Baptist preacher Tim LaHaye had written evangelical pastors in California: "A wife stealer, who divorced his wife of 30 years, broke up another man's home, and took a mother from her four children, stands a good chance to win the approval of Republican voters in California. If he is elected it will be the same as public approval of his wicked actions." He also told his fellow ministers he would preach a sermon against Rockefeller. Other religious leaders condemned Rockefeller. He had been scheduled to speak at Loyola University, but Cardinal James F. McIntyre withdrew the invitation for Rockefeller to appear at this Roman Catholic institution. McIntyre and the archdiocese were not willing to imply an endorsement for a divorced and remarried man.[32]

Last-minute ads for Goldwater had capitalized on the fact that Happy Rockefeller gave birth a mere 72 hours before the polls opened. Indeed, Los Angeles residents heard more radio than anywhere else in the United States because of long automobile commutes. It was probably radio advertising plus discussion on talk radio that mattered more about the baby, rather than print media. One ad proclaimed, "Why are women for Goldwater? Because he is a responsible family man." Another went further: "Mother, . . . why are we for Barry Goldwater? Because: Children need the inspiration of example. If all children are to grow up respecting truth, morality, courage, and justice, we must show them that we too respect these principles."[33]

Rockefeller told journalists after losing to Goldwater in California that the party of "Lincoln, of Teddy Roosevelt, of Bob Taft and Dwight Eisenhower" was in jeopardy as was "freedom," "human dignity," and "equal opportunity for all Americans." On June 3, the Rockefeller team held a postmortem on the California loss. They reckoned that their position was "in essence the same as it was after New Hampshire—a holding operation." To try to keep delegates from abandoning the New York governor in favor of Goldwater, Rockefeller backers argued his delegates should move to the candidate most likely to block Goldwater at the GOP convention. As a result of the loss Rockefeller redefined his presidential bid as a favorite son effort "generally against the Goldwater candidacy." A week later the Rockefeller campaign talked about whether there was a way to stop Goldwater. One participant noted, "General Eisenhower could probably do it, but won't."[34]

On June 4, Rockefeller campaign leaders met again. During part of the meeting former baseball player Jackie Robinson, who had long been working with the campaign, made a blunt assertion that the African American community "will work as hard as possible to defeat Goldwater." Campaign staffers asked Robinson to wait until he spoke with Rockefeller before speaking publicly.[35]

He did not wait long. Jackie Robinson and Barry Goldwater clashed over Goldwater's fitness to be president in the summer of 1964. Goldwater took umbrage to Robinson's criticisms. He wrote a letter to Robinson and released it to the press. In it he expressed anger that Robinson had judged him without meeting or talking with him. Robinson's reply, also released to the press, gave Goldwater no sympathy. He disagreed with the presumptive GOP nominee on everything from national security to civil rights, saying he "fear[ed]" for the future should "our government" be "placed in your stewardship."[36]

With three contested primaries and three different winners—Lodge in New Hampshire, Rockefeller in Oregon, and Goldwater in California—in stepped the traditional power brokers to attempt to discern the Republican nominee. In 1964, only 540 of the 1,308 total convention delegates had been selected by primary balloting. The rest came from a combination of state, district, and local conventions along with party committees making the choice in some instances. In most states congressional districts mattered more than the state overall, meaning a candidate could be the second or third choice statewide but have a strong grassroots organization in enough congressional districts to still win a majority of convention delegates from the state. Candidates who prevailed under this system usually had staff well versed in the peculiarities of each state's delegate selection process. For the Republicans in 1964 Goldwater's team earned that distinction. Clif White had developed a delegate strategy in 1961. His tactics concentrated on three separate regions of the country—the West, the South, and the Midwest—where he thought Goldwater would run strongest. In the West, White targeted businessmen who felt strangled by federal government regulations. Similarly, he maintained southerners disgusted by corrupt, one-party Democratic politics, usually revolving around backroom courthouse deals, would welcome Goldwater's message. In the Midwest, Taft conservatives received White's attention. The plan worked; Goldwater got almost a third of his first ballot delegate strength from the South.[37]

Once the California primary ended, machinations began to block Goldwater's nomination. Goldwater described a secret meeting Nixon had at the Waldorf-Astoria in New York during Memorial Day weekend. He complained Nixon "was plotting behind closed doors to take over the convention and give all the current candidates the boot. Yet we had the power to block anyone's nomination." Goldwater stressed he would never support Nixon because of Nixon's capitulation to Rockefeller in 1960.[38]

Despite Goldwater's bravado, moderates had good reason to think a convention challenge to Goldwater might work. Goldwater was a minority candidate, favored by just 13 percent of white voters in the spring of 1964. Not much changed by the summer of 1964. In late June, the Gallup Poll of all voters gave Scranton a sizeable lead over Goldwater for the GOP nomination, 63 percent to 26 percent and 11 percent undecided. When just Republicans were asked, Scranton's lead over Goldwater in polling was lower, 55 percent to 34 percent. Polling among independents mirrored polling among all voters. Independents especially favored Scranton instead of the Arizona senator. It proved insufficient, though, to sway Goldwater's most committed delegates, especially those from the South and the West. Indeed, these conservatives not only were distrustful of Scranton but also they were at war with moderates in their states. Goldwater did not worry about the polls that gave Scranton a huge lead going into the convention because he enjoyed tremendous delegate strength.[39]

Would Scranton participate in a combined stop Goldwater movement? He had always been coy about the matter. Seven months earlier he had told the press: "I've said over and over again, sir, that if there were an honest and sincere draft, I think any honest and sincere person would accept this. But I don't think you have any honest and sincere drafts anymore that you don't know about in advance, in which case I would certainly stop it." Scranton did indicate a willingness to be a favorite son under two conditions only: "one, if at the time the convention comes around, there is still a difference of opinion as to who is going to be the nominee, and secondly, if the delegation wanted me to do this. No personal desire of my own."[40]

After the California primary Eisenhower and Scranton met on June 6. The president called for the meeting because he did not savor the idea of a Goldwater nomination. Eisenhower's purpose seemingly was to recruit Scranton to run. The challenges were multifold, not the least of which was Scranton himself. Right after California he went on a television news program and said he would accept the vice-presidential nomination, an offer that had not been tendered. Scranton believed that anyone chosen had the responsibility to say yes. Humble by nature Scranton did not intend to sound "craven," as one journalist described the remark. Still, he horrified the stop-Goldwater Republicans when he said no "basic differences" existed between him and the Arizona senator. Eisenhower persuaded Scranton to make himself "more available" to a draft movement.[41]

Scranton left the Gettysburg, Pennsylvania meeting, which lasted over an hour, sensing that Eisenhower wanted him to fight Goldwater for the nomination. He traveled from Gettysburg to a meeting of the nation's governors in Cleveland, Ohio. He declared he had Eisenhower's backing to challenge Goldwater. When the press reported that sentiment, Eisenhower instructed Scranton to call him. He did so because the Goldwater team had learned of the Eisenhower-Scranton move. Denison Kitchel, the campaign manager, lobbied a Goldwater supporter who had been a member of Eisenhower's administration to encourage the president to remain neutral in the nominating process. When Ike and Scranton talked on the phone, the former president insisted he would "not be part of any 'cabal' to stop Barry." Scranton thus abandoned his plans to challenge Goldwater and even used an appearance on *Meet the Press* to suggest Goldwater was an able and fit candidate for the presidency. The GOP governors in attendance in Cleveland—there were only sixteen in the nation but thirteen of them opposed Goldwater—flailed about to try to figure out how to stop Goldwater. They turned to George Romney who had promised he would fight the Arizonan's "suicidal destruction of the Republican Party." Oregon governor (and future US senator) Mark Hatfield told Romney, "George, you're six months too late. If you can't add, I'll add it for you. Goldwater's got it."[42]

National events—namely Goldwater's vote against cloture on the civil rights bill on June 10—pushed Scranton to reconsider yet again entering the race. He wanted to prevent his party from "go[ing] down in history as the white-supremacy party." On June 11, Scranton met with advisors. When he asked Hugh Scott, a moderate senator from Pennsylvania, for advice, Scott replied the risk of running was great but the reward—win or lose— was greater. Quickly Scranton worked the phones to line up supporters and donors. He called but did not reach Goldwater. As such, he wrote Goldwater the next day: "because of principle I have made the decision now announced. Certainly you will respect that." Further telephone conversations with Eisenhower, also disgusted by Goldwater's cloture vote, convinced Scranton to make a quixotic, five-week campaign for the nomination, but it was too late to create a boom.[43]

Scranton crisscrossed the nation in search of delegates, spending $800,000 in the process. To win, Scranton needed every uncommitted delegate along with 200 or so Goldwater delegates. He also needed all the Rockefeller and Lodge delegates, all the favorite-son campaigns to remain

While traveling on June 24, 1964, from Charleston, West Virginia, to Miami, Florida, Governor William W. Scranton told reporters aboard his plane "that the nomination of Senator Barry Goldwater for President would set up our party for a defeat of major proportion." Courtesy the Associated Press.

opposed to Goldwater, strong support from the eastern establishment, a public endorsement from Eisenhower, and public opinion to turn in his favor. Efforts to bring the eastern establishment on board fizzled. Someone with the Scranton campaign observed, "We called all the old names; but they weren't there any longer. . . . It was as if the Goldwater people had rewired the switchboard of the Party and the numbers we had were all dead."[44]

Scranton formally announced his intent to challenge Goldwater at the Maryland State Republican Convention. He told a national television audience on June 28 that the Republican Party and the country faced catastrophe should Goldwater prevail in his presidential campaign. Additionally, Scranton judged Goldwater's vote against the Civil Rights Act as an endorsement of segregation. Liberal and moderate Republicans were thrilled when Scranton decided to challenge Goldwater at the national convention. Four days after Scranton announced, Rockefeller on June 15 endorsed the Pennsylvania governor, noting with "Governor Scranton as the candidate, the moderate cause can still be won. I urge all those who share this view to enlist now in that cause." Three days later, though, there had been no direct contact between the top Rockefeller officials and the top Scranton officials. Rockefeller staffers described the Scranton effort as "chaotic" and lacking any "concept of the operation ahead of them."[45]

As the convention drew nearer, Goldwater gained in the lead. This trend frustrated delegates who supported other candidates. A Texas Republican and Rockefeller supporter complained that the Texas delegation to the Republican National Convention was "bound by blood oath to Goldwater." That individual noted that "the Texas Republican convention last Tuesday was not a convention in fact but a coronation ceremony. . . . This is democracy in action, Birch style."[46]

Indeed, the inflammatory nature of Goldwater and his extremist supporters ensured the GOP convention would produce controversy and protest. Such discord began before the convention was gaveled to order. The Congress of Racial Equality (CORE) and other civil rights groups planned "noisy" protests against both Goldwater and Scranton at the Republican National Convention. Scranton drew this negative attention because he had had "no communications" with civil rights leaders. Jackie Robinson persuaded James Farmer to "do what he can to keep down" rallies against Scranton in San Francisco. This did not end matters. The NAACP "call[ed] up the Republican Party to repudiate the candidacy of Goldwater." Robinson warned civil rights leaders that "violent demonstrations . . . would trigger the nomination for Goldwater." He promised Rockefeller campaign officials that there were only two groups that might stage rowdy protests with the rest being "under as much control as possible."[47]

Over 40,000 people joined a civil rights march on Market Street on the eve of the Republican National Convention. Demonstrators marched to the San Francisco Civic Center to protest the likely nomination of Goldwater. In attendance were Farmer, John Lewis of the Student Non-Violent Coordinating Committee (SNCC), A. Philip Randolph of the Brotherhood of Sleeping Car Porters, and Robinson. Lewis told the crowd, "No political party can expect to survive that nominates a man like Barry Goldwater." Randolph said Goldwater was a modern-day Jefferson Davis. Robinson dismissed Goldwater as a "bigot."[48]

They were not alone in using the streets of San Francisco. Hordes of conservatives also packed the streets chanting, "We are the Goldwater *armyyyyyyy* of liberation!" They wanted liberty from establishment Republicans, from the communist threat, from the civil rights movement, and from moderation in civil society. In other words, they practiced the politics of resentment and backlash. Fear also motivated them, fear of an ex-

Ku Klux Klan members march in favor of Barry Goldwater's candidacy for the White House at the Republican National Convention, San Francisco, California, while at the same time an African American man pushes back, July 12, 1964. Library of Congress, Prints and Photographs Division, photograph by U.S. News & World Report Magazine Photograph Collection.

panding federal government bureaucracy, fear of racial equality, and fear of change. Norman Mailer observed of the convention, the delegates were "loaded with one hatred: the Eastern Establishment was not going to win again, this time Main Street was going to take Wall Street. So Barry had his brothers, three or four hundred of the hardest delegates in the land, and they were ready to become the lifelong enemy of any delegate who might waver to Scranton."[49]

Other dissenting groups assembled outside the convention, which was held at the Cow Palace, an arena constructed with federal money during the New Deal and located on sixty-seven acres six miles from downtown San Francisco. Peace groups harangued against nuclear proliferation and against NATO. Labor groups demanded justice for Teamster leader Jimmy Hoffa. Finally, civil rights activists carried placards reading "Goldwater for President—Jefferson Davis for Vice-President" and "Goldwater—'64, Hot Water—'65, Bread and Water—'66." Other signs read "Goldwater for Führer" and "Defoliate Mississippi." None provoked a reaction.[50]

Segregationist governor George Wallace executed a crazy plan to try to get himself on the ticket with Goldwater as the vice-presidential nominee.

He called fellow Alabaman James Martin, a Republican candidate for Congress, an avowed Goldwater partisan, and also the GOP Senate candidate who had almost toppled Lister Hill in 1962. Wallace invited Martin to come to the governor's office on a Saturday. Martin was in work clothes mowing his lawn, but he went to see Wallace without even changing clothes. Wallace wanted him to fly straight to San Francisco, meet with Goldwater, and tell him Wallace was ready and willing to be named the GOP vice-presidential nominee. The governor told Martin, "It must be apparent to a one-eyed nigguh who can't see good outa his other eye, that me and Goldwater would be a winning ticket. We'd have the South locked up, and then him and me could concentrate on the industrial states of the North and win." Martin had a private meeting with Goldwater the afternoon before the convention opened. He told a stunned Goldwater: "Mr. Wallace has suggested that he would like to be a candidate with you as your vice-presidential nominee on the Republican ticket." Nothing came of the solicitation so three days after Goldwater's nomination Wallace withdrew from the race, telling the country his mission had been accomplished.[51]

Moderates and conservatives even fought about how long the convention should last. The Goldwater forces were insisting that the first convention ballot be cast immediately following the nominating speeches. Moderates disliked this option because it favored Goldwater. They wanted to retain a longer, five-day convention schedule. Republican National Committee chair Representative William E. Miller (R-NY), who later in the convention became the vice-presidential nominee, was noncommittal. If Goldwater had secured the nomination Miller wondered what would be the point of extending the convention, but moderates countered that "it would take some time after the nomination had been made actually to find out what the situation was in respect to this."[52]

By the time the convention opened on July 13, 1,308 delegates had traveled to San Francisco primed to choose a nominee. Another 5,400 reporters were in the city to cover the proceedings. The first order of business involved drafting the platform. Conservatives wanted a document paralleling the Goldwater agenda. Liberals and moderates disagreed, but they were not sure whether and how they could retain the 1960 platform and a commitment to civil rights. Rockefeller sought but did not gain strong, pro–civil rights language. Goldwater wrote party liberals and told them he would follow the Eisenhower–John Foster Dulles foreign policy line. Scranton loyalist Hugh Scott sardonically remarked, Goldwater would "accept anything short of the *Communist Manifesto*" for the platform.[53]

Rockefeller, Romney, and Scranton all addressed the Platform Committee. Each gave reasoned, thoughtful, and detailed analysis about the role of the GOP in national affairs. According to one journalist Scranton's speech was especially strong, but the committee members sat silent. Conversely, when Goldwater addressed the committee, he entered and exited the room to chants of "We want Barry." The tone of his remarks could best be described as both angry and full of "moral fervor." The committee loved it, and loved him so much so, according to one journalist, that he "might have read a page out of the Sears-Roebuck catalogue and received the same cheering of approval."[54]

The experiences of moderate and liberal Republican leaders show just how much Goldwater had remade the GOP. The Platform Committee treated Milton Eisenhower, the brother of the president, George Romney, and Henry Cabot Lodge terribly, dismissing their moderate Republicanism out of hand. Indeed, the majority of the committee sat in utter silence when Lodge advocated a "Republican-sponsored Marshall Plan for our cities and schools." Later when he went to his hotel a Goldwater advocate told him he was "terrible," causing Lodge to return the insult word for word. Upon looking at the roster of convention delegates, Lodge remarked, "What in God's name has happened to the Republican Party! I hardly know any of these people."[55]

Goldwater intensified those charges through his management of the physical space at the convention. He had his San Francisco headquarters at the Hotel Mark Hopkins on Nob Hill. Because the only risk to his nomination was loss of delegates to Scranton, his team established a sophisticated communication system among the various hotels where delegates were staying. An "elaborate phone tie-up" allowed for "instant" communication. A Goldwater team member noted, "It also will be possible to keep quick track of the movements of Scranton, Lodge, et al." Scranton and Goldwater had previously been close friends, but Scranton's late entry into the race irked Goldwater, who had long thought of Scranton as a potential running mate. So sour had their relationship become that Goldwater had Pinkerton guards protecting his floors at the hotel with the dual mission of holding the press at bay and preventing Scranton spies from gaining any advantage.[56]

The Goldwater camp was equally cautious about the convention delegates. They completed thorough research on all delegates and alternates to the convention, noting their educational, business, religious, and political backgrounds. The manner in which delegates for candidates other than

Goldwater were discussed sometimes bordered on the offensive with homophobic language used about men rumored to be gay. An Alaska state representative and a Nixon supporter was termed someone who could be "flattered and 'wined,'" was "definitely" a "known homosexual," and was "keeping some man." Another state representative in Alaska was termed "effeminate." An uncommitted female alternate was dubbed "a real baby doll type." Notes were made on whether or not delegates had police records. The campaign assumed that Republican delegates and alternates of modest economic means might be bribed by rival candidates. A delegate from the District of Columbia was described as "screwy" and "perhaps senile."[57]

Demographically Republican delegates were young, under fifty on average, male, and middle to upper middle-class. For many, San Francisco was their first convention. They were more conservative in their political values than past GOP convention delegates. Of the GOP delegates, approximately 100—8 percent of the total—were members of the John Birch Society. Republican delegates there were also overwhelmingly white. Indeed the percentage of African American delegates was the lowest on record at just 1 percent. They endured racist insults from the southern white delegates. Many black delegates walked out of the convention. A New York African American refused to change his vote so Goldwater's nomination could be made unanimous, stating, "I'd rather be lynched than vote for this guy." Jackie Robinson explained of the convention, "I now believe I know how it felt to be a Jew in Hitler's Germany."[58]

Tom Stagg Jr., though, was one of the many gleeful delegates in San Francisco. A national committeeman from Louisiana, Stagg said of Goldwater's controversial statements: "I sure like that. I sure like that." Such observations reinforced what political pundits argued. Columnist Walter Lippmann wrote of Goldwater's movement in June 1964, "It is impossible to doubt that Senator Goldwater intends to make his candidacy the rallying point of white resistance." Nothing at the convention changed these views, on either side of the equation. After the GOP convention a *Chicago Defender* headline read "GOP Convention, 1964, Recalls Germany, 1933."[59]

Despite these concerns, Goldwater had the numbers to claim the nomination. This mathematical calculation did not stop Scranton, who worked hard to win over any delegation whose loyalty to Goldwater was in doubt. For example, he met the Illinois delegation at the airport en route to the Republican National Convention to try to persuade them to abandon Goldwater and endorse Scranton. Indeed, leaders in the Illinois delegation worried about whether the Arizonan was presidential in his behavior. Right before the Republican National Convention, Everett Dirksen told a journalist, "we've got to control him. We have got to stop this hip shooting. It is simply too dangerous in the world as it is." Two delegations—Wisconsin and Ohio—had gone to San Francisco essentially undecided. Each was pledged to a favorite son. The Young Republicans in Wisconsin had warned the delegation, "Vote our wishes in San Francisco or continue westward." Both broke for Goldwater, but the manner in which Ohio did so shocked Scranton, who had hoped to pick up those delegates. Political insiders had attested Jim Rhodes, the Ohio governor, would hold the delegation in favorite-son status until Goldwater had been denied the nomination. Instead, Rhodes told Scranton he vowed the backlash vote for Goldwater might be sufficient to provide a surprise upset in November. A California delegate told a reporter, "The nigger issue will put [Goldwater] in the White House."[60]

Scranton was nonplussed. He hoped to convince Goldwater to debate him on the floor of the convention, but a scathing, nasty letter drafted by Scranton's young staff and sent before the Pennsylvania governor had read it enraged the Goldwater camp. The Scranton letter asserted Goldwater's managers were treating the delegates as *"little more than a flock of chickens whose necks will be wrung at will."* He castigated Goldwater for advocating nuclear war, working with radical extremists, dismissing iconic GOP leaders like Taft and Eisenhower and Lincoln, and supporting "irresponsibility in the serious question of racial holocaust." All these sins, Scranton professed, comprised "Goldwaterism," the *"whole crazy-quilt"* ideology that was destroying the Republican Party.[61]

After receiving the Scranton letter on the eve of the convention, a furious Goldwater called a meeting with his top advisors. He was convinced Scranton did not write the letter. It did not bear his signature, and Goldwater termed the Pennsylvania governor a gentleman. They returned the original letter to Scranton, but also made sure copies of the letter were delivered to all delegates. He flatly rejected Scranton's call for a debate before the convention delegates. Scranton accepted responsibility for the letter, but Goldwater was not satisfied. He told the German news magazine *Der Spiegel,* "I would say he has completely ruled that out [being offered the vice presidency]." Later, Goldwater explained the letter "shocked and angered conservatives" and gave "the Democrats their campaign slogans and strategy on a platter—only Lyndon Johnson and Bill Moyers were to exceed the vulgar indecencies of Scranton's staff."[62]

The full convention still had to deliberate the platform, and given the Scranton letter, that debate had the potential to get ugly. Scranton's forces had timed it so the debate would occur during prime time, but Goldwater's people outsmarted the liberals by undertaking a word-for-word reading of the document. Histrionics resulted after prime time, though, when Clif White had the sergeants at arms remove NBC journalist John Chancellor from the floor. NBC ran footage live of the police arresting Chancellor and him telling viewers, "I want to assure you that NBC is fully staffed with other reporters who are not in [police] custody. . . . I formally say this is a disgrace. The press, radio, and television should be allowed to do their work at the convention." He signed off, "This is John Chancellor, somewhere in custody." Goldwater supporters had a different view of the press, noting, "Why they made Goldwater out to be a man who ate negro babies for breakfast."[63]

When Eisenhower addressed the delegates, Goldwater partisans vented their spleen, not at the former president but at liberals and those they defended. Ike had penciled in the lines to an otherwise bland speech of GOP party history. He told the delegates: "Let us particularly scorn the divisive efforts of those outside our family, including sensation seeking columnists . . . who couldn't care less about the good of our party." These words inspired delegates to storm toward the press as if to attack. It took a call from Clif White to the delegation chairs to bring order back to the floor. Delegates welcomed Eisenhower's controversial statement in his convention speech, "let us not be guilty of maudlin sympathy for the criminal who, roaming the streets with switchblade knife and illegal firearms seeking a helpless prey, suddenly becomes upon apprehension a poor, underprivileged person who counts upon the compassion of our society and the laxness or weaknesses of too many courts to forgive his offense."[64]

Rockefeller, Scranton, and Romney led one last fight to strip the party platform of its right-wing planks. They lost their battles to get the party to condemn the John Birch Society, endorse nuclear arms control, and advocate additional civil rights reforms. When Rockefeller addressed the convention, he complained about Goldwater's "goon squads" and "Nazi methods." The Goldwater-friendly crowd responded with chants of "We want Barry." Rockefeller turned to the television cameras and said, "This is still a free country, ladies and gentlemen." The crowd booed him off the stage. The booing of Rockefeller grew out of control when some in the Cow Palace rang cowbells and blew horns. An angry blonde woman in the galleries yelled, "You're a lousy lover! You're a lousy lover!"[65]

The hostile crowd proved to be a highly orchestrated show. The Goldwater team used their sophisticated telecommunications network to tell delegates when to demonstrate and when to take their seats. Goldwater himself maintained that with just a few more weeks planning time each delegate could have been provided a "pocket telephone." One moderate Republican recalled, "The venom of the booing and the hatred in people's eyes really was quite stunning. I remember I was standing next to an officer from the San Mateo County Sheriff's Office, who was there to keep the peace, and there he was, with his pistol unsheathed, booing along with everyone else." Hugh Scott expressed his frustration with the Republican conservatives: "My letters have been full of indignation at the indecent conduct of a bunch of hog-callers" who booed the New York governor.[66]

The conservative "hog-callers" followed script and nominated Goldwater for the presidency. As each state was called and its votes announced the Goldwater team kept track of the overall delegate tally, comparing the actual results with the carefully drafted predictions. When Ohio called fifty-seven for Goldwater and just one for Margaret Chase Smith that put the Arizona senator over 600, very close to the 655 number needed to claim the nomination. Clif White announced to the candidate with jubilation, "Just for your information on this projection you'll make it on South Carolina." He did. With that state's sixteen delegates Goldwater officially became the GOP nominee. Goldwater had a muted reaction: "I never thought it would be that close."[67]

For a brief moment it seemed like Goldwater might reach to the middle and unite the party with his selection of a running mate. Earlier, he had suggested he wanted Scranton to be his running mate, but the quixotic summer campaign to stop Goldwater and the letter to convention delegates changed Goldwater's mind. Instead, Goldwater used his vice-presidential pick to further anger party moderates and hopefully to annoy Johnson. Goldwater named Miller as his choice. Miller was not well known nationally or even in the party, but he was a conservative, perhaps more so than the standard-bearer himself. Miller was a poor choice for the number-two spot, though, if Goldwater had hoped his vice-presidential nominee would help unite the party. Miller, from New York, was no eastern Republican; he had been more opposed to Eisenhower's agenda in the 1950s than had Goldwater. Moreover, Goldwater did not consult with Eisenhower or any other party leaders on his selection. Finally, Miller was not a reassuring figure to American voters.

While putting together his acceptance speech with his speech writers, polling from Opinion Research in Princeton, New Jersey, came out that showed LBJ with an 80–20 percent lead. Goldwater told them, "Instead

On July 15, 1964, Barry Goldwater waves to delegates inside the Cow Palace at the Republican National Convention in San Francisco. Courtesy the Associated Press.

of writing an acceptance speech, we should be putting together a rejection speech and tell them all to go to hell." He did tell them to go to hell, but he did not reject the nomination. Goldwater explained, "If I walked out on that convention dais and embraced Rockefeller, conservatives in the Cow Palace and across the country would have thought it was some political ad paid for by the Democratic National Committee." He recounted the party had "just been through a bloody war on a host of issues," so he believed his speech "had to make clear that this was a historic break, . . . taking over the party from the Republican National Committee on down and setting a new course in GOP national politics."[68]

After Nixon introduced Goldwater to give his acceptance speech, the nominee entered to "Glory, Glory Hallelujah" also known as the "Battle Hymn of the Republic." Ironically, the song originated as a spiritual sung by enslaved African Americans and then morphed into a pro-Union song during the Civil War. Red, white, and blue balloons were dropped, and the crowd chanted, "We want Barry." Goldwater proclaimed, "The Good Lord raised this mighty Republic . . . not to stagnate in the swamplands of collectivism, not to cringe before the bully of Communism." He castigated

Democrats as the party responsible for "violence in our streets, corruption in our highest offices, aimlessness among our youth, anxiety among our elderly, and there's a virtual despair among the many who look beyond material successes toward the inner meaning of their lives." He said these conditions resulted not because of "political differences" but because of "a fundamentally and absolutely wrong view of man." He crucified not only Democrats but also Republican moderates with his charge: "Extremism in the defense of liberty is no vice! . . . Moderation in the pursuit of justice is no virtue!"[69]

When Goldwater spoke positively of extremism in his convention address he did so to antagonize moderates worried about the influence of the John Birch Society in American politics. Instead of trying to bring all factions of the party back together Goldwater had, in the words of Nixon, "opened new wounds and then rubbed salt in them." Other moderate Republicans reacted badly to the speech. Senator Kenneth Keating of New York, who faced a tough reelection campaign against Robert Kennedy, walked out of the convention in anger. Forty New York delegates followed him. Rockefeller said of the speech: "To extol extremism—whether 'in defense of liberty' or in 'pursuit of justice'—is dangerous, irresponsible, and frightening." Some moderates tried to reach out to the Goldwater camp to unite the party. California congressmen sent a statement to the party delegation, but after former senator William Knowland read the missive aloud he tore it up and threw it on the ground. The assembled crowd cheered.[70]

After controversy ensued about Goldwater's acceptance speech he expounded that his main purpose had been to talk about freedom, a word he used twenty-five times in the convention address. Some Republicans elucidated that Goldwater's statement about extremism derived from the ancient Roman orator Cicero. The result of the two sentences, written for Goldwater by Harry Jaffa, an Ohio State University political science professor, was to further divide Republican moderates and conservatives and to give conservatives a false target to attack, the media.

Vice-presidential nominee Miller defended Goldwater: "I think what Senator Goldwater was talking about was that 'extremism' meaning wholehearted devotion to the cause of freedom—if he had used the term 'wholehearted devotion' instead of extremism, it would have probably been not so easily misunderstood. If he had used the term 'half-hearted' instead of 'moderation,' I think he would not have been so easily misunderstood." Miller stressed that Goldwater had not meant to imply "extremism in political activity or in political action" but instead had "us[ed] a term to describe a necessity for everlasting vigilance and wholehearted devotion in an all-out effort to secure freedom and to secure justice." Journalist Ben Bradlee told Goldwater that if Kennedy had made the same quote about extremism editorial writers would have praised it. Dean Burch said: "Barry Goldwater could have recited the Lord's Prayer or the Twenty-third Psalm as his acceptance speech. He still would have been attacked."[71]

The tone and content of Goldwater's acceptance speech angered moderate Republicans. Former representative Walter Judd (R-MN) asserted, "Barry . . . seemed more defiant than conciliatory, militant than magnanimous." Nixon was even more blunt, "if he ever had a chance to win the presidency, he lost it that night with that speech. . . . I felt almost physically sick as I sat there." Goldwater defended his statement to Nixon as "examples of a quality of devotion to liberty and justice—'firmness in the right,' as Lincoln put it—for which no Republican, and, indeed, no American need apologize. It goes without saying that such devotion would not countenance illegal or improper means to achieve proper goals." Eisenhower demanded that Goldwater meet him at his hotel the morning after his acceptance speech. He dressed him down: "Barry, what the hell did you mean last night about extremism . . . ? I couldn't make any sense out of it and I thought it was a damn silly thing to say." Goldwater explained, "General, in June 1944 when you led the Allied forces across the English Channel, you were an 'extremist,' and you did it in defense of liberty." Eisenhower supposedly replied, "By golly, I get it! I see now what you mean. By golly, that makes real sense. That's great, Barry—great, just great. I'm glad you came to see me."[72]

Following the nomination, journalists and establishment political observers were quick to dismiss Goldwater. One reporter who heard the speech declared, "My God, he's going to run as Barry Goldwater." Katie Louchheim, a Democratic insider, analyzed the GOP convention: "There have been moments when the Rep[ublican] Convention on TV lacked only the script writer's signature; Mephistopheles. Except that Goldwater wasn't really Faust for he paid no price for his victory, he made no deals." Conservatives had summarily dispatched "the Rep[ublican] 'crew-cut' liberals." Indeed, the eastern wing of the party came across as "effete, foreign" compared with the "focused trained flat foots armed and aiming, western in origin but not in tradition. For the cunning and the money of the EAST was nothing to the cunning and money of the WEST." The transformation of the party had earlier been revealed when Eisenhower traveled by train to San Francisco: "at every stop Ike got madder. There were NO I Like Ikers;

they were all Goldwater fans." As people made their way to San Francisco, Goldwater supporters passed out roses to women. Someone offered flowers to journalist Mary McGrory, who refused, saying sardonically, "'I'm a member of the Eastern Communist Press.'" Did the outpouring of support mean Goldwater could carry California in the fall? Journalists asked Democratic governor Pat Brown of California. He said yes, but only "By a very slight margin." When asked if he could be quoted, Brown changed his words: "'If you're going to quote me, make it a large margin.'"[73]

Goldwater's decisions after gaining the nomination suggest the GOP nominee was more interested in ideology than victory. He selected Dean Burch to become the national committee chairman. Burch, an unknown Arizonan and an archconservative, sought a Republican Party more loyal to conservatism than dedicated to bridging the gap with moderates. A Burch assistant, John Grenier, instructed staff members to remove all portraits of Abraham Lincoln and Dwight Eisenhower from the Republican Party headquarters. The Goldwater strategy, according to one GOP insider, was to focus on "race, corruption, nostalgia, and nationalism." Goldwater opined the race issue could be exploited to "break the hold [Democrats] have on the Northern working man's vote." Moreover, discussing charges of Democratic corruption, Republicans insisted, would support the nostalgia appeal to "the 'little people,' the 'forgotten majority' that belongs to no 'organized, pressure group.'" Goldwater planned an attack on the foreign aid program and foreign policy priorities in place since the end of World War II with the goal of "translat[ing] foreign distaste for Goldwater into a wave of liquidation by foreigners of American stocks." Reported one source, "the Goldwater people hope that they can precipitate a crisis in foreign confidence which in turn could possibly bring about a domestic crisis."[74]

The GOP convention energized some conservatives about the possibility of remaking the party, but others from Texas, for example, did not think Goldwater conservative enough. It also troubled Democrats about what changes might result in general election campaigning. Clyde T. Ellis, an official with the national organization overseeing rural electricity cooperatives and a Johnson crony, advised the president, "The Goldwater group will stop at nothing to win, I think. Character assassination, a major John Birch Society tactic, will probably be their secret weapon. . . . Miller's role will no doubt be to lead the hatchet brigade, and he is good at it." More pragmatic conservatives realized that the Goldwater nomination would hurt the party with minority voters, but judged that an increase in white voters would eliminate any such problems. A Louisiana Democrat turned Republican proved this point, saying he would be for Goldwater even if he was a member of the "Vegetarian Party."[75]

Goldwater, though, did not entirely abandon the middle in July 1964. After the convention he wrote Scranton he wanted to talk to him in person. "Even though we had some rather sharp disagreements during the course of the campaign," Goldwater stressed, "I feel certain that the two of us can do more than any other two in pulling this Party back together." Goldwater made this appeal because he maintained "there is not a vast canyon between you and me, but rather a relatively small ditch that either of us can jump back and forth over at the convenience of the Party." Goldwater knew this was true because, at least for the moment, he had defeated Republican pragmatists, those like Scranton who had dominated the party since World War I and who had been more interested in getting things done than in ideology. Goldwater's victory over Republican pragmatism meant he would face off in November against the epitome of political pragmatism from either party: Lyndon B. Johnson.[76]

"THAT WAS LYNDON BAINES JOHNSON!"

"I had to take the dead man's program and turn it into a martyr's cause," Lyndon B. Johnson explained of the challenges he faced when he succeeded John F. Kennedy in the White House. Whereas Kennedy had endured political gridlock throughout his presidency, Johnson made the legislative process productive again. By doing so, he expounded, "Kennedy would live on forever and so would I." LBJ had two main political priorities: expanding the liberal New Deal welfare state and securing real civil rights reform. He did not moderate his legislative agenda to account for a divided populace. Instead, he used Kennedy's death to push reforms ranging from health care to education. With no real primary opponent other than Alabama governor and segregationist George C. Wallace's quixotic brief challenge to Johnson, then, civil rights, and its place within the liberal agenda, became the central campaign question. By ending Jim Crow segregation, Johnson cast his sun in the direction of liberty and justice for all, suggesting the possibilities for a Sunbelt style of liberalism that reached forward to a future of equality most unlike Goldwater's Far Right Sunbelt conservatism.[1]

Obtaining civil rights required several difficult prerequisites: maintaining the allegiance of Kennedy loyalists, moving the stalled Kennedy agenda through Congress, gaining the trust of the civil rights community, and winning over the American people. Johnson began by addressing a joint session of Congress before a nationally televised audience with his November 27, 1963, "Let Us Continue" speech.

Lyndon B. Johnson, new president of the United States, speaks at Andrews Air Force Base, November 22, 1963, with his wife, Lady Bird Johnson, at his side. Cecil Stoughton (Dan Lewis). White House Photographs. John F. Kennedy Presidential Library and Museum, Boston.

A mere five days after the assassination he told lawmakers and the public: "All I have I would have given gladly not to be standing here today." Other parts of the address were geared to his former congressional colleagues: "For 32 years Capitol Hill has been my home. I have shared many moments of pride with you, pride in the ability of the Congress of the United States to act, to meet any crisis, to distill from our differences strong programs of national action." In still other parts of the speech he addressed the American people. "The time has come for Americans of all races and creeds and political beliefs to understand and to respect one another. So let us put an end to the teaching and the preaching of hate and evil and violence," Johnson avowed. "Let us turn away from the fanatics of the far left and the far right, from the apostles of bitterness and bigotry, from those defiant of law, and those who pour venom into our Nation's bloodstream."[2] His purpose was to identify Kennedy as a martyr, label extremists as a threat to democracy, and emphasize the words of America's founding documents that "all

President Lyndon B. Johnson talks with Martin Luther King Jr. in the Oval Office, December 3, 1963. LBJ Library, photo by Yoichi Okamoto.

men are created equal." In doing so, he articulated his brand of consensus liberalism, which was rooted in his southwestern background.

TRB in *The New Republic* said of Johnson's address to Congress, "It was a good speech, movingly delivered on a great occasion—the kind of epilogue which Shakespeare lets a surviving character deliver over a stage strewn with hopes and corpses." Representative Adam Clayton Powell (D-NY) was even less reserved. He told Johnson: "it was really wonderful. You were at your best today. Absolutely superb. I don't know when you got the time to *do* it though. . . . I know you have good ghostwriters. But brother, that was Lyndon Baines *Johnson!*" Other lawmakers agreed; Congress interrupted Johnson thirty-four times for applause. Kennedy people were more ambiguous. For Robert F. Kennedy, the attorney general and brother of the slain president, the speech was difficult. Great animus had long marked the relationship between Bobby and Lyndon, and indeed managing Kennedy became an important sub-theme for Johnson during the first eight months of 1964. During the speech, Bobby "was pale, somber and inscrutable, applauding faithfully, but his face set and his lips compressed," JFK advisor Arthur M. Schlesinger Jr. recounted.[3]

Johnson's outreach to civil rights leaders began immediately upon entering the presidency. For example, civil rights leader James Farmer, the founder of the civil rights group Congress of Racial Equality (CORE), re-called of Johnson: "he felt at this stage that he desperately needed civil rights people in order to overcome his background, to overcome his Southern constituency and his accent. So he made a very special and definite appeal to us." Farmer explained that Johnson called him "just a few days after he assumed office," saying "'Come down and see me whenever you can. I want to talk. I need your help.' And I'm sure that I was overly impressed with" the entreaty from the president. Less well known but just as important, LBJ also cultivated the Mexican American community, showing another layer to his Sunbelt political vision.[4]

Given GOP divisions between the eastern establishment and Goldwaterites, Johnson saw little risk in pursuing civil rights before the election. He told Texas governor John Connally on February 8, 1964: "I don't see that they got anybody, though, that's appealing to people much. [Barry] Goldwater has gone crazy. He wanted to go in [to Cuba with] the Marines yesterday, and he's just nutty as a fruitcake. . . . [Nelson] Rockefeller's wife ain't going to let him get off the ground." Even though he did not "believe he's appealing enough or attractive enough" Johnson guessed William Scranton would get the nomination. To be competitive in the fall, Connally had earlier advised Johnson, "I was just going to suggest: for God's sake, meet with the businessmen. . . . You been getting a little *too* much emphasis on meeting with the civil rights boys." Johnson disagreed with Governor Connally, observing later: "I should have spent more time with that boy. His problem is he likes those oak-paneled rooms too much."[5]

To Johnson courting liberals and civil rights leaders did not mean abandoning more moderate and conservative Democrats. Still, southern political leaders put him on notice regarding what they would and would not tolerate. Senator Robert C. Byrd (D-WV) wrote Johnson that he would support him as strongly, "or possibly even better," than he had helped Kennedy, but he cautioned the new president he could not endorse civil rights reform because it "impinges upon the civil and Constitutional rights of white people." Moreover, Representative Joe Kilgore (D-TX) told White House aide Walter Jenkins that Representative Howard Worth Smith (D-VA) "was an original Johnson man," and should be courted by the White House. Clifton C. Carter, another Johnson aide, described as "a pedestrian political errand-doer" and "suspicious of anyone who came from east of the Mississippi or north of the Mason-Dixon line," told LBJ that John J. McKeithen, a protégé of Governor Earl Long and the leading Democratic candidate for governor of Louisiana, had promised, "I can't shout support of Mr. Johnson from the roof tops but when the final bell rings Louisiana and I will be in the right corner."[6]

Johnson's rise to the presidency presented a dilemma for white southern politicians. They had known Johnson for years and they respected his political skills. More important, they had long wanted someone from their region to occupy the White House. Thus, when Johnson became president many initially looked for ways to justify or excuse the civil rights rhetoric from the White House. Smith told *Meet the Press* in January that he expected the House to pass the civil rights legislation, and he acknowledged, "we are not overlooking the hope that the Senate will be able to do something about it," meaning kill the bill via a filibuster.[7]

A master legislator, Johnson brought his prodigious energy and talent to the White House where he began moving stalled Kennedy bills through Congress. Presidential advisor Jack Valenti contended in June 1964, "the professionals in the Congress and in the newspaper business" believed if Johnson "were able to pass a civil rights bill and the tax bill he would be a shoo-in for re-election." When Kennedy was assassinated, Valenti explained, "both these bills were being suffocated in the Senate with precious little chance of them being brought up for vote. The Congress was in its blackest stalemate in many years. . . . There was simply no rapport between the Executive and the Legislative branches." He praised Johnson for moving through Congress multiple appropriations bills, several education bills, a library construction bill, and a foreign aid bill all by the end of December 1963. Johnson also realized the import of his work, telling one liberal senator, "I've got to pass taxes and civil rights—or I quit."[8]

John Kenneth Galbraith, a liberal economist and unofficial presidential advisor, made it clear that "Johnson had far more power when it came to maneuvering through Congress and far more willingness to do it than Kennedy." That reason more than any other clarified for Galbraith why Johnson signed so much reform legislation into law. He did not doubt Kennedy's commitment to reform but noted the slain president was just not forceful with the legislative branch. Galbraith downplayed the notion that Johnson's legislative accomplishments were the result of emotion following Kennedy's assassination, asserting "that's the result of an undue effort to enlarge the influence of JFK."[9]

Johnson embarked on lawmaking in a nonpartisan, statesmanlike way that nonetheless encapsulated his Sunbelt political strategy of expanding the Democratic Party base. Indeed, his approach to governing grew out of his Texas roots, which were nurtured in a factionalized one-party environ-

The telephone was almost an appendage of Johnson's body. Here, he is talking on the phone on November 29, 1963. LBJ Library, photo by Yoichi Okamoto.

ment. He told one supporter: "If we can just keep the politics out of both sides for four or five months until we get some of the things that need to be done done, and let them get decided on the merits, why, we'll . . . we can get partisan the latter part of the year and go on and settle the election. I don't know, I think we're going to get a reasonably good tax bill." Johnson saw the tax bill as crucial to his election. He told Senator Russell Long (D-LA) on February 7, "you did a wonderful job. Just 20 votes against it. Now, you go in that conference and get it sacked up. We're losing $30 million a day—that's withholding—out of that economy, and I want to have a good year so I can get reelected."[10]

Johnson's advisors believed the new president needed a slogan that would define his liberalism. When Johnson had not crafted one by mid-March 1964, journalists Rowland Evans and Robert Novak observed, "until he did this, his full power as President would be incomplete." White House speechwriter Richard Goodwin suggested "the Great Society." Johnson tried it and other slogans regularly before his May 22 Great Society speech at the University of Michigan. There, Johnson articulated his unique version of consensus liberalism, which he hoped would result in "abundance and liberty for all." Unlike the New Deal liberalism of his early days in Washington, Johnson placed equal importance on ending poverty, securing racial justice, and bettering cultural opportunities for all Americans. The president described the Great Society as "a place where every child can find knowledge to enrich his mind and to enlarge his talents. It is a place where leisure is a welcome chance to build and reflect, not a feared cause of boredom and restlessness. It is a place where the city of man serves not only the needs of the body and the demands of commerce but the desire for beauty and the hunger for community."[11]

At the same time Johnson mobilized his legislative blitzkrieg, he contended with multiple electoral challenges. Bobby Kennedy flirted with pursuing the vice presidency. When Schlesinger and Bobby Kennedy traveled to Boston on December 5 to incorporate the Kennedy Library, they discussed whether he should seek the office. Schlesinger explained, "My first reaction was negative, though, when he asked me why, I found it hard to give clear reasons." Bobby noted his dislike for the office, especially "the premise of waiting around for someone to die." Schlesinger agreed that the vice presidency was not the best path to the White House. He and Bobby continued talking about the vice presidency and by December 13, Schlesinger had changed his mind. Bobby told Schlesinger about all the policy areas that needed attention—civil rights, unemployment, education—and concluded,

"The new fellow doesn't get this. He knows all about politics and nothing about human beings."[12]

Moreover, a fanciful primary challenge to Johnson, one that presaged the politics of resentment Goldwater deployed later in the fall, came from Governor Wallace. Wallace only competed in a handful of states, but those primaries did reveal the potency of racial backlash in and out of the South. In his ill-fated race for the Democratic nomination in the spring of 1964 Wallace demagogued against the Civil Rights Act, with arguments it would result in hiring quotas, neighborhood integration, school busing, and elimination of seniority benefits for union workers. In the spring primaries Wallace made a sophisticated, backlash appeal to white working-class voters. He insisted he was not a racist, but he wore the badge of segregation with pride, making an affirmative defense of states' rights.

Wallace decided to run in midwestern primaries following a speech he gave at the University of Wisconsin on February 19, 1964, but he had been skeptical he would attract voters in this white, midwestern state with a population of ethnic, working-class voters. He got his answer at a speech he gave in Milwaukee. There white ethnic voters cheered Wallace, and showed their racial concerns even though the state's African American population was low. Groused one Milwaukeean, "They beat up old ladies 83-years-old, rape our womenfolk. They mug people. They won't work. They are on relief. How long can we tolerate this? Did I go to Guadalcanal and come back to something like this?" Others agreed with this sentiment, and Wallace netted more than a third of the 780,000 votes cast. Wisconsin's governor had said more than 100,000 would be a "catastrophe," so on election night Wallace boasted, "Well, I got 264,000, so there must have been three catastrophes in Wisconsin."[13]

Republicans watched carefully the developments in Wisconsin. One Goldwater advisor said the national media had exaggerated racist thinking among Wallace voters. Goldwater advisors attributed much of the Wallace vote to discontent with the "unpopular Democratic governor." Officials in the Johnson White House came to a similar conclusion that the contest should not be read exclusively through the lens of civil rights, but should also be interpreted as a protest vote and as Republicans taking an opportunity to meddle in the Democratic Party.[14]

Based on this result Wallace entered two more Democratic primaries: Indiana and Maryland. Indiana like Wisconsin had a minimal African American population, just 6 percent, but the state received tremendous media coverage of racial unrest in Chicago. Moreover, the state had had, in the 1920s, a very active Ku Klux Klan. Governor Matthew Welsh, who was running as a favorite son stand-in for Johnson, actively campaigned against Wallace, telling crowds about Wallace, "This is the man who tolerated the presence of billboards in his state before the [Kennedy] assassination which demanded, 'K.O. the Kennedys.' This is the man whose beliefs were responsible for the deaths of innocent children in the bombing of a Sunday school class." For each charge Wallace had one response, "I have the highest regard for Governor Welsh. He is a fine man." Wallace, though, wanted to abandon his civility. Late one night, he told a journalist: "I'd like to go into one of these places and tell them what they expect to hear. . . . Hi, yall. Sho good to see yall. I'm jes an ign'rant ol' hookwormy redneck from Alabama come up to visit yall. Ain't had no education and didn't wear no shoes 'til I was thirty, but I come to ask yall for yall's vote.'" He did not do this, but, again, he performed well, claiming 30 percent of the vote.[15]

When the filing deadline arrived for Maryland there was no ready favorite son, so Johnson badgered Senator Daniel Brewster into accepting the assignment. He provided Brewster with resources and imagery to run a pro-LBJ campaign. Wallace, meanwhile, found the Maryland audiences more similar to his native Alabamans, and he struggled not to revert to using the "n-word," telling one audience what would happen if the civil rights bill became law: the federal government will "tell an employer who he's got to employ. If a man's got 100 Japanese-Lutherans working for him and there's 100 Chinese-Baptists unemployed, he's got to let some of the Japanese-Lutherans go so he can make room for some of the Chinese-Baptists. And of course, what does that do for your seniority rights? It destroys them!"[16]

Johnson discussed the Maryland race with Senator Hubert Humphrey (D-MN), an ally of the president who during their Senate years together had given the Texan entrée to the liberal bloc. He asked, "Do you know they think they're going to win with [George] Wallace in Maryland." Humphrey replied, "Well, this is what they're all waiting for." Humphrey groused that the Democratic National Committee had not "given any money for the goddang campaign up in Maryland." Humphrey had pushed DNC chair John M. Bailey, "'What in hell is up? . . . You people have got the fight of your life over here. First of all, our candidate's not a good candidate, let's face it. I mean, Brewster, God Almighty.'" Johnson wanted Humphrey to plant a story in the media highlighting southern hypocrisy. The president contended, "all these years that southerners have resented people coming into their states and they talk about the do-gooders in the North. And yet now it's the South that's going in and stirring up this trouble. . . . They're fine ones to be talking; they've been raising hell about it all these years. It's a pretty good point."[17]

Following one Maryland rally in a town rent with passions about whether there should be an open housing ordinance, a riot broke out. Wallace had given a listless speech, but the crowd still grew violent. African American protestors clashed with the National Guard troops. The riot helped Wallace. A shop owner in the town told the press white voters "see Governor Wallace on TV and they can't believe the mild little man they see is the bad man they keep reading and hearing about. What he says makes a lot of sense down here." On Election Day Wallace carried the Eastern Shore and the white-ethnic neighborhoods in Baltimore. Brewster won with 53 percent of the vote, but Wallace still crowed, "if it hadn't been for the nigger bloc vote we'd have won it all."[18]

Johnson ignored Wallace's race-baiting politics of resentment and pushed on with pursuit of full civil rights for all Americans, one component of his consensus liberalism. In doing so, he concentrated on legislating an *end* to the South and the *beginning* of the Sunbelt. The South of Johnson's youth was the Jim Crow South, but the civil rights reforms the president envisioned would commence the funeral for state-sanctioned bigotry in the United States. One consequence would be uniting the economic interests of southern states from the Atlantic to the Pacific and the emergence, by decade's end, of a universal identification for the region, the Sunbelt. Johnson met with civil rights lawyer Joseph Rauh and NAACP lobbyist Clarence Mitchell in January to discuss tactics for passing the Civil Rights Act. He indicated that he expected the bill to clear the House prior to the Lincoln Day recess. Rauh noted, "The President said he wanted the bill passed by the House without a word or a comma changed." They also devised tactics for the Senate, where the filibuster presented a very real threat. Johnson wanted lawmakers to clear the Senate calendar while the House was debating civil rights so that there would be no other urgent Senate business when they debated racial justice. That game plan mitigated the filibuster threat.[19]

Johnson stuck to the strategy he had earlier discussed with Rauh. James Farmer recalled listening to a Johnson performance in the Oval Office where he phoned and "cajol[ed]" senators to get their support for civil rights. Farmer acknowledged that LBJ "could twist those arms better" than Kennedy because he was "a southerner speaking with a southern accent." Johnson, though, lamented the difficulty of getting Dixiecrat support, telling Farmer, "Somehow I've gotta get to 'em. Somehow I gotta break down their resistance. . . . Jim, somehow I gotta get my hand under their dress." The president continued applying his unique brand of pressure. During the filibuster the White House kept close tabs on Republican senators, especially those likely to vote for cloture, the process by which a filibuster was ended by its opponents.[20]

Johnson had a lengthy conversation with Representative Charles Halleck (R-IN) on June 22 about the progress of the civil rights bill, which Johnson wanted to sign by July 4. Threaded throughout their conversation was a debate about whether the bill was partisan and what its passage might mean for the coming presidential election. Halleck promised, "We're going to get your civil rights bill." That was not enough for Johnson, who wanted more bills moved through Congress, in part to augment his consensus liberalism and in part to help his election chances. He would not prioritize or specify which bills should be considered first, telling Halleck, "We got 31 proposals at one house or the other."[21]

Halleck countered that the House should recess for the GOP convention following final passage of the Civil Rights Act as amended in the Senate. Johnson was not convinced. He viewed the matter through the lens of fairness and democracy, "Well, Charlie, why don't you let us go on—why don't you let us take these things up, let the majority decide it?" Halleck resisted out of concern for the start of the Republican National Convention. Johnson did not back down: "Well, Charlie, don't you think I ought to try to get my program passed?" Halleck countered, "I don't think you can do it." Johnson disagreed, "You oughtn't to hold up my poverty bill. That's a good bill, and there's no reason why you ought to keep a majority from beating it. If you can beat it, go on and beat it, but you oughtn't to hold it up. You ought to give me a fair shake and give me a chance to vote on it. I've got it in my budget."[22]

Halleck was frustrated with just how much legislation Johnson wanted passed that summer. In a curt manner he told Johnson, "You want this civil rights bill through, you wanted the tax bill through, and I helped you do it. And *goddamn* it, did I help you on civil rights?" Johnson agreed, but only to a point, "Yeah, you sure did. You helped Kennedy. . . . Then you helped yourself. Course you-all want civil rights as much as we do. I believe it's a nonpartisan bill. I don't think it's a Johnson bill." Halleck disagreed, "No, no, no, no, no, you're going to get all the political advantage. We are not going to get a goddamned thing."[23]

Halleck then said the House should perhaps slow down consideration of the civil rights bill and examine what the Senate had done to the measure.

Signing of the 1964 Civil Rights Act, July 2, 1964. LBJ Library, photo by Cecil Stoughton.

Johnson returned to his point that the legislation was beneficial to both parties, telling Halleck "Well, you wouldn't want to go to your convention without a civil rights bill, would you?" Halleck replied, "You know, as a matter of fact, if you scratch me very deep, Mr. President." Johnson did not let Halleck complete his threat, returning Halleck's vinegar with some honey: "I wouldn't scratch you at all because I want to pet you."[24]

Halleck was not appeased. He told the president, "Wait just a minute. Wait just a minute." Johnson laughed because he knew he was winning this battle. Halleck continued, "If I had my way, I'd let you folks be fussing with that goddamned thing before *your* convention instead of ours. But I'm perfectly willing to give you the right to sign that thing on July 4." After Halleck said "I'll do just about anything I can for you," Johnson asked for passage of the rest of his agenda. They continued their dance of Halleck's frustration met at each turn with Johnson's false flattery. Halleck told LBJ, "Look, you're an old Senate hand," and Johnson replied, "Yeah, an old House hand too." When Halleck agreed, Johnson went one step further, noting he was also "an old Halleck man." Halleck finally broke, "All right, and you're a Halleck man and I'm a Johnson man. But, Christ." Halleck's reward for working with Johnson on civil rights was the enmity of GOP conservatives.[25] Conversely, Johnson gained a major victory. He signed the historic measure into law on July 2.

White House aides debated how LBJ should handle the GOP convention, his next challenge following passage of the Civil Rights Act. LBJ requested "a line-by-line analysis and refutation of the GOP platform." He specifically wanted language to rebut two Republican claims pertaining to his integrity, first that his administration "has impeded investigations of suspected wrongdoing" among government officials and second that Johnson's secretive management of the news media "has shown a contempt of the right of the people to know the truth." Others identified different threats. India Edwards told LBJ: "none of us can tell how many bigots and 'kooks' there are in these 50 United States." She worried, "every one of them will vote for the opposition," thinking "we can turn the clock back and become an isolated nation, self-sufficient, caring nothing for the rest of the world."[26]

Simultaneous with the GOP convention, a riot in Harlem began July 16 when an off-duty police officer killed a black teenager who was attending a summer school program. The riot altered Democratic Party thinking about Goldwater, the backlash, and the presidential race. Fears of racial violence following the New York riots shaded the presidential election. Democratic insider and Johnson associate Katie Louchheim described the conversation at one Washington, DC, dinner party in late July. She recalled a male guest saying, "In N.Y. no one ventures out. His secy won't ride the subway after 5:30. Hotels with cancelled bookings, taxis with no fares." Similar fears existed in other northeastern cities. In a middle-class Cleveland, Ohio, neighborhood, Louchheim worried, "previously dem fifty to one, it was 11 to 1 Goldwater. Why? The apts were integrated. We were lost, sunk, gone."[27]

Following the riots, the GOP nominee requested a meeting with LBJ. Goldwater had proposed the federal government assume responsibility for urban law enforcement. White House officials found the proposal hypocritical because it "would do more than anything else to concentrate power in Washington—which Goldwater says he opposes." Johnson contended "nothing good can come out of" meeting Goldwater about the racial issues before the nation. The president explained, "he wants to use this as a forum. He wants to encourage a backlash. That's where his future is; it's not in peace and harmony."[28]

In a July 24 press conference, held about an hour before the meeting between the president and his GOP challenger, Johnson undercut Goldwater's efforts to blunt discussion of civil rights and claim the issue of crime as his own. When asked if he would not campaign about civil rights—LBJ had arranged for the question to be asked—the president proclaimed, "I do not believe that any issue which is before the people can be eliminated from a campaign in a free society." He promised he would "discuss and debate the hard and difficult issues" while also "rebutting and rebuking big-ots and those who seek to excite and exploit tensions." The president also acknowledged urban unrest as a concern for some. Johnson told reporters, "I am against sin, I am against lawlessness, and I am very much opposed to violence." He promised to use federal resources to combat rioting, but he also stressed law and order was a local matter. He needled Goldwater and conservative advocates of states' rights: "I seem to have read and heard that other people, too, are opposed to the federal government usurping the rights of the states."[29]

Goldwater arrived early for his meeting with the president, and com-plimented "how well" Johnson "looked." During their sixteen-minute con-versation, Goldwater said that as a "half-Jew" he wanted to do nothing that would "contribute to any riots or disorders or bring about any violence." Goldwater clarified his own view of racial equality: "All men are created equal at the instant of birth, Americans, Mexicans, Cubans, and Africans. But from then on, that's the end of equality." Goldwater surprised Johnson, though, when he said he would abandon his presidential bid if he discov-ered that his supporters had instigated racial violence. The extreme pledge was Goldwater's attempt to separate his opposition to the Civil Rights Act from racist thuggery. The former, he posited, resulted because of his read-ing of the Constitution. Goldwater reasoned, "I know your big cities in the Northeast and in the Middle West—not only on the West Coast—are just tinder boxes, and I'll be darned if I will have my grandchildren accuse their grandfather of setting fire to it."[30]

Goldwater and Johnson issued a joint statement: "The President met with Senator Goldwater and reviewed the steps he has taken to avoid the incitement of racial statements. Senator Goldwater expressed his position, which was that racial tensions should be avoided. Both agreed on this po-sition." The meeting ended with Goldwater asking if he could fly the new A-11 supersonic jet being developed to replace the U-2. Johnson noted the plane would not be ready for at least another year, and that at that date there might be a different president. Both men laughed. Goldwater exited the White House by the southeast gate so he could avoid reporters.[31]

Another dramatic issue for Democrats involved jockeying for the party's vice-presidential nomination. Johnson's secretive, manipulative approach to the decision, especially the question of whether or not to choose Ken-nedy, escalated tensions. Kennedy partisans wanted Johnson to pick the attorney general. Kennedy both wanted and did not want the offer. He viewed Johnson as an illegitimate successor to his brother, whose legacy he believed needed protecting. He also wished no involvement with John-son. According to sources close to Kennedy, he nonetheless "wanted to be named vice president by Johnson." Journalist Joseph W. Alsop said, "I pointed out to him that given their relations, it would be really a grinding chore to be a proper vice president under Lyndon Johnson. But then, I don't think he wanted to be a proper vice president." Instead, RFK wanted to use the office as a path to the presidency. Alsop declared, "If he'd been named vice president by Johnson, sweet God alone knows what would have hap-pened" given the "chemical antipathy between the two men." Jack Valenti added, "it never worked simply because there were too many people in the Johnson staff and in the Kennedy staff who fed their principals this kind of poisoning."[32]

Conversely, Johnson wanted to keep Kennedy voters happy but had no desire for a vice president who would upstage him. Early in 1964 Bobby Kennedy was a favorite in the polls to receive the vice-presidential nomina-tion. Saying no to Bobby thus risked losing support from key Democratic constituencies including Catholics, African Americans, and Kennedy vot-ers. Said one political observer, "Lyndon is boxed in—if Bobby really wants it, he can have it." Johnson wanted no part of Kennedy on the ticket, telling White House aide and former JFK advisor Kenneth O'Donnell, "If I don't need him, I'm not going to take him. I don't want to go down in history as the guy to have the dog wagged by the tail and have the Vice President elect me."[33]

Several years later Johnson bemoaned to Doris Kearns, a White House aide at the time, "I'd given three years of loyal service to Jack Kennedy. During all that time I'd willingly stayed in the background; I knew that it was his Presidency, not mine. If I disagreed with him, I did it in private, not in public." After the JFK assassination, though, Johnson argued, "I became the custodian of his will. I became the President. But none of this seemed to register with Bobby Kennedy, who acted like he was the custodian of the Kennedy dream." To the Texan "It just didn't seem fair. I'd waited for my turn. Bobby should've waited for his."[34]

Southerners were appalled at the notion of a Kennedy vice presidency. Huffman Baines, a relative of the president, told Johnson, "The people in Texas and the South hope that you can see fit to choose a running mate outside of the Kennedys . . . someone not already very unpopular and dis-liked in a vast section of the country." At a June 1964 potluck dinner with the Johnsons, Helen Mahon, wife of Representative George Mahon (D-TX) contended, "It will be murder in Texas," trying to defeat Goldwater, but she was sure "LBJ will win." At the same party one woman close to the Kennedys tried to get a sense whether LBJ would pick Bobby, to which Mahon insisted, "If it's Bob K. we'll lose." The subject of the vice presidency, though, had been an issue for southerners from the day Johnson became president. Senator George Smathers (D-FL) recounted for Johnson a conversation he had with Hubert Humphrey on the night Kennedy was assassinated. Smathers had told Humphrey the importance of having "a liberal running with" Johnson. He noted, "most of the southerners would be for [Hubert]," believing he could "keep these damn liberals in *line*, and keep things going."[35]

To solve the Bobby problem Johnson devoted considerable effort to the search for a vice president. Washington insider Clark Clifford explained: "To put it coldly and bluntly, it was well known that President Johnson had had a serious coronary attack years before, so I think the job was eagerly sought." First, LBJ thought of Sargent Shriver, the director of the Peace Corps, a Catholic, and a member of the Kennedy family by marriage. The Kennedys rejected the idea. Johnson also considered Republican cabinet member Robert McNamara, who was close with the Kennedys. Party leaders feared McNamara would turn off liberals and long-time Democratic partisans. Several senators wanted the job: Birch Bayh (D-IN), Claiborne Pell (D-RI), Eugene McCarthy (D-MN), and Humphrey.[36]

Humphrey and Johnson entered the Senate in the same year, 1949. One journalist observed that they could not have been more different at the time, Johnson coming in "from the right as a segregationist" and Humphrey "from the left as the most vocal champion of civil rights to enter the Senate since Reconstruction." They were also quite similar, observed journalist Theodore H. White, "poor boys both, their families bowed by the depression, they had wandered the country and then become classroom teachers before entering politics. They had been hungry; and they had made good." While they became friends they also "bristled at each other." Both quickly entered the Senate leadership, Johnson in 1953 and Humphrey in 1961 "by Lyndon Johnson's intercession." Earlier in the mid-1950s, though, Johnson had brought Humphrey into the Senate's "Bourbon inner circle," making him "the first Northern Democratic liberal" with an insider's voice in Senate leadership.[37]

Ted Van Dyk, a Humphrey advisor, prepared a "simple and straightforward" plan to get the vice-presidential nomination for his boss. He sent mailings to go to journalists and Democratic leaders around the nation. The United Auto Workers funded these initiatives. Journalists understood Humphrey's potential as a candidate and sought interviews with him on the network news shows. Humphrey himself was not deeply involved in this campaign, though he occasionally asked Van Dyk, "How are things going? Any news?"[38]

The Republican primary contest ultimately shaped Johnson's thinking about Kennedy. When Goldwater secured the GOP nomination, Johnson, after careful study of the polls, decided it did not matter so much whom he chose for his vice president. White House advisor Lawrence O'Brien recalled, "He'd pull them out of his inside pocket, and we'd go over them one more time. Of course the polls were simply showing what obviously they would, that of all these various candidates none of them strengthened Johnson's position, and Hubert Humphrey was a wash." Still, Johnson worried that Kennedy supporters might try something at the convention.[39]

On July 23 Johnson "summoned" John Kenneth Galbraith to Washington. The two met for three hours in the evening and again the next morning for an hour. The president sought input on a list of eighteen potential vice-presidential nominees, including Humphrey, Kennedy, McNamara, Adlai Stevenson, McCarthy, and Shriver. Johnson had "complain[ed] of the coldness of the Kennedy people toward him." After learning of the meeting from Galbraith, Schlesinger concluded, "I have the impression that LBJ is playing a vast game with everybody on the vice presidency and doing so with great relish. He evidently talks to everyone about the problem and leaves behind a trail of cryptic hints and possibilities which only tease and torment both aspirants and observers."[40]

Knowing there was no good way to eliminate Kennedy, Johnson hoped Bobby would withdraw. Kennedy had no interest in doing LBJ a favor even though he had decided he did not want the job. Johnson took two steps to make a Bobby selection impossible. First, he said he would not announce his choice before the convention. Second, he met with RFK on July 29. Johnson praised Bobby's political talents but made clear he would not select him. He wanted Kennedy to announce he would not be a candidate, but when Kennedy did not Johnson issued a public statement that he would not consider any cabinet member for the vice presidency. A few days later Bobby recounted for Schlesinger and other friends what the president had said. Kennedy indicated they had discussed the requirements for the vice presidency, but Schlesinger did not list any particulars. He did impart Bobby's version of Johnson's assessment: "In my judgment, you don't have them."[41]

Johnson gave his own account of the meeting with Kennedy. He told Clark Clifford that he had made his decision out of the need to shore up

Democratic support in the Midwest. Johnson related that he asked Kennedy to remain as attorney general, but Bobby declined. They then discussed possible successors. As to the larger purpose of the conversation, Johnson observed, "He seemed to have expected what happened, but cherished a kind of hope he . . . he kind of swallowed deeply a time or two. . . . He wasn't combative in any way, and I was—I leaned over backwards not to be the slightest arrogant." Johnson worked out a strategy with Clifford whereby Clifford or another mutual friend of Kennedy and Johnson could try to explain to Bobby that Johnson wanted to see Bobby follow him in the White House. Johnson wanted the message conveyed to Kennedy that LBJ had "no envy and no jealousy" toward him, that Johnson would likely not seek a second term, and that Bobby would have "friendly president" in the White House.[42]

A *New York Herald Tribune* article claimed that Johnson's rejection of Bobby as a running mate dealt a "bitter blow" that resulted in an "end to a gay and glittering era that became known as 'The New Frontier.'" The president was furious and blamed the Kennedys for leaking the story. In turn he entertained reporters from the *New York Herald Tribune*, the *New York Times*, and the *Washington Post*. There he regaled them with an off-the-record conversation about his encounter with Kennedy. Johnson made fun of Bobby's squeaky voice and his unease at being told he would not be named vice-presidential candidate. Johnson even claimed Bobby begged for the nomination. Bobby heard about the session and was enraged with Johnson, who denied he had had such a meeting.[43]

After Kennedy had been removed from public speculation, political observers concluded Humphrey was the favorite to get the nomination. Humphrey had been working behind the scenes to facilitate his nomination. Still Johnson wavered. Earlier in the spring he reasoned to White House aide Bill Moyers: "I don't think Hubert would be happy as my VP. Moreover, I would have lots of problems with him: He's so exuberant, so enthusiastic, he'd get off the reservation all the time. He talks too much to be Vice President." Throughout their Senate years together Johnson and Humphrey had worked to bridge the liberals and conservatives. The process by which Johnson went from decision to announcement was cloaked in secrecy. Louchheim observed, "Everyone is maneuvering and folks are suspect."[44]

James Rowe Jr., who was friends with both men, let Humphrey know that LBJ was supportive of his efforts to campaign for the nomination. The president insisted that Humphrey's people provide him with a daily summary of their activities. LBJ had a similar process in place with McCarthy, who he had also encouraged to make himself available for the nomination. The Humphrey people had been told that Lady Bird Johnson preferred McCarthy, who had a more moderate voting record than did Humphrey. Moreover, McCarthy had shown greater support for the oil and gas industry and big business generally.[45]

Prior to the convention, Humphrey's team built support for his candidacy in all the state and territorial delegations. They arranged for a telephone switchboard in Humphrey's suite upstairs at the Shelburne Hotel to facilitate communication with the delegates in Atlantic City. Humphrey's people had prepared Johnson-Humphrey signs and buttons that would "materialize magically if and when Johnson put Humphrey's name into vice presidential nomination." They also wanted endorsements for their candidate. Van Dyk recalled how Humphrey handled that issue with California governor Pat Brown. The California governor preferred to postpone; *Life* magazine was writing a story about him as a vice-presidential possibility. Because Brown wanted the article published so he could have a keepsake for his grandchildren, Humphrey told him "to take his time and endorse whenever he pleased." Van Dyk countered that the proximity of the convention meant the endorsement was needed immediately. Humphrey countered, "Pat just wanted his moment and I couldn't take it away from him."[46]

Johnson even sought advice from evangelist Billy Graham about whom he should put on the ticket. Graham narrated a White House dinner in the summer of 1964, before the Democratic National Convention, when Johnson went over the list of fourteen names he was considering. Ruth Graham did not like for her husband to give political advice, thinking he should stick to matters religious. After dinner when Johnson and Graham were alone LBJ asked again, and Graham argued for Humphrey.[47]

Throughout Johnson tortured Humphrey with suggestions he might change his mind and choose someone else. Johnson did so in part because he wanted to keep speculation rife among the press and in part because he wanted to control Humphrey. The day before Johnson finally announced his selection he met with Humphrey in the White House, telling him he must "understand that this is like a marriage with no chance of divorce. I need complete and unswerving loyalty." The president also belittled Humphrey, telling him, "If you didn't know you were going to be vice president a month ago, you're too damn dumb to have the office."[48]

Johnson second-guessed his decision to pick Humphrey and postponed finalizing until the bitter end. When Johnson asked Chicago mayor Richard Daley yet again whether he should name Humphrey as the vice-presidential candidate, an irritated Daley replied, "Why, it is. I've told you!" One of the reasons he gave himself for doubting Humphrey was the frequency with which Humphrey talked to the press. Johnson instructed his aide Jenkins to meet with Humphrey. He wanted Jenkins to convey to Humphrey that "he's just got to quit antagonizing the South."[49]

As the convention drew near the White House faced another potentially serious threat to their goal for a harmonious, unifying convention. Specifically, White House advisors worried about race rioting in Atlantic City. Said one official, "because of the congested nature of Atlantic City, and because of the shady elements that the beaches attract anyway, any demonstration could erupt into a dangerous situation." Of especial concern was unilateral action by Atlantic City and/or New Jersey officials, causing White House officials to advocate "get[ting] some coordination going, specifically with our security people and our civil rights people." Federal officials surveilled the large northern cities prior to the convention to ferret out any "chartered buses which might be carrying known troublemakers to Atlantic City and the Democratic Convention—and halting them." Moreover, Johnson loyalists convinced civil rights leaders not to hold demonstrations before, during, or after the convention to prevent a backlash. Only James Farmer of CORE and John Lewis of the Student Non-Violent Coordinating Committee (SNCC) refused to comply. Farmer explained, "The backlash had been there all along, and it was not going to get any worse. The people who were on our side remained on our side, and those who had been against us, but non-vocal about it, had simply become vocal. That had been my philosophy of the backlash—that minds had not changed."[50]

They should have paid more attention to the possibility of demonstrations within the convention, especially from delegates seeking civil rights reform of Democratic Party machinery. The Mississippi Freedom Democratic Party (MFDP) was founded in April 1964 as the political branch of SNCC and the Council of Federated Organizations (COFO). It challenged the legality of the all-white, regular Democratic Party in Mississippi. That party did not allow black participation in precinct meetings, meaning African Americans from Mississippi had no opportunity to be named as delegates to the Democratic National Convention. Aaron Henry, a druggist from Clarksville, Mississippi, co-founded the MFDP. He believed that since the MFDP stood with the Democratic Party on its national agenda, supported Johnson's candidacy, and backed civil rights reform it would be seated and the white regulars, who opposed Johnson, Great Society liberalism, and civil rights would be turned away. Leaders of the MFDP, namely Victoria Gray, Edwin King, and Henry, rejected calls for a compromise that would either seat no delegates from Mississippi or some from the MFDP and some from the regular party. They told the press, "either course of action represents, at best, a compromise with racism."[51]

Henry wrote Johnson on August 22 about the MFDP agenda. He thanked Johnson for his "benevolent neutrality" regarding the Credentials Committee deliberations about which delegation from Mississippi to seat. Henry expressed his surety that the MFDP would prevail because "a truly Democratic and open vote of the convention can never seat the so-called Mississippi Democratic Party," meaning the regular party of white Mississippians. He concluded, "whatever the outcome of the fight to be seated, we want you to know we will support you with all our hearts in the coming election."[52]

The White House had received 416 telegrams in favor of seating the MFDP delegation and only one in support of the regular delegation. As such, Johnson and his advisors continued the search for compromise. Juanita Roberts, one of LBJ's secretaries, gave the president a note with an idea about how to defuse the controversy over the MFDP delegates. Because Robert Kennedy was giving his seat to his sister-in-law for reasons of illness, the question was put to the president whether a Mississippi Democratic delegate loyal to the national Democratic Party "got a virus." Could that person give his seat to a MFDP member? When Roberts raised this matter with the president: "he said 'God that's a good idea . . . ' And then he turned to the telephone and called W[alter] J[enkins] (at Atlantic City, Convention Hall). He did not say just exactly what the note reads, but he talked to WJ in 'what if' ways planting the idea of seeing if a substitution could be made. He crumpled up this note and threw it in the waste basket. I retrieved it."[53]

Bigger challenges existed within the Credentials Committee, which was meeting in Atlantic City. First, the space for the meeting—a room designed for 300 people—was not sufficient for the vast number of participants and observers. Jenkins told LBJ: "Joe Rauh is raising hell that he can't even get his witnesses in. The television people are raising hell because they will have to have a pool camera, and they want to have separate cameras." Both Rauh and the networks wanted the meeting moved to a large ballroom, which would hold 1,000 people. Jenkins disagreed, "My own feeling is that the more you get in there, the more chance you have for trouble." Johnson concurred: "My inclination is to keep it in the room where they are because

I think that they—Joe Rauh would try to storm it and try to have a bunch of applause like they do in these conventions. That's a Communist effort" to pack the meetings with supporters.[54]

Rauh opened testimony before the Credentials Committee indicating he and the MFDP had "only an hour to tell you the story of terror and tragedy in Mississippi." Aaron Henry related that the attorney general in Mississippi had issued an "injunction against our attending this very convention." He argued economic, educational, judicial, and social injustice were all the product of racism. Over 90 percent of the African American population in the state was unable to register to vote. Henry elucidated how he and his colleagues had been blocked from working through the regular Mississippi Democratic Party.[55]

Sharecropper and civil rights activist Fannie Lou Hamer was among the MFDP delegates who testified. She told of how she and seventeen other African Americans attempted to register to vote on August 31, 1962. "We was met in Indianola by Mississippi men, Highway Patrolmens and they only allowed two of us in to take the literacy test at the time," explained Hamer. "After we had taken this test and started back to Ruleville, we was held up by the City Police and the State Highway Patrolmen and carried back to Indianola where the bus driver was charged that day with driving a bus the wrong color." They paid the fine and returned to Ruleville. Hamer was then fired from her job as a timekeeper and sharecropper on a plantation for trying to vote. "I had to leave that same night. On the 10th of September, 1962, 16 bullets was fired into the home of Mr. and Mrs. Robert Tucker for me. That same night two girls were shot in Ruleville, Mississippi. Also Mr. Joe McDonald's house was shot in."[56]

Hamer then described an incident from June 1963 when she had attended a voter registration workshop and was rewarded with arrest at a Winona, Mississippi, bus stop. No sooner was Hamer in a cell than she heard "sounds of licks and screams. I could hear the sounds of licks and horrible screams, and I could hear somebody say, 'Can you say, yes, sir, nigger?'" Soon thereafter three white men inquired where she was from. When they learned Ruleville, one of them "used a curse word, and he said, 'We are going to make you wish you was dead.'" The men ordered two African American prisoners to beat her. Recounted Hamer, "The first Negro prisoner ordered me, by orders from the State Highway Patrolman for me, to lay down on a bunk bed on my face, and I laid on my face. The first Negro began to beat, and I was beat by the first Negro until he was exhausted." As the second African American was beating her, Hamer explained, "I began

Fannie Lou Hamer, a Mississippi Freedom Democratic Party delegate, addressing the Credentials Committee at the Democratic National Convention, Atlantic City, New Jersey, August 22, 1964. Library of Congress, Prints and Photographs Division, photograph by U.S. News & World Report *Magazine Photograph Collection.*

to work my feet, and the State Highway Patrolman ordered the first Negro who had beat to set on my feet to keep me from kicking my feet. I began to scream and one white man got up and began to beat me in my head and tell me to hush." She told the Credentials Committee, "All of this is on account we want to register, to become first-class citizens, and if the freedom Democratic Party is not seated now, I question America, is this America, the land of the free and the home of the brave where we have to sleep with our telephones off of the hooks because our lives be threatened daily because we want to live as decent human beings, in America?"[57]

Johnson, Rauh, and labor leader Walter Reuther had multiple conversations about how to handle the MFDP. Rauh wanted to know how the Johnson administration could seat the Mississippi delegation when the state's governor, also the head of the delegation, had said NAACP was short for "niggers, alligators, apes, coons, and possums." Reuther ignored the point, and instead argued that permitting the MFDP to be seated would cause Johnson to lose to Goldwater. "We both think the backlash is so tremendous that we're going to lose the election if you go through with this. You can't possibly win, but if you should win, the pictures of all the black delegates going in to replace the white is going to add to the backlash, and we are convinced that Goldwater will be president."[58]

Johnson ordered the use of heavy-handed techniques to control the convention. The FBI ran counterintelligence on both Bobby Kennedy and MFDP activists. Johnson worried that Kennedy might still try to claim the vice presidency and that the MFDP might create a disturbance on the floor of the convention. Hoping to curry Johnson's favor, the FBI left nothing to chance. They placed a wiretap in Martin Luther King Jr.'s hotel room, they surveilled SNCC and CORE workers, and they deployed undercover agents to "infiltrate . . . key groups." They penetrated the Gem Motel where Henry and his colleagues based their operations. The FBI used fraudulent NBC press passes to interview civil rights workers and gain intelligence on MFDP strategy for the convention.[59]

Johnson also orchestrated the response to the MFDP. He wanted O'Donnell and Humphrey "to handle this Mississippi thing," but when Humphrey reported that they were developing a plan for "seating *both* of these delegations," the president stressed, "You can't do that at all. There's no compromise. You can seat one or the other. You can't seat both of them, because if you do, the other one walks out." After a long conversation about why Humphrey's initial proposal would not work, the Minnesotan suggested an alternate approach, "that we seat the regular delegation, and that we . . . and that we have as an alternative the establishment of a commission within the party to take a look at this whole business." Johnson agreed. Humphrey promised, "Now, we're going to try to sell that."[60]

Humphrey bragged that he was "quite the salesman" when he negotiated with the MFDP. That proposal would keep the following delegations in the convention: Texas, Georgia, Florida, and North Carolina. What Arkansas and Louisiana would do remained uncertain. Because it took so long to work out a compromise the various delegations grew restless. None of the work of the convention could proceed until the problem with the Mississippi delegation was resolved. Johnson did not want to be blamed for the delays. He held that the liberals should be made "responsible for the delay."[61]

When Humphrey offered the MFDP two seats, Hamer replied, "We didn't come all this way for no two seats!" Hamer reflected the view of most in the MFDP, but Henry disagreed. He was willing to compromise, but Bob Moses, an intellectual in the New Left and civil rights activist, was not. Hamer indicated she would "cut [his] throat" if he took Johnson's deal. She saw a class and educational attainment divide in action, noting later, "The strange thing to me" was that "everybody that would compromise in five minutes is the people with a real good education. Them folks will sell you—they will sell you, your mama, they mama, anybody else for a dollar." The Credentials Committee divided over what to do about the MFDP, but ultimately that body accepted the Johnson proposal to give two seats to the biracial delegation.[62]

Johnson understood there was no moral equivalency between the regular white Mississippi Democratic Party delegation and the MFDP, but he yearned to win election by a margin greater than FDR's in 1936. Doing so, he believed, would give him the mandate to enact his Great Society. As such, he ignored larger truths about racial injustice and immorality in Mississippi, in the South, and in the country as a whole. LBJ knew he was wrong to do so. Governor Carl Sanders of Georgia, a southern moderate, tried to convince Johnson there was no need to seat the MFDP because they were not Democrats and thus not entitled to recognition in Atlantic City. Johnson had none of it: "They're Democrats. And by God, they tried to attend the convention, and pistols kept them out. These people went in and begged to go and participate in the conventions. They've got half the population. They won't let them. They lock them out!" Johnson noted "the state of Mississippi wouldn't let a Negro come into their damn convention, and therefore they violated the law and wouldn't let them vote." Johnson pushed his reasoning to one logical conclusion: "by God," the regular Mississippi delegation "oughtn't to be seated" because it had violated the civil rights legislation passed in 1957 and 1960 and 1964. How could lawbreakers, Johnson queried, be seated at the convention. The result of the compromise, a derisive Johnson judged, was an implied statement to the white South, "You lily white babies, we're going to salute you." He abandoned this point because it was not compatible with the compromise that would prevent a South-wide walkout and help make possible a landslide victory in November.[63]

Johnson's pragmatism proved stronger than his idealism. He challenged Reuther, "And if you and Hubert Humphrey got any leadership, you'll get Joe Rauh off that damn television. And the only thing that can really screw us good is to seat that group of challengers from Mississippi, and that will make Texas and Louisiana and Arkansas and Georgia and all of them refuse to go along. And then we could lose some votes now." Johnson wanted to avoid a floor vote about the MFDP because, he believed, "there's not a damn vote that we get by seating these folks." Johnson kept his focus on retaining Democrats in Congress to preserve the Civil Rights Act. He explained his attitude toward the white Mississippi delegation: "The only reason I would let Mississippi come in is because I don't want to run off 14 border states like Oklahoma and like Kentucky and like Texas." Johnson concluded, "If they give us four years, I'll guarantee the Freedom delegation—somebody representing views like that—will be seated four years from now, but we can't do it all before breakfast."[64]

Conversely, Mississippi officials used multiple arguments, some specious, before the Credentials Committee to try to prove the MFDP should not be seated: the party was controlled by non-Mississippians, party organizers were members of Communist front organizations, the party only had representation in forty of Mississippi's eighty-two counties. Moreover, Governor Paul Johnson let the White House know that Mississippi's regular, white delegation would not take their convention seats, so offended were they by the compromise of offering two of Mississippi's seats to the MFDP. Other southern governors, including moderates John Connally of Texas and Carl Sanders of Georgia, enjoined Johnson they would lead their state delegations out of the convention should the MFDP be seated. Connally admonished Johnson of the MFDP standoff: "If you seat those black jigaboos, the whole South will walk out." To another ally Johnson fumed, "But, *by God*, they can't practice segregation at a convention! Now, they can practice it in their home, their house. But they've got no right. . . . If they're seated, and they're recognized in their group, it's none of their goddamn business who we make delegates."[65]

On August 25, Humphrey briefed Johnson on the MFDP situation. He noted they had assented to seat the "Mississippi regulars" as long as "they're loyal and they meet the requirements and call of the convention." They also agreed that the Democratic Party would indicate its support of "an open party" and would "establish standards of full participation in the party without regard to race, creed, or color." Finally, they concurred that two members of the MFDP would be seated as at-large delegates "not deductible from the Mississippi vote."[66]

The compromise did not appease the MFDP. Jenkins reported, "The Freedom Party are now demonstrating very heavily in what borders on being a riot outside of the Convention Hall, about 2,000 of them, and delegates cannot get through. . . . There's no violence. I think that's probably good." Moreover, according to FBI agents surveilling the MFDP, "'Martin Luther King is very, very unhappy about the way things have turned out.'" LBJ had the television coverage of the convention playing while they were talking, and he told Jenkins what he was watching: "The Freedom Party has got the seats of the regular Mississippi delegates, and they're coming in and taking them." Johnson said that only those approved under the compromise should be let in, but he also stressed, "Of course, don't embarrass them. Just put a guard around them."[67]

Johnson faced one other hurdle to his nomination: Johnson. From the time of Kennedy's assassination until the Democrats held their National Convention the following August, Johnson flirted with not running. Such statements from the Texan were more a measure of his insecurity than a preview of a decision he might make. Never was there a chance Johnson would not run, but still he tortured his aides and his wife with talk of not running. Johnson lamented the "convention won't really want me." Here his concern was with his fractured relationship with party liberals. Said Johnson, "to them my name is shit and always has been and always will be. I got their goddamn legislation passed for them, but they gave me no credit." Though programmatically Johnson pursued a liberal agenda, temperamentally his sun did not mesh with the party's northeastern liberal leaders, instead emitting an ill-defined and ill-recognized Sunbelt liberalism that sought consensus. The criticism from liberals that Johnson was not really a liberal irked him. He joked, "What's the difference between a cannibal and a liberal?" The answer, said Johnson, "A cannibal doesn't eat his friends."[68]

In January he discussed the matter with Lady Bird who knew not running would destroy her husband and by implication leave her own life in turmoil. Johnson's enemies would take glee that he abandoned the ultimate political prize. Finally, his friends would blame him should the Republicans win in November. Lady Bird told Lyndon he would seek out a "scapegoat" if he decided not to run. She asserted, "I do not want to be it.

You may drink too much for lack of a higher calling." She concluded, "Stay in. If you win, let's do the best we can for 3 years and 3 or 4 months—and then the Lord letting us live that long, announce in Feb. or Mar. 1968 that you are not a candidate for reelection."[69]

President Johnson complained to Walter Jenkins when he considered pulling out of the presidential race: "Here at the crowning point in my life when I need people's help, I haven't even got the loyalty of Ken O'Donnell, Larry O'Brien, my attorney general, or anything like that." He opined, "People, I think, have a mistaken judgment. They think I want great power. What I want is great solace, a little love. That's all I want." Jenkins disagreed: "You have a lot more of that than you think you do." Johnson did not let up, arguing, "I don't think a white southerner is the man to unite this nation in this hour. And I don't know who is. And I don't even want that responsibility." Fearing he might not win his home state, Johnson lamented, "I don't want to have to fight to carry Texas. I just don't want Texas to have to say yes to me anymore. I've asked them the last time I want to ask them. And if you don't know how that feels, well, you can go out there and start asking a man to please give you a quarter for a cup of coffee."[70]

After the Democratic National Convention opened, Johnson wrote a statement announcing he would not accept his party's nomination. He discussed his fears with several close confidantes. "Our country faces grave dangers. These dangers must be faced and met by a united people under a leader they do not doubt," Johnson protested, noting his was not "a voice that men of all parties, sections and color can follow. I have learned after trying very hard that I am not that voice or that leader." He told his friend and business partner A. W. Moursund of his statement, "You can see from what's happening in Mississippi and Alabama that the *southerners* don't want me, and the *Nigras* don't want me. And *I* don't want it. So I don't know what the hell we are fighting to . . . seeking to . . . for what purpose? Who are we going to serve?" Moursund opposed Johnson pulling out. He argued, "they'll end up nominating this little bastard Bobby Kennedy." Still, so serious did Johnson appear that George Reedy, an aide to whom Johnson complained, went home "in a nervous funk." Reedy worried Johnson would follow through and throw the convention into "chaos" for no good reason. Lady Bird would have none of her husband's depression, telling him, "to step out now would be *wrong* for your country, and I can see nothing but a lonely wasteland for your future. Your friends would be frozen in embarrassed silence and your enemies jeering." Longtime mentor Senator Richard Russell (D-GA) was more blunt,

Wide-angle view of the Convention Hall, Democratic National Convention, Atlantic City, New Jersey, August 1964. LBJ Library, photo by Cecil Stoughton.

telling his former pupil that he was acting like a "spoiled" child and that he should "take a tranquilizer."[71]

Even as he debated getting out Johnson supervised every aspect of planning for the convention and the fall campaign. White House advisor Eric Goldman recounted, "[Johnson] was like the mother of the bride, considering, controlling, fussing over every detail. . . . He specified that a forty-foot photograph of himself would flank the stage." Johnson also chose who would nominate him: Governor Pat Brown of California and Governor John Connally of Texas, both Sunbelt governors but holding different political styles with Brown an avowed liberal and Connally a moderate beholden to the business community. Johnson even dictated what the convention theme song would be—"Hello Lyndon," a riff on the popular Broadway tune, "Hello Dolly."[72]

The Democratic Party used Lady Bird as the centerpiece of their appeal to women voters. At the convention, women had the opportunity to attend leadership training programs. Panels for women throughout the convention were to include women doers and female officeholders. Conversely, GOP convention events for women had involved almost exclusively fashion shows, receptions, and house tours. Liz Carpenter, the press secretary for the first lady, wanted to "bring Bird and the girls down the night of the nominating." Carpenter questioned, "why shouldn't Bird be visible so the cameras have something to play on during the long night. Even if, (she's looked it up) it wasn't done by Mrs. T[ruman], or Eleanor. We decide, to h—— with precedent—and anyway the reporters are too lazy to find out that this is an innovation."[73]

Johnson, though, did not go to Atlantic City until the evening of August 26 after his nomination by acclamation. Once he arrived at the convention he "fairly yelled the name 'Senator Hubert Humphrey of Minnesota'" as his vice-presidential nominee. A journalist with *The New Republic* observed, "We lapped it up and so did the crowd. The White House these days is not a very emotion-stirring place, nor is it blessed with much humor." At 12:24 a.m. on August 27 the delegates nominated Humphrey by acclamation and held a huge celebration in the hall. Following that a fireworks display took place on the boardwalk with Barbra Streisand and Peter, Paul, and Mary performing. Paul Newman emceed the event. Johnson "was glowering" because he was not the center of attention. One journalist explained why there was such enthusiasm for Humphrey: "Mr. Humphrey is about our favorite man in Washington. Amidst all the recent millionaires like Rocky, FDR, JFK, Barry, and Lyndon, it is nice to run into an old-fashioned, modest-income type once in a while. Humphrey still says he married his wife, Muriel, 'for her money'; she had $600 and he was so broke he had left college to run the family drugstore at Huron, S.D."[74]

For the last night of the convention—after the nominations but before the candidates' speeches—Johnson's team planned a tribute to Kennedy and other Democratic leaders who had died since 1960: Eleanor Roosevelt and Sam Rayburn. A film about Kennedy's life and presidency was produced to show the delegates. Music from *Camelot* was included. Jacqueline Kennedy had told journalist Theodore White that she and Jack had enjoyed listening to the musical, and as a result the nickname Camelot had already been given to the Kennedy years. The White House was pleased with the film, but wondered whether the musical choice was wise. "*Camelot* is certainly a tear-jerker. Of course, *Camelot* was a highly schmaltzy musical about a semi-mythical kingdom. I have quite mixed feelings about its propriety at a convention. Certainly, the delegates will be left weeping," White House aide S. Douglass Cater asserted. "It would be less dramatic but probably less risky to show that film sequence without the music. I have vague unrest about engaging in such an emotional bender just before the Johnson acceptance speech."[75]

Kennedy's speech, which followed the film, was also an homage to his slain brother. Johnson had made sure neither Bobby nor the JFK film would be seen by the delegates until after his nomination; he feared a last-minute delegate stampede to put Kennedy on the ticket. O'Brien characterized the president at that moment as suffering "absolute paranoia." Johnson made sure the Kennedy people were "far removed from" all the convention planning. O'Brien termed it "the funniest thing" he "had ever experienced." Still, Bobby did goad Johnson beginning with the twenty-two-minute ovation delegates gave him when he was introduced. He wanted to silence the delegates, but Senator Henry Jackson (D-WA) told Kennedy, "Let it go on. . . . Just let them do it Bob. . . . Let them get it out of their system." If that were not enough to rile Johnson certainly the end of Kennedy's remarks did. He concluded his convention speech with a quote from *Romeo and Juliet* that Jackie Kennedy had given him:

> When he shall die
> Take him and cut him out in little stars
> And he will make the face of heaven so fine
> That all the world will be in love with night,
> And pay no worship to the garish Sun.

Johnson was furious, thinking, according to one biographer, "garish sun my ass."[76]

Following Robert Kennedy's speech, Humphrey gave his acceptance speech, which was a stellar statement of Democratic ideals. When Humphrey ticked off a list of bipartisan policy accomplishments that gained Democratic and Republican votes, he asserted "But not Senator Goldwater!" The crowd loved it, and the line became a refrain they used throughout the speech. When Humphrey finished, LBJ addressed the delegates in a listless speech. The president asked his aide Walter Jenkins how frequently he received applause. Jenkins said after every line, but the *New York Times* provided a harsher assessment, editorializing the speech resulted in "Death by Boredom."[77]

Overall, the convention received poor reviews for style. TRB in *The New Republic* observed, "It would be nice to paint it heroically. We can't. Mostly it was a dreary wasteland of Lyndon-knows-best. Convention speakers like John McCormack kept saying unctuously that Providence guided JFK to pick LBJ in 1960. There was also a speech in favor of women. Yes, honest, just in favor of women. A woman made it, and said how important women are, particularly, we guess, Democratic women." Theodore White also was critical of the convention, especially Johnson's acceptance speech, calling it "the poorest he made in the campaign." White explained, "His speech was a consensus of the worst thinking of the best thinkers attached to the White House. Willard Wirtz, Richard Goodwin, McGeorge Bundy, Horace Busby and Bill Moyers together proved that no great speech can be written by a committee. Johnson's speech was dull."[78]

Even so, Johnson now owned his party. He had won the opportunity to fight Barry Goldwater for the right to define what consensus liberalism and Sunbelt politics meant in a Great Society. How then did Johnson approach his task? The answer, in a word, was dismissively of Goldwater and his brand of Sunbelt conservatism. Whereas the GOP nominee ran toward his regional identity, Johnson ran away from his. Put differently, Goldwater looked backward with a narrow world view and Johnson forward with a vast, inclusive view. After the convention Johnson told newspaper publisher and friend Houston Harte that the Goldwater Republican Party was a "bunch of screwballs" who would bring about "the death of the" GOP because Goldwater advocated "drop[ping] atomic bombs on everybody. I don't believe the people will stand for that."

As dreary as Lyndon's convention was, at least they focused on a substantive public policy agenda for the nation. Kennedy loyalist Arthur Schlesinger observed, "The convention wholly ratified LBJ's control of the party, in case anyone had any doubt, and it supplied further evidence of his political wizardry, if such evidence were required. It was his convention—every controversial issue deflected and disposed of; no roll calls; plus the hectic melodrama of the vice presidency. And his presence dominated the convention," Schlesinger deplored. "It would have been hard to tell from the external trappings that Kennedy had been President of the United States during three of the last four years; in the symbolism of the convention, he was a remote icon, along with Truman and Roosevelt." The shift meant a new identity for the Democratic Party: "And the LBJ party emerged: western rather than eastern; middle-aged rather than youthful; conciliatory rather than aggressive; bland rather than intellectual; centrist rather than liberal. These adjectives refer perhaps to form rather than substance." After making this veiled criticism Schlesinger acknowledged, LBJ would not deviate from the Kennedy legacy on policy questions, but he ended with one last dismissal of Johnson: "The test will come when he runs out of ideas. Up to this point he has been living intellectually off the Kennedy years."[79]

6

BACKLASH, FRONTLASH, SMEARLASH

When did the fall campaign begin? To what degree was it shaped by the backlash and frontlash tensions? Neither question is as simple as it might seem at first glance. Thinking about the November contest, certainly in the White House, began well before the traditional Labor Day start to fall campaigns, and to understand the critical day-to-day components of the September–November race makes necessary looking at work done prior to Labor Day 1964, including White House outreach to Republicans, fundraising, the pursuit of newspaper endorsements, and candidate strategy. Other contextual aspects of the contest speak less to when the campaign began and more to the question of backlash and frontlash, both of which were rooted in the emerging Sunbelt takeover of national politics.

Backlash simply put was the notion that critical segments of white voters would no longer support the Democratic Party because of civil rights. Frontlash was the reverse: the contention that Republicans would leave the GOP because of Barry Goldwater's political agenda. Both were rooted in Sunbelt extremisms. The first "extremism" posited that the apartheid against African Americans could no longer be tolerated. The second "extremism" held that the federal government was too large and intrusive. No general consensus had solidified, but support for civil rights was closer to majoritarian status than was opposition to a strong federal government. Republicans used reports of scandal and immorality in bold political ways to increase animus against Washington, DC. The party hoped calling out Lyndon Johnson for offending the mores of good governance would enable Goldwater to win the White House.

LBJ countered by complaining in rallies that fall of the "smearlash." He stressed Republicans were "desperate," "dangerous," and "not cautious." The president concluded the GOP was unethical in its campaign rhetoric while the Democrats were not: "We have no unkind words to say about anyone. We don't indulge in any muckraking or any mudslinging, because we don't think that is what the American people will listen to."[1] These Sunbelt extremes collided in complicated ways to shape the 1964 contest.

Goldwater's team decided to make the race a question of ethics and morality, which meant questioning Lyndon Johnson's character. Journalist Theodore H. White observed, "But how does an advertising firm go about attacking a President? How does one besmirch the majesty and uniform of the office? How, for example, as one of the Republicans complained to me, do you ask how a Texas Congressman and Senator, never earning more than $22,500 a year, accumulates a fortune of $7 million?"[2]

By early February the Republicans began their campaign against LBJ with "personal attacks upon the President" and "claims that everything that is wrong in the world would be put right if a Republican were elected President." While throwing mud was not new in American politics, the degree of personal vitriol used to deny Johnson's qualifications for office was unprecedented. Goldwater challenged Johnson's personal and business ethics, equating Johnson's moral limitations with a perceived larger national moral crisis. At key junctures in the campaign, though, Goldwater parried when a thrust of his verbal sword would have been more effective. Advisors to Johnson insisted that the president "ignore" the attacks and focus on doing his job of running the country. Said one White House insider, "It is rather interesting that the hysteria of the Republicans has even begun to be reflected in speeches by Governor [Nelson] Rockefeller. It is obvious that the only constructive notes will be sounded by former President [Dwight D.] Eisenhower and cannot be followed by other Republicans."[3]

Several scandals engulfed the 1964 presidential election. Though the charges never fully eclipsed Johnson's moment in the sun they threatened harm. Most notable was Bobby Baker. He had been the secretary to the Senate majority, and he had amassed tremendous power on Capitol Hill in the 1950s, earning the nickname "Little Lyndon" for his work with Johnson. In late 1963, Baker had been charged with financial impropriety, which compelled him to resign his Senate position. Republicans tried to exploit the Baker scandal in 1964. Johnson told journalists, "I hardly knew Bobby

Baker!" The statement defied credibility because as White House press secretary George Reedy explained, "My God! Bobby was one of his messiahs." Still, Washington insiders believed the Baker story did not matter outside the capital, characterizing it as "a sick story of interest to this sick town."[4]

Additionally, investigative journalists suggested Johnson's Austin, Texas, radio and television empire resulted from corrupt business dealings. Republicans contended the Johnson monopoly allowed the president to make inordinate profits because he violated FCC rules and regulations. One Republican complained that North American Aviation was "the *major* purchaser of advertising time on the LBJ Co. TV station in Austin." This individual cried foul; the company "does not sell ANYTHING of any consequence to the consumer public." Instead, its business was with the federal government, and it resold its Austin advertising time to other parties for less than it had originally paid. Additional rumors circulated that the Johnson White House had coerced campaign donations out of defense contractors with the threat that if they did not support Johnson they would lose their military contracts. White elucidated why these charges never gained much traction: "Johnson had in no sense ever been guilty of the 'hard take.' The complicated higher finance of monopoly television stations and government franchises could not be made a clear issue for the girl behind the counter or the man in the mill."[5]

Throughout the campaign Johnson had to face down negative public opinion in other ways. For example, reporters and the public had reacted negatively to pictures showing Johnson lifting his pet beagles by the ears. Moreover, in late March 1964 Johnson had taken four reporters on a ride through his Texas Hill Country ranch over the Easter holiday. Drinking Pearl beer, Johnson reputedly drove over 90 miles an hour on two-lane roads. The press coverage suggested he was rash and irresponsible. A *Time* magazine article angered Johnson. It began: "A cream-colored Lincoln Continental driven by the President of the US flashed up a long Texas hill, swung into the left lane to pass two cars poking along under 85 m.p.h. . . . The President charged on, his paper cup of Pearl beer within easy sipping distance" even after he nearly hit an oncoming car. The *Time* article noted one of Johnson's passengers "groaned . . . when the ride was over: 'That's the closest [Speaker of the House] John McCormack has come to the White House yet.'" The writer claimed the president was "a cross between a teenage Grand Prix driver and a back-to-nature Thoreau in cowboy boots." It recounted how the president had provided a "very graphic description of the sex life of a bull" to an audience of men and women. White House advisors worried the article might "creat[e] an indelible image of a reckless President, cutting away his popular support." Certainly, newspapers around the country published "moralizing editorials . . . that deplored the beer-drinking, fast-driving President." To Republicans the episode was yet more "proof of moral decay in the Johnson Administration."[6]

Johnson showed his warm side to the Washington press corps immediately following the coverage of his Easter weekend driving habits. He had aide Bill Moyers walk with him to the Southeast Gate of the White House to greet the assembled tourists. The president shouted to the crowd, "Would you like to take a walk with me?" After the gates were opened one journalist observed that "a hundred tourists swarmed about him." Johnson requested, "All of you ugly men get up front and all of you pretty girls come back here with me." The following day Johnson crossed Pennsylvania Avenue from Blair House toward the White House, and along the way he again relished mixing with the tourists. Journalists concluded, "what the people saw was not the stereotyped Texas wheeler-dealer, but an outgoing, compulsively gregarious, peripatetic President."[7]

Johnson countered the stories of his reckless driving and of possible corruption by casting aspersions on Goldwater. The president encouraged journalists to discuss the impropriety of Goldwater receiving a television set from his staffers. He questioned Goldwater's personal finances, suggesting hypocrisy. Johnson told a friendly journalist: "Well, we've got a bunch of goddamned thugs here taking us on. Now, this Goldwater, talking about morality! If we wanted to deal in morality, what we could show on that guy!" The president said he had proof that Goldwater's eighty-nine-year-old mother was "drawing a tax deduction from the Goldwater stores, that are owned by Associated Dry Goods, for forty-nine hundred a year. And she's too damned old to even get to the store!" Goldwater had been the chief Senate fundraiser for Republicans from 1955 to 1963. The Texan stressed that he had never involved himself with collecting money in his congressional years. Johnson ranted to Humphrey: "and if they want to go into everybody's collected money, well, just how much has Mr. [Barry] Goldwater, this presidential candidate? He came in and he ran this committee of the Republicans all these years and he collected more money from more people than anybody in the country." Johnson complained that Goldwater had "collected money from every damned oil man in Texas, distributed it around to all of them."[8]

Johnson was not simply reactive to GOP ethics charges. He understood the importance of public opinion, and to ensure he won that battle Johnson went after the GOP elite in business and politics. Such would help his fund-raising and increase newspaper endorsements. Johnson's strategy to pick up wayward Republicans proved seamless with his efforts to win corporate support. His thinking about these two intertwined constituencies derived from his experience in Texas politics, where faction or subgroup identity had been much more important than Democratic Party membership, which mattered little in a one-party southern state. Fort Worth business-man Ray Shaffer told White House staffer Jack Valenti, "if the Democrats don't come up with some 'red bottomed' running mate for the President, it will be the first time in my life that I have supported a Democrat for Pres-ident. Many of my Republican friends share this feeling with me." In late June 1964, press secretary to Lady Bird Johnson Liz Carpenter told Johnson that he would likely be getting the endorsement of the *Detroit News*, a Re-publican-leaning paper. She advised arranging a luncheon with leaders of the paper. Later that summer, Palmer Hoyt, the editor and publisher of the *Denver Post*, asked LBJ, "Are you trying to take over the Republican Party by nominating Barry Goldwater? It looks like you might get more Republican votes than normally go to a Democratic candidate for the presidency."[9]

Just as important to the Johnson campaign as winning over Republicans was gaining the support of the business community. Almost as soon as he became president LBJ began courting corporate America. He invited the most important CEOs to the White House and while there he had his pic-ture taken individually with each of them. Later in January he invited them to dine in the White House. Each dinner party followed a similar formula. The evening began with handshakes, a meal, a presidential speech, and then a fond farewell. White House advisor Eric Goldman recalled, "LBJ was a master at this gastronomical politicking. His speeches, wandering far from the text, were persuasively non-partisan and had an appealing un-dertone of 'We responsible people—you and I—understand that a pretty ir-responsible fellow is presuming to run this nation.'" Then he wooed them with a preview of the State of the Union address. With such tactics and his enthusiastic support for a tax cut, Johnson convinced corporate America he would not undertake policies harmful to business.[10]

White House officials worked with their Wall Street contacts to ascer-tain the impact of Goldwater on the economy. Walter Heller, the chair of the Council of Economic Advisors, cautioned, *"there might be a financial backlash if the stock market began to take Goldwater's chances seriously."* He reported his conversation with financial writer Sylvia Porter, who indicated, *"after Goldwater's nomination, many mutual funds and trusts* began to cut back on stock buying, putting their money instead into certificates of deposit, government bills, and so forth." Porter repeated what one Wall Street insider told her, "We all believe in the balanced budget, publicly, just like we're publicly against having a mistress—but privately, it's another matter. *Goldwater's budget policy would hurt the economy* and business profits."[11]

Heller showed that corporate profits had increased under Democratic leadership, with an average before-tax profit level of $42 billion during the Eisenhower years and an average of $50 billion in the Kennedy-Johnson years. Corporate profits were also better on average when after-tax dollars were compared: $21 billion in the Eisenhower years and $26 billion in the Kennedy-Johnson years. Statistics alone would not win the argument. Clifton C. Carter, White House liaison to the Democratic National Committee, told the president that a national committee of businessmen was needed "in order that we may try to pre-empt this field while the Republicans are scrambling around for a nominee."[12]

Theories of backlash and frontlash wove through Johnson's efforts to claim GOP backing. Johnson viewed backlash as unthinking and reactive and frontlash as thoughtful and potentially the first step in a political realignment. Moyers contended, "we [must] move in a very great hurry to insure that our dissident Republican friends are corralled before they wander off the pasture." Later in the fall White House staffers discussed with Moyers the difference between Republicans leaving their party and Democrats defecting from Johnson. "The Republican defection to the President is a scare defection—Goldwater scares people. The Democratic defection to Goldwater is anti-Negro, is worst among Poles in Chicago, is elsewhere scattered and whipped up by the clandestine John Birch Society, now surfacing."[13]

Courting GOP businessmen limited what Democrats could do in other arenas, namely attacks on the Republican record. This strategy meant Johnson would run against Goldwater and not the GOP, divorcing Goldwater from his party and its record. Johnson agreed and told a Texas oilman, "You cannot raise a big enough crop of ex-Republicans to suit me, but I don't know of a better man to do the plowing in this field than you." As such, White House advisor Lawrence O'Brien counseled strongly against attacking the Eisenhower administration on national defense issues. He noted that doing so would upset "Eisenhower partisans—the very groups we are trying to bring into our camp." D. O. Andreas, a Minnesota businessman, told Humphrey: "if you will direct your campaign largely against 'the gang that has taken over the Republican party,' you will most certainly fall heir to a large segment of the liberal Republican vote."[14]

Similar reports came to Johnson from other sources. Secretary of the Interior Stewart Udall told LBJ of Lewis Douglas's disenchantment with Goldwater. Douglas had served briefly in Franklin D. Roosevelt's first administration as director of the budget, but left after quarreling with the president over federal spending. He never abandoned the Democratic Party, but he never voted that ticket for the presidency after 1932. Moreover, he supported Goldwater in his 1952 and 1958 Senate races. According to Udall, Douglas termed the Goldwater nomination "a 'tragic mistake.'" With Douglas a director on several major Wall Street corporate boards, Udall reasoned, "His open support would undoubtedly have an impact in the business community similar to that of the Henry Ford II endorsement."[15]

Leading northern and liberal Republicans refused to endorse Goldwater that fall, including Michigan governor George Romney, New York governor Nelson Rockefeller, New York senator Jacob Javits, and New York senator Kenneth Keating. Johnson's campaign through unknown means procured Rockefeller's research files on Goldwater. Several other Republican moderates close to Eisenhower, including former cabinet member Arthur Flemming and Milton Eisenhower, opted not to endorse or vote for Goldwater but to stay in the Republican Party. To keep Goldwater from picking up moderate and mainstream Republicans Johnson relied on Texan and former Treasury Secretary Robert Anderson to court his old boss. Anderson reported to Johnson on his conversations with Eisenhower, "you absolutely won the guy." He gained support from other prominent Republicans, including corporate leaders and Ambassador Henry Cabot Lodge, who promised he would travel around the United States touting administration policy in Vietnam. Anderson told Johnson, "I've seen people that have never voted the Democratic ticket in their life—strong Republicans—and for the first time in their life, they're going to vote for you." Such thinking caused Johnson to believe, "for every backlash that the Democrats lose, we pick up 3 frontlash."[16]

Since the New Deal, Democrats outnumbered Republicans in terms of voter registration and party identification. As such most Democratic candidates stressed their party membership, but not Johnson in 1964. Doing so would have hindered the frontlash. By targeting arguments to every voting constituency in the country, Johnson hoped to leave Republicans nothing to discuss other than "beagles and speedometers," references to stories about his dogs and his driving habits. Deemphasizing a party identification helped make his argument that he would be president for all the people. It also made it easier for Republicans to endorse and campaign for Johnson. In one print ad that ran in major US dailies including the *Chicago Tribune*, the *Los Angeles Times*, and the *New York Times*, a leading Republican declared: "A President who shoots from the hip and lip would involve a bigger risk than I care to assume. I'd be a lot more comfortable if the man on our end of the Hot Line were as flexible as he is rigid, as conciliatory as he is tough, and somewhat more egghead than hot-head. . . . I'm comfortable with Lyndon Johnson and so I'm going to vote for him."[17]

The Republican Businessmen for Johnson and other groups like it proved integral to funding the Johnson campaign, which relied on large donations from the "fat cat" business community. For example, the 4,000 wealthy members of the President's Club gave a minimum of $1,000 each. Ford was among Johnson's largest donors. In all over 3,000 CEOs joined the effort, which became known as the National Independent Committee for President Johnson and Senator Humphrey. Some of the Sunbelt business leaders who migrated to Johnson viewed the Texas Democrat as the true conservative in the 1964 race. After the election was over, New Dealer and Democratic Party insider Thomas Corcoran advised LBJ to thank the business leaders who "took bushel baskets of abusive letters about 'treason'" for endorsing the Democratic ticket.[18]

The frontlash initiative with businessmen made possible a volume of large campaign contributions that a Democratic presidential contender had never before seen from the business community. When he announced the National Independent Committee for Johnson and Humphrey from the White House, Johnson articulated a universalist political strategy of frontlash designed to help Republican business leaders support the Democrats. Said Johnson, "I did not, I do not, and I shall never seek to be a labor President, or a business President, a President for liberals or a President for conservatives, a President for the North or a President for the South—but only President for all the people."[19]

So how did Johnson approach fundraising beyond courting big donors? Trace evidence suggests his role was substantial. Johnson asked his staff to arrange meetings for him with the "big givers" from California and New York. He criticized the manner in which the Democratic National Committee handled fundraising. Johnson told Clifton Carter: "Tell them over at the [Democratic] National Committee to quit claiming they're picking up all this money that they're not picking up. They claim they picked up a million dollars out yonder. They don't do it. They didn't pick up $500,000 net. And I'd put the net figure because if we pick up that, people are not going to want to give money." Still in early August, Johnson reported to Walter Reuther, the president of the United Auto Workers, that the national party was flush with cash, that voter registration was up, and that the party's research efforts into Goldwater and vice-presidential nominee William E. Miller were well under way. Regarding voter registration, Johnson noted, "they had to put on 12 extra girls to take the calls from people that were changing from Republican to Democrat."[20]

In 1964, the Republican Party deployed new fundraising methods to appeal to small donors. When the eastern establishment ran the party the majority of donations came from big business and corporate America, with Nixon receiving just 40,000 individual donations in his losing 1960 race. In 1964, fundraiser and direct-mail expert Richard Viguerie sent over 15 million mass mailings, resulting in donations totaling $5.8 million from 650,000 individual contributors, most of whom gave less than $500 each. Indeed, just 28 percent of Goldwater's donations came from contributions of more than $500 compared with 69 percent of Johnson's donations. The average Goldwater donation per contributor was $15.21. Viguerie had come to the Goldwater campaign from the Young Americans for Freedom, and he became a leading figure in Republican circles well into the twenty-first century. In all the party raised $17.9 million in 1964, with the remainder coming from state fundraising quotas, dinners, and television appeals. The latter included Ronald Reagan's "A Time for Choosing" broadcast, which brought in $700,000. That was not the highest-grossing television appeal. Dean Burch raised over $800,000 in one evening's television appearance.[21]

In fundraising Goldwater also did well with corporate America, getting donations from the director of Aetna, Walt Disney, the du Pont family, officials from General Electric, the president of Gimbels, Walter Knott, the chairman of the board of the Libbey-Owens-Ford Glass Company, the Eli Lilly family, the president of the San Francisco Giants, Texas oilmen and ranchers, the medical community, and the owner of the Waldorf-Astoria. Textile entrepreneur Roger Milliken, the "Daddy Warbucks" of the Republican Party, was the most important financier working on Goldwater's campaign. Still, Johnson had the clear advantage with corporate America. Leading CEOs saw Goldwater as volatile and mercurial, bad for the economy, but small-business leaders backed Goldwater with financial donations out of fear of increased government intervention in the economy. Because of Johnson's successes with Republicans in the business community Goldwater advisor Stephen Shadegg complained that business commitment for

Goldwater was thin. Dan Gainey, a key Goldwater fundraiser, said after the election, "I just couldn't bring myself to vote for him," meaning Goldwater.[22]

Early in the summer the effort to earn newspaper endorsements began. At a gathering of leading journalists including Gardner "Mike" Cowles, William S. Paley, William Randolph Hearst, Jack Howard, Leonard Goldenson, Wes Gallagher, Barney Kilgore, and Turner Catledge all agreed that Goldwater's candidacy was "absurd." When asked if anyone was going to vote for the Republican challenger none of the journalists said a word.[23]

Before the conventions were over Johnson began amassing national newspaper endorsements, a trend that continued. The editorial board of the *Kansas City Star* voted to endorse Johnson, "the first time in history that this paper . . . has ever supported a Democratic Presidential candidate." Valenti told LBJ the *Atlantic Monthly* would endorse his candidacy in the October issue, "the first time that this magazine has endorsed any candidate since Woodrow Wilson." Johnson did well in newspaper endorsements; he earned almost 60 out of 100 endorsements from the top papers in the country. In the previous twenty years, those same papers opted for the Republican candidate 77 percent of the time.[24]

The most interesting negotiation for endorsements was with the Chandler family, who owned the *Los Angeles Times*. Valenti told Johnson in early September of his conversation with Otis Chandler, the paper's publisher, and their efforts to get Johnson to meet with his parents. Less than a decade earlier the paper had been a "mouthpiece" for "intensely conservative politics," and one branch of the family supported the John Birch Society. Otis Chandler, when he took over the paper at the beginning of the decade, declared his independence. Valenti contended Johnson should dine with the elder Chandlers. Johnson concurred with the plan. A week later, Valenti told the president, "Otis thinks Goldwater is poison and is pained by the prospect of having to endorse him." He expressed his hope that his parents would consent "NOT" to endorse Goldwater after meeting with Johnson.[25]

Valenti had discussed the situation with Palmer Hoyt, the editor and publisher of the *Denver Post*, a paper that had endorsed Johnson, who counseled that the focus should be placed on Dorothy Buffum Chandler because she would likely make the decision. He conveyed how Johnson should handle the meeting: "Key your discussion to what you intend this country to be—and what you foresee for the free enterprise system. Hit this hard. Norman Chandler is impressed by the support you are getting from big business." Hoyt stressed that Johnson should not "attack Goldwater" but instead "make positive statements about what you have done and what you intend to do—keyed to cooperation with business." Valenti concluded, "Otis says that even if he has to endorse Goldwater, he will do it mildly and will give us all the breaks on the news pages."[26] Despite these preparations, Johnson did not win over the Chandlers.

Besides the *Los Angeles Times*, Goldwater gained only two other major newspaper endorsements: the *Chicago Tribune* and the *Cincinnati Enquirer*. The *Saturday Evening Post*, typically loyal to the GOP, wrote of the Republican nominee, "Goldwater is a grotesque burlesque of the conservative he pretends to be. He is a wild man, a stray, an unprincipled and ruthless jujitsu artist like Joe McCarthy."[27]

None of this changed coverage of the campaign. Whereas Goldwater gave lapel pins to his traveling press corps, Johnson gave access, holding regular background meetings with bureau chiefs. He sometimes fed the press's interest in name calling by offering criticisms of Goldwater. Reedy told Johnson in mid-August, "I don't believe there is any way in which you can avoid news stories that say you are taking 'a jab at Goldwater.'" Instead he advised Johnson to discuss "the problem completely off the record with the Bureau Chiefs tonight. In doing so you should be completely good humored and fully aware of their problem—which is that they cannot read your mind and that the practical impact of almost any statement that you make today *is* a jab at Goldwater simply because of his determination to oppose you at every step." Reedy insisted the bureau chiefs were "more likely to balance it out and put the shoe on the foot where it belongs—Senator Goldwater's foot" if Johnson explained his position more fully.[28]

Valenti told Reedy and White House aide Bill Moyers that decisions must be made soon regarding whether Johnson would go on news shows like *Meet the Press* and *Face the Nation*. He continued, "It will be difficult to say YES to one or two and NO to the others." A few weeks later White House officials again discussed what to do about invitations from news talk shows. Washington attorneys and political wise men Abe Fortas and Clark Clifford counseled Johnson should stay away from all of them because the programs "are too commercial, not controllable, and unsuitable for the President of the United States ('they are not dignified rostrums.')" Moreover, they clarified that a Johnson appearance "either before or after Goldwater" would "build the Senator an audience he could not otherwise get." Finally, they acknowledged that "us[ing] the same platform as Goldwater would be admitting that the Senator is on an equal footing with the President." Johnson acceded to this conclusion.[29]

White House advisor S. Douglass Cater told Johnson, and LBJ assented:

Not only did Johnson pursue white ethnic voters and African American voters but also Hispanic voters. LBJ Library, photo by Donald Stoderl.

"So far, we have not done a good job in making maximum use of the nightly TV news programs (Huntley-Brinkley and Cronkite)." Cater learned from journalist Theodore White "the problem is to provide a visual story early enough in the day for it to get to New York to be processed. Away from the East Coast, this means that we should be planning a newsworthy statement by 12 noon or 1 p.m. at the latest." Failure to do so meant networks would run "a catch-as-catch-can story each night. From what I have seen, it does not do justice to your discussion of the issues."[30] News coverage, though, did not matter that much given Johnson's overwhelming lead in the polls.

Johnson's advantage over Goldwater was both a result and a cause of backlash and frontlash, which fed into thinking about voter registration and about discussion of these electoral tensions. Indeed, competing for the African American vote showed the complexity of race in the 1964 contest. The DNC pushed the White House to reschedule the off-the-record meeting with the Southern Regional Conference of Negro Democrats. Such meetings had been held with similar African American groups from the

Northeast and the Midwest, and a party official contended, "The Negro vote in North Carolina, Georgia, South Carolina, Florida and some of the other states can be decisive."[31] The Johnson team, though, also wanted to hold white southern voters, thus the caution.

Goldwater benefited from the civil rights backlash in parts of the country. For example, a Goldwater campaign official noted that a CORE picket in West Virginia "obviously . . . helped us." Additionally, when Goldwater spoke before a Winston-Salem audience, a "scuffle" broke out between an African American woman and a retired white male railroad worker. The police charged both of them with simple assault, but not before multiple African Americans and whites intensified the conflict. Whites "holler[ed] for the man to stand up for his rights," while the assembled African Americans challenged the police to "hit" the woman. A columnist for the *Chicago Sun Times* argued, "every time there is violence by Negroes, Goldwater gains supporters. The Republican picture is looking up, and the first to admit it are Democrats" who spoke off the record.[32]

Goldwater spent substantial time exploring the nonvoter, looking for ways to bring that segment of the population into his camp. The survey research that the Republican campaign conducted revealed that while more nonvoters identified with the Democrats, they also tended to hold conservative political views, be less well educated, and come from a lower socioeconomic position than those who voted. Finally, their reasons for not voting fell into one of two categories: they lacked interest in the process or they were tugged in two directions, meaning support for the Democratic Party but opposition to civil rights. Denison Kitchel, of the Goldwater campaign, told *Meet the Press*, "I think that a great many members of labor unions . . . are Republicans."[33]

The dichotomy between the backlash and the frontlash shaped every aspect of thinking about white ethnic voters. In late July, Indiana governor Matthew E. Welsh told Johnson, "The problem of 'backlash' among ethnic groups *does* exist—but it can be effectively countered." He cited as an example how he outran his opponent in a Polish and Hungarian area in South Bend. Welsh indicated that Johnson's visit to the area to inspect a federal program helped keep voters loyal to the Democratic Party during the primary: "you 'lifted their sights' and they followed their normal voting pattern—straight organization Democrat!" The governor concluded: "I would strongly urge that you make a personal appearance in those areas where the ethnic vote is of consequence."[34]

Cater offered Johnson a more sophisticated analysis of the ethnic back-

Johnson campaigning among white and black industrial workers in the Midwest. LBJ Library, photo by Cecil Stoughton.

lash, using data from Indiana. There, polls suggested 15 percent of voters would abandon the Democratic Party for Goldwater, but those same polls revealed "a 'frontlash'" wherein 30 percent of Republicans were identified as Johnson voters. Cater deduced, "the 'front lash' is running two to one over the 'backlash.'" He asserted other polls corroborated the finding. An early August Gallup poll showed GOP defections more than double Democratic ones, at 26 percent and 11 percent, respectively. Nevertheless, Cater stressed Johnson should not "minimize the problem of the 'backlash.'" Interviews in eighty Milwaukee taverns that catered to Polish-Americans suggested little to no anger about the Civil Rights Act. Johnson pollster Dick Scammon surmised, "*as of now* you can carry all but four or five states outside the South."[35]

By the time the general election began, Goldwater found some success, but not enough to win, when he campaigned among white, working-class voters, who were concerned about race, integration, and Social Security. They tended to agree with Goldwater on the first two issues but not the latter. This divergence caused northern working-class voters to stay with the Democrats, even as they gave advice to Goldwater about how to appeal to blue-collar voters. One such voter told the campaign to play on racial fears of crime and busing with yard signs that read "'Streets must be made safe

again. Vote Goldwater' or 'Don't experiment with our children. Keep neighborhood schools. Vote Goldwater.'"³⁶

The Democrats saw Illinois as "the big pivotal Midwest swing state."
John Bartlow Martin, a journalist, ambassador to the Dominican Republic,
and liberal Democratic insider, explained it was a state Goldwater should
win because "Downstate and the Chicago suburbs are conservative Republican" while "Democrats never have done as well as they should in such
industrial cities as Danville, Decatur, and Peoria." Neither party nor union
leadership could overcome the proclivities of workers who were either
"farmboys or Kentuckians and Tennesseans." Democratic votes came from
Chicago and African American East St. Louis, meaning the party needed
big wins there.³⁷

That was not enough, said Martin, who believed Republican votes were
necessary to win in Illinois. He argued a frontlash was possible in Illinois
because of a divide between regular Republican Party members and Goldwater volunteers. Martin contended, "the regular Republicans resent them
bitterly," in part because of the prominence of the John Birch Society and
other radical right groups. Racism drove working-class voters to Goldwater,
explained Martin. Whites feared for their job security and their property
values when blacks moved into the area. Friendships broke up over the
issue. Martin recounted signage that said, "'If you want a Negro in the next
plant, vote Democrat.'" Moreover, party activists had "passed out white el-
ephants and black donkeys" on Republican Day at the State Fair. Johnson
would not get those votes, but would get middle-class, professional Republican votes. He summarized conversation from an Illinois dinner party "of
young Republicans and independents, semi-egghead" who "'couldn't quite
stomach Johnson' but would reluctantly vote for him: Goldwater was just
too much of a threat to survival. . . . And, as one man said, 'it is not *respectable*' to be for Goldwater."³⁸

John A. Gronouski, the Postmaster General, wrote LBJ his concerns
about the ethnic vote. He warned, "Goldwater already has literally hundreds
of people working among the ethnic group communities in Chicago, New
York, Milwaukee and other big cities, particularly in the midwest and East."
The Democratic National Committee outreach to ethnic voters was paltry in
comparison, just "two people working in our whole national ethnic group
campaign—one man and his secretary." Such evidence suggested, according to Gronouski, that the campaign was not organized at the grassroots
level. He cautioned that "voluntary state coordinators" would not "do the
intensive work that needs to be done during the next couple of months."

Johnson's "schedule-makers," Gronouski intoned, must "concern themselves with appearances by you in the critical areas before ethnic groups."[39]

Johnson's frontlash resulted from the negative reaction of moderate and liberal Republicans to Goldwater. This frontlash produced much volatility within the party. Before the Democrats even staged their convention, the Goldwater campaign surveyed the Republican political landscape around the country and found significant disunity. Such was understandable given the divisive San Francisco convention. New York presented a number of challenges. Several unions that usually supported Republicans were not backing Goldwater, and African American leaders "remain[ed] hostile to [the] National ticket." Just as problematic were liberal state Republican officeholders already outspoken in opposition to Goldwater. Goldwater advisors recommended giving campaign leaders a couple of weeks to fix the problems. In Massachusetts, divisions remained among supporters of former candidates Henry Cabot Lodge, Bill Scranton, and the nominee. The Goldwater camp affirmed vice-presidential nominee Bill Miller "should be sent in QUICKLY."[40]

Later in August, Scranton hosted a Republican Party unity meeting in Pennsylvania. For as much political talent as was assembled in Hershey the results were modest at best. Attendees included Scranton, Goldwater, Miller, Dwight D. Eisenhower, Richard M. Nixon, Dean Burch, George Romney, and Nelson Rockefeller. Goldwater showed no leadership. He consented to holding the conference to try to keep up "appearances," but otherwise was not eager to participate. After the election, Eisenhower remarked, "I voted for Goldwater, but I did not vote for him, I voted for the Party." With the exception of Scranton and Nixon, the moderate Republicans left Hershey and the national ticket behind focusing exclusively on their own state races and treating the GOP nominee "as if he were cursed with political halitosis." Scranton campaigned for Goldwater in Pennsylvania and the Midwest, but Nixon went to thirty-six states to give speeches for the Republican nominee. The Hershey meeting proved significant, not because strategy was determined there but because the schisms in the party resulting from the GOP National Convention hardened. Put differently, the conference helped confirm why Republicans would lose in the fall.[41]

Goldwater began the meeting by stating, "we are about two or three weeks ahead of the schedule we had set to bring this unity about." Next Goldwater explained why he had chosen Miller as his running mate. The two had worked closely since 1956 to raise money for the Republican Party and to help Republican senatorial candidates. "Bill is a tough fighter, not that we are going to wage that kind of campaign, but we can expect from the opposition certainly a lot of it," Goldwater contended. "And I wanted a man with me who could return the fire, so to speak." He also hailed Miller's legal skills and the geographic balance as a New Yorker he brought to a Sunbelt-themed ticket. Goldwater had hoped Miller could attack Johnson as ethically challenged, but Miller had his own problems. He had tried to bribe a fellow member of Congress, had not disclosed all his income while in Congress, had had a conflict of interest between his investments and his legislative responsibilities, and he also falsified his employment record, suggesting he had been a Nuremberg prosecutor when he had not.[42]

Goldwater anticipated Miller would "drive Johnson nuts" with his acerbic wit and his fierce partisanship, but instead the Democrats ignored Miller. Johnson dismissed Miller as a "Brooks Brothers style" character assassin in a telephone conversation with John Connally. White House staffer Eric Goldman recalled, "I was particularly repelled by the Republican vice-presidential candidate, William Miller. It was not only the policies the man represented; he had about him a slick sleaziness which made me wince at the thought that the election could conceivably put him in a position where he would be President of United States."[43]

At the Hershey meeting Goldwater explained the organization of the campaign. He noted F. Clifton White would oversee "the citizen civilians." Celebrities Clare Boothe Luce and Jimmy Doolittle were honorary chairs of the group. Parallel to this group and also under White's jurisdiction was "the 'Goldwater Club,'" a citizen's group that would "work with or through the Republican Party wherever this can be done." Rockefeller instructed Goldwater to send "a mailing . . . to all of the County Chairmen" to clarify the operational structure. Such action, Rockefeller insisted, would "do a great deal at this point to calm a lot of jittery nerves." He stressed Goldwater should work directly with county chairs because "they are the boys on the firing line."[44]

Journalists judged Goldwater's campaign organization to be "absolutely first-class, except that it reminded one of the clay mockups of the new models in Detroit's automobile industry. It was meticulously designed, hand-sanded, striking in appearance—but it had no motor." Goldwater had insufficient staff, especially speechwriters. Those closest to Goldwater were "bitter" because "all those eloquent conservative and right-wing intellectuals who had so urged the great cause on their champion" were not playing leadership roles in the campaign. One Goldwater loyalist intoned, "Where were they when we made our charge up San Juan Hill? They blew the trumpets—but when we charged, nobody followed. Where was Buckley? Where was Kirk? Where was Davenport? Where were Bozell and Burnham? At least you got to say this for a liberal s.o.b. like Schlesinger—when his candidates go into action, he's there writing speeches for them."[45]

Goldwater disliked campaigning, a handicap for Republicans. Stump speeches were not natural for him, and he often stumbled over his words. Just as bad was his "obvious distaste for handshaking." Nor did his staff match the text of his speeches to the audiences he was addressing. For example, Goldwater disparaged Social Security when speaking in St. Petersburg, Florida, the area of the country with the highest percentage of Social Security recipients. He criticized the Tennessee Valley Authority while in Knoxville, Tennessee.[46]

Still, Goldwater traveled extensively from early September to early November, logging almost 65,000 air miles aboard his campaign plane the Yai Bi Ken, almost 3,000 rail miles, 12 miles in a tugboat, a couple of hundred on horseback, and untold road miles. Goldwater appeared in forty-five states and over a hundred cities. His crowds were large and enthusiastic. An aide explained Goldwater made one mistake in all these local appearances: he never discussed local problems, leaving audiences concerned that the Arizonan did not understand or care about their problems. Journalist Mary McGrory avowed, "He does not even trouble to mention the town in which he finds himself."[47]

Goldwater tried to have it both ways regarding extremists—the key voting demographic responsible for triggering the frontlash and pushing moderate Republicans into the arms of Johnson. He knew he needed the votes and the campaign work from the Far Right, but he also realized their full inclusion would offend party insiders. The Hershey meeting excluded the most rabid, Far Right Goldwater supporters. When Goldwater addressed the issue of extremism, he sounded dismissive of his core voters, noting: "I seek the support of no extremist, of the left or of the right. I have far too much faith in the good sense and stability of my fellow Republicans to be impressed by talk of a so-called 'extremist take-over' of the Party." He promised, "We repudiate the character assassins, vigilantes, communists, and any group such as the Ku Klux Klan which seeks to impose its views through terror or threat or violence." Earlier, when the GOP convention refused to condemn the Ku Klux Klan, Dean Burch divulged, "We're not in the business of turning away votes."[48]

Eisenhower underscored the importance of language and especially avoiding phrasing that could be offensive, when talking about issues like "good police protection." Ike admitted, "I made a crack about switch-blade knives [at the convention]. Well, I got a letter this morning, or a copy sent to me, that this has been taken in Harlem to mean that I took a crack at Negroes. This is news to me because I didn't associate switch-blade knives with Negroes." Eisenhower confessed his first instinct was to "throw this thing in the waste basket," but because Roy Wilkins, the head of the NAACP, had written the letter, he said he was "going to have an aide write to this fellow and say, well, for God's sake, that's the last thing in my mind; as a matter of fact, I thought switch-blade knives were always—and I hope there are no Italians here—identified with Italians."[49]

When the Hershey conversation turned to race, both Miller and Goldwater avowed that the Republican Party should not be identified as the party of hatred but instead that moniker should be placed on the Democrats. As Miller put it, "All the leaders of the Ku Klux Klan for years and years and years have been Democrats." Goldwater told those assembled, "I will put my record on civil rights against any man in the United States." He then displayed a tremendous ignorance about the realities of racism in the South: "the issue of racism down there is not the big screaming thing that it is in the North. In the cities in the South they are making real progress; in the suburban areas, out in the country, is where you will find the die-hard segregationists who are Democrats, not Republicans." Someone in Johnson's office penned in the margin of the transcript "were" to note that no longer could one say that southern segregationists were exclusively Democrats.[50]

Goldwater's comments about civil rights at the Hershey meeting reveal his own self-deceit and tone-deaf understanding of the struggle for racial equality. Goldwater avowed why he thought he had garnered such opposition from African Americans and the NAACP: "I voted against one amendment to a civil rights bill that would have injected the Federal Government actively into it." Doing so, he said, won him the enmity of civil rights "conformists," people he suspected were "run by the UAW." Goldwater observed of that organization, "you go along with them one hundred per cent or you don't go along." Completely ignoring his position on the Civil Rights Act of 1964 Goldwater asserted, "And that's the background of most of my problems with the Negro people." He explained Roy Wilkins had ignored all his requests to address the NAACP, "Never a word from him. So this is not an easy thing to handle. I will do my best, but I will promise you with every degree of seriousness and strength that I have that I will never talk about racism." Goldwater argued, "I don't even intend to talk about civil

Republican Party leaders hold a party unity meeting, August 12, 1964, in Hershey, Pennsylvania. From left: Representative William Miller, vice-presidential nominee; former president Dwight D. Eisenhower; Senator Barry Goldwater, presidential nominee; former vice president Richard M. Nixon; and Pennsylvania governor William Scranton. Courtesy the Associated Press.

rights. I think it's such an explosive issue. And I tried to get the President to hold off on this thing."[51]

The White House debated what strategy Johnson should use. Ultimately, Johnson concluded a negative campaign was necessary if the frontlash was to work. While Johnson enjoyed positive public opinion ratings, his policies were less popular. Voters credited him with the economic prosperity and with convincing Congress to pass legislation that had been stymied during the Kennedy administration. Other aspects of the Johnson agenda were less popular, including plans to increase the federal budget by $4.5 billion, civil rights reform, proposals for Medicare, urban renewal, and the war on poverty. Indeed, 58 percent of voters surveyed rated the White House record as fair or poor. Two other factors encouraged Johnson to strike a negative tone: his experience in Texas politics, which often included underhanded gambits, and his judgment that a negative strategy would result in a larger margin of victory.[52]

Johnson had not even appointed a campaign manager when the Democratic National Convention was gaveled to order and instead oversaw a campaign with an "appalling" "duplication of effort." Johnson's choices made sense given his view of the campaign and the presidency. Namely, he organized state and regional operatives to work alongside state party organizations because he did not fully trust the DNC, which was staffed with Kennedy loyalists and which he believed early in 1964 was working to secure the vice presidency for Robert F. Kennedy. Johnson also drew connections with local candidates to increase turnout and increase his margin of victory. These decisions meant that Johnson created his own structure. He gave little thought to the long-term sustainability of the Democratic Party, but instead worked for the moment.[53]

For the 1964 race Johnson was his own campaign manager. There was no designated campaign staff in the modern sense of the term. Johnson's public pose, though, was one of being above the politics of the fall election. He masqueraded as being too busy as president to spend much time on matters of the campaign when in reality he was obsessed with the contest and the possibility of losing. The tactic worked so well that when Democratic voters expressed concern the campaign was not active enough, Johnson became angry with his aides. One insider observed, "He treated them awful." Nor did he show much more respect to his wife, Lady Bird, once asking her whether she was "working for Goldwater." The list of things that irritated Johnson about the campaign was quite long, including the graphic design of campaign buttons. A particular button that had headshots of him and Humphrey, equally sized, made him furious. He wanted his image to be more prominent.[54]

Journalist Theodore White had a somewhat different understanding of the Johnson campaign, stressing its organizational structure mirrored what Johnson used in the White House, "bizarre," multi-layered, and "a radial, not a pyramidal, model." The three advisors central to the operation and with the greatest access to Johnson were Jenkins, Moyers, and Valenti, all young men. Jenkins was the "transmission belt for all presidential directives"; he could take over forty separate messages from Johnson in one telephone call and deliver them to the proper recipients. Moyers, described as "frail, overworked and dedicated," functioned as the "chief idea channel of the campaign." Prior to working for Johnson he had been ordained as a Baptist minister. He received all the speech material from the different cabinet departments, and he worked with Willard Wirtz, the Secretary of Labor, to direct the efforts of the speechwriters. Valenti was "ever cheerful" and "unwearying" while acting as "the President's shadow, companion, counselor and personal attendant." Next in importance, Johnson relied on three of the smartest Washington lawyers with extensive political experience to provide perspective and guidance: Clark Clifford, Abe Fortas, and James Rowe. Former Kennedy allies Kenneth O'Donnell and Lawrence O'Brien also proved useful. On paper, they *"were* the campaign directors," overseeing the state organizations. In yet another orbit was John Bailey and the Democratic National Committee. Bailey had tremendous experience in politics, but "in his life there has been only one political romance— with John F. Kennedy, to whom he gave his heart and to whom his heart still belongs." This made it difficult for Bailey to form a close relationship with Johnson, and his major responsibility was voter registration and voter turnout, or as he described it, "the housekeeping job." The final sphere of importance was Humphrey and his team. As vice-presidential candidate Humphrey turned his prodigious energy to "swinging lustily around the country, spreading happiness and savaging Goldwater."[55]

The Johnson campaign appeared to be a "slapdash, jerry-built" effort with but one exception: "the Anti-Campaign" that Johnson constructed. It was, according to journalists Rowland Evans and Robert Novak, a "clandestine 'black propaganda' organized by a dozen brainy Washington-based Democrats, some in and some out of the government." White House aide Myer Feldman oversaw this "Five O'clock Club" of young attorneys and government officials. They worked on "counteroffensive" maneuvers of "deviltry" to keep Goldwater off balance and to help Johnson gain a landslide victory. They followed all the Goldwater-Miller statements and prepared responses that showed where the GOP was wrong. They gave Goldwater's traveling press corps critical questions to ask the candidate. They importuned friendly newspaper columnists to write more anti-Goldwater editorials. They even beseeched Ann Landers to use her advice column to help the president. Not all in the Johnson circle liked this committee. Press secretary George Reedy observed: "That was a childish sort of operation, which had no purpose, and did absolutely nothing but I think maybe create a little bit of sympathy for Goldwater."[56]

Not only did Johnson spend too much time on campaign strategy, he also obsessed about public polling. He almost always had copies of the latest favorable poll in his pocket. The Gallup Poll organization agreed to "cooperate" with the Johnson campaign "on a confidential basis" and share data they collected but had not published. The organization also consented to "conduct 'flash' telephone surveys . . . on specific developments." Jack Valenti told LBJ, "Our main strength lies not so much in the FOR Johnson but in the AGAINST Goldwater," meaning that "we ought to treat Goldwater not as an equal, who has credentials to be President, but as a *radical*, a preposterous candidate who would ruin this country and our future." To that end, Valenti called for "humor, barbs, jokes, ridicule" but no "answer[ing] his charges seriously." Valenti wanted to treat Miller in the same fashion, "as some April Fool's gag" and not "Vice Presidential material," depicting his "absentee record" and the "lack of confidence in him by his own constituents." Valenti stressed that the public must remain afraid of Goldwater and what he might do, especially since the Republicans were increasingly focusing on efforts to *"demean the President."* Valenti emphasized Democrats must be on the attack: "Hit Goldwater-Miller HARD through other voices on their own immorality of the Republican party." He concluded, "President stays above the battle. He is President and acts like one."[57]

What battle plan would Johnson use to gain sufficient states to carry the Electoral College? In the mid-twentieth century liberal Democrats concentrated on the Midwest from Kansas City north to Minneapolis and then the northeast over to Boston and south to Baltimore. Leaving aside the South, which likely would not vote for Johnson because of civil rights, the only other sometimes Democratic state was California. If 1964 had been a typical year, then Johnson would have focused on those regions, but with the Goldwater nomination LBJ saw the opportunity to claim a nationwide landslide. "There were the Senatorial and Congressional weaklings of his ticket whom he could thus help by flying visits; there was his own nostalgic connection with the South, for Lyndon Johnson wanted his Southland with him as much as Kennedy had wanted his New England."[58]

Foreign policy proved one more consideration for Democrats and Republicans. The pertinent questions were, first, whether and how much should Democrats capitalize on Goldwater's views on atomic weapons and second, would voters listen to Goldwater's criticism of Vietnam policy. Johnson worried little how and whether foreign policy would shape the election. Indeed, there was not a substantial foreign policy debate in the fall campaign but nevertheless Goldwater's pronouncements did provide substantial Democratic fodder to suggest he was unfit for the White House. Goldwater hoped his greater decisiveness and his bluntness would give him an advantage with foreign policy, but in reality the Arizonan turned these into a deficit. Clark Clifford contended Goldwater's intemperate statements "scared a lot of people to death," specifically his call to use nuclear weapons in Southeast Asia. Clifford recounted the slogan that emerged from Goldwater's promise: "within the Republican party there'd been two great figures, Lincoln was the great emancipator and Goldwater was the great defoliator."[59]

Earlier in October 1963, Goldwater had attended a political caucus in Hartford, Connecticut, with state GOP leaders. While there, Goldwater held a press conference. Reporters asked him about Eisenhower's assertion that the US military could reduce the number of NATO divisions from six down to one. Goldwater agreed, especially if NATO commanders were authorized to use tactical nuclear weapons without securing authorization from the military hierarchy. Upon hearing the candidate's answer, Goldwater's press adviser halted the conference, but the image of Goldwater as a bomb thrower had been etched in the American psyche. Journalist Theodore White argued because of Goldwater's statements about nuclear weaponry and military policy more generally the 1964 election became a referendum on "peace and the *risk* of war." Dennison Kitchel observed, "When I went to bed . . . I would lie awake asking myself at night, how do you get at the bomb issue? My candidate had been branded bomb dropper—and I couldn't figure out how to lick it. And the advertising people, people who could sell anything, toothpaste or soap or automobiles—when it came to a political question like this they couldn't offer anything either."[60]

Vietnam intruded into the campaign in part because of international events and in part because of Goldwater's strategy. The Arizona senator charged that Democrats were soft on communism and the country should fight in North Vietnam and China if necessary. Such statements grew more potent after the Gulf of Tonkin incident wherein it was reported the North Vietnamese had fired on US warships and the United States issued retaliatory air strikes. In response, Congress passed the Gulf of Tonkin Resolution. When charges of further North Vietnamese aggression reached the White House, Johnson's advisors stressed the president must not make promises to keep American troops out of Vietnam as Woodrow Wilson had done in 1916 and Franklin D. Roosevelt had done in 1940. Indeed, Johnson had talked regularly about the threats in Vietnam and his intent to maintain US commitments there, even increasing involvement to match the greater danger presented by the North Vietnamese. He mixed such specific rhetoric with calls for peace more generally. He was not interested in escalation for the sake of escalation. In late September he expressed his skepticism about a reported attack against a US position: Johnson told Robert McNamara, "I don't want them just being some change-o'-life woman running up and saying that, by God, she was being raped just because a man walks in the room!"[61]

Goldwater made Vietnam an issue when he talked of using low-level nuclear weapons to defoliate Communist supply lines from North to South Vietnam. What he did not realize was that such statements hurt his candidacy. He did so in an interview with Howard K. Smith on the ABC news program, *Issues and Answers*. On that same show Goldwater suggested he would not hesitate to escalate the war into "Red China," arguing "either that, or we have a war dragged out and dragged out. A defensive war is never won." When the media published stories about Goldwater's statements, the candidate complained he had been quoted out of context. Certainly, he did qualify his statements and certainly he drew on ideas long discussed in the Pentagon. Yet, as he attempted to clarify and minimize the damage, he made other remarks that exacerbated matters and invited a foreign policy backlash: "If I had my choice, I would go into South China. It would be fairly easy. You have one railroad. You have a number of bridges. You would knock out the railroad: if that did not convince them, you would knock out the roads."[62]

Ultimately, Johnson supporters made foreign policy a Democratic advantage when they used humor to reinforce the image of Goldwater as an extremist. For example, the Americans for Democratic Action distributed a satiric treatment of what the United States might look like under a Goldwater presidency. The pamphlet "Through a Looking Glass Darkly: A Political Fantasy" fulminated about the Far Right–wing government ADA officials feared Goldwater might lead. The pamphlet suggested a President Goldwater might take the United States out of the United Nations, sell the TVA, eliminate half the State Department employees, and lease the empty space in the State Department to a private corporation. Moreover, Johnson proponents had fun with Goldwater's slogan, "In Your Heart You Know He's Right!" saying alternately "In Your Heart You Know He Might" and "In Your Guts You Know He's Nuts!"[63]

By Labor Day Johnson enjoyed a two-to-one lead over Goldwater. He hoped to win in such a way that his victory would not be tied to remembrances of Kennedy but instead would be affirmation of his political skills and ambition. Moreover, he also wanted a wider margin of victory than any previous president in US history, meaning besting FDR's 1936 victory of 60.8 percent of the vote. Throughout the campaign Johnson worried over every detail and feared the worst possible outcome. He had no respect for Goldwater, believing if he won terrible consequences would result for the country. Business leader Cornelius Vanderbilt sent a message to Johnson after the GOP convention that *"the entire buildup of the GOLDWATER group*

Democrats had two responses to the Goldwater slogan, depicted on the campaign button shown on the lower left: "yes, far right" and "in your guts you know he's nuts." Author's personal collection.

follows the line of the Nazis, pre-WWII." Other quarters of the nation contributed to the narrative that Goldwater was not fit to be president. *Fact* magazine surveyed the 12,000 psychiatrists practicing in the United States, and only 657 agreed Goldwater was fit to be president. Another 1,189 concluded he suffered from paranoia. Democrats believed there was no limit to what Goldwater might do to try to win. They worried the Arizonan would capitalize on a growing civil rights backlash.[64]

Johnson commented to Richard Goodwin, a White House speech writer, "What the man on the street wants is not a big debate on fundamental issues. He wants a little medical care, a rug on the floor, a picture on the wall, a little music in the house, and a place to take Molly and the grandchildren when he retired." To LBJ that meant more New Deal economic liberalism, but this formula was not stable. The genesis of that social contract was linked to the Great Depression, but according to some, was foundering in the 1960s. Johnson understood. Goldwater drew his strength from "the outgrowth of long, long public unrest with Big Government, Big Spending," Johnson intoned, "and feeling that 'Washington doesn't understand our problems.'"[65]

The two candidates began campaigning around Labor Day. Goldwater opened his fall campaign on September 3 on the courthouse steps in Prescott, Arizona, as had been his habit in all of his Senate races. Goldwater's uncle had served as mayor of Prescott for twenty-six years. The event did not go well for Goldwater: the date and time of the event was changed at the last minute, no national broadcast coverage was secured, press accommodations were in a different location from the press room, and the crowd was small, just 4,000 people.[66]

Johnson opened his campaign in Detroit over Labor Day weekend. Speaking to a crowd of 100,000, he deviated from the typical partisan speeches previous Democratic candidates had used on that occasion. He aimed high, but missed when he attempted a more statesmanlike approach akin to what FDR had used in his three reelection bids. The president suggested his remarks were not political, but the Democratic National Committee funded the travel from Washington, DC. Johnson wanted to articulate a frontlash economic philosophy, but he never successfully merged that with his New Deal heritage. LBJ discussed with Bill Moyers what he wanted from his Labor Day address. He asked for "a little of this Holy Roller populist stuff," including "at least two biblical quotations . . . that every one of them have heard." In dictating ideas for his speech to Moyers, Johnson grew vaguer and vaguer all the while borrowing phrasing and ideas from Martin Luther King Jr.'s "I Have a Dream" speech. The result was a bland speech that promised a better life for all Americans.[67]

Johnson did not follow his Labor Day campaign speech with more campaigning as did Goldwater. He had good reason for delaying his formal campaign. White House staffer George Reedy explained, "It became obvious right from the start that the most effective campaign speeches for Lyndon Johnson were being made by Barry Goldwater" when he talked about selling the TVA, or reducing Social Security, or bombing the Kremlin. Moreover, Johnson's closest advisors had, both before and after the conventions, told the president to stay in the White House and show the American people through "periodic use of the television networks . . . that the man behind the big desk in the Oval Office was taking good care of the people's business."[68]

Goldwater's team conversely had wanted "a majestic dialogue on the two American philosophies, the conservative and the liberal." Their desired format was a series of seven speeches on the critical issues: the draft and national defense, a major reduction to income taxes, social overreach by the Supreme Court, the role of the federal government, the meaning of freedom, and civil rights. Kitchel complained that Johnson did not campaign in September and that he showed no interest in undertaking a campaign of the style Goldwater envisioned. Johnson's only travel was presidential and nonpartisan. Kitchel concluded, "Lyndon Johnson was so far away from it, we couldn't find an opponent. We were punching at a pillow." Later Goldwater fumed just how much differently the campaign would have been had Jack Kennedy not been shot: "I could tell him what I felt about his proposals. 'That's no good, Jack,' I would say, or 'That part is okay. That's fine.' And he'd listen. He would have debated me. It would have been good for the campaign. It would have been a good campaign."[69]

Instead, after his Labor Day opening speech, Johnson directed Lawrence O'Brien to call a series of confidential regional meetings, which would reveal the political situation in every state. This directive was intended to remedy the president's feeling of being "out of touch," with national political affairs. O'Brien's job was to "be the presidential eyes and ears." To attend the regional meetings took six weeks of travel to and from Washington so he could "talk politics to a dozen or so top leaders in every state. In sessions behind locked doors, lasting three or four hours, every detail of the campaign was ruthlessly laid out." After such meetings, "O'Brien locked himself in his hotel room and wrote a voluminous confidential report for the President, which was sent by Western Union to the White House the instant it was finished." Evans and Novak contended that "the O'Brien reports became The Word. Their recommendations were carved up and passed among the staff of the White House" where they "came quickly to have the same urgent classification as a National Intelligence Estimate from the CIA."[70]

Johnson was better prepared to enter the fall campaign. His election team was organized in a manner that fit his own style, the contest of 1964, and pursuit of a frontlash strategy. Goldwater, on the other hand, never figured out how to move from a convention message geared toward the party's right wing to all American voters. Never fully determining a position about backlash hurt Goldwater with voters. He just could not overcome Johnson's enthusiasm for the campaign and election. Said Katie Louchheim: "You never know with the President. He does everything himself. He chairs the meetings, does the work, and on the days when he decides he is also the first lady's Press secy, it's rough." Nor could Goldwater diminish the voter desire for "a *Can Do* President during the coming years."[71] Indeed, Johnson's sun portended results while Goldwater's did not.

7

"GOVERNMENT IS NOT AN ENEMY OF THE PEOPLE. IT IS THE PEOPLE"

In the fall campaign Barry Goldwater and Lyndon Johnson debated whether the federal government operated in the best interest of the American people. On that issue more than any other the stark differences between their two suns became obvious. Negative messaging was crucial to both Democrats and Republicans, but they went about it in very divergent ways. Both relied on the publication of books as well as television commercials, but both deployed these resources in contrasting ways. Johnson's operation was more centralized. He had two goals: maximize the frontlash and convince American voters of the continued efficacy of the federal government. Often grandiose, the words he spoke were about consensus and a Great Society for all. Words spoken on his behalf, especially campaign ads, were harsh and audacious.

Goldwater's negative message criticizing government activism unfolded in decentralized fashion. The result was a discordant message, mixing themes of immorality and antistatism. He made a political appeal to those Americans who feared loss of status to individuals they deemed unworthy of full citizenship. In so doing he encouraged dissension and revealed lurid, bilious tendencies in American politics, especially the use of morality politics to divide Americans. Ultimately their contest over the meaning of the government—whether or not it was the enemy of the people—was not resolved in 1964 but was the opening round in a political siege fought for the remainder of the century and into the twenty-first century about the utility of liberalism and conservatism as governing ideologies.

To promote his candidacy, Johnson published his book, *My Hope for America*. White House aide S. Douglass Cater compiled the manuscript from speeches Johnson had made as president. Random House, the publisher, planned an original run of 400,000 copies. Cater explained the genesis of the book: "I saw that Goldwater was flooding the market with various Goldwater books, and there was no Johnson book by him." The Goldwater books included *Where I Stand*, which was a "rather shoddy paperback" printed on poor-quality paper. Still, according to one Johnson partisan, the Goldwater book was making an impact because "a couple of 'reasonable' people reading" it reacted with "'indecision' about voting for the President." To counteract the right-wing offensive, the White House worked hard to get *My Hope for America* syndicated in the nation's newspapers as well as made available through book stores.[1]

When the first two advance copies arrived at the White House on September 19, Cater told LBJ: "It has been 26 days since we approached Random House, which makes book publishing history." Later Cater reported, "one of the editors worked with me 20 hours a day for a week running." Cater advised dispersing approximately 50,000 copies of the book to "opinion leaders" like Walter Lippmann. He wanted *My Hope for America* to go to all leaders recently invited to the White House; all presidential appointees; all DNC officials; all Democratic office holders down to the county chair level; all mayors; all labor union leaders; all members of the clergy; all high school teachers; all members of the AAUP; all local leaders of the League of Women Voters, the Business and Professional Women, and the American Association of University Women; all local American Legion and VFW commanders; and business leaders identified by advisors to the campaign. By mid-October, Cater estimated that 48.2 million copies of the book had been disseminated. The *New York Times* said of the spate of books published to influence the 1964 campaign: "Never before have paperback books of any category been printed and distributed in such volume in such a short time."[2]

Not all of the books published in 1964 were favorable to Johnson. *A Choice, Not an Echo*, by Phyllis Schlafly, *A Texan Looks at Lyndon*, by J. Evetts Haley, and *None Dare Call It Treason*, by John Stormer created real problems for Democrats. The Republican Party and the John Birch Society were both doling out the books as were other right-wing organizations. Though Stormer was not a member of the JBS, one conservative Goldwater supporter described *None Dare Call It Treason* as "vintage John Birch Society propaganda" and "hopelessly simplistic as geopolitical analysis." White

House advisor Lawrence O'Brien recounted, "a national effort is being made to get these books into the hands of voters, particularly in the non-industrial, marginal States of the Midwest, West, and South." He stressed to LBJ that the "books are being *read*" and they "are hurting." He did not want Johnson to respond to the books, though, arguing that work should be done by surrogates.[3]

The right-wing books proved popular. Reputedly Haley's diatribe against Johnson sold over 7 million copies. A Johnson aide complained "carload[s]" of the Haley book were dispatched in Arkansas, Missouri, and Oklahoma, and rumors suggested Spanish translations had been made available along the US-Mexico border. When interested voters contacted the Republican National Committee or Citizens for Goldwater-Miller for copies of *None Dare Call It Treason* or *A Texan Looks at Lyndon* or *A Choice, Not an Echo*, party officials directed the callers to a Houston, Texas, distribution company that handled book sales. The party refused to benefit from the books, but the same was not true for the right-wing groups that created the books. They profited handsomely. The Houston company also sold an anti-Goldwater book, *Barry Goldwater: Extremist on the Right* by Fred J. Cook. The Democratic National Committee, unlike the RNC, did sell Cook's book, and it earned a commission from the publisher on its sales.[4]

More wide-reaching than book publications were television ads. After Labor Day Goldwater seemed to have a "far superior" television advertising strategy than did Johnson. The GOP had hired the Interpublic Group of New York, the largest marketing-communications company in the world. Interpublic used modern computing technology to evaluate the last three presidential campaigns from several different angles, including partisanship, state level results, and ethnicity. The purpose was identification of swing states and development of plans to reach those voters. They also studied the sizeable television markets to discern how to reach more voters for less money. There was just one problem with this initiative. Interpublic could never establish a clear line of communication with Goldwater or his campaign.[5]

Johnson and his staff, though, proved very hands on with their advertising strategy. In this area of the campaign Johnson did not deviate from what Kennedy had intended. The Kennedy administration had been considering hiring Madison Avenue firm Doyle Dane Bernbach (DDB) for the 1964 campaign prior to Kennedy's murder. DDB had created the popular and successful "Think Small" ads for Volkswagen and had a reputation for being "on the cutting edge of the new media technology." Johnson's team signed a contract with DDB on March 19, 1964, despite DNC concerns that the agency was too expensive. DDB wanted the assignment. The creative director told Bill Moyers: "We are ardent Democrats who are deadly afraid of Goldwater." During the 1960s most advertising agencies were strongly Republican. DDB confessed desire for a Johnson landslide, explaining "we risked the possible resentment of some of our giant Republican clients."[6]

Because there were many more Democrats among the voting public than Republicans, Democratic advertisements underscored the party, while GOP advertisements accentuated individual candidates. Indeed, the Johnson advertisements did not match the "nonpartisan," frontlash message from the candidate, but the discordance between the conflicting messages worked because Goldwater was the GOP nominee. He faced his own messaging difficulties. There were key distinctions in the types of ads Democrats and Republicans ran. The Democrats most often ran short ads, having only eight programs preempted, but the GOP typically ran half hour commercials that required preempting thirteen separate programs. Moreover, Goldwater was prominently featured in most GOP ads; Johnson was but a bit player in Democratic spots. Their relative positions, one the sitting president known across the country and the other a senator from Arizona and less well known, illustrated in part their varying advertising styles. Another contrast between the two involved the use, or not, of the vice-presidential contenders. Goldwater's ads routinely mentioned Bill Miller, suggesting their administration would be a team effort. Johnson's ads did not allude to Hubert Humphrey. The tone of the ads diverged as well with Democratic ads first attacking Goldwater on the issues, second making a proactive argument for Johnson's accomplishments, and third urging Americans to vote. Republican ads meanwhile deployed two themes: first defending Goldwater from Democratic charges and then attacking LBJ for letting the morality of the country atrophy.[7]

Johnson worried that Goldwater might shuck his extremist reputation. Moyers discussed the concern with DDB. Their reply was the infamous "Daisy Ad," which, Moyers clarified, "remind[ed] people that Barry Goldwater had spoken loosely and lightly and recklessly about the overarching issue of nuclear power." At the core of Johnson's campaign blitz was the usage of negative television advertising, clearly a smearlash, despite his claim that only Republicans engaged in such negative tactics. The campaign budgeted $3 million for local stations and $1.7 million for network programming. The Daisy Ad, which was aired on Monday, September 7 on NBC's *Monday Night at the Movies*, was the first commercial issued from the Johnson campaign.

These images depict the girl picking petals from a daisy in the infamous "Daisy Ad." A few seconds later the camera closes in on her eye, which then shows a nuclear explosion. Courtesy of the Democratic National Committee.

It featured a young girl pulling petals off a flower, actually a black-eyed Susan, and counting to ten. The camera narrowed to her right eye before the screen went dark and a nuclear bomb exploded into a mushroom cloud. Johnson himself provided the voiceover: "These are the stakes—to make a world in which all of God's children can live, or to go into the dark. We must love each other, or we must die." An announcer concluded, "Vote for President Johnson on November 3. The stakes are too high for you to stay home." The White House had only planned for one airing of the commercial, and when the angry calls came in they adhered to this schedule, not for fear that they had gone too far but because they knew the ad had worked. After feigning outrage about the Daisy Ad, Johnson called Moyers aside and asked him, "You sure we ought to run it just once?"[8]

The Daisy commercial was new and different in that it traded in the currency of emotion, not reason, in making the case to vote for Johnson. It was the first television advertisement to use fear as a motivator. The ad did not create the fear of nuclear war, but instead channeled extant fears among the American people. Other critical components of the ad included the use of narrative and symbolism. For example, the little girl embodied the nation's safety at risk from a Goldwater presidency. The argument in the ad was not rational so it was impossible to dispute the ad's point of view. Moreover, it was the first ad to generate coverage by the news media. Widely criticized as unfair by the news media in the years that followed, the ad nevertheless did draw on many statements Goldwater had made about his willingness to use nuclear weapons. To attack the ad, as some have done, requires a certain ignorance of Goldwater's record. O'Brien saw "nothing unfair" in the decision "because we were just holding him to his own statements."[9]

Though Johnson never used the Daisy Ad again, similar spots did air. Reedy counseled Johnson, "The one thing we ought to get at is mothers that are worried about having radioactive poisoning in their kid's milk," birth defects in children, and men concerned "about becoming sterile." One featured a girl eating an ice cream cone with a woman talking in the background about the danger of ending the nuclear test ban treaty as Goldwater advocated: "there is a man who . . . doesn't like this treaty. He's . . . voted against it. He wants to go on testing more bombs. His name is Barry Goldwater, and if he's elected, they might start testing all over again." The commercial ended with the same warning about voting for Johnson. Like the Daisy Ad it only ran once. Moyers contended, "The big issue in the country was Strontium 90. Mothers were marching. The dairy industry was greatly concerned. Kennedy had addressed it before his death. That issue played into our hands because Goldwater had called for more nuclear testing."[10]

Goldwater was nonplussed. He eviscerated the ads, saying of them voters "are horrified and the intelligence of Americans is insulted by weird television advertising by which this administration threatens the end of the world unless all-wise Lyndon Johnson is given the nation for his very own." Years later Goldwater complained, "The commercials completely misrepresented my position, which called for treaty guarantees and other safeguards for the United States. . . . Those bomb commercials were the start of dirty political ads on television. It was the beginning of what I call 'electronic dirt.'" According to Goldwater, journalist Ben Bradlee said the bomb commercials were "a fucking outrage."[11]

A Republican insider complained about how Johnson manipulated the media, first, by his Austin television station deciding not to air two of Goldwater's nationally televised speeches, and second, by going on television live to address the nation about a myriad of topics as president. Indeed, Johnson used television appearances more frequently than had either Eisenhower or Kennedy. Johnson also maneuvered the press corps. "Reporters are puppets. They simply respond to the pull of the most powerful strings," Johnson told Doris Kearns. "Every story is always slanted to win the favor of someone who sits somewhere higher up. There is no such thing as an objective news story. There is always a private story behind the public story. And if you don't control the strings to that private story, you'll never get good coverage."[12]

Goldwater relied on a completely different advertising strategy, thirty-minute television programs. He delivered a half-hour paid television address where he tried to undo the damage done by Democratic attacks, specifically that he was trigger-happy. The speech did not work. Goldwater never changed the battlefield from the one Johnson had chosen. According to Goldwater advisor Stephen Shadegg, "No one was happy with the speech. It was defensive, it dealt in generalities, and it opened with Goldwater's repeating the charges his opponents were making, i.e. that he was impulsive, imprudent, and trigger-happy."[13]

Several of Goldwater's half-hour commercials attempted to remake his image. Goldwater took to morning television in a "happy, gossipy" paid program entitled *Brunch with Barry* in late October 1964. Senator Margaret Chase Smith (R-ME), who had challenged Goldwater in the primaries, moderated the twenty-five-minute panel discussion, which included the GOP candidate and five women. Goldwater used the extended campaign advertisement to try to soften his image while also holding firm to his anti-communist message. In the program he attacked "segregation by compulsion" and "integration by compulsion." John Wayne provided the narration for a thirty-minute program that sketched out Goldwater's biography. The Arizonan explained he had entered politics to create a world safe for his children. He told voters that "Politics [was] young people getting married and forming families, buying homes."[14]

Goldwater's team recruited Eisenhower, hoping an endorsement from the popular former president would shift the momentum in Goldwater's favor. Because Ike had earlier implied Goldwater was not suited for the presidency, the Goldwater campaign opted instead to film a conversation between the two men. The session in Gettysburg, Pennsylvania, proved disastrous. Ike wanted to say that the charges of nuclear irresponsibility levied against Goldwater were "bullshit," but he knew the language was inappropriate for television. He settled on using the word "tommyrot" to try and vindicate the GOP nominee. Throughout the interview process Eisenhower appeared disinterested and his syntax was often garbled, witness his assertion the United States must "preserve the outbreak of war." Goldwater looked like a supplicant seeking approval that would never be sufficient.[15]

That thirty-minute conversation was aired on September 22 against two low-brow television programs, Petticoat Junction and Peyton Place. The latter earned ratings of 27.4 and 25.0 compared with just 8.6 for the Goldwater ad. Eisenhower never directly endorsed the GOP nominee. Later Goldwater observed of the broadcast, "the most charitable thing I can say about the film is that it wasn't effective."[16]

Some half-hour Goldwater advertisements were targeted to particular regions or states. Goldwater wanted to win Texas, and he used a former LBJ congressional challenger, Hardy Hollers, to suggest Johnson was not a proper American. Hollers stated his opposition to Johnson for president in 1964 on a Doctors for Goldwater statewide TV program in Texas. He compared Johnson to "Hitler and his crew of very curious people" and argued the Civil Rights Act of 1964 gave the president "all the power A. Hitler ever had." Another speaker on this program said Hubert Humphrey was a Socialist, that Johnson was "pretty much branded with the same brand," and that socialism and communism were about the same.[17]

Neither candidate was especially eager to go out on the campaign trail. Johnson enjoyed pressing the flesh but doing so in 1964 was not necessarily in his interest. One of Johnson's strongest arguments for his election was being president, therefore going on the campaign trail contradicted his use of the White House itself as a prop and symbol. Goldwater on the other hand did not enjoy campaigning. Both had preconceived notions about where and how they should campaign. The South was crucial to the strategy of each. Their priorities reveal the very different ways they interpreted the rising Sunbelt.

Since the end of the summer the White House had been looking for ways to keep the South Democratic and if not that then at least southern officeholders in sync with the party. Governor Farris Bryant of Florida, who was term-limited out of office, told the White House that Governor George C. Wallace of Alabama would do "everything humanly possible under cover to help Goldwater." Indeed, before the summer was even over some of the more racially rabid southern Democrats had begun swinging toward Goldwater with the most well-known being Wallace. As had been the case during the GOP convention when Wallace lobbied for the number two spot on that ticket, Goldwater and his team were not sure how to handle Wallace. GOP vice-presidential candidate William E. Miller questioned whether Goldwater should accept support from Wallace. Said Miller, "No, I don't think so. Governor Wallace is a Democrat."[18]

Governor Orval Faubus in Arkansas focused on his race against Republican Winthrop Rockefeller, which "is his only concern." In August, the Goldwater campaign had learned that "Faubus will NOT endorse Johnson" but instead supported Goldwater. Campaign leaders did not want this made public because "this would hurt nationally." Indeed, the race in Arkansas proved complicated because Rockefeller polled well with Johnson voters and Faubus had the support of Goldwater voters. The Goldwater campaign believed that a candidate visit to the state might secure a Republican win there, but they also acknowledged "it is an 'iffy' sort of thing, and the electoral rewards are small. Goldwater would be better off spending such time in Ohio or Illinois. Besides, a joint Goldwater-Rockefeller appearance might lose votes for both."[19]

In late September, Ralph McGill, the editor and publisher of the *Atlanta Constitution,* told Johnson, "What disturbs me about the rural South . . . is something which began during the months when George Wallace was campaigning for the nomination." Specifically, McGill elucidated that John Grenier, "the Republican Committee's Simon Legree in charge of Southern delegates at San Francisco," had made great use of "demagoguery" to inflame voter passions. He did so by sending GOP operatives to Alabama, Georgia, Louisiana, North Carolina, and South Carolina where they were tasked with "drift[ing] from town to town getting hold of the racist type leadership." As they traveled these operatives "sowed the rumor" that 10 percent of white mill workers would lose their jobs to African Americans. "They also frightened the small-town barbershops, restaurants, and beauty parlors," McGill cautioned, "with exaggerated stories of how the public accommodations law would flood them with Negro customers." Such tactics caused mill workers who had benefited from Johnson administration cotton policy to grumble about its civil rights policy, a classic example of the backlash working for Goldwater. Indeed, McGill concluded, these small town institutions were "in an ugly mood."[20]

Southerners who participated in Goldwater's campaign trips to the region noted the overwhelming excitement for the candidate. One reported, "I have yet to hear a Southerner say he is going to vote for Johnson." Another said the Arizona senator was more popular than the Beatles, exhorting "they just went nuts over" Goldwater. Later Goldwater campaign workers observed in October, "Early in the campaign, both the stringer and newspaper columnists pointed to a Goldwater sweep in Florida. But now they say Johnson is coming on fast, and a few predict that Johnson will win. The rest rate Florida a toss-up."[21]

The region where Johnson least wanted to campaign was the Northeast where he assumed he would not be welcome. The conventional wisdom also suggested Goldwater was unpopular there. Johnson nevertheless began his campaigning in earnest on September 28 in New England. He enjoyed large, enthusiastic crowds in Vermont, New Hampshire, Maine, Connecticut, and Rhode Island, revealing just how successfully he had transcended the Sunbelt and convinced voters to welcome his sun of inclusivity. The president was shocked by the warm and enthusiastic greeting he received there, and he dragged an AP reporter to the rope line so he could see the "proof the people *did* like" Johnson and "write *that* in your story."[22]

Such popular enthusiasm spurred Democrats to heighten their response to Goldwater. Johnson strategists missed no opportunity to draw attention to Goldwater's recklessness. Surrogate speakers were a central part of this approach. The Democratic National Committee used Franklin Roosevelt Jr., Stewart Udall, and Harry S. Truman to rebut Goldwater. They wanted the Democratic responses delivered from the city where Goldwater would be speaking before he made his speech, turning rebuttals into prebuttals. A White House aide explained, "We are not waiting until Goldwater actually speaks, as that would be too late to get decent coverage." More unexpected, though was the use of popular culture. In late September Bill Moyers wrote to the president that they had in the White House a copy of the movie, *Fail*

*LBJ campaigning to an enthusiastic New England crowd, September 28. LBJ
Library, photo by Cecil Stoughton.*

Safe, "which we have arranged to be released in about ten days. It should
have pretty good impact on the campaign in our favor, since it deals with
irresponsibility in the handling of nuclear weapons."[23]

Despite all this, journalists asserted at the end of September Goldwater
still had a modicum of hope. His next major task was a four-day whistle
stop tour of the Midwest. The tour was necessary to claim three crucial
states—Ohio, Indiana, and Illinois—and expand on his base of support
in the South. Polling suggested the Midwest was strongly Democratic, but
late September–early October was the last chance to shift the momentum
toward the GOP. The whistle stop, though, lacked any sense of urgency.
Goldwater's speeches failed to achieve his goal for the trip—that was to assuage concerns that he would lead the country into World War III. Instead,
Goldwater in just one speech made almost thirty warlike, pugnacious references toward the Soviet Union and communism more generally. By the end
of the whistle stop some journalists concluded, "Goldwater was running
not so much against Johnson as against himself—or the Barry Goldwater
the image-makers had created." One Ohio Republican operative observed
in late September, "I don't know what there is now that can save this thing
except maybe an act of God, and you know those things don't come along
too often in a lifetime."[24]

With election day about a month away reports came in about how Johnson would fare around the country. In early October Lawrence F. O'Brien, who had been tasked with overseeing this reporting, updated Johnson on how the race looked in the Mountain West, the Midwest, and the border South. Michigan was described as the "best organized Northern State. You should win big here." Moreover, the president looked like he might become the first Democrat to take Indiana since 1936. States that remained close included Arkansas, Colorado, Kansas, Kentucky, Missouri, Nebraska, North Dakota, Oklahoma, and Wisconsin. O'Brien told Johnson, "You are about to make history in New England. You should become the first Democratic candidate for President in history to win all six New England states." The campaign had set its sights in that region back in the summer. Reports were not universally glowing, though. In mid-October Johnson received substantial pressure to visit New Mexico because it was "not safe for the President." He flew to Albuquerque on October 27 and was a greeted by enthusiastic crowds. The next day approximately 60,000 people lined his motorcade route, and 35,000 attended his speech.[25]

Attention shifted back to the South and the Sunbelt pretty quickly. Goldwater campaigned in South Carolina on September 17, 1964, the day after Strom Thurmond announced he was switching parties and supporting the GOP nominee. Over 20,000 turned out to welcome Goldwater, and traffic backed up for three miles on Interstate 85 near the Greenville-Spartanburg airport. Welcoming the candidate were marching bands and Goldwater Girls. The crowd was so enthusiastic that the cordon of police officers could not keep order. Fisticuffs ensued between law enforcement and teenagers who wanted to get closer to their idol. Forty-five people required medical attention, mostly for fainting, but two people had heart attacks. In response, South Carolina Democrats asked that Johnson come to the state. They noted that Thurmond's "defection" had weakened the Democratic Party in the state and meant LBJ might lose there. When Thurmond switched parties and stumped for Goldwater in the South he attracted racially conservative whites to the GOP and gave the emerging southern strategy a tinge of racism. Indeed, 1964 started the trajectory of the Deep South voting for the Republican candidate and not the Democratic contender in part because the GOP showed no interest in winning southern black votes.[26]

Journalist Richard Rovere, who covered the Goldwater campaign's mid-September tour of the old Confederacy, ruminated on the absence of African Americans in the cities they visited. "It was weird," Rovere avowed. "In a Negroless Memphis or Atlanta or New Orleans, many of

Goldwater Girls, 1964, campaigning for the Republican nominee. Charles Moore Photographic Archive, e_clm_0496, Dolph Briscoe Center for American History, University of Texas at Austin.

us had the feeling of having lost our bearings. We would peer out beyond the edges of the crowds and down side streets to see if we could spot a single Negro, and, whenever we saw one, advise one another of our rare discovery." Rovere had been a political journalist for three decades, but he observed of this southern trip in 1964: "never until I went South with Barry Goldwater had I heard any large number of Americans boo and hoot at the mention of the name of the President of the United States. In Alabama and Louisiana, there were thunderous, stadium-filling boos, all of them cued by a United States Senator."[27] Here in this setting Goldwater was comfortable mixing the politics of resentment with conservatism, showing his sun to be dark.

Rovere described the southern Goldwater rallies as more than political events. "They were revels, they were pageants, they were celebrations," claimed Rovere, "The aim of the revelers" was to enable "great numbers of unapologetic white supremacists to hold great carnivals of white supremacy." He concluded, "As long as they could put on shows of this kind, no Negro would ever want in." One observer of the 1964 race recounted Confederate flags were more common at Goldwater rallies than American flags and "Dixie" was played more frequently than the national anthem. At a

Spartanburg, South Carolina rally the grand dragon of the South Carolina Ku Klux Klan sat on the stage.[28]

Goldwater's understanding of freedom privileged protecting free-market capitalism from government intrusion and regulation, not guaranteeing civil rights for those left out of the American Dream. He insisted he was not biased against African Americans, but civil rights leaders had a more complicated view. Roger Wilkins intimated that Goldwater believed he was not a racist but that he also thought, "the strength of the country was in white male entrepreneurs, and so let the white guys do what they need to do to be entrepreneurs, and sure, they get wealthy, but they use their wealth to create things, and that creates jobs and the country is strong and healthy." Such thinking explains why Republicans convinced themselves it was okay to use race to appeal for votes. Louisville, Kentucky Republicans disseminated flyers depicting Sammy Davis Jr., a popular African American entertainer, hugging a white woman. She was actually his wife. The president, Davis quoted in the flyer, was "for full integration, for preferential treatment in getting a job, for the right to live anywhere, for the right to marry anyone."[29]

Rovere attested the Goldwater movement in the South was "a racist movement and very little else. Goldwater seemed fully aware of this and not visibly distressed by it. He did not, to be sure, make any direct racist appeals." Never in this southern campaign did Goldwater talk openly about race or segregation or civil rights. Instead, Rovere argued, "He talked about them all the time in an underground, or Aesopian, language—a kind of code that few in his audiences had any trouble deciphering. In the code, 'bullies and marauders' means 'Negroes.' 'Criminal defendants' means 'Negroes.' 'States' rights' means 'opposition to civil rights.' 'Women' means 'white women.'" Such coded language did not need translation for northern audiences, but other phrasings did. Rovere provided the dictionary: "in the Old Confederacy, 'Lyndon Baines Johnson' and 'my opponent' mean 'integrationist.' 'Hubert Horatio' (it somehow amuses Goldwater to drop the 'Humphrey') means 'super-integrationist.' 'Federal judiciary' means 'integrationist judges.'"[30]

Goldwater, though, was not a cartoon character. Indeed, his attitude toward the Civil Rights Act, after it became law, was nuanced in ways that most liberals ignored. Goldwater asserted, "I think the legislative branch has now spoken for the majority." He promised he would "stand with the majority just as Harry Truman did when he vetoed the Taft-Hartley Act. He later used it six times even though he didn't like it." Still, whether Goldwater intended it or not his voters heard race when he discussed crime. Meanwhile, Republican vice-presidential candidate William Miller condemned Johnson for using the FBI to investigate the three missing civil rights workers in Philadelphia, Mississippi but not "protect[ing] the property and civil rights of thousands of people in Philadelphia, Pennsylvania," a reference to an August 1964 race riot there. Moreover, Goldwater said Washington, DC, a city with a large African American population, was "plagued by lawlessness, haunted by fears."[31]

Goldwater and Johnson hoped to have very different conversations about crime, reflecting their very different suns. Goldwater attributed the increased prevalence of crime as a reflection of society's—and liberalism's—degeneracy. Johnson wished to discuss federal solutions. Goldwater blamed federal paternalism for creating the conditions where crime flourished and Johnson emphasized more federal intervention was required. In mid-October, LBJ announced, "The war on poverty . . . is a war against crime and a war against disorder." He attacked Goldwater for voting against federal programs that would ameliorate the problem. "There is something mighty wrong when a candidate for the highest office bemoans violence in the streets but votes against the war on poverty, votes against the Civil Rights Act, and votes against major educational bills," Johnson opined. "The thing to do is not to talk about crime; the thing to do is to fight and work and vote against crime."[32]

From the old Confederacy to the southwest gender played important but subtle roles in the campaign. While Goldwater made the same appeal to women as he did to men, advocating a return to small government, his campaign also developed, in the words of one historian, "a maternal pro-Goldwater discourse." Indeed, Goldwater proved to be a compelling figure for many suburban, Sunbelt women. They volunteered in large numbers for his campaign in Southern California. Women and girls volunteered to be Goldwater Gals and Goldwater Girls, respectively. They functioned as hostesses and cheerleaders at campaign events, and they wore matching outfits, the Goldwater Gals clad in cowgirl uniforms and gold hats and the Goldwater Girls in long gold skirts, gold bandanas, and bright blue collars with gold embroidery or in blue skirts, white shirts, and red sashes and white cowboy hats. Hillary Rodham Clinton was perhaps the most famous Goldwater Girl.[33]

Conversely, Democratic women used traditional trappings to chart new territory for women in politics. The most notable example was the Lady Bird Special. Lady Bird Johnson became the first first lady to campaign independently for her husband's election. She did so regularly in 1964, but the most important example was a four-day, eight-state, 1,700-mile whistle stop tour of the Deep South. Johnson gave forty-seven speeches to over 200,000 people, many of them truculent toward the Democratic Party and her husband. The October 6–9 trip made for great press, related Liz Carpenter, with the major television networks giving it five minutes of coverage each night of the journey. This national audience appreciated Lady Bird's liberal message, but many whites in her native South did not welcome her support for civil rights.[34]

LBJ staff members believed Lady Bird was the best person to argue for an activist federal government in the South. One of Johnson's aides said the first lady "is *highly appealing* and *effective* on the platform. She comes across as intelligent and knowledgeable and *unlike* Eleanor Roosevelt thoroughly feminine." Johnson used the whistle stop to emphasize her husband's advocacy for consensus, a difficult task given her itinerary. The first lady told the crowd when she departed from Alexandria, Virginia, her feelings about the whistle stop: "anxiety" mixed with "anticipation." She chastised non-southerners for deriding the South as nothing more than "'corn pone' and 'rednecks.' . . . None of this is good for the future of our country. We must search for the ties that bind us together, not settle for the tensions that tend to divide us." She dismissed southern animosity toward the Civil Rights Act of 1964: "It would be a bottomless tragedy for our country to be racially divided. And here I want to say emphatically, this is not a challenge only in the South. It is a national challenge. . . . The laws that have been passed are national laws."[35]

The juxtaposition of southern black responses to the Lady Bird Special with those of southern racist whites proved stark. Reporters noted the "unspoken bond of sympathy displayed" by African Americans toward Lady Bird. Black Americans gathered along the railroad route in the towns too small for the train to even stop. No African American officials were members of the platform party, and very few local black dignitaries rode the train. Still, local white politicians took note of this grassroots support for the party that had been, historically, the party of segregation and discrimination. Not everywhere were white audiences happy to see Johnson. Goldwater partisans carried signs that read, "Barry for the USA, Lyndon for the USSR." The worst of the protests occurred in Deep South cities. In Columbia, South Carolina, angry, jeering crowds disrupted Lady Bird's speech. Some of the ugliest demonstrations occurred in areas of the South where the African American population outstripped whites. One sign in the crowd in Charleston read "Black Bird Go Home."[36]

President Johnson greets Lady Bird Johnson in New Orleans at the conclusion of the Lady Bird Special, October 9, 1964. LBJ Library, photo by Cecil Stoughton.

If Lady Bird's whistle stop was a gamble then LBJ's New Orleans speech at the conclusion of her journey was nothing short of radical. Johnson gave about thirty-five minutes of prepared remarks akin to what he said at every other campaign stop. Then he abandoned his text, and spoke for another thirty-five minutes off-the-cuff. Johnson delivered before a stunned, integrated audience what two leading journalists, Katherine Graham and Mary McGrory, called the best political speech they had ever heard. He argued prosperity could not come to a divided nation that still observed the Mason-Dixon line and the color line. Instead, consensus liberalism was required. LBJ reminded his audience of what Robert E. Lee stated after the Civil War, that southerners must "raise their sons to be Americans." He then made two points about the divisive Civil Rights Act: "we have a Constitution and we have got a Bill of Rights, and we've got the law of the land. And two-thirds of the Democrats in the Senate voted for it, and three-fourths of the Republicans. And I signed it, and I am going to enforce it. . . . I'm not going to let them build up the hate . . . by appealing to their prejudice."[37]

He began with a history lesson about former senator Huey Long, a figure well-known in Louisiana. Johnson avowed, "The things that I am talking about from coast-to-coast . . . are the things that he talked about thirty years ago." Johnson then enumerated the Long agenda: educational access for everyone, employment access for everyone, social security for everyone, and medical care for the aged and ill, everyone. Long was "way ahead of them all because he was against poverty, *really* against it, and for the ordinary man, *really* for him." Johnson used Long to make the point that the South had long been held prostrate before the East, economically dependent on that region. Then he addressed the deleterious impact of race on southern politics by telling a story Sam Rayburn had shared about Senator Joseph Weldon Bailey, a Texas Democrat who died in 1929. Johnson recalled how Bailey viewed the South's economy: "we had been at the mercy of certain economic interests. . . . They have worked our women for five cents an hour, they have worked our men for a dollar a day, they have exploited our soil, they had let our resources go to waste, they had taken everything out of the grounds they could, and they had shipped it to other sections." Johnson explained that Bailey had wanted "to go back" to Mississippi where he was born "and make them one more Democratic speech." When Johnson reached his climax—expanding on Bailey and race-baiting in southern politics—the entire audience of 1,900 people sat stunned, and then gave the president a five-minute standing ovation. Johnson used Bailey's oratory to illustrate the danger of Goldwater. "Poor old State, they haven't heard a real Democratic speech in thirty years," Johnson stressed. Borrowing from Bailey, the president concluded, "All they ever hear at election time is 'Nigger, Nigger, Nigger!'"[38]

A white southerner from the audience observed to Jack Valenti after Johnson's New Orleans speech, "You know, I never really liked Johnson. I always thought he didn't really have it here," pointing to his heart, "but tonight, gawd-damn, he shoved it right up us and made us like it. That takes a fair amount of guts and I got to say Johnson showed us that tonight, that he did."[39]

This New Orleans speech was pure, authentic Johnson. Like everything else about his politics Johnson learned speechmaking in the rural South, where the victor was most often "the man who can out-shout, out-dramatize, out-campaign, out-smile and out-entertain the raw voters." Johnson wanted to be heir to Franklin D. Roosevelt, but stylistically, at least in southern settings, he more often resembled Huey Long. Some journalists also compared him to Harry S. Truman, especially his 1948 whistle stop campaign. Johnson's southern style, said journalist Theodore H. White, "at its best, is native American art, and it was probably in this idiom that America was governed for one hundred years." Johnson, though, was never fully comfortable in that voice, fearing it revealed a regionalism that would harm his search for consensus. Mary McGrory wrote in the *Washington Star* that Johnson wanted "to make it chic to be a Democrat" so that disaffected suburbanites would return to the party. White recounted, "Johnson, like so many other Southwesterners, has been brainwashed by the Eastern press and the manners of the great leaders of the past thirty years until any reference to this homely style in print enrages him as mockery."[40]

During the campaign Goldwater also spoke of things like freedom and civil rights, but when he did so he stood in stark contrast to the Goldwater who a few months earlier had voted against the Civil Rights Act of 1964. The action spoke louder than the words for voters. Moreover, in other speeches, Goldwater doubled-down on racial division and racial segregation. He emphasized anti-busing rhetoric in speeches given in Madison Square Garden and in Chicago in the last month of the campaign. Harry Jaffa, a conservative political science professor, and William Rehnquist, a Goldwater supporter and Phoenix attorney and future chief justice of the Supreme Court, drafted Goldwater's Chicago remarks. He told that audience of 2,500 it was "wrong" to "take some children" out of their schools and "bus them to others just to get a mixture of ethnic and racial groups that somebody thinks is desirable." He asserted "forced integration is just as wrong as forced segregation." Some journalists compared the speech— one of the few in which Goldwater discussed race—with Johnson's New Orleans address. The two speeches, though, could not have been more distinct. Johnson's, like his campaign, was inclusive of all Americans whereas Goldwater's was a defense of the racial status quo cloaked in the language of a "colorblind" Constitution.[41]

Race and region were just one part of this Sunbelt presidential campaign. The merger of religion and morality played an equally important role, and in the process shaped not only Goldwater's Sunbelt conservatism but also Johnson's consensus liberalism. Starting in the summer Johnson's campaign looked for ways to gain support from the religious community while also severing Goldwater from his efforts to moralize American politics. Even before the conventions were over Bill Moyers told Johnson, "we have an opportunity to arouse many religious groups to oppose Goldwater." Later in the fall, White House advisor Mike Manatos informed Moyers that Goldwater had recently admitted he did not attend church, causing Manatos to wonder whether "this attitude could be woven into somebody's speech somewhere along the line." People of faith within the Goldwater ranks believed equally strongly their candidate had the greater appeal to Christian voters. A Protestant minister sympathetic to Goldwater said of the 1964 contest, "I don't want to flaunt my collar, but truly this is a year when a good many will pray before they vote. Our moral future appears at stake."[42]

Mainstream Protestant theologians, though, broke with tradition and endorsed a candidate in 1964, Lyndon Johnson. They did so because Goldwater horrified them. The *Christian Century*, a long-standing and revered publication, editorialized: "We flatly state our opposition to Senator Goldwater. We are opposed to him not so much because he is a conservative—which in fact he is not, contrary to his claim—but because he is an ideologist. His position is doctrinaire, and is not based on the considerations of practical politics which have hitherto dominated American elections." They argued his civil rights views "would set our country back half a century, would exacerbate the color question and undermine the position of the poorer third of our population. . . . Goldwater? No!" Even Episcopal Church leaders, the denomination of which Goldwater was a member, disavowed his candidacy because of "the shrill and unreasoning extremists who are supporting him and whose support he refuses to repudiate." Episcopalian leaders queried, "Should a man who is this blind to the dangers of the lunatic fringe in our country be entrusted with the Presidency? We think not." Even the priest who baptized him noted, "frankly he scares me."[43]

Not all religious people rejected Goldwater. California evangelicals played an important role in mobilizing grassroots support for Goldwater. They collaborated with white southerners also troubled by political liberalism. Some conservative evangelical pastors in the Golden State turned their sermons over to extended political advertising for Goldwater, equating a vote for the Arizonan with Christian rectitude. For example, officials with Central Baptist Church in Anaheim, California, positioned a Goldwater table on the church's front lawn, far enough from the doors to remain in compliance with tax laws, and also arranged a rally for congregants at Knott's Berry Farm the weekend before the election. Central members joined a crowd of over 30,000 people at the amusement park. Actors John Wayne and Ronald Reagan appeared as did right-wing folk singers. The *Wall Street Journal* described such rallies: "The evangelistic fervor of his rallies, at times embellished with choir singing and prayers, lifts most audiences to high emotional pitch."[44]

With at least one well-known clergy the politics of morality merged with Sunbelt appeals. Both candidates sought favor from Billy Graham. Graham avoided taking sides in 1964, even though Goldwater talked regularly about moral decay. He insisted churches should stay out of politics, but he did make clear that "President Johnson will get my prayers day and night." This did not happen by accident. Johnson long worried Graham would endorse Goldwater so he courted the popular southern evangelist, inviting him and his wife, Ruth, to dine and stay at the White House. Johnson and Graham had known each other for about a decade but were not close. Johnson knew Graham had backed Nixon in 1960. He also knew many conservative evangelicals wanted Graham to run for the presidency. Graham rebuffed such efforts. Not once, as Graham later told Nixon, did Johnson try to discuss politics with the pastor during that first White House visit. Instead, they swam, ate, and prayed. There was, according to White House aide Bill Moyers, "an almost visceral attraction" between the two men, who came from similar Sunbelt backgrounds, Graham from North Carolina and Johnson Texas.[45]

Johnson sought Graham's advice on a host of issues including what to do after his aide and close friend Walter Jenkins was arrested for homosexual activity. At one point, Johnson lectured Graham: "Now Billy, you stay out of politics." Graham did so in 1964, and in that way mirrored many urban Republicans who could not support Goldwater. Politics did not stay away from Graham, though. Goldwater sought his support throughout the fall, stressing the similarity in their views. Any hint that Graham might be a Goldwater partisan disappeared in October when Graham visited the White House during the aftermath of the Walter Jenkins scandal. The pastor was nervous about making the trip, and he discussed his concerns with Nixon before going to provide Johnson with the requested "spiritual counsel." Nixon believed Graham had to comply but that he should insist he would "expose" Johnson if the president used the visit for political gain. Other evangelists were less circumspect. Both Billy James Hargis and Bob Jones Jr. offered enthusiastic praise for Goldwater's candidacy.[46]

So what was the Jenkins scandal and how did it intersect with the politics of morality? The early October transgression fueled Republican charges of Democratic immorality, but Goldwater was ambivalent about manipulating the sad tale for political benefit. Jenkins had attended a Washington, DC, cocktail party on October 7. Later that evening he was arrested in a YMCA men's room for what was then legally defined as indecent sexual behavior. Rumors circulated soon thereafter, but the matter did not become widely known until a *Washington Star* reporter discovered Jenkins's arrest report. The reporters persisted and discovered Jenkins had been charged with a similar crime in 1959. That was enough for editors to run the story.[47]

The question then became what would Johnson do. Those closest to the president insisted he must not fire Jenkins. Lady Bird told Lyndon of her intention to call the Jenkins and offer support, including a job for Walter at KTBC in Austin. Johnson opposed his wife's plans to insert herself in the matter, but she did not back down. "We will lose the entire love and devotion of all the people who have been with us," Lady Bird explained. "A gesture of support to Walter on our part is best." Lyndon did not demur, "Don't create any more problems than I've got. . . . You just can't do that to the presidency, honey." Lady Bird had none of it: "You're a brave, good guy, and if you read where I've said some things in Walter's support, they will be along the line that I have just said to you." Johnson gave Jenkins an extended leave of absence and directed close allies to convince Jenkins to resign. Walter Jenkins and his family ultimately moved back to Austin, and the Johnsons did what they could to take care of him, including giving him a percentage of the profits from the LBJ Ranch.[48]

Goldwater refused to talk publicly about the incident, but off-the-record he told journalists, "what a way to win an election, Communists and cocksuckers." According to William F. Buckley Jr., Goldwater had ordered his staff not to exploit the Jenkins arrest out of concern for his wife and six children. Still, Goldwater activists carried signs, "Either Way with LBJ." The Johnson campaign, though, took steps to discourage Goldwater from further capitalizing on Jenkins's problems. They reminded the Arizonan of published reports most recently in the May 1964 *Good Housekeeping* that he had had two nervous breakdowns in the 1930s (in reality the episodes followed periods of overwork and were resolved with vacations). The Jenkins incident did not distract voters if only because it was superseded by international events: Nikita Khrushchev's resignation as Soviet premier, the victory of the Labour Party in British elections leading to their control of the government, and mainland China's successful explosion of a nuclear bomb.[49]

Goldwater benefited from a surrogate who helped make his closing argument. Former actor and aspiring politician Ronald Reagan hit hard on the theme of moral decay, helping flesh out Sunbelt conservatism. The Goldwater campaign did not arrange or pay for the speech; friends of Reagan did. His main purpose was to suggest the liberal excesses of the federal government since the New Deal. Reagan recalled his motivation for wanting to help Goldwater in 1964: "Lyndon Johnson had begun to make most of the tax-and-spend Democrats of the past seem miserly by comparison. I thought we sorely needed Goldwater to reverse the trend. I said I'd do anything to help get him elected." Indeed, the politics of taxation

Ronald Reagan is shown with Barry Goldwater. Reagan is giving a speech for the Goldwater campaign at the International Hotel in Los Angeles. Courtesy Ronald Reagan Library.

drew voters to Goldwater. Tax resistance was increasingly prevalent among the prosperous middle class in the years after World War II. Participants were doubly angry: first about rising income and property taxes and second about increasing federal government intrusion in private matters. Part of Goldwater's appeal to the tax resisters came from his western image, which signified individualism and opposition to a world with taxes.[50]

Taped before a live audience, Reagan's "Time for Choosing" speech was later aired on national television on October 27. "The Speech" had its genesis with Reagan's speechmaking in the 1950s when he promoted General Electric to the American people. Reagan gave as many as 100 speeches for Goldwater, most in California because Reagan did not enjoy flying. He made his speeches without notes and without a Teleprompter. Reagan wrote the speech himself. In it, he lambasted liberals and liberalism, telling Americans "there is no such thing as a left or right. There is only an up or down—up to a man's age-old dream, the ultimate in individual freedom consistent with law and order—or down to the ant heap of totalitarianism." To Reagan, bureaucracy was killing the soul of America. The speech boosted GOP fundraising, and as a result the party paid to have it rebroadcast, as many as six times in some television markets. Journalist David Broder concurred, noting it was "the most successful national debut since William Jennings Bryan electrified the 1896 Democratic convention in the 'Cross of Gold' address." The speech played a major role in Reagan's decision to run for governor of California two years later. Said Richard Viguerie, "That stirring endorsement of Goldwater created a new political star and a new spokesman for conservatism—a far more effective spokesman than Goldwater."[51]

The 1964 race, though, was not just a presidential election but also a down-ballot contest. Republicans and Democrats had different approaches to the congressional races. While Goldwater focused mainly on his own race, moderate Republicans—the party regulars—tried to salvage the rest of the ticket. Johnson and the Democrats, though, paid attention to these races. For Johnson working the down ballot races meant first and foremost improving the image of Congress, so people would be excited to vote on the legislative races. Journalists Rowland Evans and Robert Novak contended, "Johnson's most significant legislative breakthrough was to establish an image in Congress, as with the public, of presidential mastery over Congress. . . . He [had] lustily expended the enormous powers of the presidency to tame the Congress. And in so doing, he strengthened his presidency." Johnson believed that public opinion of Congress would correlate with his success in the general election. He asked labor leader Walter Reuther to help increase public support for the legislative branch: "I wish you would get it out among the columnists and others that this is the greatest Congress that we've ever had. This is greater than any Roosevelt Congress." He then listed progress in multiple policy arenas: taxation, civil rights, agriculture, foreign aid, and poverty.[52]

Larry O'Brien advised Johnson about Democratic chances in the Senate and House races. Of the thirty-three Senate races that year, only three Democrats faced substantial challenges and another three had challengers who might pose a threat. Five Republican seats looked vulnerable to a Democratic challenge. O'Brien estimated Democrats could increase their Senate seats from sixty-seven to as many as seventy. He was even more optimistic about the situation in the House where Democrats prior to the election held a 257-178 advantage. He did not see Democrats losing any of the twenty-nine seats where party incumbents faced challengers. The thirty-eight Republican seats being contested, though, O'Brien believed were vulnerable to Democratic attack. While he hoped for an increase of thirty-eight Democratic seats, his goal was more modest: approximately twenty additional seats.[53]

LBJ paid substantial attention to Texas, revealing his ego and his paranoia. He worried, "We've got problems. They're going to beat [Texas senator Ralph] Yarborough in this state, just beat him sure as hell. And I wouldn't be surprised if they don't beat me." Later Johnson said of Yarborough's opponent: "And this damn [George H. W.] Bush is just mean as he can be. I never thought he would—made such gains as he's made down here. But we've got to pull Yarborough in as a fellow that's helped build this whole constructive program."[54]

By the fall of 1964, moderate Republicans had given up on the presidency but not their political philosophy. The Committee to Support Moderate Republicans formed to secure the election of down-ballot Republicans. Asserting "moderate Republicanism" was the "most needed" and "most responsible force on the American political scene," Charles P. Taft was a leader in the organization and the more liberal brother of deceased conservative senator Robert Taft (R-OH). He argued, "our country is in a state of political crisis. And this crisis is due in large part to the fact that our kind of Republicans are in disarray. We must face that fact. And we must pull ourselves together and do something about it!" This organization worked for moderate Republican US Senate and House candidates. In what was a decidedly Democratic year, only three of the candidates they supported lost their races.[55]

Indeed, Republicans were partially successful. One result of the frontlash was split ticket voting. Republicans who won in states that Johnson carried included John H. Chafee in Rhode Island, George Murphy in California, Charles H. Percy in Illinois, George Romney in Michigan, Hugh Scott in Pennsylvania, and Robert Taft Jr. in Ohio. In other cases the ticket

Johnson campaigning with Bobby Kennedy, October 1964. LBJ Library, photo by Cecil Stoughton.

splitting was not prolific enough to protect Republicans, but was neverthe-less noticeable. The best example was in the New York Senate race. Johnson carried the state by 2.6 million votes, but Bobby Kennedy defeated the Re-publican incumbent by only 720,000 votes.[56]

A fascinating struggle transpired behind the scenes about how the re-sults of this contest would be reported. By 1964 the networks had settled into a vicious competition to be the first to predict the election results. During the California primary over 50,000 poll watchers, at an expense of $1 million, sought the scoop for who would win the state. Network budget offices worried that such efforts would ultimately require each network to have workers in each precinct in the country to report totals, a prohibitive expense. To thwart the trend the networks formed the Network Election Service, a single bureau joined with the Associated Press and the United Press International to share information about voting turnout and results. None of this was necessary; Johnson swept the map with some otherwise strongly Republican towns in New England reporting mid-afternoon on election day for Johnson.[57]

When the election results came in LBJ claimed an overwhelming and near complete election victory: in the popular vote with 43,128,956 or 61.1 percent for Johnson and 27,177,873 or 38.5 for Goldwater; the num-ber of states won, forty-four and six, respectively; and the Electoral College with a 486–52 margin. He bested Franklin D. Roosevelt's 1936 margin in

Johnson watching the election returns on November 3. LBJ Library, photo by Cecil Stoughton.

terms of percentage by a mere 0.3 percent but in terms of vote by a much larger 15,951,083 compared with 11,078,204 for FDR, but not in number of states won or the Electoral College spread. Johnson lost five Deep South states—Louisiana, Mississippi, Alabama, Georgia, and South Carolina—plus Goldwater's own Arizona, whereas FDR only lost two, Vermont and Maine. Democrats also did well in congressional races, picking up a net thirty-eight additional seats in the House of Representatives and two in the Senate, giving a partisan distribution of 295–140 in the House and 68–32 in the Senate. This meant that Democrats controlled just over two-thirds of the seats in both chambers. At the gubernatorial level, though, Republicans achieved a net gain of one, but Democrats still held a decided advantage in the state houses with thirty-three governorships to just seventeen for Republicans.[58]

Goldwater had a drink with the reporters who covered his campaign once they returned to Phoenix at the end of the race. The Arizonan replied to requests he give his final thoughts on the campaign: "We may not have spelled out the issues as well as we could. That was the point of it all—the point of the entire campaign. If only Jack Kennedy were here. If Jack were here, we would have had a good campaign." Goldwater told Stephen Shadegg seven months after the election, "my defeat was insured on July the 15th by the stiletto job Rockefeller and Scranton and others had done on me" when they attempted to derail his nomination at the GOP National Convention. A year after the fact Shadegg contended he had become certain Goldwater would lose as early as September 1964.[59]

The different manner in which Goldwater conveyed his congratulations to Johnson and Rockefeller expressed his condolences to Goldwater reveals much about the status of the GOP, especially the gentility of the old eastern establishment and the crass petulance of the Sunbelt conservatives. Goldwater refused to call Johnson and congratulate him before going to bed on election night. He reasoned that the results—a landslide for the Democrats by any measure—were not yet official until vote counts were certified. Close political friends who had gathered with him for election night suggested it was a requirement, but Goldwater had none of it. When he awoke the following morning his wife, Peggy, told him he had to dictate a statement for his secretary to prepare for the press. She added, "Be nice." Goldwater replied, "All right, dear." Conversely, Rockefeller wrote Goldwater a handwritten note on the stationery of the Hotel Ritz in Madrid after LBJ won his overwhelming victory. "A line to tell you that I am *sorry* that after your tremendous personal effort the campaign result was disappointing," said Rockefeller. "I know that you are glad and relieved that it is over."[60]

Goldwater remained bitter. He made multiple vehement charges against Johnson and the Democrats for what he termed their immoral behavior. At one point, Goldwater asserted, "You will search in vain for *any* reference to God or religion in the Democratic platform." Goldwater wrote harshly about the Johnson campaign, saying of Bill Moyers, "he portrayed himself as a poor preacher boy, but he was actually involved in the dirtiest work of the Johnson campaign." In response to Democratic sneering that Goldwater did not know what he was doing, the GOP candidate wrote, "the real tragedy is that Johnson, Moyers, and company also knew what they were doing, knew precisely where they were going, and still behaved with paranoia and cold deceit." Goldwater surmised the Johnson campaign had a spy working inside the Goldwater operation. He also suspected but did not prove that the Johnson campaign sprinkled itching powder down the necks of people carrying anti-LBJ signs at rallies where the president spoke.[61]

The *Washington Post* editorialized that the November election put one central question before voters: "Do you wish the government to continue its intervention in affairs which before 1932 were largely left to private decision?" Voters, said the *Post*, answered yes. Walter Lippmann found a slightly contrastive meaning in the election, namely that Johnson had remade the Democratic Party so that it "represents the vast center of American public life." The *New York Times* termed the election a victory for "moderate liberalism." Some observers contended voters did not make decisions in 1964 for ideological reasons, meaning that the country did not necessarily vote for the liberalism promised in Johnson's Great Society. Others disagreed. Polling data in the National Election Study, perhaps the best statistical analysis of the 1964 contest, suggests that Americans purposefully voted for liberalism that year. Put simply, according to this data, voters trusted Johnson and feared Goldwater. Arthur Schlesinger Jr. had a more partisan view, "The election results of 1964 seemed to demonstrate Thomas Dewey's prediction about what would happen if the parties were realigned on an ideological basis: 'The Democrats would win every election and the Republicans would lose every election.'"[62] To all the best wisdom, then, it seemed Goldwater's regional sun had set, replaced by Johnson's national sun. Over the horizon glowed the promise of harmony and consensus.

CONCLUSION

Barry Goldwater was not elected president in 1964, but his Sunbelt values still rose over national politics in the decades that followed. After the election, conservative Republicans recognized that while Goldwater would never be president, "there still is a huge conservative machine, if only somebody can keep it together." The mood of the electorate shifted more and more in sync with his Sunbelt views of public policy. Liberal New York Republican John Lindsay observed of the GOP post Goldwater, "Its power structure was now oriented West and South. It was hostile to the East and deeply suspicious of the egalitarianism of the cities. It had been a centrist party which for decades had occupied the middle ground between Right and Left. Now it had veered Right." Goldwater agreed that his efforts in 1964 had contributed to the downfall of liberalism and all Lyndon Johnson had advocated in his frontlash campaign. He reflected fifteen years after his presidential race: "Today as I sit in the Senate in the year 1979 it is interesting to me to watch liberals, moderates and conservatives fighting each other to see who can come out on top the quickest against those matters that I talked so fervently and so much about in 1964." The Arizonan took great pleasure "that almost every one of the principles I advocated in 1964 have become the gospel of the whole spread of the spectrum of politics." Seemingly, Goldwater's version of Sunbelt politics surpassed Johnson's consensus liberalism. The Arizonan reckoned, "there really isn't a heck of a lot left."[1]

If Goldwater was right, why did he lose? Journalist and scholar Godfrey Hodgson concluded three factors had hindered Goldwater's chances: the primary season attacks on him from other Republicans; the antipathy of the media toward his candidacy; and the assassination of Kennedy. There were other, more minor reasons for his loss, namely mistakes inside the campaign. First, there was no clear chain of command. Second, those who developed the ideology for the campaign were separated from the people who ran it. Third, Goldwater insiders did not have the skill and experience to navigate a general election campaign, especially since they faced a master politician in Lyndon Johnson. Fourth, infighting among the campaign staff plagued the Goldwater effort. Fifth, they never offered an affirmative definition of conservatism powerful enough to counter the rhetoric of liberals. Last, the chief difference between Goldwater and Johnson was the former wanted to be right and the latter president.

People familiar with the intimate details of the Goldwater campaign offered varying reasons for his loss. Goldwater's pollster explained how his candidate lost the general election during the primaries. The other Republican candidates said many critical things of Goldwater that Johnson's team used against the GOP nominee. The pollster expounded: "The charge of extremism was hung on Goldwater during the primary period and lasted throughout the entire campaign." Miller said of the election, "The American people were just not in the mood to assassinate two Presidents in one year." Ayn Rand was less than pleased with Goldwater's performance in the general election, observing after his defeat: "There was no discussion of capitalism. There was no discussion of statism. There was no discussion of the blatantly vulnerable record of the government's policies in the last thirty years. There was no discussion. There were no issues."[2]

George H. W. Bush, a Texas Republican who lost his race for the US Senate in 1964, wrote in the National Review that despite Goldwater's "constructive" and "forthright" discussion of policy, "the so-called 'nut' fringe" destroyed his image with "undecided" voters. In making these claims, Bush ignored Goldwater's own words. "The undecided voter wouldn't get a sensible message on where Goldwater stood, he'd get some fanatic on his back tearing down Lyndon. Goldwater didn't want to repeal Social Security but some of his more militant backers did. He didn't want to bomb the UN but these same backers did," Bush argued. "They pushed their philosophy in Goldwater's name, and scared the hell out of the plain average non-issue-conscious man on the street."[3]

The politics of 1964 did produce significant shifts in the GOP. Observed journalist Jack W. Germond, "1964 was the year the 'eastern establishment' that had nominated Thomas E. Dewey and Dwight D. Eisenhower became a terminal case." The realignment did not entirely make sense to Germond; he found scant difference between "the eastern establishment" and "their more conservative counterparts" on a host of issues: national security, foreign policy, and budget issues. "The progressives were, nonetheless, much more inclined to rely on activist government to solve problems," admitted Germond. "And, above all, they were much different from their conservative colleagues in their aggressive support for civil rights, the issue that more than any other shaped politics for two generations of Americans."[4]

The election had consequences for the conservative movement. One important development was the expansion of a conservative intellectual infrastructure. The foundations, policy think tanks, and educational programs that conservatives funded following Goldwater's defeat included the Bradley Foundation, the Heritage Foundation, the Institute for Humane Studies, the Intercollegiate Studies Institute, the Liberty Fund, the Olin Foundation, and the Richard and Helen DeVos Foundation. Some scholars have argued the most significant fact of the 1964 race was not the electoral trouncing of conservatism but the speedy recovery of the intellectual and political movement.

Years later GOP activist Richard Viguerie observed that the 1964 election was "phase I" for the "conservative movement," in which it "learn[ed] *how to nominate a candidate for president.*" Viguerie contended other important lessons were learned in 1964: "The mainstream media are incurably liberal. They will never give conservatives a fair chance, so you have to do an end-run around them. Boy, did we learn this lesson the hard way!" He expressed conservative ire over the epithets applied to them: "fascists, Nazis, bigots, racists, and reckless crazies who might destroy the world in a nuclear holocaust." The conservative response was construction of "our own channels of communication," which included newspapers, magazines, and books. Viguerie also touted what was learned about the grass roots from the campaign, namely the impact of "properly mobilized" volunteers when they possessed a "shared ideology" against "the combined forces of Wall Street, the entrenched political machines, and the mainstream media." He noted that Goldwater had twice as many volunteers as Johnson even though the Democrats had a 50 percent larger voter base. Viguerie explained the import of direct mail, a tactic little used in politics before 1964, "I applied the techniques used successfully in the commercial world to the political realm, learning as I went along."[5]

Were all the legacies of the 1964 contest positive? Historians have condemned Goldwater's strategy—"hunting where the ducks are" or seeking the votes of white racists. Such tactics set back Eisenhower's and Nixon's earlier Republican efforts to compete in the South. Indeed, Goldwater's methods meant abandoning the Eisenhower approach in the region, which had been pursuit of white moderates. During the 1964 contest southern segregationists staged a hostile takeover of the Republican Party. Goldwater, though, denied he had pursued a southern strategy: "that's never been a strategy of mine or anybody else's. . . . I don't care who the Democrat was or who the Democrat will be the next time, the South has been going more and more Republican since '48, but you might go clear back to the days of Al Smith. The Republican presidential candidates have not done badly in the South." Others disagreed. The Ripon Society, a group of liberal Republicans, concluded, "until 1964, Republican growth in the South was centered in the urban and suburban communities, which enjoyed an atmosphere of more racial moderation, higher educational attainment and greater economic prosperity." Ripon queried, "Is our party the party of Lincoln or the party of Thurmond?" Some historians have even traced the legacy of Goldwater forward to the twenty-first century, arguing a direct line connected the Goldwater movement to the Tea Party.[6]

Young, progressive Republicans used the writings of Lewis Carroll to understand the politics of 1964: "The year 1964 was a strange and bizarre political year. As in Alice's Wonderland many things were as they should not have been and one incredible development followed another." Indeed, the 1964 contest portended a racial realignment. It brought a seismic shift in how voters viewed the parties on civil rights. As a result of the election, voters overwhelmingly identified Democrats as the party friendly to civil rights. Several weeks after the election, Goldwater justified his views: the African American vote would not have changed much with a liberal or moderate Republican at the head of the ticket. Statistics tell this story well, revealing important ironies to this "revolution in American politics." LBJ, "the first Southern President since the Civil War," won the African American vote by 90 percent but still faced defeat in the Deep South where he lost "by large margins." Johnson's win in much of the outer South—for sure Virginia, North Carolina, Tennessee, Arkansas, and possibly Florida— came only because of newly enfranchised African Americans. Goldwater won rural southern whites in almost equally overwhelming proportion, carrying Mississippi with 87 percent, Alabama with 70 percent, South Carolina with 57 percent, and Georgia with 54 percent.[7] In many counties in these states only whites were allowed to register or vote in 1964. The 1964 Civil Rights Act was supposed to fix this problem, but its impact on voting was less robust than architects of the bill had hoped. The result: civil rights leaders made voting rights their major objective going forward, with the result being passage of the Voting Rights Act in 1965.

The 1964 contest has been routinely acknowledged as one of the most ideological in US history. Individual rights versus collectivism: this was the conflict between Goldwater conservatives and Great Society liberals. Not in 1964, but not long thereafter, conservatives convinced Americans that liberals no longer primarily worked to secure expanded individual liberties but instead for entitlements through social engineering and ever more heightened federal power over individual lives. Conservatives learned from the Goldwater debacle that they would have to court the votes of party moderates and also avoid rhetoric that estranged them. President Gerald Ford recalled of the 1960s, "It was difficult because the Democratic party was not unified, and the Republican party had its own splits: from the hard right to the moderates like myself. So it was a transitional period in American politics." As such, some scholars have refuted the notion of the Goldwater vote as a "conservative hard core" because the very "meaning of conservatism" changed in the decades following 1964. Instead these academics have suggested the Goldwater vote "indicates a sizable population skeptical of liberal rhetoric." Most notable among the modifications to conservatism came in the areas of morality and sexuality where no litmus test existed in the 1960s but emerged in the decades that followed.[8]

Definitions of liberalism and conservatism evolved as did perceptions of the two parties. The Democratic Party lost its identity as the proponent of economic security for all in favor of advocating rights of the marginalized. The results also shaped how Johnson governed. White House aide George Reedy said of the 1964 results that the president and his close advisers operated as if LBJ had won "a mandate from the people not only to carry on the policies of the Johnson administration but any other policies that might come to mind." For Johnson his victory proved the wisdom of his frontlash liberalism. Reedy later disputed that conclusion, noting "a sizable share of his victory had come from people who were literally frightened into the Democratic camp by the grotesque and preposterous campaign tactics of the opposition." Longtime Johnson advisor Horace Busby disagreed with Reedy: "Johnson is a man without ideology. The New Deal needed an ideology—it needed enemies. They were fighting against the economic royalists." Because he had so deeply internalized his frontlash politics of "consensus," said Busby, Johnson "sucks his feelings up from the gut. He was one of the poor. He can't see the need for any enemies." Busby con-

Johnson and Humphrey celebrating their victory at the LBJ Ranch the day after the election. LBJ Library, photo by Cecil Stoughton.

cluded, "What he wants most is that his programs should go down in history not as Democratic Party programs, but as American programs."[9]

The year 1964 proved to be an electoral triumph for liberals not just at the White House level. Liberal House Democrats decided to attack the problem of not passing Kennedy legislation by increasing Democratic numbers in the House. In 1963, the Democratic Study Group expanded to include partisan electoral work. Through "better organization," better information gathering, and better fundraising they sought to elect "Democrats from marginal Republican districts." Among congressional races, the more liberal the candidate, the more likely a victory. Those members of Congress rated as most liberal all were reelected. Only one Democrat in the House who voted for the Civil Rights Act was defeated, but half of those who voted against it lost their races. All Senate Democrats who voted for the measure survived. John M. Bailey, the chair of the Democratic National Committee, explained the impact of Goldwater on other Republicans: "The Democrats carried legislatures they never carried before." He recalled the results of this down ballot success, "Of course, the Eighty-Ninth Congress has been a great success. We had sort of a landslide." White House aide Lawrence O'Brien concurred, "The fact is the first session of the Eighty-Ninth was most productive in the history of the country."[10]

As a result, in 1965 an "impotent" GOP and a resurgent, motivated Democratic Party in the Eighty-Ninth Congress provided LBJ with tremendous legislative victories. Said one Congress watcher, "the result was an unparalleled outpouring of legislation during the first session," including agricultural programs, creation of the Department of Housing and Urban Development, the Elementary and Secondary Education Act, environmental protections for air and water, highway beautification, housing initiatives, the Immigration and Naturalization Act, Medicare, a constitutional amendment on presidential continuity, regional economic planning and development, and the Voting Rights Act. During the first session of the Eighty-Ninth Congress, LBJ asked lawmakers to consider 469 proposals of which 323 were enacted for a 68.9 percent success rate. Statistics from House roll call votes reinforce this point. Lawmakers voted the Johnson position 94 percent of the time. Democratic success rates fell only slightly in the second session of the Eighty-Ninth Congress, with Johnson asking for 371 proposals and gaining 207, a 55.8 percent approval rate. Similarly, he prevailed on 91 percent of the roll calls where he had declared a preference.[11]

Despite the success of party initiatives in 1964, Johnson was unable to continue such work in subsequent years. The escalation of the Vietnam War offers one possible explanation, and indeed Johnson was already engaged in military planning in mid-1964. Another factor was significant. No Democratic Party contemporary and no scholar has ever determined that Johnson was a phenomenal party builder. To the contrary, the consensus view suggests Johnson was uninterested in party affairs, but the Texan had the luxury to not worry given the size of Democratic majorities in the House, the Senate, the statehouses, and the electorate. Moreover, blunting partisanship was both central to Johnson's electoral strategy and his governing strategy. Said a liberal labor leader, "We pulled in a hell of a lot of people in that election. And then Lyndon Johnson dismantled the whole thing, just didn't want that there, was electing the wrong kind of Democrats as far as he was concerned."[12]

George Reedy explained why. Johnson's conclusion about 1964 mirrored "his longstanding belief that party organization played a very minor role in the political life of the nation." The reasoning went deeper; according to Reedy, Johnson "resent[ed]" the DNC for undermining the Democratic congressional leadership in the 1950s in favor of then party standard-bearer, Adlai Stevenson. Nor, said Reedy, did Johnson approve of the "influx of the more sectarian 'liberals' into party headquarters." Finally, he blamed the DNC because in 1960 John F. Kennedy controlled most of the state-level party organizations. As such when Johnson entered the White House, "he began moving almost immediately to bring the Democratic National Committee under firm control." He "camouflaged" this effort by leaving the DNC staff alone while also moving the committee's power to Clifton C. Carter, a longtime LBJ ally. Even though Carter had long been loyal to LBJ when Carter advocated boosting party organization Johnson pulled control back to the White House. Said Reedy, he wrongly believed the 1968 election "would follow the pattern of 1964, in which the personal campaign of the president himself would be the crucial factor and organization would be wholly unnecessary."[13]

Why? Johnson never abandoned his frontlash thinking about politics. "His actual message," journalists Rowland Evans and Robert Novak contended, "neither profound nor demagogic, was sheer Great Society consensus. America is *one* family, not North or South, not Republican or Democrat, not white or black. America is love, not hate; reason, not extremism; peace, not nuclear war." Journalist Theodore H. White observed, "The ultimate paradox of 1964 was that the Americans had chosen one of the most passionately political of all Presidents, who proposed, if he could, to make the Presidency a non-political office." On that score, Johnson failed. He wanted his sun to shine consensual liberalism, but instead partisanship intensified in Washington over the course of his administration, especially following the 1966 midterm elections. How could it have been otherwise given Johnson's frontlash strategy? In 1964, the majority party invited Republicans and independents to vote Democratic, but an opposite consequence was just as important: long term the Johnson methods unintentionally encouraged Republicans to find more effective arguments to use against consensus liberalism. As one Republican senator put it: "That damn Lyndon Johnson hasn't just grabbed the middle of the road. He's a bit to the Right of center, as well as a bit to the Left of center. And with Johnson hogging the whole road, Right, Left and center, where the devil can we go except the ditch?"[14]

APPENDIX A

REPUBLICAN PRIMARY RESULTS

	Votes	Percentage
March 10, New Hampshire		
Henry Cabot Lodge*	33,007	35.5
Barry M. Goldwater	20,692	22.3
Nelson A. Rockefeller	19,504	21
Richard M. Nixon*	15,587	16.8
Margaret Chase Smith	2,120	2.3
Harold E. Stassen	1,373	1.5
Others	465	0.5
William W. Scranton*	105	0.1
April 2, Wisconsin		
John W. Byrnes	299,612	99.7
Unpledged delegates	816	0.3
April 14, Illinois		
Barry M. Goldwater	512,840	62
Margaret Chase Smith	209,521	25.3
Henry Cabot Lodge*	68,122	8.2
Richard M. Nixon*	30,313	3.7
George C. Wallace*	2,203	0.3
Nelson A. Rockefeller*	2,048	0.2
William W. Scranton*	1,842	0.2
George W. Romney*	465	0.1
Others*	437	0.1
April 21, New Jersey		
Henry Cabot Lodge*	7,896	41.7
Barry M. Goldwater*	5,309	28
Richard M. Nixon*	4,179	22.1
William W. Scranton*	633	3.3
Nelson A. Rockefeller*	612	3.2
Others*	304	1.6

(continued on next page)

	Votes	Percentage
April 28, Massachusetts		
Henry Cabot Lodge*	70,809	76.9
Barry M. Goldwater*	9,338	10.1
Richard M. Nixon*	5,460	5.9
Nelson A. Rockefeller*	2,454	2.7
William W. Scranton*	1,709	1.9
Others*	711	0.8
Lyndon B. Johnson*	600	0.7
Margaret Chase Smith*	426	0.5
George C. Lodge*	365	0.4
George W. Romney*	262	0.3
April 28, Pennsylvania		
William W. Scranton*	235,222	51.9
Henry Cabot Lodge*	92,712	20.5
Richard M. Nixon*	44,396	9.8
Barry M. Goldwater*	38,669	8.5
Lyndon B. Johnson*	22,372	4.9
Nelson A. Rockefeller*	9,123	2
Others*	5,269	1.2
George C. Wallace*	5,105	1.1
May 2, Texas		
Barry M. Goldwater	104,137	74.7
Henry Cabot Lodge*	12,324	8.8
Nelson A. Rockefeller	6,207	4.5
Richard M. Nixon*	5,390	3.9
Harold E. Stassen	5,273	3.8
Margaret Chase Smith	4,816	3.5
William W. Scranton*	803	0.6
Others*	373	0.3
*May 5, Washington, DC***		
May 5, Indiana		
Barry M. Goldwater	267,935	67
Harold E. Stassen	107,157	26.8
Others	24,588	6.2
May 5, Ohio		
James A. Rhodes	615,754	100

May 12, Nebraska

Barry M. Goldwater	68,050	49.1
Richard M. Nixon*	43,613	31.5
Henry Cabot Lodge*	22,622	16.3
Nelson A. Rockefeller*	2,333	1.7
Others*	1,010	0.7
William W. Scranton*	578	0.4
Lyndon B. Johnson*	316	0.2

May 12, West Virginia

Nelson A. Rockefeller	115,680	100

May 15, Oregon

Nelson A. Rockefeller	94,190	33
Henry Cabot Lodge	79,169	27.7
Barry M. Goldwater	50,105	17.6
Richard M. Nixon	48,274	16.9
Margaret Chase Smith	8,087	2.8
William W. Scranton	4,509	1.6
Others	1,152	0.4

May 19, Maryland

Unpledged delegates	57,004	58.2
Others	40,994	41.8

May 26, Florida

Unpledged delegates	58,179	57.8
Barry M. Goldwater	42,525	42.2

June 2, California

Barry M. Goldwater	1,120,403	51.6
Nelson A. Rockefeller	1,052,053	48.4

June 2, South Dakota

Unpledged delegates	57,653	68
Barry M. Goldwater	27,076	32

Primary Vote Totals

Barry M. Goldwater	2,267,079	38.2
Nelson A. Rockefeller	1,304,204	22
James A. Rhodes	615,754	10.4
Henry Cabot Lodge	386,661	6.5
John W. Byrnes	299,612	5.0

(continued on next page)

	Votes	Percentage
William W. Scranton	245,401	4.1
Margaret Chase Smith	224,970	3.8
Richard M. Nixon	197,212	3.3
Unpledged delegates	173,652	2.9
Harold E. Stassen	113,803	1.9
Others	75,303	1.3
Lyndon B. Johnson	23,288	0.4
George C. Wallace	7,308	0.1
George W. Romney	727	0
George C. Lodge	365	0

*Write-in

**No primary figures available for Republican vote.

Source: *Presidential Elections, 1789–1992* (Washington, DC: Congressional Quarterly, 1995), 176–178

DEMOCRATIC PRIMARY RESULTS

	Votes	Percentage
March 10, New Hampshire		
Lyndon B. Johnson*	29,317	95.3
Robert F. Kennedy*	487	1.6
Henry Cabot Lodge*	280	0.9
Richard M. Nixon*	232	0.8
Barry M. Goldwater*	193	0.6
Others*	159	0.5
Nelson A. Rockefeller*	109	0.4
April 7, Wisconsin		
John W. Reynolds***	522,405	66.2
George C. Wallace	266,136	33.8
April 14, Illinois		
Lyndon B. Johnson*	82,027	91.6
George C. Wallace*	3,761	4.2
Robert F. Kennedy*	2,894	3.2
Others*	841	0.9
April 21, New Jersey		
Lyndon B. Johnson*	4,863	82.3
George C. Wallace*	491	8.3
Robert F. Kennedy*	431	7.3
Others*	124	2.1
April 28, Massachusetts		
Lyndon B. Johnson*	61,035	73.4
Robert F. Kennedy*	15,870	19.1
Henry Cabot Lodge*	2,269	2.7
Others*	1,436	1.7
Edward M. Kennedy*	1,259	1.5
George C. Wallace*	565	0.7

(continued on next page)

	Votes	Percentage
Adlai E. Stevenson*	452	0.5
Hubert H. Humphrey*	323	0.4

April 28, Pennsylvania

Lyndon B. Johnson*	209,606	82.8
George C. Wallace*	12,104	4.8
Robert F. Kennedy*	12,029	4.8
William W. Scranton*	8,156	3.2
Others*	6,438	2.5
Henry Cabot Lodge*	4,895	1.9

May 2, Texas**

May 5, Indiana

Matthew E. Welsh***	376,023	64.9
George C. Wallace	172,646	29.8
Others	30,367	5.2

May 5, Ohio

Albert S. Porter***	493,619	100

May 5, Washington, DC

Unpledged delegates	41,095	100

May 12, Nebraska

Lyndon B. Johnson*	54,713	89.3
Robert F. Kennedy*	2,099	3.4
George C. Wallace*	1,067	1.7
Henry Cabot Lodge*	1,051	1.7
Others*	904	1.5
Richard M. Nixon*	833	1.4
Barry M. Goldwater*	603	1

May 12, West Virginia

Unpledged delegates	131,432	100

May 15, Oregon

Lyndon B. Johnson	272,099	99.5
George C. Wallace*	1,365	0.5

May 19, Maryland

Daniel B. Brewster***	267,106	53.1
George C. Wallace	214,849	42.7

Unpledged delegates	12,377	2.5
Others	8,275	1.6

May 26, Florida
Lyndon B. Johnson	393,339	100

June 2, California****
Unpledged delegates/Edmund G. Brown	1,693,813	68
Unpledged delegates/Sam Yorty	798,431	32

June 2, South Dakota
Unpledged delegates	28,142	100

Primary Vote Totals
Unpledged delegates/Edmund G. Brown	1,693,813	27.1
Lyndon B. Johnson	1,106,999	17.7
Unpledged delegates/Sam Yorty	798,431	12.8
George C. Wallace	672,984	10.8
John W. Reynolds***	522,405	8.4
Albert S. Porter***	493,619	7.9
Matthew E. Welsh***	376,023	6.0
Daniel B. Brewster***	267,106	4.3
Unpledged delegates	213,046	3.4
Others	48,544	0.8
Robert F. Kennedy	33,810	0.5
Henry Cabot Lodge	8,495	0.1
William W. Scranton	8,156	0.1
Edward M. Kennedy	1,259	0.0
Richard M. Nixon	1,065	0.0
Barry M. Goldwater	796	0.0
Adlai E. Stevenson	452	0.0
Hubert H. Humphrey	323	0.0
Nelson A. Rockefeller	109	0.0

*Write-in

**No primary authorized.

***Favorite son candidate pledged to support Johnson at the convention.

****Governor Edmund G. Brown headed the winning slate of delegates and Mayor Sam Yorty headed the losing slate.

Source: Presidential Elections, 1789–1992 (Washington, DC: Congressional Quarterly, 1995), 176–178

APPENDIX C GENERAL ELECTION RESULTS, POPULAR VOTE TOTALS 1964

States	Total Vote	Lyndon B. Johnson Democrat	%	Barry M. Goldwater Republican	%	Eric Hass Socialist Labor	%	Clifton DeBerry Socialist Workers	%	Other	%	Plurality	Party
Alabama*	689,818	0		479,085	69.5	0		0		210,733	30.5	268,353	R
Alaska	67,259	44,329	65.9	22,930	34.1	0		0		0		21,399	D
Arizona	480,770	237,753	49.5	242,535	50.4	482	0.1	0		0		4,782	R
Arkansas	560,426	314,197	56.1	243,264	43.4	0		0		2,965	0.5	70,933	D
California	7,057,586	4,171,877	59.1	2,879,108	40.8	489		378		5,734	0.1	1,292,769	D
Colorado	776,986	476,024	61.3	296,767	38.2	302		2,537	0.3	1,356	0.2	179,257	D
Connecticut	1,218,578	826,269	67.8	390,996	32.1	0		0		1,313	0.1	435,273	D
Delaware	201,320	122,704	60.9	78,078	38.8	113	0.1	0		425	0.2	44,626	D
DC	198,597	169,796	85.5	28,801	14.5	0		0		0		140,995	D
Florida	1,854,481	948,540	51.1	905,941	48.9	0		0		0		42,599	D
Georgia	1,139,335	522,556	45.9	616,584	54.1	0		0		195		94,028	R
Hawaii	207,271	163,249	78.8	44,022	21.2	0		0		0		119,227	D
Idaho	292,477	148,920	50.9	143,557	49.1	0		0		0		5,363	D
Illinois	4,702,841	2,796,833	59.5	1,905,946	40.5	0		0		62		890,887	D
Indiana	2,091,606	1,170,848	56.0	911,118	43.6	1,374	0.1	0		8,266	0.4	259,730	D
Iowa	1,184,539	733,030	61.9	449,148	37.9	182		159		2,020	0.2	283,882	D
Kansas	857,901	464,028	54.1	386,579	45.1	1,901	0.2	0		5,393	0.6	77,449	D
Kentucky	1,046,105	669,659	64.0	372,977	35.7	0		0		3,469	0.3	296,682	D
Louisiana	896,293	387,068	43.2	509,225	56.8	0		0		0		122,157	R

Maine	380,965	262,264	68.8	118,701	31.2	0		0		0		143,563	D
Maryland	1,116,457	730,912	65.5	385,495	34.5	0		0		50		345,417	D
Massachusetts	2,344,798	1,786,422	76.2	549,727	23.4	4,755	0.2	0		3,894	0.2	1,236,695	D
Michigan	3,203,102	2,136,615	66.7	1,060,152	33.1	1,704	0.1	3,817	0.1	814		1,076,463	D
Minnesota	1,554,462	991,117	63.8	559,624	36	2,544	0.2	1,177	0.1	0		431,493	D
Mississippi	409,146	52,618	12.9	356,528	87.1	0		0		0		303,910	R
Missouri	1,817,879	1,164,344	64.0	653,535	36	0		0		0		510,809	D
Montana	278,628	164,246	58.9	113,032	40.6	0		332		1,018	0.4	51,214	D
Nebraska	584,154	307,307	52.6	276,847	47.4	0		0		0		30,460	D
Nevada	135,433	79,339	58.6	56,094	41.4	0		0		0		23,245	D
New Hampshire	288,093	184,064	63.9	104,029	36.1	0		0		0		80,035	D
New Jersey	2,847,663	1,868,231	65.6	964,174	33.9	7,075	0.2	8,183	0.3	0		904,057	D
New Mexico	328,645	194,015	59.0	132,838	40.4	1,217	0.4	0		575	0.2	61,177	D
New York	7,166,275	4,913,102	68.6	2,243,559	31.3	6,118	0.1	3,228	0.1	268		2,669,543	D
North Carolina	1,424,983	800,139	56.2	624,844	43.8	0		0		0		175,295	D
North Dakota	258,389	149,784	58.0	108,207	41.9	0		224		174	0.1	41,577	D
Ohio	3,969,196	2,498,331	62.9	1,470,865	37.1	0		0		0		1,027,466	D
Oklahoma	932,499	519,834	55.7	412,665	44.3	0		0		0		107,169	D
Oregon	786,305	501,017	63.7	282,779	36	0		0		2,509	0.3	218,238	D
Pennsylvania	4,822,690	3,130,954	64.9	1,673,657	34.7	5,092	0.1	10,456	0.2	2,531	0.1	1,457,297	D
Rhode Island	390,091	315,463	80.9	74,615	19.1	0		0		13		240,848	D
South Carolina	524,779	215,723	41.1	309,048	58.9	0		0		8		93,325	R
South Dakota	293,118	163,010	55.6	130,108	44.4	0		0		0		32,902	D
Tennessee	1,143,946	634,947	55.5	508,965	44.5	0		0		34		125,982	D
Texas	2,626,811	1,663,185	63.3	958,566	36.5	0		0		5,060	0.2	704,619	D

(continued on next page)

APPENDIX C (*continued*)

States	Total Vote	Lyndon B. Johnson Democrat	%	Barry M. Goldwater Republican	%	Eric Hass Socialist Labor	%	Clifton DeBerry Socialist Workers	%	Other	%	Plurality	Party
Utah	401,413	219,628	54.7	181,785	45.3	0		0		0		37,843	D
Vermont	163,089	108,127	66.3	54,942	33.7	0		0		20		53,185	D
Virginia	1,042,267	558,038	53.5	481,334	46.2	2,895	0.3	0		0		76,704	D
Washington	1,258,556	779,881	62.0	470,366	37.4	7,772	0.6	537		0		309,515	D
West Virginia	792,040	538,087	67.9	253,953	32.1	0		0		0		284,134	D
Wisconsin	1,691,815	1,050,424	62.1	638,495	37.7	1,204	0.1	1,692	0.1	0		411,929	D
Wyoming	142,716	80,718	56.6	61,998	43.4	0		0		0		18,720	D
Totals	70,644,592	43,129,566	61.1	27,178,188	38.5	45,219	0.1	32,720	0.1	258,899	0.4	15,951,378	

*The "Other" column for Alabama is the vote for unpledged Democratic electors as Johnson was not on the ballot in that state.

Source: Presidential Elections, 1789–1992 (Washington, DC: Congressional Quarterly, 1995), 67, 121

GENERAL ELECTION RESULTS, ELECTORAL COLLEGE TOTALS 1964

States	Total Electoral Votes	Johnson	Goldwater
Alabama	10	0	10
Alaska	3	3	0
Arizona	5	0	5
Arkansas	6	6	0
California	40	40	0
Colorado	6	6	0
Connecticut	8	8	0
Delaware	3	3	0
DC	3	3	0
Florida	14	14	0
Georgia	12	0	12
Hawaii	4	4	0
Idaho	4	4	0
Illinois	26	26	0
Indiana	13	13	0
Iowa	9	9	0
Kansas	7	7	0
Kentucky	9	9	0
Louisiana	10	0	10
Maine	4	4	0
Maryland	10	10	0
Massachusetts	14	14	0
Michigan	21	21	0
Minnesota	10	10	0
Mississippi	7	0	7
Missouri	12	12	0
Montana	4	4	0
Nebraska	5	5	0
Nevada	3	3	0
New Hampshire	4	4	0
New Jersey	17	17	0

(continued on next page)

States	Total Electoral Votes	Johnson	Goldwater
New Mexico	4	4	o
New York	43	43	o
North Carolina	13	13	o
North Dakota	4	4	o
Ohio	26	26	o
Oklahoma	8	8	o
Oregon	6	6	o
Pennsylvania	29	29	o
Rhode Island	4	4	o
South Carolina	8	o	8
South Dakota	4	4	o
Tennessee	11	11	o
Texas	25	25	o
Utah	4	4	o
Vermont	3	3	o
Virginia	12	12	o
Washington	9	9	o
West Virginia	7	7	o
Wisconsin	12	12	o
Wyoming	3	3	o
Totals	538	486	52

Source: *Presidential Elections, 1789–1992* (Washington, DC: Congressional Quarterly, 1995), 67

LYNDON B. JOHNSON'S INAUGURAL ADDRESS, JANUARY 20, 1965

My fellow countrymen:

On this occasion the oath I have taken before you and before God is not mine alone, but ours together. We are one nation and one people. Our fate as a nation and our future as a people rest not upon one citizen but upon all citizens.

That is the majesty and the meaning of this moment.

For every generation there is a destiny. For some, history decides. For this generation the choice must be our own.

Even now, a rocket moves toward Mars. It reminds us that the world will not be the same for our children, or even for ourselves in a short span of years. The next man to stand here will look out on a scene that is different from our own.

Ours is a time of change—rapid and fantastic change—bearing the secrets of nature, multiplying the nations, placing in uncertain hands new weapons for mastery and destruction, shaking old values and uprooting old ways.

Our destiny in the midst of change will rest on the unchanged character of our people and on their faith.

THE AMERICAN COVENANT They came here—the exile and the stranger, brave but frightened—to find a place where a man could be his own man. They made a covenant with this land. Conceived in justice, written in liberty, bound in union, it was meant one day to inspire the hopes of all mankind. And it binds us still. If we keep its terms we shall flourish.

JUSTICE AND CHANGE First, justice was the promise that all who made the journey would share in the fruits of the land.

In a land of great wealth, families must not live in hopeless poverty. In a land rich in harvest, children just must not go hungry. In a land of healing miracles, neighbors must not suffer and die untended. In a great land of learning and scholars, young people must be taught to read and write.

For more than 30 years that I have served this Nation I have believed that this injustice to our people, this waste of our resources, was our real enemy. For 30 years or more, with the resources I have had, I have vigilantly fought against it. I have learned and I know that it will not surrender easily.

But change has given us new weapons. Before this generation of Americans is finished, this enemy will not only retreat, it will be conquered.

Justice requires us to remember: when any citizen denies his fellow, saying: "His color is not mine or his beliefs are strange and different," in that moment he betrays America, though his forebears created this Nation.

LIBERTY AND CHANGE Liberty was the second article of our covenant. It was self-government. It was our Bill of Rights. But it was more. America would be a place where each man could be proud to be himself: stretching his talents, rejoicing in his work, important in the life of his neighbors and his nation.

This has become more difficult in a world where change and growth seem to tower beyond the control and even the judgment of men. We must work to provide the knowledge and the surroundings which can enlarge the possibilities of every citizen.

THE WORLD AND CHANGE The American covenant called on us to help show the way for the liberation of man. And that is today our goal. Thus, if as a nation, there is much outside our control, as a people no stranger is outside our hope.

Change has brought new meaning to that old mission. We can never again stand aside, prideful in isolation. Terrific dangers and troubles that we once called "foreign" now constantly live among us. If American lives must end, and American treasure be spilled, in countries that we barely know, then that is the price that change has demanded of conviction and of our enduring covenant.

Think of our world as it looks from that rocket that is heading toward Mars. It is like a child's globe, hanging in space, the continent stuck to its side like colored maps. We are all fellow passengers on a dot of earth. And each of us, in the span of time, has really only a moment among our companions.

How incredible it is that in this fragile existence we should hate and destroy one another. There are possibilities enough for all who will abandon mastery over others to pursue mastery over nature. There is world enough for all to seek their happiness in their own way.

Our Nation's course is abundantly clear. We aspire to nothing that belongs to others. We seek no dominion over our fellow man, but man's dominion over tyranny and misery.

But more is required. Men want to be part of a common enterprise, a cause greater than themselves. And each of us must find a way to advance the purpose of the Nation, thus finding new purpose for ourselves. Without this, we will simply become a nation of strangers.

UNION AND CHANGE The third article is union. To those who were small and few against the wilderness, the success of liberty demanded the strength of union. Two centuries of change have made this true again.

No longer need capitalist and worker, farmer and clerk, city and countryside, struggle to divide our bounty. By working shoulder to shoulder together we can increase the bounty of all. We have discovered that every child who learns, and every man who finds work, and every sick body that is made whole—like a candle added to an altar—brightens the hope of all the faithful.

So let us reject any among us who seek to reopen old wounds and rekindle old hatreds. They stand in the way of a seeking nation.

Let us now join reason to faith and action to experience, to transform our unity of interest into a unity of purpose. For the hour and the day and the time are here to achieve progress without strife, to achieve change without hatred; not without difference of opinion but without the deep and abiding divisions which scar the union for generations.

THE AMERICAN BELIEF Under this covenant of justice, liberty, and union we have become a nation—prosperous, great, and mighty. And we have kept our freedom. But we have no promise from God that our greatness will endure. We have been allowed by Him to seek greatness with the sweat of our hands and the strength of our spirit.

I do not believe that the Great Society is the ordered, changeless, and sterile battalion of the ants. It is the excitement of becoming-always becoming, trying, probing, falling, resting, and trying again—but always trying and always gaining.

In each generation, with toil and tears, we have had to earn our heritage again. If we fail now then we will have forgotten in abundance what we learned in hardship: that democracy rests on faith, that freedom asks more than it gives, and the judgment of God is harshest on those who are most favored.

If we succeed it will not be because of what we have, but it will be because of what we are; not because of what we own, but rather because of what we believe.

For we are a nation of believers. Underneath the clamor of building and the rush of our day's pursuits, we are believers in justice and liberty and in our own union. We believe that every man must some day be free. And we believe in ourselves.

And that is the mistake that our enemies have always made. In my lifetime, in depression and in war they have awaited our defeat. Each time, from the secret places of the American heart, came forth the faith that they could not see or that they could not even imagine. And it brought us victory. And it will again.

For this is what America is all about. It is the uncrossed desert and the unclimbed ridge. It is the star that is not reached and the harvest that is sleeping in the unplowed ground. Is our world gone? We say farewell. Is a new world coming? We welcome it, and we will bend it to the hopes of man.

And to these trusted public servants and to my family, and those close friends of mine who have followed me down a long winding road, and to all the people of this Union and the world, I will repeat today what I said on that sorrowful day in November last year: I will lead and I will do the best I can.

But you, you must look within your own hearts to the old promises and to the old dreams. They will lead you best of all.

For myself, I ask only in the words of an ancient leader: "Give me now wisdom and knowledge, that I may go out and come in before this people: for who can judge this thy people, that is so great?"

Source: Lyndon B. Johnson, "The President's Inaugural Address," January 20, 1965, *The American Presidency Project*, eds. Gerhard Peters and John T. Woolley, http://www.presidency.ucsb.edu/ws /?pid=26985.

NOTES

INTRODUCTION

1   "What about 1964?" December 7, 1963, in Richard L. Strout, *TRB: Views and Perspectives on the Presidency* (New York: Macmillan, 1979), 256–258 (first quote); Telephone conversation # 2908, Lyndon B. Johnson and George Reedy, April 8, 1964, 11:45AM, Recordings and Transcripts of Telephone Conversations and Meetings, Lyndon B. Johnson Library, Austin, Texas, https://www.discoverlbj.org/item/tel-02908 (remaining quotes).

2   Allen J. Matusow, *The Unraveling of America: A History of Liberalism in the 1960s* (New York: Harper Torchbooks, 1984), 132–133 (first quote); Tom Wicker, *JFK and LBJ: The Influence of Personality upon Politics* (1968; repr., Chicago: Ivan R. Dee, 1991), 230 (second quote).

3   Wicker, *JFK and LBJ*, 213.

4   Elizabeth Tandy Shermer, "Drafting a Movement: Barry Goldwater and the Rebirth of the Arizona Republican Party," in Elizabeth Tandy Shermer, ed., *Barry Goldwater and the Remaking of the American Political Landscape* (Tucson: University of Arizona Press, 2013), 60 (first quote); Jerome L. Himmelstein, *To the Right: The Transformation of American Conservatism* (Berkeley: University of California Press, 1990), 68 (last two quotes).

5   Jonathan Darman, *Landslide: LBJ and Ronald Reagan at the Dawn of a New America* (New York: Random House, 2014), 156–157.

6   George H. Nash, *The Conservative Intellectual Movement in America, since 1945* (Wilmington, Del.: Intercollegiate Studies Institute, 1996), 273.

7   Mary C. Brennan, *Turning Right in the Sixties: The Conservative Capture of the GOP* (Chapel Hill: University of North Carolina Press, 1995), 16 (first quote); J. William Middendorf II, *A Glorious Disaster: Barry Goldwater's Presidential Campaign and the Origins of the Conservative Movement* (New York: Basic Books, 2006), 107 (next five quotes); Perlstein, *Before the Storm*, 474 (last quote).

8   Steve Fraser, *The Age of Acquiescence: The Life and Death of American Resistance to Organized Wealth and Power* (New York: Little, Brown, 2015), 386–387 (first quote); David T. Courtwright, *No Right Turn: Conservative Politics in a Liberal America* (Cambridge, Mass.: Harvard University Press, 2010), 57 (last quote).

9   Kevin Mattson, *Rebels All! A Short History of the Conservative Mind in Postwar America* (New Brunswick, N.J.: Rutgers University Press, 2008), 69.

10 Theodore H. White, *The Making of the President 1964*, reprint ed. (New York:

Antheneum House, 1965; New York: Harper Perennial Political Classics, 2010), 330. Citations refer to the Harper Perennial edition.

11   White, *The Making of the President*, 377–383, 385 (emphasis in original).

12   Richard H. Rovere, *The Goldwater Caper* (New York: Harcourt, Brace & World, 1965), 9, 40 (first five quotes); Rowland Evans and Robert Novak, *Lyndon B. Johnson: The Exercise of Power: A Political Biography* (New York: New American Library, 1966), 465 (last quote).

13   Sean P. Cunningham, *American Politics in the Postwar Sunbelt: Conservative Growth in a Battleground Region* (New York: Cambridge University Press, 2014), 111.

14   Earl Black and Merle Black, *The Rise of Southern Republicans* (Cambridge, Mass.: Belknap Press of Harvard University Press, 2002), 4 (first quote); Timothy N. Thurber, *Republicans and Race: The GOP's Frayed Relationship with African Americans, 1945–1974* (Lawrence: University Press of Kansas, 2013), 177 (second quote).

CHAPTER 1   THE MYTH OF REPUBLICAN MODERATION IN THE 1950S

1   Heather Cox Richardson, *To Make Men Free: A History of the Republican Party* (New York: Basic Books, 2014), 229; W. J. Rorabaugh, *The Real Making of the President: Kennedy, Nixon, and the 1960 Election* (Lawrence: University Press of Kansas, 2009), 11–30.

2   Data gleaned from Gallup Poll # 1952-0508: Presidential Election/Eisenhower, November 14–19, 1952; Gallup Poll # 541, December 31, 1954–January 5, 1955; Gallup Poll # 1956-0574: Egypt/Voter Registration/Elections, November 9–14, 1956; Gallup Poll # 1960-0638: 1960 Presidential Election, November 17–22, 1960, all available from Roper Center iPOLL, https://ropercenter-cornell-edu .ezproxy.lib.uh.edu/CFIDE/cf/action/ipoll/index.cfm.

3   *The Eisenhower Diaries*, edited by Robert H. Ferrell (New York: W. W. Norton, 1981), 170 (first quote); Kim Phillips-Fein, *Invisible Hands: The Businessmen's Crusade against the New Deal* (New York: W. W. Norton, 2009), 56 (second quote).

4   *Remembering Kerens* (Kerens, Tex.: Friends of the Kerens Library, 1998), 38–39 (quote); "Judge Mays Speaks for Ike at Kerens Says Local Candidates Query 'Cruel,'" *Corsicana Daily Sun*, October 27, 1952.

5   Sherman Adams, *Firsthand Report: The Story of the Eisenhower Administration* (New York: Harper and Brothers, 1961), 12–19.

6   Dwight D. Eisenhower, *The White House Years: Mandate for Change, 1953–1956* (Garden City, N.Y.: Doubleday, 1963), 27 (first two quotes); Adams, *Firsthand Report*, 12–19 (last two quotes).

7   Jack Bell, *The Splendid Misery: The Story of the Presidency and Power Politics at Close Range* (Garden City, N.Y.: Doubleday, 1960), 14–27 (quotes); James T. Patterson, *Mr. Republican: A Biography of Robert A. Taft* (Boston: Houghton Mifflin, 1972), 572–578.

8   Eisenhower, *Mandate for Change*, 55 (quote); Earl Black and Merle Black, *The*

Rise of Southern Republicans (Cambridge, Mass.: The Belknap Press of Harvard University, 2002), 24–25, 61–66, 207–209, 257; Dewey W. Grantham, *The Life and Death of the Solid South: A Political History* (Lexington: University Press of Kentucky, 1988), 127–129.

9   Samuel Lubell, *Revolt of the Moderates* (New York: Harper & Brothers, 1956), 8–10 (first quote); *Eisenhower Diaries*, 226, 233 (second through fourth quotes); Emmet John Hughes, *The Ordeal of Power: A Political Memoir of the Eisenhower Years* (New York: Atheneum, 1963), 124 (last quote).

10   *Eisenhower Diaries*, 234 (first two quotes); Adams, *Firsthand Report*, 20–22 (last quote).

11   Adams, *Firsthand Report*, 25–26 (quote); Gayle B. Montgomery and James W. Johnson, *One Step from the White House: The Rise and Fall of Senator William F. Knowland* (Berkeley: University of California Press, 1998), 132–141.

12   Adams, *Firsthand Report*, 25–26 (first four quotes); *Eisenhower Diaries*, 239, 270 (remaining quotes).

13   Lubell, *Revolt of the Moderates*, 18.

14   *Ike's Letters to a Friend, 1941–1958*, edited by Robert Griffith (Lawrence: University Press of Kansas, 1984), 116–117.

15   Robert Alan Goldberg, *Barry Goldwater* (New Haven, Conn.: Yale University Press, 1995), 24–91.

16   *The Diary of James C. Hagerty: Eisenhower in Mid-Course, 1954–1955*, edited by Robert H. Ferrell (Bloomington: University of Indiana Press, 1983), 95, 119–120.

17   *Diary of James C. Hagerty*, 9 (first quote); Eisenhower, *Mandate for Change*, 428–429 (remaining quotes).

18   David W. Reinhard, *The Republican Right Since 1945* (Lexington: University Press of Kentucky, 1983), 122.

19   *Diary of James C. Hagerty*, 129, 133, 163.

20   *Eisenhower Diaries*, 288–289, 291–292.

21   Lubell, *Revolt of the Moderates*, 216–218.

22   Ibid., 218–220; Louis Harris, *Is There a Republican Majority? Political Trends, 1952–1956* (New York: Harper & Brothers, 1954), 201–214.

23   *Diary of James C. Hagerty*, 241.

24   *Ike's Letters to a Friend*, 136–138 (first four quotes); Hughes, *The Ordeal of Power*, 176 (last quote).

25   Dwight D. Eisenhower, *The White House Years: Waging Peace, 1956–1961* (Garden City, N.Y.: Doubleday, 1965), 3–9.

26   Reinhard, *Republican Right*, 130.

27   *Ike's Letters to a Friend*, 173–174.

28   Dwight D. Eisenhower, "Radio and Television Remarks Following the Election Victory," November 7, 1956, *The American Presidency Project*, eds. Gerhard Peters and John T. Woolley, http://www.presidency.ucsb.edu/ws/?pid=10698 (first quote); Bell, *Splendid Misery*, 413 (second quote).

29   Lubell, *Revolt of the Moderates*, 185, 235.

30 Eisenhower, *Waging Peace*, 377–378, 380.
31 Steven E. Ambrose, *Eisenhower: The President*, vol. 2 (New York: Simon and Schuster, 1984), 488–489; Bell, *Splendid Misery*, 410 (quote).
32 Bell, *Splendid Misery*, 418.
33 Eisenhower, *Waging Peace*, 594–596.
34 Reinhard, *Republican Right*, 153–155.
35 Eisenhower, *Waging Peace*, 601 (emphasis in original).
36 Hughes, *The Ordeal of Power*, 333–334 (emphasis in original).
37 Ibid. 335–338; Lewis L. Gould, *Grand Old Party: A History of the Republican Party* (New York: Random House, 2003), 334.
38 Richardson, *To Make Men Free*, 231–232, 262–263; John Micklethwait and Adrian Wooldridge, *The Right Nation: Conservative Power in America* (New York: Penguin Press, 2004), 40–41.

CHAPTER 2   A NEW FRONTIER FOR THE DEMOCRATIC PARTY?

1 Kari Frederickson, *The Dixiecrat Revolt and the End of the Solid South, 1932–1968* (Chapel Hill: University of North Carolina Press, 2001), 118–186; W. J. Rorabaugh, *The Real Making of the President: Kennedy, Nixon, and the 1960 Election* (Lawrence: University Press of Kansas, 2009), 27–28.
2 Rorabaugh, *The Real Making of the President*, 68–92; Randall B. Woods, *LBJ: Architect of American Ambition* (New York: Simon and Schuster, 2006), 378 (quote).
3 Thomas C. Reeves, *A Question of Character: A Life of John F. Kennedy* (New York: The Free Press, 1991), 167–182.
4 Woods, *LBJ*, 357–358 (first quote); Rowland Evans Jr., recorded interview by Roberta W. Greene, July 30, 1970, p. 18, Robert F. Kennedy Oral History Program, John F. Kennedy Presidential Library, Boston, Massachusetts (hereinafter RF-KOHP, JFKL), (second quote); Joseph W. Alsop, recorded interview by Roberta W. Greene, June 10, 1971, p. 13, RFKOHP, JFKL (last quote).
5 Woods, *LBJ*, 353 (quote).
6 Woods, *LBJ*, 355–356, 360–366, 379; Robert Dallek, *Lone Star Rising: Lyndon Johnson and His Times, 1908–1960* (New York: Oxford University Press, 1991), 559–561, 569–591.
7 Claudia Alta "Lady Bird" Johnson, recorded interview by Sheldon Stern, March 9, 1979, p. 17, John F. Kennedy Library Oral History Program (hereinafter OHP), JFKL.
8 Barry M. Goldwater, recorded interview by Jack Bell, January 24, 1965, p. 11, OHP, JFKL.
9 Kennedy Remarks, Alben Barkley Democratic Club Banquet—Maryland, Saturday Evening, May 14, 1960, in "The Democratic Party: The Spirit of '60," Box 1029, Subseries 1 Speeches and the Press: Speeches, Statements, and Sections, 1958–1960, Series 15 Speeches and the Press, Pre-Presidential Papers (hereinafter PPP), Presidential Campaign Files, 1960 (hereinafter PCF) (first quote); Kennedy Acceptance Speech, July 15, 1960, in "Convention Acceptance Speech, 'The New Frontier,' 15 July 1960," Box 137, Series 11 Special Events through the

Years, President's Office Files (hereinafter POF), Presidential Papers (hereinafter PP) (second and third quotes); and Transcript, Kennedy and Richard M. Nixon, First Joint Radio Television Broadcast, September 26, 1960, 8:30–9:30 p.m. (CDT), CBS—Chicago, in "Television debates: CBS transcript: First debate [Folder 1 of 2]," Box 1052, Subseries 6 Speeches and the Press: Press Secretary's Subject File, 1960, Series 15 Speeches and the Press, PPP, PCF (last two quotes) all in Papers of John F. Kennedy (hereinafter JFKP), JFKL.

10 Kennedy Remarks, The 1960 Election—and 1968, in "The Democratic Party: 1960 Election and 1968," Box 1029, Subseries 1 Speeches and the Press: Speeches, Statements, and Sections, 1958–1960, Series 15 Speeches and the Press, PPP, PCF, JFKP, JFKL.

11 John M. Bailey, recorded interview by Charles T. Morrissey, April 27, 1966, pp. 90–91, OHP, JFKL (quotes); Rorabaugh, *The Real Making of the President*, 1–7, 184–186.

12 Jill Cowan and Priscilla Wear, recorded interview by William J. vanden Heuvel, March 16, 1965, p. 10 (first quote), Thruston B. Morton, recorded interview by Stephen Hess, August 4, 1964, p. 15 (second quote), and Carl B. Albert, recorded interview by Charles T. Morrissey, May 17, 1965, pp. 20–23 (last quote), all in OHP, JFKL.

13 James N. Giglio, *The Presidency of John F. Kennedy* (Lawrence: University Press of Kansas, 1991), 38–40 (first quote); Robert Dallek, *Flawed Giant: Lyndon Johnson and His Times, 1961–1973* (New York: Oxford University Press, 1998), 10–11; Arthur M. Schlesinger Jr., *A Thousand Days: John F. Kennedy in the White House* (Boston: Houghton Mifflin, 1965), 707–710 (last quote).

14 Clinton P. Anderson, recorded interview by John F. Stewart, April 14, 1967, p. 41 (first quote), and Theodore C. Sorensen, recorded interview by Carl Kaysen, May 3, 1964, p. 137 (second quote), both in OHP, JFKL.

15 Robert Dallek, *An Unfinished Life: John F. Kennedy, 1917–1963* (New York: Back Bay Books, 2003), 328–336, 378–380; Woods, *LBJ*, 378–379.

16 Theodore C. Sorensen, *Kennedy* (New York: Harper & Row, 1965), 480–482.

17 Dallek, *An Unfinished Life*, 577–578.

18 Ibid., 578–579.

19 Andrew Biemiller, recorded interview by Sheldon Stern, May 24, 1979, p. 64, OHP, JFKL (quote); Dallek, *An Unfinished Life*, 579; Schlesinger, *A Thousand Days*, 756.

20 Alsop interview, October 29, 1979, p. 43, RFKOHP, JFKL (quotes); Telephone conversation, Kennedy and George Smathers, 1962, in "Telephone Recordings: Dictation Belt 50.3. Signed Bill; Southern Congressmen/Senators," Subseries Telephone Recordings Addition, Series Telephone Recordings, and Telephone conversation, Kennedy and Carl Albert, June 12, 1963, in "Telephone Recordings: Dictation Belt 22A.2. Defeat of Bill in House Due to Integration Backlash," Subseries Telephone Recordings Original Accession, Series Presidential Recordings, both in POF, PP, JFKP, JFKL.

21 Dallek, *An Unfinished Life*, 380–388, 494, 510–518, 589–600; Giglio, *Presidency of John F. Kennedy*, 43–44, 159–178.

22 Dallek, *An Unfinished Life*, 600–603 (quotes); Woods, *LBJ*, 409–412.

23 Dallek, *An Unfinished Life*, 604–606, 640–650.

24 Sorensen interview, May 3, 1964, pp. 133–134, OHP, JFKL.

25 Thomas Grey "Tom" Wicker, recorded interview by Ronald J. Grele, March 22, 1966, pp. 150–152, OHP, JFKL.

26 Wicker interview, pp. 145–148, OHP, JFKL.

27 Jack Valenti recorded interview by Sheldon M. Stern, May 25, 1982, pp. 6–7, OHP, JFKL.

28 Valenti interview, pp. 6–7, OHP, JFKL (first three quotes); Woods, *LBJ*, 367 (sixth quote), 379–380, 381–382 (remaining quotes).

29 Dallek, *An Unfinished Life*, 686–687; Richard Reeves, *President Kennedy: Profile of Power* (New York: Simon & Schuster, 1993), 655.

30 Sorensen interview, May 20, 1964, p. 168, OHP, JFKL (quotes); Reeves, *President Kennedy*, 656–657. Adjusted for inflation, $10,000 in 1963 had the same buying power as $80,000 in 2017.

31 Charles Roche to John Bailey, Democratic Party Activities, November 1963–November 1964, in "Memoranda regarding state organizations for campaign, 1964, 1963," Box 138, Series 11 Special Events through the Years, POF, PP, JFKP, JFKL; Dallek, *An Unfinished Life*, 688 (quotes).

32 Reeves, *President Kennedy*, 655–656.

33 Dallek, *An Unfinished Life*, 688–689 (first quote); Recording of a meeting Kennedy had with Robert F. Kennedy, Lawrence F. O'Brien, John Bailey, Kenneth O'Donnell, Theodore Sorensen, and Dick Maguire, November 11, 1963, in "Meetings: Tape 121/A57. 1964 Democratic Convention Plans; Otepka Security Case; Indonesia; the EEC and International Grain Prices [Entire Tape]," Subseries Presidential Recordings Meetings, Series Presidential Recordings, in POF, PP, JFKP, JFKL (last quote).

34 Dallek, *An Unfinished Life*, 691; Henry Fairlie, *The Kennedy Promise: The Politics of Expectation* (Garden City, N.Y.: Doubleday, 1973), 346 (quotes).

35 Woods, *LBJ*, 415.

36 Wicker interview, pp. 179–204, OHP, JFKL.

37 Bailey interview, p. 117 (first quote), and James T. Corcoran, recorded interview by William Hartigan, March 8, 1976, pp. 12–13 (last quote), both in OHP, JFKL.

38 Johnson interview, pp. 45–47, OHP, JFKL.

39 Valenti interview, pp. 10–12, OHP, JFKL.

40 Wicker interview, pp. 179–204, OHP, JFKL.

41 Reeves, *President Kennedy*, 661.

42 Wicker interview, pp. 179–204, OHP, JFKL.

43 Ibid., pp. 229–231.

44 Valenti interview, pp. 12–14, OHP, JFKL.

45 Evans interview, pp. 15–16, RFKOHP, JFKL.

46 Arthur M. Schlesinger Jr., *Journals, 1952–2000* (New York: Penguin Press, 2007), 207–208 (first quote); Biemiller interview, p. 77, OHP, JFKL (second quote); Dallek, *Flawed Giant*, 50 (last quote).

CHAPTER 3 A REPUBLICAN CIVIL WAR BEGINS

1   Can a Conservative Republican Win?, n.d. [c. 1961 or 1962], in Folder 1, Box 156, William A. Rusher Papers, Manuscript Division, Library of Congress, Washington, DC (hereinafter MD, LC) (first three quotes); Phyllis Schlafly, *A Choice, Not an Echo* (Alton, Ill.: Pere Marquette, 1964), 6 (remaining quotes).

2   Can a Conservative Republican Win?, Rusher Papers, MD, LC.

3   Theodore H. White, *The Making of the President 1964*, reprint ed. (New York: Antheneum House, 1965; New York: Harper Perennial Political Classics, 2010), 66–73 (quote). Citations refer to the Harper Perennial edition.

4   Robert Alan Goldberg, *Barry Goldwater* (New Haven, Conn.: Yale University Press, 1995), 3–64.

5   Rick Perlstein, *Before the Storm: Barry Goldwater and the Unmaking of the American Consensus* (New York: Hill and Wang, 2001), 19.

6   Patrick Allitt, *The Conservatives: Ideas and Personalities Throughout American History* (New Haven, Conn.: Yale University Press, 2009), 188 (first quote); Barry Goldwater, *The Conscience of a Conservative* (Shepherdsville, Ky.: Victor Publishing Company, Inc., 1960), 10–11 (remaining quotes; emphasis in original).

7   Robert D. Novak, *The Agony of the G.O.P. 1964* (New York: Macmillan, 1965), 25–35.

8   Barry M. Goldwater with Jack Casserly, *Goldwater* (New York: Doubleday, 1988), 116.

9   Richard Norton Smith, *On His Own Terms: A Life of Nelson Rockefeller* (New York: Random House, 2014), 410–428; Joseph E. Persico, *The Imperial Rockefeller: A Biography of Nelson A. Rockefeller* (New York: Simon and Schuster, 1982).

10 Allen J. Matusow, *The Unraveling of America: A History of Liberalism in the 1960s* (New York: Harper Torchbooks, 1984), 135.

11 George L. Hinman to Nelson A. Rockefeller, October 30, 1961, in Folder 118, Box 20, Series J.2, Politics—George L. Hinman, Record Group 4, Nelson A. Rockefeller Personal Papers, Rockefeller Family Collection, Rockefeller Archive Center, Sleepy Hollow, New York (hereinafter Series J.2, Hinman, NARPP, RFC, RAC).

12 Stephen E. Ambrose, *Eisenhower: The President*, vol. 2 (New York: Simon and Schuster, 1984), 645 (first quote); Goldwater to William E. Miller, July 2, 1962, in Folder 118, Box 20, Series J.2, Hinman, NARPP, RFC, RAC (last quote).

13 Allan J. Lichtman, *White Protestant Nation: The Rise of the American Conservative Movement* (New York: Grove Press, 2008), 237.

14 Earl Black and Merle Black, *The Rise of Southern Republicans* (Cambridge, Mass.: Belknap Press of Harvard University Press, 2002), 28.

15 Timothy N. Thurber, *Republicans and Race: The GOP's Frayed Relationship with African Americans, 1945–1974* (Lawrence: University Press of Kansas, 2013), 172–173, 176–177.

16 Confidential Memo, May 29, 1962, in Folder 4, Box 155, Rusher Papers, MD, LC.

17 RRD, Memorandum to the Files, December 10, 1962, in Folder 119, Box 20, Series J.2, Hinman, NARPP, RFC, RAC.

18 M. Stanton Evans, *Revolt on the Campus* (Chicago: H. Regnery, 1961), 124.

19 Goldberg, *Goldwater*, 163 (first quote); Lee Edwards, *Goldwater: The Man Who Made a Revolution* (Washington, DC: Regnery Publishing, 1995), 154 (last quote).

20 Mary C. Brennan, *Turning Right in the Sixties: The Conservative Capture of the GOP* (Chapel Hill: University of North Carolina Press, 1995), 164 n.25; Goldberg, *Goldwater*, 150–151.

21 Arthur Krock to Charles P. Taft, July 29, 1963, in "Republican Party Programs and Policies, 1963–63," Box I:215, Charles P. Taft Papers, MD, LC (first quote); Harry O'Donnell to the Governor, et al., February 21, 1962, in Folder 163, Box 28, Series J.2, Hinman, NARPP, RFC, RAC (second quote); Smith, *Rockefeller*, 371 (last quote).

22 John Deardourff to Hinman and Bob Douglass [c. July 25, 1962], in Folder 118, Box 20, Series J.2, Hinman, NARPP, RFC, RAC (first five quotes); Matusow, *The Unraveling of America*, 135 (last quote).

23 Novak, *Agony of the G.O.P.*, 73–74 (first quote); Hinman to Claude J. Jasper, November 14, 1964, in "Draft Goldwater (Chicago Meeting)," Box 119, Barry M. Goldwater Papers, Special Collections, Arizona State University, Tempe, Arizona (hereinafter SC, ASU) (last two quotes).

24 Edward H. Miller, *Nut Country: Right-Wing Dallas and the Birth of the Southern Strategy* (Chicago: University of Chicago Press, 2015), 122–125, 127–129.

25 J. D. Stetson Coleman to Goldwater, November 17, 1962, in "Draft Goldwater (Chicago Meeting)," Box 119, Goldwater Papers, SC, ASU (quotes); Black and Black, *The Rise of Southern Republicans*, 25, 28–29.

26 Hinman to Rockefeller, November 23, 1962, in Folder 372, Box 59, Series J.2, Hinman, NARPP, RFC, RAC (first two quotes); Thurber, *Republicans and Race*, 180–181 (remaining quotes).

27 Lichtman, *White Protestant Nation*, 236 (first quote); Thurber, *Republicans and Race*, 176 (second quote).

28 White, *The Making of the President*, 88–90.

29 Mike Wallace, at 10:00 a.m. over WCBS-TV (New York) and CBS Television Network, January 3, 1963, in Folder 115, Box 20, Series J.2, Hinman, NARPP, RFC, RAC; Questions, December 23, 1962, in "Draft Goldwater (Chicago meeting)," Box 119, Goldwater Papers, SC, ASU (quote).

30 Daniel K. Williams, *God's Own Party: The Making of the Christian Right* (New York: Oxford University Press, 2010), 72 (first quote); Donald T. Critchlow, *The Conservative Ascendancy: How the GOP Right Made Political History* (Cambridge, Mass.: Harvard University Press, 2007), 66–67; David T. Courtwright, *No Right Turn: Conservative Politics in a Liberal America* (Cambridge, Mass.: Harvard University Press, 2010), 55 (last quote).

31 William A. Rusher to Goldwater, January 18, 1963 (first quote), and Rusher to Goldwater, January 23, 1963 (third and fourth quotes) both in "Draft Goldwater (Chicago meeting)," Box 119, Goldwater Papers, SC, ASU; White, *The Making of the President*, 93 (second quote).

32 Sara Fitzgerald, *Elly Peterson: "Mother" of the Moderates* (Ann Arbor: University of Michigan Press, 2011), 49.

33 Novak, *Agony of the G.O.P.*, 177.

34 Gary Donaldson, *Liberalism's Last Hurrah: The Presidential Campaign of 1964* (Armonk, N.Y.: M. E. Sharpe, 2003), 61 (first quote); Perlstein, *Before the Storm*, 191 (second quote).

35 Polly A. Yarnall to David J. Blanchard, April 9, 1963, in "Citizens for Goldwater-Miller (staff directory)," Box 119, Goldwater Papers, SC, ASU (emphasis in original).

36 Edwards, *Goldwater*, 180 (first four quotes); David W. Reinhard, *The Republican Right since 1945* (Lexington: University Press of Kentucky, 1983), 180 (last quote).

37 National Sample Survey, Prepared for William W. Scranton, Governor, The State of Pennsylvania, May 1963, in Folder 17, Box 31, William Scranton Papers, Special Collections, Penn State University, State College, Pennsylvania (first quote); White, *The Making of the President*, 89–92 (last quote; emphasis in original).

38 Reinhard, *Republican Right*, 177–178 (first quote); Transcript of News Conference, Governor Rockefeller, July 30, 1963, in Folder 570, Box 54, Series 21, Hugh Morrow, Record Group 15, Nelson A. Rockefeller Gubernatorial Records (hereinafter Series 21, Morrow Files, NARG), RFC, RAC (remaining quotes).

39 Jackie Robinson to Rockefeller, July 29, 1963 (first two quotes), and Robinson, "The G.O.P.: for White Men Only?" magazine article, n.d. (last quote), both in Folder 339, Box 54, Series J.2, Hinman, NARPP, RFC, RAC; Arnold Rampersad, *Jackie Robinson: A Biography* (New York: Ballantine Books, 1997), 384.

40 Bulletin for August, 1963, Approved by the Executive Committee, Robert Welch to Rockefeller, in Folder 570, Box 54, Morrow Files, NARG, RFC, RAC.

41 J. William Middendorf II, *A Glorious Disaster: Barry Goldwater's Presidential Campaign and the Origins of the Conservative Movement* (New York: Basic Books, 2006), 43 (first two quotes); Raymond Moley, "The Young Republicans," *Newsweek*, August 12, 1963, in Folder 570, Box 54, Morrow Files, NARG, RFC, RAC (next three quotes); Geoffrey Kabaservice, *Rule and Ruin: The Downfall of Moderation and the Destruction of the Republican Party, from Eisenhower to the Tea Party* (New York: Oxford University Press, 2012), 64–66 (last quote).

42 Senator Barry Goldwater Interviewed, WOR-TV, New York, September 19, 1963, in Folder 115, Box 20, Series J.2, Hinman, NARPP, RFC, RAC.

43 CBS News Special Report, September 13, 1963, WCBS-TV and CBS-TV Network, in Folder 115, Box 20, Series J.2, Hinman, NARPP, RFC, RAC.

44 James W. Silver, *Mississippi: The Closed Society* (1964; repr., Jackson: University Press of Mississippi, 2012), 83–104.

45 Gerald R. Ford recorded interview by Vicki Daitch, July 8, 2003, p. 6, John F. Kennedy Library Oral History Program, John F. Kennedy Presidential Library, Boston, Massachusetts (first quote); Stephen Shadegg, *What Happened to Goldwater? The Inside Story of the 1964 Republican Campaign* (New York: Holt, Rinehart and Winston, 1965), 82 (second quote); Untitled, undated statement, in Folder 7, Box 155, Rusher Papers, MD, LC (remaining quotes; emphasis in original).

46 White, *The Making of the President*, 98–99.

47 Ibid. (first quote); Goldwater with Casserly, *Goldwater*, 151–154 (remaining quotes).

48 White, *The Making of the President*, 101 (first quote); Shadegg, *What Happened to Goldwater?*, 85; Barry Goldwater, "Remarks Announcing Candidacy for the Republican Presidential Nomination," January 3, 1964, *The American Presidency Project*, eds. Gerhard Peters and John T. Woolley, http://www.presidency.ucsb.edu/ws/?pid=77813 (second and third quotes); Statement by Peter O'Donnell Jr., Chairman National Draft Goldwater Committee, January 16, 1964, in Folder 8, Box 155, Rusher Papers, MD, LC (last quote).

49 Murray Friedman, *The Neoconservative Revolution: Jewish Intellectuals and the Shaping of Public Policy* (New York: Cambridge University Press, 2005), 97 (first quote); Jennifer Burns, *Goddess of the Market: Ayn Rand and the American Right* (New York: Oxford University Press, 2009), 204–205 (last quote).

50 Donald T. Critchlow, *Phyllis Schlafly and Grassroots Conservatism: A Woman's Crusade* (Princeton, N.J.: Princeton University Press, 2005), 123–125; Kabaservice, *Rule and Ruin*, 90 (first quote); Memo, Cincinnati, June 26, 1964, in "Goldwater 1964 Presidential Campaign, Ohio (notebook) (3 of 3)," Box 141, Goldwater Papers, SC, ASU (remaining quotes).

51 Goldwater Press Conference, Fayetteville, N.C., January 18, 1964, in Folder 115, Box 20, Series J.2, Hinman, NARPP, RFC, RAC (first quote); John Birch Society, March 3, 1964, in Folder 570, Box 54, Morrow Files, NARG, RFC, RAC (remaining quotes).

52 Dear Gerry, p. 61, April 19, 1964, in Folder 1, Box 79, Katie Louchheim Papers, 1997 Addition, MD, LC (first quote); Goldwater to Shadegg, February 29, 1964, in Folder 20, Box 27, Stephen C. Shadegg Papers, SC, ASU (last quote).

53 Progress Report #3, O'Donnell to Goldwater State Chairmen and Key Goldwater People, October 10, 1963, in "Draft Goldwater Progress Reports," Box 119, Goldwater Papers, SC, ASU (first quote); Critchlow, *Phyllis Schlafly and Grassroots Conservatism*, 125 (second quote); Reinhard, *Republican Right*, 183 (last quote).

54 White, *The Making of the President*, 104–107.

55 Notes on Interview with David Hewitt, *Hanover Gazette* (first quote), and Notes on Interview with Ed Bennett, *Claremont Eagle* (second quote), both in Folder 623, and Wilson Sullivan, "Report from New Hampshire, The Press and the Primary" (remaining quotes), in Folder 622, all in Box 60, Morrow Files, NARG, RFC, RAC.

56 White, *The Making of the President*, 109.

57 White, *The Making of the President*, 106–107 (first four quotes); O'Donnell to Goldwater, January 12, 1964, in Folder 8, Box 155, Rusher Papers, MD, LC (next three quotes; emphasis in original); Shadegg, *What Happened to Goldwater?*, 93 (last quote).

58 Perlstein, *Before the Storm*, 282–283.

59 White, *The Making of the President*, 106–107 (first quote); Rockefeller, "Keeping Government Close to the People," Press Release, February 27, 1964, in Folder 631 (second quote), and Rockefeller, "The Goldwater Threat to Social Security,"

Press Release, February 6, 1964, in Folder 628 (last quote), both in Box 60, Morrow Files, NARG, RFC, RAC (emphasis in original).

60 White, *The Making of the President*, 113 (first quote); Rockefeller to Henry Cabot Lodge, January 7, 1964, in Folder 207, Box 34, Series J.2, Hinman, NARPP, RFC, RAC (second quote); Frank to Ralph de Toledano, February 18, 1964, in "Goldwater 1964 Presidential Campaign, New Hampshire (notebook)," Box 141, Goldwater Papers, SC, ASU (last quote).

61 National Draft Lodge Headquarters, Press Release, February 29, 1964 (first two quotes), and National Draft Lodge Headquarters, Press Release, February 11, 1964 (last quote), both in Folder 207, Box 34, Series J.2, Hinman, NARPP, RFC, RAC.

62 New Hampshire Report, March 1, 1964, in "Goldwater 1964 Presidential Campaign, New Hampshire (notebook)," Box 141 (first quote), and Washington State Report, March 26, 1964, in "Goldwater 1964 Presidential Campaign, Washington (notebook)," Box 143 (second and third quotes), both in Goldwater Papers, SC, ASU; New York Republican State Chairman, Fred A. Young, Issued the Following Statement, March 11, 1964, in Folder 603, Box 59, Morrow Files, NARG, RFC, RAC (remaining quotes).

63 Smith, *Rockefeller*, 442–443.

64 New Hampshire Report, March 13, 1964, in "Goldwater 1964 Presidential Campaign, New Hampshire (notebook)," Box 141 (first four quotes), and Washington State Report, Memo to National News-Research, March 19, 1964, in "Goldwater 1964 Presidential Campaign, Washington (notebook)," Box 143 (remaining quotes), both in Goldwater Papers, SC, ASU.

65 Perlstein, *Before the Storm*, 298 (first quote); Nick Thimmesch, *The Condition of Republicanism* (New York: W. W. Norton, 1968), 39 (second quote); Kevin J. Smant, *Principles and Heresies: Frank S. Meyer and the Shaping of the American Conservative Movement* (Wilmington, Del.: ISI Books, 2002), 145 (remaining quotes).

66 Kevin Mattson, *Rebels All! A Short History of the Conservative Mind in Postwar America* (New Brunswick, N.J.: Rutgers University Press, 2008), 69.

CHAPTER 4 PYRRHIC TRIUMPH OR EXTREMIST VICTORY?

1 Allen J. Matusow, *The Unraveling of America: A History of Liberalism in the 1960s* (New York: Harper Torchbooks, 1984), 137.

2 David W. Reinhard, *The Republican Right since 1945* (Lexington: University Press of Kentucky, 1983), 185.

3 Frederick W. Kuechenmeister to James Streeter, March 4, 1964, in "Goldwater 1964 Presidential Campaign, New Jersey (notebook)," Box 141, Barry M. Goldwater Papers, Special Collections, Arizona State University, Tempe, Arizona (hereinafter SC, ASU).

4 Denison Kitchel to State Chairmen, Co-Chairmen, Finance Chairmen and Other Key Goldwater People [c. March 1964], in "Memos, Reports, Correspondence," Box 121, Goldwater Papers, SC, ASU.

5 Malcolm B. Johnson to National News-Research, February 25, 1964 (first

quote), and Florida Report [c. June 20, 1964], (second quote; emphasis in original), both in "Goldwater 1964 Presidential Campaign, Florida (notebook) 2 of 2," Box 138, Goldwater Papers, SC, ASU.

6   Report from Fred H. Taylor, February 3 [1964], in "Goldwater 1964 Campaign, Alabama (notebook)," Box 137, Goldwater Papers, SC, ASU (quote).

7   See delegate reports in "Goldwater 1964 Presidential Campaign, Virginia (notebook)," Box 143, Goldwater Papers, SC, ASU.

8   Theodore H. White, *The Making of the President 1964*, reprint ed. (New York: Antheneum House, 1965; New York: Harper Perennial Political Classics, 2010), 119–120 (first quote). Citations refer to the Harper Perennial edition. Oregon Politics Report, March 19, 1964, in "Goldwater 1964 Presidential Campaign, Wisconsin (notebook) 2 of 2," Box 142, Goldwater Papers, SC, ASU (last quote).

9   Tristram Coffin to George Reedy, April 16, 1964, in "PL 2 Elections and Campaigns, March 17–April 30, 1964," Box 83, White House Central Files, Lyndon B. Johnson Papers, Lyndon B. Johnson Library, Austin, Texas (hereinafter WHCF, LBJP, LBJL).

10   White, *The Making of the President*, 117–118.

11   Richard Norton Smith, *On His Own Terms: A Life of Nelson Rockefeller* (New York: Random House, 2014), 430 (first quote); White, *The Making of the President*, 119–120 (last quote).

12   Oregon Politics Report, May 6, 1964, in "Goldwater 1964 Presidential Campaign, Wisconsin (notebook) 2 of 2," Box 142, Goldwater Papers, SC, ASU (first and last quotes); Minutes of meeting of Operations Committee, Rockefeller National Campaign Committee, Wednesday, April 22, 1964, Confidential, in Folder 122, Box 16, Series J.1—Politics, Record Group 4, Nelson A. Rockefeller Personal Papers, Rockefeller Family Collection, Rockefeller Archive Center, Sleepy Hollow, New York (hereinafter Series J.1, Politics, NARPP, RFC, RAC) (second quote).

13   Oregon Politics Report, April 2, 1964, in "Goldwater 1964 Presidential Campaign, Wisconsin (notebook) 2 of 2," Box 142, Goldwater Papers, SC, ASU (emphasis in original).

14   Stephen C. Shadegg manuscript, May 18, 1964, in Folder 20, Box 27, Stephen C. Shadegg Papers, SC, ASU (first four quotes); Smith, *Rockefeller*, 438 (last two quotes).

15   California Summary, March 14, 1964 (first two quotes), and Summary: California (San Francisco) Rec'd April 3 [1964], (last quote), both in "Goldwater 1964 Presidential Campaign, California (notebook special reports 4 of 4)," Box 138, Goldwater Papers, SC, ASU.

16   White, *The Making of the President*, 125 (first quote); Rick Perlstein, *Before the Storm: Barry Goldwater and the Unmaking of the American Consensus* (New York: Hill and Wang, 2001), 343 (last quote).

17   RLN—PAR [March 1964], in Folder 8, Box 155, William A. Rusher Papers, Manuscript Division, Library of Congress, Washington, DC (hereinafter MD, LC).

18   Perlstein, *Before the Storm*, 337.

19 White, *The Making of the President*, 130, 132.

20 Ibid., 125–127 (first quote); Geoffrey Kabaservice, *Rule and Ruin: The Downfall of Moderation and the Destruction of the Republican Party, from Eisenhower to the Tea Party* (New York: Oxford University Press, 2012), 91 (second and third quotes); Perlstein, *Before the Storm*, 333 (last quote).

21 "Decision Time for State GOP," *Los Angeles Times*, May 17, 1964 (quote); Rockefeller for President Press Release [c. May 17, 1964], in Folder 603, Box 59, Series 21, Hugh Morrow, Record Group 15, Nelson A. Rockefeller Gubernatorial Records (hereinafter Series 21, Morrow Files, NARG), RAC.

22 "Comparison of Eisenhower Statement of May 24, 1964, with Rockefeller and Goldwater Statements and Record," Revised May 27, 1964, in Folder 866, Box 33, Record Group IV, 3A, 18, Graham Molitor Papers, RAC (first quote); White, *The Making of the President*, 146–149 (last quote).

23 Perlstein, *Before the Storm*, 350.

24 Perlstein, *Before the Storm*, 350–351.

25 David Farber, *The Rise and Fall of Modern American Conservatism: A Short History* (Princeton, N.J.: Princeton University Press, 2010), 109–110 (emphasis in original).

26 Robert Alan Goldberg, *Barry Goldwater* (New Haven, Conn.: Yale University Press, 1995), 191 (first two quotes); Perlstein, *Before the Storm*, 339–340 (remaining quotes).

27 Lisa McGirr, *Suburban Warriors: The Origins of the New American Right* (Princeton, N.J.: Princeton University Press, 2001), 135–136.

28 Donald T. Critchlow, *The Conservative Ascendancy: How the GOP Right Made Political History* (Cambridge, Mass.: Harvard University Press, 2007), 69; Matusow, *The Unraveling of America*, 136.

29 White, *The Making of the President*, 127–130.

30 Ibid., 132–135 (emphasis in original).

31 Texas Delegate, George Bush, in "Goldwater 1964 Presidential Campaign, Texas (notebook) (2 of 2)," Box 143, (first quote), and Report for the Week of May 29 to June 5, 1964, in "Goldwater 1964 Presidential Campaign, California (notebook special reports 4 of 4)," Box 138, (remaining quotes), both in Goldwater Papers, SC, ASU.

32 Kabaservice, *Rule and Ruin*, 90–91, 95 (first two quotes; emphasis in original); Daniel K. Williams, *God's Own Party: The Making of the Christian Right* (New York: Oxford University Press, 2010), 73 (last quote).

33 Goldberg, *Goldwater*, 194.

34 Transcript of News Conference, Governor Nelson A. Rockefeller, June 3, 1964, in Folder 614, Series 21, Morrow Files, NARG, RFC, RAC (first four quotes); Minutes of post-California meeting held in Mr. Well's office, Wednesday, June 3, 1964, Confidential (fifth and sixth quotes), and Minutes of Operations Committee, Rockefeller National Campaign Committee, Thursday, June 11, 1964, Confidential (last quote), both in Folder 122, Box 16, Series J.1, Politics, NARPP, RFC, RAC.

35 Minutes of meeting of Operations Committee, Rockefeller National Campaign

Committee, June 4, 1964, Confidential, in Folder 122, Box 16, Series J.1, Politics, NARPP, RFC, RAC.

36 Robinson to Goldwater, August 7, 1964, in Folder 562, Box 54, Series 21, Morrow Files, NARG, RFC, RAC.

37 Goldberg, *Goldwater*, 188.

38 Barry M. Goldwater with Jack Casserly, *Goldwater* (New York: Doubleday, 1988), 169–170.

39 Gallup Poll # 694, June 25–30, 1964, available from Roper Center iPOLL, https://ropercenter-cornell-edu.ezproxy.lib.uh.edu/CFIDE/cf/action/ipoll /index.cfm; George H. Gallup, *The Gallup Poll: Public Opinion, 1935–1971*, vol. 3, 1959–1971 (New York: Random House, 1972), 1890.

40 Transcript of News Conference, Governor Rockefeller and Governor William A. Scranton, November 21, 1963, in Folder 608, Box 59, Series 21, Morrow Files, NARG, RFC, RAC.

41 White, *The Making of the President*, 149–155 (first quote); Reinhard, *Republican Right*, 188–189 (remaining quotes).

42 White, *The Making of the President*, 153 (first quote); Reinhard, *Republican Right*, 189 (second quote); Goldberg, *Goldwater*, 195–196 (last quote).

43 Goldberg, *Goldwater*, 198 (first quote); William Scranton to Goldwater, June 12, 1964, in Folder 20, Box 36, William Scranton Papers, Special Collections, Penn State University, State College, Pennsylvania (hereinafter SC, PSU) (last quote).

44 White, *The Making of the President*, 161–164, 166.

45 Statement by Governor Nelson A. Rockefeller, for immediate release, June 15, 1964, in Folder 588, Box 57, Series 21, Morrow Files, NARG, RFC, RAC (first quote); Minutes of Operations Committee of Former Rockefeller National Campaign Committee, June 18, 1964, Confidential, in Folder 122, Box 16, Series J.1, Politics, NARPP, RFC, RAC (remaining quotes).

46 Maurice I. Carlson to Jean K. Tool, June 22, 1964, in Folder 131, Box 17, Series J.1, Politics, NARPP, RFC, RAC.

47 Minutes of Meeting of Rockefeller for Scranton, Operations Committee, June 24, 1964, Confidential (first two quotes), Minutes of Meeting of Operations Committee, Rockefeller for Scranton Committee, Monday, June 22, 1964, Confidential (third quote), Minutes of Operations Committee Meeting, Rockefeller for Scranton Committee, Monday, June 29, 1964, Confidential (fourth quote), and Minutes of Final Meeting of Operations Committee, Rockefeller for Scranton Committee, Thursday, July 2, 1964, Confidential (remaining quotes), all in Folder 122, Box 16, Series J.1, Politics, NARPP, RFC, RAC.

48 Jonathan M. Schoenwald, *A Time for Choosing: The Rise of Modern American Conservatism* (New York: Oxford University Press, 2001), 142.

49 Kevin M. Schultz, *Buckley and Mailer: The Difficult Friendship That Shaped the Sixties* (New York: W. W. Norton, 2015), 76–77 (emphasis in original).

50 White, *The Making of the President*, 209–210 (first two quotes); Perlstein, *Before the Storm*, 371 (remaining quotes).

51 Dan T. Carter, *The Politics of Rage: George Wallace, the Origins of the New Con-*

servatism, and the Transformation of American Politics (New York: Simon and Schuster, 1995), 219–222.

52 George L. Hinman to Rockefeller, June 26, 1964, in Folder 117, Box 15, Series J.1, Politics, NARPP, RFC, RAC.

53 Goldberg, *Goldwater*, 194–195.

54 White, *The Making of the President*, 202.

55 Perlstein, *Before the Storm*, 374.

56 Report for Week of June 19–26, [1964], in "Goldwater 1964 Presidential Campaign, California (notebook special reports 4 of 4)," Box 138, Goldwater Papers, SC, ASU.

57 See delegate reports in "Goldwater 1964 Presidential Campaign, Alaska (notebook)," Box 137, see the file "Goldwater 1964 Presidential Campaign, Connecticut (notebook)," and see delegate reports in "Goldwater 1964 Presidential Campaign, District of Columbia (notebook)," both in Box 138, and see delegate reports in "Goldwater 1964 Presidential Campaign, West Virginia (notebook)," Box 143, all in Goldwater Papers, SC, ASU.

58 Kabaservice, *Rule and Ruin*, 118.

59 Robert D. Novak, *The Agony of the G.O.P. 1964* (New York: Macmillan, 1965), 2 (first quote); Edward H. Miller, *Nut Country: Right-Wing Dallas and the Birth of the Southern Strategy* (Chicago: University of Chicago Press, 2015), 191n.68 (second quote); Timothy N. Thurber, *Republicans and Race: The GOP's Frayed Relationship with African Americans, 1945–1974* (Lawrence: University Press of Kansas, 2013), 191 (last quote).

60 Byron C. Hulsey, *Everett Dirksen and His Presidents: How a Senate Giant Shaped American Politics* (Lawrence: University Press of Kansas, 2000), 204 (first quote); Perlstein, *Before the Storm*, 373–374 (remaining quotes).

61 Scranton to Goldwater, July 12, 1964, in "Memos, Reports, Correspondence," Box 121, Goldwater Papers, SC, ASU (emphasis in original).

62 Goldberg, *Goldwater*, 199–200 (first quote); Goldwater with Casserly, *Goldwater*, 181–183 (remaining quotes).

63 Perlstein, *Before the Storm*, 382 (first two quotes); Dear Gerry, p. 89, July 24, 1964, in Folder 2, Box 79, Katie Louchheim Papers, 1997 Addition, MD, LC (last quote).

64 White, *The Making of the President*, 210. The context for Ike's reference to switchblades was a recent Supreme Court decision affirming for the accused the right to silence.

65 Donald T. Critchlow, *Phyllis Schlafly and Grassroots Conservatism: A Woman's Crusade* (Princeton, N.J.: Princeton University Press, 2005), 131 (first four quotes); Randall B. Woods, *LBJ: Architect of American Ambition* (New York: Simon and Schuster, 2006), 528 (last quote).

66 White, *The Making of the President*, 212 (first quote); Kabaservice, *Rule and Ruin*, 113 (second quote); Hugh Scott to George Hinman, July 29, 1964, in Folder 372, Box 59, Series J.2, Politics—George L. Hinman, Record Group 4, NARPP, RFC, RAC (last quote).

67 White, *The Making of the President*, 214–215, 217.

68 Goldwater with Casserly, *Goldwater*, 185–186.

69 White, *The Making of the President*, 226–228.

70 Kabaservice, *Rule and Ruin*, 116–117.

71 William E. Miller on *Meet the Press*, July 19, 1964, in "TV Transcripts—Miller, William E., 7/19/1964," Box 219, Lawrence E. Spivak Papers, MD, LC (first four quotes); Goldwater with Casserly, *Goldwater*, 187 (last quote).

72 Goldberg, *Goldwater*, 206–207 (first two quotes); Reinhard, *Republican Right*, 199 (third quote); Schoenwald, *A Time for Choosing*, 146 (remaining quotes).

73 White, *The Making of the President*, 228 (first quote); Dear Gerry, p. 87, July 24, 1964, in Folder 2, Box 79, Louchheim Papers, 1997 Addition, MD, LC (remaining quotes; emphasis in original).

74 Leonard Coe Scruggs to Harry McPherson, July 22, 1964, in PL2—Elections and Campaigns, August 6–14, 1964, Box 83, WHCF, LBJP, LBJL.

75 Clyde T. Ellis to Lyndon B. Johnson, July 27, 1964, in PL2—Elections and Campaigns, August 15–25, 1964, Box 83, WHCF, LBJP, LBJL (first quote); Alternate Reports in "Goldwater 1964 Presidential Campaign, Louisiana (notebook)," Box 140, in Goldwater Papers, SC, ASU (last quote).

76 Goldwater to Scranton, July 18, 1964, in Folder 5, Box 33, Scranton Papers, SC, PSU.

CHAPTER 5 "THAT WAS LYNDON BAINES *JOHNSON!*"

1 Doris Kearns, *Lyndon Johnson and the American Dream* (New York: Harper & Row, 1976), 178.

2 Lyndon B. Johnson, "Address before a Joint Session of the Congress," November 27, 1963, *The American Presidency Project*, eds. Gerhard Peters and John T. Woolley, http://www.presidency.ucsb.edu/ws/?pid=25988.

3 "What about 1964?" December 7, 1963, in Richard L. Strout, *TRB: Views and Perspectives on the Presidency* (New York: Macmillan, 1979), 255 (first quote); Telephone conversation # 85, LBJ and Adam Clayton Powell, November 27, 1963, 2:22PM, Recordings and Transcripts of Telephone Conversations and Meetings (hereinafter RTTCM), Lyndon B. Johnson Library, Austin, Texas (hereinafter LBJL), https://www.discoverlbj.org/item/tel-00085 (second quote; emphasis added); Arthur M. Schlesinger Jr., *Journals, 1952–2000* (New York: Penguin Press, 2007), 210 (last quote).

4 James Farmer recorded interview by John F. Stewart, March 10, 1967, p. 19, John F. Kennedy Library Oral History Program, John F. Kennedy Library, Boston, Massachusetts (hereinafter OHP, JFKL).

5 Telephone conversation # 1967, LBJ and John Connally, February 8, 1964, RTTCM, LBJL, https://www.discoverlbj.org/item/tel-01967 (first two quotes); Telephone conversation # 304, LBJ and Connally, December 5, 1963, 6:40PM, RTTCM, LBJL, https://www.discoverlbj.org/item/tel-00304 (third quote; emphasis added); James Reston Jr., *The Lone Star: The Life of John Connally* (New York: Harper & Row, 1989), 434 (last quote).

6 Robert C. Byrd to LBJ, December 7, 1963, in "PL/ST 48," Box 76 (first two

quotes), Walter Jenkins to LBJ, December 9, 1963, in "PL/ST 9," Box 39 (third quote), and Clifton C. Carter to LBJ, January 15, 1964, in "PL/ST 18," Box 47, (sixth and seventh quotes), all in White House Central Files, Lyndon B. Johnson Papers (hereinafter WHCF, LBJP), LBJL; Theodore H. White, *The Making of the President 1964*, reprint ed. (New York: Antheneum House, Inc., 1965; New York: Harper Perennial Political Classics, 2010), 258. Citations refer to the Harper Perennial edition (fourth and fifth quotes).

7   Lawrence E. Spivak, producer, *Meet the Press*, January 26, 1964, in "TV Transcripts, Smith, Howard W.," Box 218, Lawrence E. Spivak Papers, Manuscript Division, Library of Congress, Washington, DC (hereinafter MD, LC).

8   Dictated by Jack Valenti, June 13, 1964, in "PL 2 Elections and Campaigns, May 1–June 14, 1964," Box 83, WHCF, LBJP, LBJL (first three quotes); Telephone conversation # 1204, LBJ and Eugene McCarthy, January 6, 1964, 7:46PM, RTTCM, LBJL, https://www.discoverlbj.org/item/tel-01204 (last quote).

9   John Kenneth Galbraith, recorded interview by Vicki Daitch, September 12, 2002, p. 30, OHP, JFKL.

10   Telephone conversation # 1335, LBJ and John Knight, January 13, 1964, 11:26AM, RTTCM, LBJL, https://www.discoverlbj.org/item/tel-01335 (first quote); Telephone conversation # 1957, LBJ and Russell Long, February 7, 1964, 7:30PM, RTTCM, LBJL, https://www.discoverlbj.org/item/tel-01957 (last quote).

11   Rowland Evans and Robert Novak, *Lyndon B. Johnson: The Exercise of Power, A Political Biography* (New York: New American Library, 1966), 424, 426 (first two quotes); LBJ, "Remarks at the University of Michigan," May 22, 1964, *The American Presidency Project*, eds. Gerhard Peters and John T. Woolley, http://www.presidency.ucsb.edu/ws/?pid=26262 (remaining quotes).

12   Schlesinger, *Journals*, 211–212, 214–215.

13   Dan T. Carter, *The Politics of Rage: George Wallace, the Origins of the New Conservatism, and the Transformation of American Politics* (New York: Simon and Schuster, 1995), 206–208.

14   Wisconsin Report, April 9, 1964, in "Goldwater 1964 Presidential Campaign, Wisconsin (notebook) 2 of 2," Box 143, Barry M. Goldwater Papers, Special Collections, Arizona State University, Tempe, Arizona (hereinafter SC, ASU).

15   Carter, *Politics of Rage*, 209–211.

16   Ibid., 212–213.

17   Telephone conversation # 3450, LBJ and Hubert Humphrey, May 13, 1964, 7:25PM, RTTCM, LBJL, https://www.discoverlbj.org/item/tel-03450.

18   Carter, *Politics of Rage*, 214–215.

19   Notes on Meeting: President Johnson, Clarence Mitchell and Joe Rauh, January 21, 1964, in Folder 4, Box 26, Joseph Rauh Papers, MD, LC.

20   James Farmer, recorded interview by Sheldon Stern, April 25, 1979, p. 21, OHP, JFKL.

21   Telephone conversation # 3810, LBJ and Charles Halleck, June 22, 1964, 6:24PM, RTTCM, LBJL, https://www.discoverlbj.org/item/tel-03810.

22   Ibid.

23 Ibid (emphasis added).

24 Ibid.

25 Ibid (emphasis added).

26 Paul Southwick to George Reedy, July 14, 1964, in "PL 6-3 Republican Party, November 22, 1963–July 19, 1964," Box 116 (first three quotes), and India Edwards to LBJ, July 22, 1964, in "PL2—Elections and Campaigns, August 15–25, 1964," Box 83 (remaining quotes), both in WHCF, LBJP, LBJL.

27 Michael W. Flamm, *In the Heat of the Summer: The New York Riots of 1964 and the War on Crime* (Philadelphia: University of Pennsylvania Press, 2017), 1; Dear Gerry, p. 88, July 24, 1964, in Folder 2, Box 79, Katie Louchheim Papers Addition, MD, LC (quotes).

28 Dick Nelson to Reedy, July 17, 1964, in "PL 6-3 Republican Party, November 22, 1963–July 19, 1964," Box 116, WHCF, LBJP, LBJL (first quote); Telephone conversation # 4321, LBJ and Connally, July 23, 1964, 5:31PM, RTTCM, LBJL, https://www.discoverlbj.org/item/tel-04321 (remaining quotes).

29 Flamm, *In the Heat of the Summer*, 205–206.

30 Telephone conversation # 4338, LBJ and Nicholas Katzenbach, July 25, 1964, 10:15AM, RTTCM, LBJL, https://www.discoverlbj.org/item/tel-04338 (first four quotes); Robert Alan Goldberg, *Barry Goldwater* (New Haven, Conn.: Yale University Press, 1995), 218 (fifth quote), 215–216 (last quote).

31 Goldberg, *Goldwater*, 216.

32 Joseph W. Alsop, recorded interview by Roberta W. Greene, June 10, 1971, pp. 6, 7, 12, Robert Kennedy Oral History Program of the John F. Kennedy Library (first four quotes); Valenti recorded interview by Sheldon M. Stern, May 25, 1982, pp. 14–15, OHP, JFKL (last quote).

33 Robert Dallek, *Flawed Giant: Lyndon Johnson and His Times, 1961–1973* (New York: Oxford University Press, 1998), 135–136.

34 Kearns, *Lyndon Johnson*, 200.

35 Huffman Baines to LBJ, March 18, 1964, in "PL 2 Elections and Campaigns, March 17–April 30, 1964," Box 83, WHCF, LBJP, LBJL (first quote); Dear Gerry, pp. 75–76, June 10, 1964, in Folder 1, Box 79, Louchheim Papers Addition, MD, LC (second through fourth quotes); Telephone conversation # 16, LBJ and George Smathers, November 23, 1963, 2:10PM, RTTCM, LBJL, https://www.discoverlbj.org/item/tel-00016 (remaining quotes; emphasis added).

36 Transcript, Clark Clifford Oral History Interview II, p. 7, July 6, 1969, by Paige Mullhollan, LBJL.

37 White, *The Making of the President*, 284.

38 Ted Van Dyk, *Heroes, Hacks, and Fools: Memoirs from the Political Inside* (Seattle: University of Washington Press, 2007), 28.

39 Dallek, *Flawed Giant*, 138–141.

40 Schlesinger, *Journals*, 228–229.

41 Ibid., 229.

42 Telephone conversation # 4393, LBJ and Clifford, July 29, 1964, 2:17PM, RTTCM, LBJL, https://www.discoverlbj.org/item/tel-04393.

43 Randall B. Woods, *LBJ: Architect of American Ambition* (New York: Simon and Schuster, 2006), 531.

44 Dallek, *Flawed Giant*, 137 (first quote); Dear Gerry, p. 92, July 24, 1964, in Folder 2, Box 79, Louchheim Papers Addition, MD, LC (last quote).

45 Van Dyk, *Heroes, Hacks, and Fools*, 29.

46 Ibid., 30–31.

47 Ronnie Dugger, *The Politician: The Life and Times of Lyndon Johnson, the Drive for Power—from the Frontier to Master of the Senate* (New York: W. W. Norton, 1982), 158.

48 Dallek, *Flawed Giant*, 159.

49 Telephone conversation # 5231, LBJ and Richard Daley, August 26, 1964, 5:55PM, RTTCM, LBJL, https://www.discoverlbj.org/item/tel-05231 (first quote); Telephone conversation # 5203, LBJ and Jenkins, August 25, 1964, 9:00PM, RTTCM, LBJL, https://www.discoverlbj.org/item/tel-05203 (last quote).

50 Nelson to Jenkins, June 2, 1964, in "PL 1 Conventions, November 22, 1963–July 22, 1964," Box 78, WHCF, LBJP, LBJL (first two quotes); White, *The Making of the President*, 248 (third quote); Transcript, James Farmer Oral History Interview II, p. 2, July 20, 1971, by Paige Mulhollan, LBJL (last quote).

51 Chris Myers Asch, *The Senator and the Sharecropper: The Freedom Struggles of James O. Eastland and Fannie Lou Hamer* (Chapel Hill: University of North Carolina Press, 2008), 210–211; Mississippi Freedom Democratic Party Press Release, July 27, 1964, in "PL 1/ST 24 Conventions, Seating Mississippi Delegation at Democratic Convention," Box 81, WHCF, LBJP, LBJL (quote).

52 Aaron Henry to LBJ, August 22, 1964, in "PL 1/ST 24 Conventions, Seating Mississippi Delegation at Democratic Convention," Box 81, WHCF, LBJP, LBJL.

53 MJDR [Juanita Roberts] to LBJ, August 24, 1964 (first quote), and MJDR [Roberts] to Dorothy [Terito], n.d. (second quote), both in "PL 1/ST 24 Conventions, Seating Mississippi Delegation at Democratic Convention," Box 81, WHCF, LBJP, LBJL.

54 Telephone conversation # 5107, LBJ and Jenkins, August 21, 1964, 8:30PM, RTTCM, LBJL, https://www.discoverlbj.org/item/tel-05107.

55 Partial Proceedings of the Democratic National Convention, 1964, Credentials Committee, Atlantic City, New Jersey, August 22, 1964, in Folder 5, Box 29, Rauh Papers, MD, LC.

56 Ibid.

57 Ibid.

58 Dallek, *Flawed Giant*, 164.

59 Ibid., 162.

60 Telephone conversations # 4917 and # 4918, LBJ and Humphrey, August 14, 1964, 11:05AM, RTTCM, LBJL, https://www.discoverlbj.org/item/tel-04917 and https://www.discoverlbj.org/item/tel-04918 (emphasis added).

61 Telephone conversation # 5156, LBJ and Jenkins, August 24, 1964, 4:31PM?, RTTCM, LBJL, https://www.discoverlbj.org/item/tel-05156.

62 Asch, *The Senator and the Sharecropper*, 212–213.

63 Robert David Johnson, *All the Way with LBJ: The 1964 Presidential Election* (New York: Cambridge University Press, 2009), 186.

64 Telephone conversation # 4840, LBJ and Walter Reuther, August 9, 1964, 8:51AM, RTTCM, LBJL, https://www.discoverlbj.org/item/tel-04840.

65 Julian E. Zelizer, *The Fierce Urgency of Now: Lyndon Johnson, Congress, and the Battle for the Great Society* (New York: Penguin Press, 2015), 152 (first quote); Telephone conversation # 5188, LBJ and Jenkins, August 25, 1964, 7:07PM, RTTCM, LBJL, https://www.discoverlbj.org/item/tel-05188 (last quote; emphasis added).

66 Telephone conversation # 5181, LBJ and Humphrey, August 25, 1964, 2:31PM, RTTCM, LBJL, https://www.discoverlbj.org/item/tel-05181.

67 Telephone conversation # 5210, LBJ and Jenkins, August 25, 1964, 9:33PM, RTTCM, LBJL, https://www.discoverlbj.org/item/tel-05210.

68 Dallek, *Flawed Giant*, 123 (first two quotes); Woods, *LBJ*, 520 (last quote).

69 Woods, *LBJ*, 520–521.

70 Telephone conversation # 5177, LBJ and Jenkins, August 25, 1964, 11:23AM, RTTCM, LBJL, https://www.discoverlbj.org/item/tel-05177.

71 Dallek, *Flawed Giant*, 123–124 (quotes one, two, and five through nine; emphasis in original); Telephone conversation # 5180, LBJ and A. W. Moursund, August 25, 1964, 12:00PM, RTTCM, LBJL, https://www.discoverlbj.org/item/tel-05180 (next two quotes; emphasis added).

72 Dallek, *Flawed Giant*, 160–161.

73 Dear Gerry, p. 92, July 24, 1964, in Folder 2, Box 79, Louchheim Papers Addition, MD, LC.

74 "Johnson-Humphrey vs. Goldwater-Miller," September 5, 1964, in Strout, *TRB*, 270 (first two quotes and last quote); Van Dyk, *Heroes, Hacks, and Fools*, 33–34 (third quote).

75 S. Douglass Cater to Bill Moyers, July 15, 1964, in "Memos to the White House Staff, May–November 1964 and [1967]," Box 13B, Aides Files—Files of S. Douglass Cater, LBJP, LBJL.

76 Transcript, O'Brien Oral History Interview VII, p. 9, February 12, 1986, by Michael L. Gillette, LBJL (first four quotes); Dallek, *Flawed Giant*, 165 (fifth quote); Woods, *LBJ*, 538 (remaining quotes).

77 Johnson, *All the Way*, 196–197.

78 "Johnson-Humphrey vs. Goldwater-Miller," September 5, 1964, in Strout, *TRB*, 269 (first quote); White, *The Making of the President*, 307 (remaining quotes).

79 Woods, *LBJ*, 528 (first three quotes); Schlesinger, *Journals*, 232 (remaining quotes).

CHAPTER 6 BACKLASH, FRONTLASH, SMEARLASH

1 Lyndon B. Johnson, "Remarks in St. Louis, Missouri," October 21, 1964, *The American Presidency Project*, eds. Gerhard Peters and John T. Woolley, https://www.presidency.ucsb.edu/node/242104.

2   Theodore H. White, *The Making of the President 1964*, reprint ed. (New York: Antheneum House, 1965; New York: Harper Perennial Political Classics, 2010), 350. Citations refer to the Harper Perennial edition.

3   Memorandum, February 4, 1964, in "PL 6-3 Republican Party, November 22, 1963–July 19, 1964," Box 116, White House Central Files, Lyndon B. Johnson Papers, Lyndon B. Johnson Presidential Library, Austin, Texas (hereinafter WHCF, LBJP, LBJL).

4   Allen J. Matusow, *The Unraveling of America: A History of Liberalism in the 1960s* (New York: Harper Torchbooks, 1984), 144–146 (first quote); Randall B. Woods, *LBJ: Architect of American Ambition* (New York: Simon and Schuster, 2006), 526 (second and third quotes); Abe Fortas to Walter Jenkins, March 26, 1964, in "PL2 Elections—Campaigns, March 17–April 30, 1964," Box 83, WHCF, LBJP, LBJL (last quote).

5   Typescript on the Johnson-owned television station, n.d., in "Goldwater for President Committee, Thompson Files 1 of 3," Box 121, Barry M. Goldwater Papers, Special Collections, Arizona State University, Tempe, Arizona (hereinafter SC, ASU) (first two quotes; emphasis in original); White, *The Making of the President*, 350 (last quote).

6   Rowland Evans and Robert Novak, *Lyndon B. Johnson: The Exercise of Power, A Political Biography* (New York: New American Library, 1966), 407–409.

7   Ibid., 422–423.

8   Telephone conversation # 5501, Lyndon B. Johnson and William S. White, September 5, 1964, 11:50AM, Recordings and Transcripts of Telephone Conversations and Meetings (hereinafter RTTCM), LBJL, https://www.discoverlbj .org/item/tel-05501 (first two quotes); Telephone conversation # 3450, LBJ and Hubert Humphrey, May 13, 1964, 7:25PM, RTTCM, LBJL, https://www.discov erlbj.org/item/tel-03450 (remaining quotes).

9   Ray O. Shaffer to Jack Valenti, January 10, 1964, in "PL 6-3 Republican Party, November 22, 1963–July 19, 1964" (first quote), and Palmer Hoyt to LBJ, July 15, 1964, in "PL 6-3 Republican Party, November 22, 1963–July 19, 1964" (second quote), both in Box 116, WHCF, LBJP, LBJL.

10   Eric F. Goldman, *The Tragedy of Lyndon Johnson* (New York: Dell Publishing, 1968, 1969), 228.

11   Walter W. Heller to LBJ, August 4, 1964, in "PL 6-3 Republican Party, July 20, 1964–September 19, 1964," Box 117, WHCF, LBJP, LBJL (emphasis in original).

12   Clifton C. Carter to LBJ, January 7, 1964, in "PL2—Elections and Campaigns, January 4–31, 1964," Box 82, in WHCF, LBJP, LBJL.

13   Bill Moyers to Carter, July 18, 1964, in "PL 2 Elections and Campaigns, June 15–July 23, 1964," Box 83 (first quote), and Memorandum for Moyers on Indiana and Illinois, October 1, 1964, in "PL/ST 13," Box 43 (last quote), both in WHCF, LBJP, LBJL.

14   LBJ to Robert F. Windfohr, January 2, 1964, in "PL/ST 43," Box 69 (first quote), Memo to LBJ, July 1, 1964, in "PL—Political Affairs, November 22, 1963–August 6, 1964," Box 1 (second quote), and D. O. Andreas to H. H., August 3,

1964, in "PL 2 Elections and Campaigns, July 24–August 5, 1964," Box 83 (last quote), all in WHCF, LBJP, LBJL.

15 Stewart L. Udall to LBJ, July 29, 1964, in "PL 2 Elections and Campaigns, July 24–August 5, 1964," Box 83, WHCF, LBJP, LBJL.

16 Woods, *LBJ*, 541.

17 Woods, *LBJ*, 541 (first quote); Kathleen Hall Jamieson, *Packaging the Presidency: A History and Criticism of Presidential Campaign Advertising*, 2nd ed. (New York: Oxford University Press, 1992), 193–194 (last quote).

18 Transcript, Lawrence F. O'Brien Oral History Interview IX, p. 16, April 9, 1986, by Michael L. Gillette, LBJL (first quote); Thomas Corcoran to LBJ, November 10, 1964, in "PL/Republicans for Johnson, November 22, 1963–August 20, 1964," Box 26, WHCF, LBJP, LBJL (last quote).

19 Evans and Novak, *Lyndon B. Johnson*, 470.

20 Jenkins to Valenti, September 29, 1964, in "PL/ST 32," Box 56, WHCF, LBJP, LBJL (first quote); Telephone conversation # 3826, LBJ and Carter, June 23, 1964, 1:36PM, RTTCM, LBJL, https://www.discoverlbj.org/item/tel-03826 (second quote); Telephone conversation # 4839, LBJ and Walter Reuther, August 9, 1964, 8:51AM, RTTCM, LBJL, https://www.discoverlbj.org/item/tel -04839 (last quote).

21 Richard A. Viguerie, *Conservatives Betrayed: How George W. Bush and Other Big Government Republicans Hijacked the Conservative Cause* (Los Angeles: Bonus Books, 2006), 185; Jonathan M. Schoenwald, *A Time for Choosing: The Rise of Modern American Conservatism* (New York: Oxford University Press, 2001), 160, 164.

22 Joseph Crespino, *Strom Thurmond's America* (New York: Hill and Wang, 2012), 128 (first quote); Kim Phillips-Fein, *Invisible Hands: The Businessmen's Crusade against the New Deal* (New York: W. W. Norton, 2009), 135–136, 139–142 (last quote).

23 S. Douglass Cater to LBJ, July 10, 1964, in "PL 6-3 Republican Party, November 22, 1963–July 19, 1964," Box 116, WHCF, LBJP, LBJL.

24 Eric F. Goldman to LBJ, July 17, 1964, in "PL 2 Elections and Campaigns, June 15–July 23, 1964," (first quote), Valenti to LBJ, August 25, 1964, in "PL 2 Elections and Campaigns, August 15–August 25, 1964," (second quote), both in Box 83, WHCF, LBJP, LBJL.

25 James Sterngold, "A Family Struggle for the Soul of Times Mirror," *New York Times*, November 27, 1995 (first two quotes); Valenti to LBJ, September 10, 1964, in "PL 2 September 6, 1964—September 14, 1964," Box 84, in WHCF, LBJP, LBJL (last two quotes; emphasis in original).

26 Valenti to LBJ, September 10, 1964, in "PL 2 September 6, 1964—September 14, 1964," Box 84, in WHCF, LBJP, LBJL.

27 John Micklethwait and Adrian Wooldridge, *The Right Nation: Conservative Power in America* (New York: Penguin Press, 2004), 58.

28 George Reedy to LBJ, August 18, 1964, in "PL 6-3 Republican Party, July 20– September 19, 1964," Box 117, WHCF, LBJP, LBJL.

29 Valenti to Moyers and Reedy, August 20, 1964, in "PL 2, August 15–August

25, 1964" (first quote; emphasis in original), and Moyers to LBJ, September 3, 1964, in "PL 2 August 26, 1964—September 5, 1964" (remaining quotes), both in Box 83, WHCF, LBJP, LBJL.

30 Cater to LBJ, October 16, 1964, in "Memos to the President, September–November 1964," Box 13B, Aides Files—Files of S. Douglass Cater (hereinafter Aides Files—Cater), LBJP, LBJL.

31 Louis Martin to Valenti, July 7, 1964, in "PL 2 Elections and Campaigns, June 15–July 23, 1964," Box 83, WHCF, LBJP, LBJL.

32 Craig Truax to Dean Burch, August 3, 1964, in "Memos, Reports, Correspondence," Box 121 (first quote), Newspaper Reaction to Goldwater Tour of the South—North Carolina, n.d. (next three quotes), and The Midwest—Illinois, n.d. both in "Goldwater for President Committee, Thompson Files (Southern States) 3 of 3," Box 122 (last quote), all in Goldwater Papers, SC, ASU.

33 Denison Kitchel on *Meet the Press*, June 14, 1964, in "TV Transcripts—Kitchel, Denison, 6/14/1964," Box 219, Lawrence E. Spivak Papers, Manuscript Division, Library of Congress, Washington, DC (hereinafter MD, LC).

34 Matthew E. Welsh to LBJ, July 27, 1964, in "PL 2 Elections and Campaigns, August 6–August 14, 1964," Box 83, WHCF, LBJP, LBJL (emphasis in original).

35 Cater to LBJ, August 12, 1964, in "Memos to the White House Staff, May–November 1964 and [1967]," Box 13B, Aides Files—Cater, LBJP, LBJL (emphasis in original).

36 Phillips-Fein, *Invisible Hands*, 143.

37 John Bartlow Martin to Moyers, October 1, 1964, in "PL/ST 14," Box 45, WHCF, LBJP, LBJL.

38 Ibid. Emphasis in original.

39 John A. Gronouski to LBJ, August 10, 1964 (first two quotes), and Paul M. Popple to Valenti, August 20, 1964 (remaining quotes), both in "PL 2 Elections and Campaigns, August 15–25, 1964," Box 83, WHCF, LBJP, LBJL.

40 Truax to Burch, August 3, 1964, in "Memos, Reports, Correspondence," Box 121, Goldwater Papers, SC, ASU (emphasis in original).

41 White, *The Making of the President*, 337 (first and third quotes); Robert Alan Goldberg, *Barry Goldwater* (New Haven, Conn.: Yale University Press, 1995), 221 (second quote).

42 Confidential Proceedings of Closed Session Meeting of Republican Unity Conference, August 12, 1964, in "PL 6-3 Republican Party, July 20–September 19, 1964," Box 117, WHCF, LBJP, LBJL (quotes); Robert David Johnson, *All the Way with LBJ: The 1964 Presidential Election* (New York: Cambridge University Press, 2009), 222–223.

43 Lee Edwards, *Goldwater: The Man Who Made a Revolution* (Washington, DC: Regnery Publishing, 1995), 330–331 (first quote); Telephone conversation # 4145, LBJ and John Connally, July 3, 1964, 11:38AM, RTTCM, LBJL, https://www.discoverlbj.org/item/tel-04145 (second quote); Goldman, *The Tragedy of Lyndon Johnson*, 226 (last quote).

44 Confidential Proceedings of Closed Session Meeting of Republican Unity Con-

ference, August 12, 1964, in "PL 6-3 Republican Party, July 20–September 19, 1964," Box 117, WHCF, LBJP, LBJL.

45 White, *The Making of the President*, 332, 335, 336.

46 Schoenwald, *A Time for Choosing*, 152.

47 J. William Middendorf II, *A Glorious Disaster: Barry Goldwater's Presidential Campaign and the Origins of the Conservative Movement* (New York: Basic Books, 2006), 179–180.

48 Confidential Proceedings of Closed Session Meeting of Republican Unity Conference, August 12, 1964, in "PL 6-3 Republican Party, July 20–September 19, 1964," Box 117, WHCF, LBJP, LBJL (first two quotes); Timothy N. Thurber, *Republicans and Race: The GOP's Frayed Relationship with African Americans, 1945–1974* (Lawrence: University Press of Kansas, 2013), 194 (last quote).

49 Confidential Proceedings of Closed Session Meeting of Republican Unity Conference, August 12, 1964, in "PL 6-3 Republican Party, July 20–September 19, 1964," Box 117, WHCF, LBJP, LBJL.

50 Ibid.

51 Ibid.

52 Robert Dallek, *Flawed Giant: Lyndon Johnson and His Times, 1961–1973* (New York: Oxford University Press, 1998), 168–169.

53 Evans and Novak, *Lyndon B. Johnson*, 465–467.

54 Dallek, *Flawed Giant*, 171–172.

55 White, *The Making of the President*, 365–369 (emphasis in original).

56 Evans and Novak, *Lyndon B. Johnson*, 468–469 (first three quotes); White, *The Making of the President*, 365–369 (next three quotes); Transcript, Reedy Oral History Interview I(c), p. 2, December 20, 1968, by T. H. Baker, LBJL (last quote).

57 Moyers to LBJ, August 15, 1964, in "PL2—Elections and Campaigns, August 15–25, 1964," Box 83 (first three quotes), and Valenti to LBJ, September 7, 1964, in "PL 2 Elections and Campaigns, September 6—September 14, 1964," Box 84 (remaining quotes; emphasis in original), both in WHCF, LBJP, LBJL.

58 White, *The Making of the President*, 371.

59 Transcript, Clark Clifford Oral History Interview II, p. 9, July 6, 1969, by Paige Mullhollan, LBJL.

60 White, *The Making of the President*, 311, 316, 347 (emphasis in original).

61 Mitchell Lerner, "Vietnam and the 1964 Election: A Defense of Lyndon Johnson," *Presidential Studies Quarterly* 25 (Fall 1995): 751–766; Woods, *LBJ*, 547–549 (quote).

62 Goldberg, *Goldwater*, 191–192.

63 Mary C. Brennan, *Turning Right in the Sixties: The Conservative Capture of the GOP* (Chapel Hill: University of North Carolina Press, 1995), 95.

64 Dallek, *Flawed Giant*, 166–168 (emphasis in original).

65 David Farber, *The Rise and Fall of Modern American Conservatism: A Short History* (Princeton, N.J.: Princeton University Press, 2010), 112 (first quote); Dallek, *Flawed Giant*, 134 (remaining quotes).

66 Middendorf, *A Glorious Disaster*, 157–161.

67 Telephone conversation # 5507, LBJ and Moyers, September 5, 1964, 4:20PM, RTTCM, LBJL, https://www.discoverlbj.org/item/tel-05507.

68 George Reedy, *Lyndon B. Johnson, A Memoir* (New York: Andrews and McMeel, 1982), 17 (first quote); Evans and Novak, *Lyndon B. Johnson*, 471 (last quote).

69 White, *The Making of the President*, 347, 360.

70 Evans and Novak, *Lyndon B. Johnson*, 467.

71 Dear Gerry, p. 91, July 24, 1964, in Folder 2, Box 79, Katie Louchheim Papers Addition, MD, LC (first quote); Cater to LBJ, June 3, 1964, in "PL 2 Elections and Campaigns, May 1–June 14, 1964," Box 83, WHCF, LBJP, LBJL (last quote; emphasis in original).

CHAPTER 7 "GOVERNMENT IS NOT AN ENEMY OF THE PEOPLE. IT IS THE PEOPLE"

1 Transcript, S. Douglass Cater Oral History Interview I, p. 7, April 29, 1969, by David G. McComb, Lyndon B. Johnson Presidential Library, Austin, Texas (hereinafter LBJL) (first quote); Cater to Lyndon B. Johnson, September 1, 1964, in "Memos to the President, September–November 1964," Box 13B, Aides Files—Files of S. Douglass Cater, Lyndon B. Johnson Papers (hereinafter Aides Files—Cater, LBJP) (second quote), and Bob Hunter to Cater, September 28, 1964, in "PL 2 September 25, 1964–September 30, 1964," Box 84, White House Central Files (hereinafter WHCF), LBJP (remaining quotes) both in LBJL.

2 Cater to LBJ, September 19, 1964 (first quote), Cater to LBJ, September 24, 1964 (second quote), and Cater to LBJ, September 21, 1964 (third quote), all in "Memos to the President, September–November 1964," Box 13B, Aides Files—Cater, LBJP, LBJL; Rick Perlstein, *Before the Storm: Barry Goldwater and the Unmaking of the American Consensus* (New York: Hill and Wang, 2001), 477 (last quote).

3 Lee Edwards, *Goldwater: The Man Who Made a Revolution* (Washington, DC: Regnery Publishing, 1995), 288 (first two quotes); Lawrence F. O'Brien to LBJ, October 4, 1964, in "PL 2 October 2, 1964–October 4, 1964," Box 84, WHCF, LBJP, LBJL (remaining quotes; emphasis in original).

4 Robert David Johnson, *All the Way with LBJ: The 1964 Presidential Election* (New York: Cambridge University Press, 2009), 229–230 (quote). There is no indication in WorldCat that a Spanish language translation of *A Texan Looks at Lyndon* was published, but author Rick Perlstein agrees there was. See Perlstein, *Before the Storm*, 477–478.

5 Theodore H. White, *The Making of the President 1964*, reprint ed. (New York: Antheneum House, Inc., 1965; New York: Harper Perennial Political Classics, 2010), 338. Citations refer to the Harper Perennial edition.

6 Kathleen Hall Jamieson, *Packaging the Presidency: A History and Criticism of Presidential Campaign Advertising*, 2nd ed. (New York: Oxford University Press, 1992), 172–173, 186.

7 Ibid., 175–177.

8 Ibid. (first quote); "Peace Little Girl (Daisy)," in *Museum of the Moving Image:*

The Living Room Candidate, Presidential Campaign Commercials, 1952–2016 (hereinafter MMI), http://www.livingroomcandidate.org/commercials/1964 /peace-little-girl-daisy (second and third quotes); Robert Dallek, *Flawed Giant: Lyndon Johnson and His Times, 1961–1973* (New York: Oxford University Press, 1998), 175–176 (last quote).

9 Robert Mann, *Daisy Petals and Mushroom Clouds: LBJ, Barry Goldwater, and the Ad that Changed American Politics* (Baton Rouge: Louisiana State University Press, 2011), 109–116; Transcript, Lawrence O'Brien Oral History Interview IX, p. 7, April 9, 1986, by Michael L. Gillette, LBJL (quotes).

10 Randall B. Woods, *LBJ: Architect of American Ambition* (New York: Simon and Schuster, 2006), 540 (first two quotes); "Ice Cream," in *MMI*, http://www.liv ingroomcandidate.org/commercials/1964/ice-cream (third quote); Jamieson, *Packaging the Presidency*, 201 (last quote).

11 Jamieson, *Packaging the Presidency*, 201 (first quote); Barry M. Goldwater with Jack Casserly, *Goldwater* (New York: Doubleday, 1988), 199, 201 (remaining quotes).

12 Doris Kearns, *Lyndon Johnson and the American Dream* (New York: Harper & Row, 1976), 247.

13 Jamieson, *Packaging the Presidency*, 205.

14 Stephen Shadegg, *What Happened to Goldwater? The Inside Story of the 1964 Republican Campaign* (New York: Holt, Rinehart and Winston, 1965), 251 (first quote); Heather Hendershot, *What's Fair on the Air? Cold War Right-Wing Broadcasting and the Public Interest* (Chicago: University of Chicago Press, 2011), 175–176 (second and third quotes); Darren Dochuk, *From Bible Belt to Sunbelt: Plain-Folk Religion, Grassroots Politics, and the Rise of Evangelical Con-servatism* (New York: W. W. Norton, 2011), 253–254 (last quote).

15 Perlstein, *Before the Storm*, 441–442.

16 Jamieson, *Packaging the Presidency*, 207.

17 Ronnie Dugger, *The Politician: The Life and Times of Lyndon Johnson, the Drive for Power—from the Frontier to Master of the Senate* (New York: W. W. Norton, 1982), 452n7.

18 Clifton C. Carter to LBJ, August 15, 1964, in "PL 2 Elections and Campaigns, August 15–August 25, 1964," Box 83, WHCF, LBJP, LBJL (first quote); William E. Miller on *Meet the Press*, July 19, 1964, in "TV Transcripts—Miller, William E., 7/19/1964," Box 219, Lawrence E. Spivak Papers, Manuscript Division, Library of Congress, Washington, DC (hereinafter MD, LC) (second quote).

19 Carter to LBJ, August 15, 1964, in "PL 2 Elections and Campaigns, August 15–August 25, 1964," Box 83, WHCF, LBJP, LBJL (first quote); Craig Truax to Dean Burch, August 3, 1964, in "Memos, Reports, Correspondence," Box 121 (second and third quotes; emphasis in original), and Newspaper Reaction to Goldwater Tour of the South—Arkansas, n.d., in "Goldwater for President Committee, Thompson Files (Southern States) 3 of 3," Box 122 (last quote), both in Goldwater Papers, SC, ASU.

20 Ralph McGill to LBJ, September 30, 1964, in "PL 2 October 5, 1964," Box 84, WHCF, LBJP, LBJL.

21 Dick Thompson to Pam Rymer, n.d., in "Goldwater for President Committee, Thompson Files (Southern States) 3 of 3," Box 122 (first two quotes) and State by State Analysis, Newspapers/Polls—Florida, October 19, 1964, in "States, State by State Analysis (newspapers, polls)," Box 137 (last quote), both in Goldwater Papers, SC, ASU.

22 Rowland Evans and Robert Novak, *Lyndon B. Johnson: The Exercise of Power, A Political Biography* (New York: New American Library, 1966), 474–475 (emphasis in original).

23 Fred Dutton to Jack Valenti, October 27, 1964, in "EX PL 2, October 26, 1964–October 28, 1964," Box 85 (first quote), and Bill Moyers to LBJ, September 29, 1964, in "PL 2 September 25, 1964–September 30, 1964," Box 84 (last quote), both in WHCF, LBJP, LBJL.

24 White, *The Making of the President*, 340–346, 351.

25 O'Brien to LBJ, October 4, 1964, in "PL 2 October 2, 1964–October 4, 1964," Box 84 (first quote), O'Brien to LBJ, October 9, 1964, in "PL 2 October 9, 1964," Box 85 (second quote), and SHR to Walter Jenkins, October 12, 1964, in "PL/ST 31," Box 56 (last quote), all in WHCF, LBJP, LBJL.

26 Joseph Crespino, *Strom Thurmond's America* (New York: Hill and Wang, 2012), 165–166; Edgar A. Brown to Jenkins, October 13, 1964, in "PL/ST 40," Box 68, WHCF, LBJP, LBJL (quote); Earl Black and Merle Black, *The Rise of Southern Republicans* (Cambridge, Mass.: Belknap Press of Harvard University Press, 2002), 33, 205, 209.

27 Richard H. Rovere, *The Goldwater Caper* (New York: Harcourt, Brace & World, 1965), 135.

28 Ibid., 134, 140–142.

29 Bernard von Bothmer, *Framing the Sixties: The Use and Abuse of a Decade from Ronald Reagan to George W. Bush* (Amherst: University of Massachusetts Press, 2010), 69 (first quote); Timothy N. Thurber, *Republicans and Race: The GOP's Frayed Relationship with African Americans, 1945–1974* (Lawrence: University Press of Kansas, 2013), 197 (last quote).

30 Rovere, *The Goldwater Caper*, 143–144.

31 Edwards, *Goldwater*, 257 (first two quotes); Thurber, *Republicans and Race*, 198 (last two quotes).

32 Michael W. Flamm, *Law and Order: Street Crime, Civil Unrest, and the Crisis of Liberalism in the 1960s* (New York: Columbia University Press, 2005), 1–2, 32–34, 36–37, 46–48.

33 Michelle M. Nickerson, *Mothers of Conservatism: Women and the Postwar Right* (Princeton, N.J.: Princeton University Press, 2012), 157–158 (quote); Lisa McGirr, *Suburban Warriors: The Origins of the New American Right* (Princeton, N.J.: Princeton University Press, 2001).

34 Meredith Hindley, "Lady Bird Special: Mrs. Johnson's Southern Strategy," *Humanities* 34 (May/June 2013), available online at http://www.neh.gov/humanities/2013/mayjune/feature/lady-bird-special; Maurine H. Beasley, *First Ladies and the Press: The Unfinished Partnership of the Media Age* (Evanston, Ill.: Northwestern University Press, 2005), 93.

35 Cater to LBJ, August 13, 1964, in "PP5 Johnson, Lady Bird, July 15, 1964–October 1, 1964," Box 62, WHCF, LBJP, both in LBJL (first quote; emphasis in original); Remarks by Johnson, Alexandria, Virginia, October 6, 1964, in "Virginia, October 6, 1964," Box 79, White House Social Files—Liz Carpenter Files (hereinafter WHSF—LCF), LBJL (remaining quotes).

36 Helen Fuller, "The Powerful Persuaders: Lady Bird's Trip Through the South," *The New Republic* 151 (October 24, 1964): 11–12 (first quote); "Story of the Lady Bird Special," n.d., in "TR1/Johnson, Mrs.," Box 2, WHCF, LBJP, LBJL (second quote); Gary Donaldson, *Liberalism's Last Hurrah: The Presidential Campaign of 1964* (Armonk, N.Y.: M.E. Sharpe, 2003), 274 (last quote).

37 Woods, *LBJ*, 544 (first quote); Eric F. Goldman, *The Tragedy of Lyndon Johnson* (New York: Dell Publishing, 1968, 1969), 290–293 (remaining quotes).

38 Goldman, *The Tragedy of Lyndon Johnson*, 290–294 (first six quotes; emphasis in original); Woods, *LBJ*, 544 (last quote).

39 Jack Valenti, *A Very Human President, A First-Hand Report* (New York: W. W. Norton, 1975), 208.

40 White, *The Making of the President*, 376 (first, second, and fourth quotes); Johnson, *All the Way*, 139 (third quote).

41 Matthew F. Delmont, *Why Busing Failed: Race, Media, and the National Resistance to School Desegregation* (Oakland: University of California Press, 2016), 94.

42 Moyers to LBJ, July 17, 1964, in "PL 2 Elections and Campaigns, June 15–July 23, 1964," Box 83 (first quote), and Mike Manatos to Moyers, October 16, 1964, in "PL 2 October 14, 1964–October 18, 1964," Box 85 (second quote), both in WHCF, LBJP, LBJ; Northwest Correspondent's Report, July 27, 1964, in Folder 15, Box 28, Stephen C. Shadegg Papers, SC, ASU (last quote).

43 "The Goldwater Candidacy and the Christian Conscience: The Response of Protestant Theologians" [August 6, 1964], in "PL 2 Elections and Campaigns, August 6–August 14, 1964," Box 83, WHCF, LBJP, LBJL.

44 Dochuk, *From Bible Belt to Sunbelt*, 229–234, 246–248.

45 Daniel K. Williams, *God's Own Party: The Making of the Christian Right* (New York: Oxford University Press, 2010), 69, 74, 76–77 (first quote); Steven P. Miller, *Billy Graham and the Rise of the Republican South* (Philadelphia: University of Pennsylvania Press, 2004), 96–108 (last quote).

46 Williams, *God's Own Party*, 69, 74, 76–77 (first quote); Miller, *Billy Graham*, 96–108 (remaining quotes).

47 Michael R. Beschloss, ed., *Reaching for Glory: Lyndon Johnson's Secret White House Tapes, 1964–1965* (New York: Simon and Schuster, 2001), 54–102.

48 Woods, *LBJ*, 551–552.

49 Dallek, *Flawed Giant*, 180–181 (first quote); Woods, *LBJ*, 551 (second quote); Alvin Toffler, "The Woman behind Barry Goldwater," *Good Housekeeping* (May 1964): 58, 60, 62, 64–65.

50 von Bothmer, *Framing the Sixties*, 29 (quote).

51 Ronald Reagan, "Address on Behalf of Senator Barry Goldwater: 'A Time for Choosing,'" October 27, 1964, in *The American Presidency Project*, eds. Gerhard

Peters and John T. Woolley, http://www.presidency.ucsb.edu/ws/?pid=76121 (first quote); James T. Patterson, *The Eve of Destruction: How 1965 Transformed America* (New York: Basic Books, 2012), 20 (second quote); Richard A. Viguerie, *Conservatives Betrayed: How George W. Bush and Other Big Government Republicans Hijacked the Conservative Cause* (Los Angeles: Bonus Books, 2006), 187 (last quote).

52   Evans and Novak, *Lyndon B. Johnson*, 382 (first quote); Telephone conversation # 4839, LBJ and Walter Reuther, August 9, 1964, 8:51AM, Recordings and Transcripts of Telephone Conversations and Meetings, LBJL, https://www.dis coverlbj.org/item/tel-04839 (last quote).

53   O'Brien to LBJ, August 22, 1964, in "PL 2 Elections and Campaigns, August 6–14, 1964," Box 83, WHCF, LBJP, LBJL.

54   LBJ and Reuther telephone conversation, August 9, 1964.

55   Charles P. Taft to Dear Friend, September 30, 1964, in Folder 561, Box 54, Series 21, Hugh Morrow, Record Group 15, Nelson A. Rockefeller Gubernatorial Records, Rockefeller Family Collection, Rockefeller Archive Center, Sleepy Hollow, New York (hereinafter RFC, RAC).

56   Goldman, *The Tragedy of Lyndon Johnson*, 303.

57   White, *The Making of the President*, 398–399.

58   "The 1964 Election Results," *CQ Almanac 1964*, 20th ed. (Washington, DC: Congressional Quarterly, 1965),1021–1068, http://library.cqpress.com/cqal manac/cqal64-1302939; Election of 1964, and Election of 1936, both in *The American Presidency Project*, eds. Gerhard Peters and John T. Woolley, see http://www.presidency.ucsb.edu/showelection.php?year=1964 and http://www.presidency.ucsb.edu/showelection.php?year=1936, respectively.

59   Goldwater with Casserly, *Goldwater*, 219–220 (first quote); Flamm, *Law and Order*, 206n.78 (last quote).

60   William F. Buckley Jr., *Flying High: Remembering Barry Goldwater* (New York: Basic Books March 2010), 166 (first two quotes); Nelson to Barry, n.d. but mailed November 13, 1964, in Folder 119, Box 20, Series J.2, Politics—George L. Hinman, Record Group 4, Nelson A. Rockefeller Personal Papers, RFC, RAC (remaining quotes; emphasis in original).

61   Robert B. Horwitz, *America's Right: Anti-establishment Conservatism from Goldwater to the Tea Party* (Cambridge, U.K.: Polity Press, 2013), 39 (first quote; emphasis in original); Goldwater with Casserly, *Goldwater*, 166 (remaining quotes).

62   G. Calvin Mackenzie and Robert Weisbrot, *The Liberal Hour: Washington and the Politics of Change in the 1960s* (New York: Penguin Books, 2008), 109 (first three quotes); Perlstein, *Before the Storm*, 516 (last quote).

CONCLUSION

1   John A. Andrew III, *The Other Side of the Sixties: Young Americans for Freedom and the Rise of Conservative Politics* (New Brunswick, N.J.: Rutgers University Press, 1997), 205 (first quote); John V. Lindsay, *Journey into Politics, Some Informal Observations* (New York: Dodd, Mead, 1967), 125–126 (second quote); Kim

Phillips-Fein, *Invisible Hands: The Businessmen's Crusade against the New Deal* (New York: W. W. Norton, 2009), 212 (remaining quotes).

2   Kathleen Hall Jamieson, *Packaging the Presidency: A History and Criticism of Presidential Campaign Advertising*, 2nd ed. (New York: Oxford University Press, 1992), 185 (first quote); Edward H. Miller, *Nut Country: Right-Wing Dallas and the Birth of the Southern Strategy* (Chicago: University of Chicago Press, 2015), 131 (second quote); Jennifer Burns, *Goddess of the Market: Ayn Rand and the American Right* (New York: Oxford University Press, 2009), 208 (last quote).

3   Jonathan M. Schoenwald, *A Time for Choosing: The Rise of Modern American Conservatism* (New York: Oxford University Press, 2001), 158–159.

4   Jack W. Germond, *Fat Man in a Middle Seat: Forty Years of Covering Politics* (New York: Random House, 1999), 55.

5   Richard A. Viguerie, *Conservatives Betrayed: How George W. Bush and Other Big Government Republicans Hijacked the Conservative Cause* (Los Angeles: Bonus Books, 2006), 183–185, 191 (emphasis in original).

6   Matthew D. Lassiter, *The Silent Majority: Suburban Politics in the Sunbelt South* (Princeton, N.J.: Princeton University Press, 2006), 230–231 (first, third, and fourth quotes); Barry M. Goldwater, recorded interview by Jack Bell, January 24, 1965, p. 25, John F. Kennedy Library Oral History Program, John F. Kennedy Presidential Library, Boston, Massachusetts (hereinafter OHP, JFKL) (second quote); Theda Skocpol and Vanessa Williamson, *The Tea Party and the Remaking of Republican Conservatism* (New York: Oxford University Press, 2012).

7   The Ripon Society, *From Disaster to Distinction: The Rebirth of the Republican Party* (New York: Pocket Books, 1966), 13 (first quote); Rowland Evans and Robert Novak, *Lyndon B. Johnson: The Exercise of Power, A Political Biography* (New York: The New American Library, 1966), 481 (remaining quotes).

8   Gerald R. Ford recorded interview by Vicki Daitch, July 8, 2003, p. 5, OHP, JFKL (first quote); Philip Jenkins, *Decade of Nightmares: The End of the Sixties and the Making of Eighties America* (New York: Oxford University Press, 2006), 76, 81 (remaining quotes).

9   George E. Reedy, *The Twilight of the Presidency* (New York: World Publishing, 1970), 66 (first two quotes); Theodore H. White, *The Making of the President 1964*, reprint ed. (New York: Antheneum House, Inc., 1965; New York: Harper Perennial Political Classics, 2010), 423 (remaining quotes). Citations refer to the Harper Perennial edition.

10   John A. Blatnik, recorded interview by Joseph E. O'Connor, February 4, 1966, p. 30, OHP, JFKL (first two quotes); John M. Bailey, recorded interview by Charles T. Morrissey, April 27, 1966, pp. 76, 119–120, OHP, JFKL (third and fourth quotes); Transcript, Lawrence F. O'Brien Oral History Interview XI, p. 2, July 24, 1986, by Michael L. Gillette, Lyndon B. Johnson Presidential Library, Austin, Texas (last quote). Ralph Harding (D-ID) lost his reelection bid in 1964. The handful of other Democrats who voted for the bill but were not reelected lost out in the primary, often because of redistricting.

11   Charles O. Jones, *The Minority Party in Congress* (Boston: Little, Brown, 1970), 72–74.

12 Jack T. Conway, recorded interview by Larry J. Hackman, December 29, 1972, p. 104, Robert F. Kennedy Oral History Program of the JFKL.

13 Reedy, *Twilight of the Presidency*, 66–67.

14 Evans and Novak, *Lyndon B. Johnson*, 475 (first quote); White, *The Making of the President*, 425 (second quote); Byron C. Hulsey, *Everett Dirksen and His Presidents: How a Senate Giant Shaped American Politics* (Lawrence: University Press of Kansas, 2000), 206 (last quote).

BIBLIOGRAPHIC ESSAY

The archival material and the secondary literature on the 1964 presidential election is vast. This bibliographic essay is limited to a discussion of those sources that were most useful in framing and developing my account of the contest. Indeed, scholars and students interested in learning more about the 1964 presidential election will find a wealth of primary and secondary source material to facilitate their efforts. Archival sources are abundant. Both of the party standard-bearers left voluminous records as did those who challenged for the Republican Party nomination. The Lyndon B. Johnson Presidential Library in Austin, Texas, houses a cornucopia of important material. Most important are the Political Affairs files (PL) within the White House Central Files (WHCF). Other useful components of the WHCF include the Trip files (TR) and the President Personal files (PP). Researchers will also benefit from the Office Files of White House Aides, specifically those for Horace Busby, S. Douglass Cater, Richard Goodwin, Bill Moyers, Lawrence O'Brien, George Reedy, and Henry Wilson. Researchers will also want to consult the voluminous oral history collection. Students and scholars interested in Lady Bird Johnson's role in the contest will be rewarded with a search of the White House Social Files (WHSF). Finally, researchers will want to examine the Recordings and Transcripts of Telephone Conversations. These conversations can be searched through the LBJ Library's website and as of September 1, 2018, all conversations cited in the manuscript were available for download. For anyone wanting to study Johnson's election as president there is no substitute for hearing him in his own voice discuss the political landscape of 1964.

For those interested in studying Republican efforts in 1964, the starting point is the Barry Goldwater Papers at the Special Collections at Arizona State University in Tempe, Arizona. Also at this repository are the following important collections: Dean Burch Papers, Karl Hess Papers, Harry Rosenzweig Papers, and Stephen C. Shadegg Papers. Combined, these materials give voice to Goldwater's political strategy. Next in importance are the materials at the Rockefeller Archive Center in Sleepy Hollow, New York. Documents in this repository tell the story of East Coast, moderate Republicans and their efforts to thwart a conservative takeover of the party. Researchers will want to consult the Nelson A. Rockefeller Gubernatorial Records for the Hugh Morrow Campaign Files and the Nelson A. Rockefeller Personal Papers for the George L. Hinman Files and the Politics Files. Additionally at the Rockefeller Archive Center researchers should examine the Graham Molitor Papers. The William Scranton Papers in the Special Collections at Pennsylvania State

University in State College, Pennsylvania reveal Scranton's hesitancy to challenge Goldwater after the primaries.

Other collections that shed light on politics in 1964 include the Katie Louchheim Papers, the Joseph Rauh Papers, the William Rusher Papers, the Lawrence Spivak Papers, and the Charles P. Taft Papers, all at the Manuscript Division, Library of Congress, Washington, DC.

Students interested in studying Kennedy's involvement with national politics can find much of the materials digitized in the John F. Kennedy Presidential Library in Boston, Massachusetts. See the Presidential Campaign Files in the Papers of John F. Kennedy, Pre-Presidential Papers. In the Papers of John F. Kennedy, Presidential Papers consult the President's Office Files, Press Secretary's Subject Files, and the Presidential Recordings. Of additional interest are two oral history collections at the Kennedy Library, the Robert F. Kennedy Oral History Program and the John F. Kennedy Library Oral History Program.

Countless edited collections of correspondence, published diaries, and other printed primary sources have helped to flesh out the story. To gain insight into the Republican Party during the 1950s see: Herbert Brownell with John P. Burke, *Advising Ike: The Memoirs of Attorney General Herbert Brownell* (Lawrence: University Press of Kansas, 1993); *The Eisenhower Diaries*, edited by Robert H. Ferrell (New York: W. W. Norton, 1981); *Ike's Letters to a Friend, 1941–1958*, edited by Robert Griffith (Lawrence: University Press of Kansas, 1984); *The Diary of James C. Hagerty: Eisenhower in Mid-Course, 1954–1955*, edited by Robert H. Ferrell (Bloomington: University of Indiana Press, 1983); and Richard M. Nixon, *RN: The Memoirs of Richard Nixon* (New York: Grosset & Dunlap, 1978). For insights into the Kennedy presidency, liberals, and the Democratic Party see Arthur M. Schlesinger Jr., *Journals, 1952–2000* (New York: Penguin Press, 2007). Richard L. Strout, *TRB: Views and Perspectives on the Presidency* (New York: Macmillan, 1979), contains the lead editorial columns from the *New Republic*. The Johnson phone tapes are voluminous and can be tricky to navigate. A series of edited volumes contains some of the most important conversations. See: Michael R. Beschloss, ed., *Taking Charge: The Johnson White House Tapes, 1963–1964* (New York: Simon and Schuster, 1997); Michael R. Beschloss, ed., *Reaching for Glory: Lyndon Johnson's Secret White House Tapes, 1964–1965* (New York: Simon and Schuster, 2001).

Online resources include *The American Presidency Project*, edited by Gerhard Peters and John T. Woolley, http://www.presidency.ucsb.edu; the *Presidential Recordings Digital Edition*, http://prde.upress.virginia.edu; *Museum of the Moving Image: The Living Room Candidate, Presidential Campaign Commercials, 1952–2016*, http://www.livingroomcandidate.org; Lyndon B. Johnson's Daily Diary Collection, http://www.lbjlibrary.net/collections/daily-diary.html; Election Polls—Vote by Groups, 1960–1964, Gallup http://news.gallup.com/poll/9454/election-polls-vote-groups-19601964.aspx; and the Roper Center iPOLL, https://ropercenter.cornell.edu.

Partisan accounts written about the 1964 election and its larger context and consequences are vast. For titles intended to help make Goldwater president see: Barry Goldwater, *The Conscience of a Conservative* (Shepherdsville, Ky.: Victor Publishing Company, 1960); Barry M. Goldwater, *Where I Stand* (New York: McGraw-Hill,

1964); J. Evetts Haley, *A Texan Looks at Lyndon: A Study in Illegitimate Power* (Canyon, Tex.: Palo Duro Press, 1964); Phyllis Schlafly, *A Choice, Not an Echo* (Alton, Ill.: Pere Marquette, 1964); John A. Stormer, *None Dare Call It Treason* (Florissant, Mo.: Liberty Bell Press, 1964). Titles written to benefit LBJ include: Lyndon B. Johnson, *My Hope for America* (New York: Random House, 1964); Fred J. Cook, *Barry Goldwater: Extremist of the Right* (New York: Grove Press, 1964).

Disappointed conservatives wrote about their experiences with the Goldwater campaign. See: Stephen Shadegg, *What Happened to Goldwater? The Inside Story of the 1964 Republican Campaign* (New York: Holt, Rinehart and Winston, 1965); Richard A. Viguerie, *Conservatives Betrayed: How George W. Bush and Other Big Government Republicans Hijacked the Conservative Cause* (Los Angeles: Bonus Books, 2006); F. Clifton White with William J. Gill, *Suite 3505: The Story of the Draft Goldwater Movement* (New Rochelle, N.Y.: Arlington House, 1967); F. Clifton White and William J. Gill, *Why Reagan Won: A Narrative History of the Conservative Movement, 1964–1981* (Chicago: Regnery Gateway, 1981).

Moderate Republicans have also written about 1964. See: George F. Gilder and Bruce K. Chapman, *The Party That Lost Its Head* (New York: Alfred A. Knopf, 1966); John V. Lindsay, *Journey into Politics, Some Informal Observations* (New York: Dodd, Mead, 1967); The Ripon Society, *From Disaster to Distinction: The Rebirth of the Republican Party* (New York: Pocket Books, 1966); Hugh Scott, *Come to the Party* (Englewood Cliffs, N.J.: Prentice-Hall, 1968).

Partisan accounts favorable to Johnson include George E. Reedy, *The Twilight of the Presidency* (New York: World Publishing, 1970), and Jack Valenti, *A Very Human President, A First-Hand Report* (New York: W. W. Norton, 1975).

Memoirs and other contemporary accounts about politics in the 1950s and 1960s fill multiple library shelves. For the most helpful titles on the Eisenhower years see: Sherman Adams, *Firsthand Report: The Story of the Eisenhower Administration* (New York: Harper and Brothers, 1961); Dwight D. Eisenhower, *The White House Years: Mandate for Change, 1953–1956* (Garden City, N.Y.: Doubleday, 1963); Dwight D. Eisenhower, *The White House Years: Waging Peace, 1956–1961* (Garden City, N.Y.: Doubleday, 1965); Louis Harris, *Is There a Republican Majority? Political Trends, 1952–1956* (New York: Harper & Brothers, 1954); Emmet John Hughes, *The Ordeal of Power: A Political Memoir of the Eisenhower Years* (New York: Atheneum, 1963); Arthur Larson, *A Republican Looks at His Party* (New York: Harper & Brothers, 1956); Samuel Lubell, *Revolt of the Moderates* (New York: Harper & Brothers, 1956); and Joe Martin, *My First Fifty Years in Politics*, as told to Robert J. Donovan, (New York: McGraw-Hill, 1960).

Memoirs focused on the 1960s include Richard Bolling, *House Out of Order* (New York: E.P. Dutton, 1965), which provides useful insights into Congress. Barry M. Goldwater with Jack Casserly, *Goldwater* (New York: Doubleday, 1988), is the best first-hand, published account of Goldwater's thinking. Lyndon Johnson's *The Vantage Point* (New York: Holt, Rinehart and Winston, 1971) is less revealing. Kevin Phillips, *The Emerging Republican Majority* (1969; repr., Princeton, N.J.: Princeton University Press, 2015), is a classic account of GOP strategy to displace Democratic hegemony in national politics. Ted Van Dyk, *Heroes, Hacks, and Fools: Memoirs from the Political Inside* (Seattle: University of Washington Press, 2007), provides an inside view of Hubert Humphrey. George Reedy has written a reflective book about the Johnson era: *Lyndon B. Johnson, A Memoir* (New York: Andrews and McMeel, 1982).

Other titles worth exploring include: Bernard Cosman and Robert J. Huckshorn, eds., *Republican Politics: The 1964 Campaign and Its Aftermath for the Party* (New York: Frederick A. Praeger, 1968); Charles O. Jones, *The Minority Party in Congress* (Boston: Little, Brown, 1970); John H. Kessel, *The Goldwater Coalition: Republican Strategies in 1964* (Indianapolis, Ind.: Bobbs-Merrill, 1968).

Journalists have written about politics in the 1950s and 1960s. For the best accounts of the Eisenhower era see: Jack Bell, *The Splendid Misery: The Story of the Presidency and Power Politics at Close Range* (Garden City, N.Y.: Doubleday, 1960), and Robert J. Donovan, *Eisenhower: The Inside Story* (New York: Harper & Brothers, 1956). Journalistic accounts of the 1964 election are Robert D. Novak, *The Agony of the G.O.P. 1964* (New York: Macmillan, 1965); Richard H. Rovere, *The Goldwater Caper* (New York: Harcourt, Brace & World, 1965); and Theodore H. White, *The Making of the President 1964*, reprint ed. (New York: Antheneum House, 1965; New York: Harper Perennial Political Classics, 2010). Following his coverage of the Kennedy election in 1960 White became the preeminent journalist covering national politics, but as a source for the 1964 contest readers should be aware of his Democratic bias. This perspective caused him to struggle to understand what was happening in the GOP. The volume is still very helpful for the near first-hand accounts he provides of events from this momentous campaign.

For the best journalistic accounts of the Johnson administration see Rowland Evans and Robert Novak, *Lyndon B. Johnson: The Exercise of Power, A Political Biography* (New York: New American Library, 1966), and Tom Wicker, *JFK and LBJ: The Influence of Personality upon Politics* (1968; repr., Chicago: Ivan R. Dee, 1991).

Other titles by journalists worth exploring include: *Conversations with Walter Lippmann* (Boston: Little, Brown, 1965); Jack W. Germond, *Fat Man in a Middle Seat: Forty Years of Covering Politics* (New York: Random House, 1999); Nick Thimmesch, *The Condition of Republicanism* (New York: W. W. Norton, 1968).

Several books have been written about the 1964 election. The most thoroughly researched treatment of Goldwater and the Republicans is Rick Perlstein, *Before the Storm: Barry Goldwater and the Unmaking of the American Consensus* (New York: Hill and Wang, 2001). J. William Middendorf II offers an insider's perspective that has the benefit of research in additional sources. See: Middendorf, *A Glorious Disaster: Barry Goldwater's Presidential Campaign and the Origins of the Conservative Movement* (New York: Basic Books, 2006). The best treatment of the election from the perspective of Johnson is Robert David Johnson, *All the Way with LBJ: The 1964 Presidential Election* (New York: Cambridge University Press, 2009), which makes heavy use of the phone tapes. Also worth noting is Gary Donaldson, *Liberalism's Last Hurrah: The Presidential Campaign of 1964* (Armonk, N.Y.: M. E. Sharpe, 2003), which makes a declensionist argument. Jonathan Darman, *Landslide: LBJ and Ronald Reagan at the Dawn of a New America* (New York: Random House, 2014), is a breezy account for popular audiences. Robert Mann, *Daisy Petals and Mushroom Clouds: LBJ, Barry Goldwater, and the Ad that Changed American Politics* (Baton Rouge: Louisiana State

University Press, 2011), is focused on the one advertisement that changed the nature of campaign advertising.

Multiple works look at midcentury political history. For a carefully researched, well-written account of campaign advertising see: Kathleen Hall Jamieson, *Packaging the Presidency: A History and Criticism of Presidential Campaign Advertising*, 2nd ed. (New York: Oxford University Press, 1992). For details on the White House and the press see: Maurine H. Beasley, *First Ladies and the Press: The Unfinished Partnership of the Media Age* (Evanston, Ill.: Northwestern University Press, 2005), and W. Dale Nelson, *Who Speaks for the President? The White House Press Secretary from Cleveland to Clinton* (Syracuse, N.Y.: Syracuse University Press, 1998). The best book on legislative policy during the Great Society is Julian E. Zelizer, *The Fierce Urgency of Now: Lyndon Johnson, Congress, and the Battle for the Great Society* (New York: Penguin Press, 2015). Two innovative looks at the 1950s and 1960s as cultural ideas are Bernard von Bothmer, *Framing the Sixties: The Use and Abuse of a Decade from Ronald Reagan to George W. Bush* (Amherst: University of Massachusetts Press, 2010), and Daniel Marcus, *Happy Days and Wonder Years: The Fifties and the Sixties in Contemporary Cultural Politics* (New Brunswick, N.J.: Rutgers University Press, 2004). Two helpful works about larger political processes include Andrew E. Busch, *Outsiders and Openness in the Presidential Nominating System* (Pittsburgh, Penn.: University of Pittsburgh Press, 1997), and Daniel J. Galvin, *Presidential Party Building: Dwight D. Eisenhower to George W. Bush* (Princeton, N.J.: Princeton University Press, 2010). Busch provides an account of the complicated procedures by which the Republican Party selected a presidential nominee in 1964.

Students and scholars interested in reading more about the GOP will want to start with Geoffrey Kabaservice, *Rule and Ruin: The Downfall of Moderation and the Destruction of the Republican Party, from Eisenhower to the Tea Party* (New York: Oxford University Press, 2012), a well-researched, thoughtful account of the realignment within the GOP. Other important books are: Gary W. Reichard, *The Reaffirmation of Republicanism: Eisenhower and the Eighty-Third Congress* (Knoxville: University of Tennessee Press, 1975); Donald A. Ritchie, *A History of the United States Senate Republican Policy Committee, 1947–1997* (Washington, DC: US Government Printing Office, 1997). See also Michael Bowen, *The Roots of Modern Conservatism: Dewey, Taft, and the Battle for the Soul of the Republican Party* (Chapel Hill: University of North Carolina Press, 2011), for a more focused but equally important exploration of the fissures in the GOP.

Timothy N. Thurber, *Republicans and Race: The GOP's Frayed Relationship with African Americans, 1945–1974* (Lawrence: University Press of Kansas, 2013), is a smart, thorough study of the GOP's tangled history with race and public policy. See also by Thurber: "Forgotten Architects of the Second Reconstruction: Republicans and Civil Rights, 1945–1972," in *Making Sense of American Liberalism*, Jonathan Bell and Timothy Stanley, eds. (Urbana: University of Illinois Press, 2012). For additional reading on race as a political issue see Thomas Byrne Edsall with Mary D. Edsall, *Chain Reaction: The Impact of Race, Rights, and Taxes on American Politics* (New York: W. W. Norton, 1992).

The best detailed narrative of the GOP in the 1960s is Mary C. Brennan, *Turning*

Right in the Sixties: The Conservative Capture of the GOP (Chapel Hill: University of North Carolina Press, 1995). General overviews of the Republican Party include Lewis L. Gould, *Grand Old Party: A History of the Republican Party* (New York: Random House, 2003), and Heather Cox Richardson, *To Make Men Free: A History of the Republican Party* (New York: Basic Books, 2014). Focused overviews of the postwar years include: Nicol C. Rae, *The Decline and Fall of the Liberal Republicans: From 1952 to the Present* (New York: Oxford University Press, 1989) and David W. Reinhard, *The Republican Right Since 1945* (Lexington: University Press of Kentucky, 1983).

Many titles explore modern conservatism. For a brief introductory account of modern conservatism, see David Farber, *The Rise and Fall of Modern Conservatism: A Short History* (Princeton, N.J.: Princeton University Press, 2010). A longer synthetic treatment of the topic is Donald T. Critchlow, *The Conservative Ascendancy: How the GOP Right Made Political History* (Cambridge, Mass.: Harvard University Press, 2007). Several important books explore different aspects of the origins of this political movement. See: Donald T. Critchlow, *Phyllis Schlafly and Grassroots Conservatism: A Woman's Crusade* (Princeton, N.J.: Princeton University Press, 2005); Heather Hendershot, *What's Fair on the Air? Cold War Right-Wing Broadcasting and the Public Interest* (Chicago, Ill.: University of Chicago Press, 2011); Allan J. Lichtman, *White Protestant Nation: The Rise of the American Conservative Movement* (New York: Grove Press, 2008); Lisa McGirr, *Suburban Warriors: The Origins of the New American Right* (Princeton, N.J.: Princeton University Press, 2001); George H. Nash, *The Conservative Intellectual Movement in America, since 1945* (Wilmington, Del.: Intercollegiate Studies Institute, 1996); Michelle M. Nickerson, *Mothers of Conservatism: Women and the Postwar Right* (Princeton, N.J.: Princeton University Press, 2012); Kim Phillips-Fein, *Invisible Hands: The Businessmen's Crusade against the New Deal* (New York: W. W. Norton, 2009); Jonathan M. Schoenwald, *A Time for Choosing: The Rise of Modern American Conservatism* (New York: Oxford University Press, 2001); Daniel K. Williams, *God's Own Party: The Making of the Christian Right* (New York: Oxford University Press, 2010). John A. Andrew III, *The Other Side of the Sixties: Young Americans for Freedom and the Rise of Conservative Politics* (New Brunswick, N.J.: Rutgers University Press, 1997), is especially helpful for understanding one Republican faction crucial to the Goldwater nomination and the conservative capture of the GOP, the Young Americans for Freedom. For related books see: Gregory L. Schneider, *Cadres for Conservatism: Young Americans for Freedom and the Rise of the Contemporary Right* (New York: New York University Press, 1999), and M. Stanton Evans, *Revolt on the Campus* (Chicago: H. Regnery, 1961). Evans, a conservative journalist who knew his subjects, provides a sympathetic portrait.

Other titles to explore include: Patrick Allitt, *The Conservatives: Ideas and Personalities throughout American History* (New Haven, Conn.: Yale University Press, 2009); Matthew F. Delmont, *Why Busing Failed: Race, Media, and the National Resistance to School Desegregation* (Oakland: University of California Press, 2016); Seth Dowland, *Family Values and the Rise of the Christian Right* (Philadelphia: University of Pennsylvania Press, 2015); Murray Friedman, *The Neoconservative Revolution: Jewish Intellectuals and the Shaping of Public Policy* (New York: Cambridge University Press, 2005); Jerome L. Himmelstein, *To the Right: The Transformation of American*

Conservatism (Berkeley: University of California Press, 1990); Godfrey Hodgson, *The World Turned Right Side Up: A History of the Conservative Ascendancy in America* (Boston: Houghton Mifflin, 1996); Robert B. Horwitz, *America's Right: Anti-Establishment Conservatism from Goldwater to the Tea Party* (Cambridge, U.K.: Polity Press, 2013); Rebecca E. Klatch, *A Generation Divided: The New Left, the New Right and the 1960s* (Berkeley: University of California Press, 1999); Kevin Mattson, *Rebels All! A Short History of the Conservative Mind in Postwar America* (New Brunswick, N.J.: Rutgers University Press, 2008); John Micklethwait and Adrian Wooldridge, *The Right Nation: Conservative Power in America* (New York: Penguin Press, 2004); Theda Skocpol and Vanessa Williamson, *The Tea Party and the Remaking of Republican Conservatism* (New York: Oxford University Press, 2012); and Robert Brent Toplin, *Radical Conservatism: The Right's Political Religion* (Lawrence: University Press of Kansas, 2006).

For titles that explore anti-communism, see David M. Oshinsky, *A Conspiracy So Immense: The World of Joe McCarthy* (New York: The Free Press, 1983), and Richard M. Fried, *Nightmare in Red: The McCarthy Era in Perspective* (New York: Oxford University Press, 1990). For a different perspective see Jennifer A. Delton, *Rethinking the 1950s: How Anticommunism and the Cold War Made America Liberal* (New York: Cambridge University Press, 2013).

For overview treatments of twentieth-century liberalism see: Steve Fraser, *The Limousine Liberal: How an Incendiary Image United the Right and Fractured America* (New York: Basic Books, 2016); Michael Kazin, *American Dreamers: How the Left Changed a Nation* (New York: Alfred A. Knopf, 2011); *The Liberal Consensus Reconsidered: American Politics and Society in the Postwar Era*, Robert Mason and Iwan Morgan, eds. (Gainesville: University of Florida Press, 2017); *Making Sense of American Liberalism*, Jonathan Bell and Timothy Stanley, eds. (Urbana: University of Illinois Press, 2012); Douglas C. Rossinow, *Visions of Progress: The Left-Liberal Tradition in America* (Philadelphia: University of Pennsylvania Press, 2008).

Other scholars have focused their study of liberalism on its tortured history in the 1960s. The best accounts are Gareth Davies, *From Opportunity to Entitlement: The Transformation and Decline of Great Society Liberalism* (Lawrence: University Press of Kansas, 1996); Michael W. Flamm, *In the Heat of the Summer: The New York Riots of 1964 and the War on Crime* (Philadelphia: University of Pennsylvania Press, 2017); Michael W. Flamm, *Law and Order: Street Crime, Civil Unrest, and the Crisis of Liberalism in the 1960s* (New York: Columbia University Press, 2005); G. Calvin Mackenzie and Robert Weisbrot, *The Liberal Hour: Washington and the Politics of Change in the 1960s* (New York: Penguin Books, 2008); and Allen J. Matusow, *The Unraveling of America: A History of Liberalism in the 1960s* (New York: Harper Torchbooks, 1984). Two different scholars have explored the intersections of liberalism and labor. See: Nelson Lichtenstein, *State of the Union: A Century of American Labor* (Princeton, N.J.: Princeton University Press, 2002), and Nancy MacLean, *Freedom Is Not Enough: The Opening of the American Workplace* (Cambridge, Mass.: Harvard University Press, 2008). Finally, some scholars of liberalism have looked at its decline and come to different conclusions. See: David T. Courtwright, *No Right Turn: Conservative Politics in a Liberal America* (Cambridge, Mass.: Harvard University

Press, 2010), and Tom Waldman, *Not Much Left: The Fate of Liberalism in America* (Berkeley: University of California Press, 2008).

For some of the best accounts of Democratic Party politics in the 1960s, see: Lewis L. Gould, "Never a Deep Partisan: Lyndon Johnson and the Democratic Party, 1963–1969," in *The Johnson Years, Volume Three: LBJ at Home and Abroad*, by Robert A. Divine, ed., (Lawrence: University Press of Kansas, 1994), 21–52; W. J. Rorabaugh, *The Real Making of the President: Kennedy, Nixon, and the 1960 Election* (Lawrence: University Press of Kansas, 2009); Sean Savage, *JFK, LBJ, and the Democratic Party* (Albany: State University of New York Press, 2004).

Students interested in the intersection between the Sunbelt and politics should start with Sean P. Cunningham, *American Politics in the Postwar Sunbelt: Conservative Growth in a Battleground Region* (New York: Cambridge University Press, 2014). Much of the Sunbelt literature also speaks to the complex topic of modern conservatism. For some of the best such studies, see: Sean P. Cunningham, *Cowboy Conservatism: Texas and the Rise of the Modern Right* (Lexington: University Press of Kentucky, 2010); Darren Dochuk, *From Bible Belt to Sunbelt: Plain-Folk Religion, Grassroots Politics, and the Rise of Evangelical Conservatism* (New York: W. W. Norton, 2011); *Sunbelt Rising: The Politics of Place, Space, and Region*, Michelle Nickerson and Darren Dochuk, eds. (Philadelphia: University of Pennsylvania Press, 2011). See also Matthew D. Lassiter, *The Silent Majority: Suburban Politics in the Sunbelt South* (Princeton, N.J.: Princeton University Press, 2006).

Readers interested in the 1964 race will also want to explore more about southern politics. Dewey W. Grantham, *The Life and Death of the Solid South: A Political History* (Lexington: University Press of Kentucky, 1988), has written a graceful synthesis of the topic. The transformation of the region from a bastion of Democratic strength to one of GOP dominance can be found in the following titles: Kari Frederickson, *The Dixiecrat Revolt and the End of the Solid South, 1932–1968* (Chapel Hill: University of North Carolina Press, 2001), and Joseph E. Lowndes, *From the New Deal to the New Right: Race and the Southern Origins of Modern Conservatism* (New Haven, Conn.: Yale University Press, 2008). Earl Black and Merle Black, *The Rise of Southern Republicans* (Cambridge, Mass.: The Belknap Press of Harvard University, 2002), is the best and most detailed account of the rise of the GOP in the South. For a powerful description of the South as a closed society, see: James W. Silver, *Mississippi: The Closed Society* (1964; repr., Jackson: University Press of Mississippi, 2012).

Other important titles on that topic include David Lublin, *The Republican South: Democratization and Partisan Change* (Princeton, N.J.: Princeton University Press, 2004); Edward H. Miller, *Nut Country: Right-Wing Dallas and the Birth of the Southern Strategy* (Chicago: University of Chicago Press, 2015). Several scholars have explored the response of whites to political and social changes in the region. See: George Lewis, *Massive Resistance: The White Response to the Civil Rights Movement* (London: Hodder Arnold, 2006); Neil R. McMillen, *The Citizens' Council: Organized Resistance to the Second Reconstruction, 1954–64* (Urbana: University of Illinois Press, 1971); and Jason Sokol, *There Goes My Everything: White Southerners in the Age of Civil Rights, 1945–1975* (New York: Vintage Books, 2006). See also *The Changing Politics of the South*, ed. William C. Havard (Baton Rouge: Louisiana State University Press, 1972).

The biographical literature about the major candidates in 1964 is immense. Within Mason and Morgan, eds., *The Liberal Consensus Reconsidered*, noted above, see especially Elizabeth Tandy Shermer, "Sunbelt Patriarchs: Lyndon B. Johnson, Barry Goldwater, and the New Deal Dissensus," for a short, thoughtful essay that provides a comparative biographical sketch of the two 1964 contenders. The essay does not delve deeply into questions of why the Southwest and the Sunbelt should be used as a frame for the election that year.

Most of the biographical scholarship is about Lyndon Johnson. The best one volume biography of LBJ is Randall B. Woods, *LBJ: Architect of American Ambition* (New York: Simon and Schuster, 2006). The most objective treatment of his presidency is Robert Dallek, *Flawed Giant: Lyndon Johnson and His Times, 1961–1973* (New York: Oxford University Press, 1998). More critical assessments are Ronnie Dugger, *The Politician: The Life and Times of Lyndon Johnson, the Drive for Power—from the Frontier to Master of the Senate* (New York: W. W. Norton, 1982); Eric F. Goldman, *The Tragedy of Lyndon Johnson* (New York: Dell Publishing Co., 1968, 1969); and Doris Kearns, *Lyndon Johnson and the American Dream* (New York: Harper & Row, 1976). For Johnson's early life see Robert Dallek, *Lone Star Rising: Lyndon Johnson and His Times, 1908–1960* (New York: Oxford University Press, 1991). See also Godfrey Hodgson, *JFK and LBJ: The Last Two Great Presidents* (New Haven, Conn.: Yale University Press, 2015).

The best biography of Goldwater is Robert Alan Goldberg, *Barry Goldwater* (New Haven, Conn.: Yale University Press, 1995). Sympathetic accounts can be found in William F. Buckley Jr., *Flying High: Remembering Barry Goldwater* (New York: Basic Books, 2010) and Lee Edwards, *Goldwater: The Man Who Made a Revolution* (Washington, DC: Regnery Publishing, 1995). For the latest research on Goldwater see Elizabeth Tandy Shermer, ed., *Barry Goldwater and the Remaking of the American Political Landscape* (Tucson: University of Arizona Press, 2013). For a thoughtful and smart biography of Rockefeller, see Richard Norton Smith, *On His Own Terms: A Life of Nelson Rockefeller* (New York: Random House, 2014). See also Joseph E. Persico, *The Imperial Rockefeller: A Biography of Nelson A. Rockefeller* (New York: Simon and Schuster, 1982). Persico was a speechwriter for Rockefeller, so he brings an insider's perspective to his subject.

Biographies of key figures in midcentury politics who played important parts in the 1964 election include Chris Myers Asch, *The Senator and the Sharecropper: The Freedom Struggles of James O. Eastland and Fannie Lou Hamer* (Chapel Hill: University of North Carolina Press, 2008); Jennifer Burns, *Goddess of the Market: Ayn Rand and the American Right* (New York: Oxford University Press, 2009); Dan T. Carter, *The Politics of Rage: George Wallace, the Origins of the New Conservatism, and the Transformation of American Politics* (New York: Simon and Schuster, 1995); Joseph Crespino, *Strom Thurmond's America* (New York: Hill and Wang, 2012); Sara Fitzgerald, *Elly Peterson: "Mother" of the Moderates* (Ann Arbor: University of Michigan Press, 2011); Lewis L. Gould, *Lady Bird Johnson: Our Environmental First Lady* (Lawrence: University Press of Kansas, 1999); Byron C. Hulsey, *Everett Dirksen and His Presidents: How a Senate Giant Shaped American Politics* (Lawrence: University Press of Kansas, 2000); Steven P. Miller, *Billy Graham and the Rise of the Republican*

South (Philadelphia: University of Pennsylvania Press, 2004); Arnold Rampersad, *Jackie Robinson: A Biography* (New York: Ballantine Books, 1997); James Reston Jr., *The Lone Star: The Life of John Connally* (New York: Harper & Row, 1989); Kevin J. Smant, *Principles and Heresies: Frank S. Meyer and the Shaping of the American Conservative Movement* (Wilmington, Del.: ISI Books, 2002).

Biographies of Dwight D. Eisenhower and John F. Kennedy include Steven E. Ambrose, *Eisenhower: The President*, vol. 2 (New York: Simon and Schuster, 1984); Robert Dallek, *An Unfinished Life: John F. Kennedy, 1917–1963* (New York: Back Bay Books, 2003); Henry Fairlie, *The Kennedy Promise: The Politics of Expectation* (Garden City, N.Y.: Doubleday, 1973); James N. Giglio, *The Presidency of John F. Kennedy* (Lawrence: University Press of Kansas, 1991); Richard Reeves, *President Kennedy: Profile of Power* (New York: Simon & Schuster, 1993); Thomas C. Reeves, *A Question of Character: A Life of John F. Kennedy* (New York: The Free Press, 1991); Arthur M. Schlesinger Jr., *A Thousand Days: John F. Kennedy in the White House* (Boston: Houghton Mifflin, 1965); and Theodore C. Sorensen, *Kennedy* (New York: Harper & Row, 1965).

Other biographies helpful to understanding this topic include: D. B. Hardeman and Donald C. Bacon, *Rayburn: A Biography* (Austin: Texas Monthly Press, 1987); Robert G. Kaufman, *Henry M. Jackson: A Life in Politics* (Seattle: University of Washington Press, 2000); James J. Kenneally, *A Compassionate Conservative: A Political Biography of Joseph W. Martin Jr., Speaker of the U.S. House of Representatives* (Lanham, Md.: Lexington Books, 2003); Gayle B. Montgomery and James W. Johnson, *One Step from the White House: The Rise and Fall of Senator William F. Knowland* (Berkeley: University of California Press, 1998); James T. Patterson, *Mr. Republican: A Biography of Robert A. Taft* (Boston: Houghton Mifflin, 1972); Kevin M. Schultz, *Buckley and Mailer: The Difficult Friendship That Shaped the Sixties* (New York: W. W. Norton, 2015).

More histories of postwar society include Steve Fraser, *The Age of Acquiescence: The Life and Death of American Resistance to Organized Wealth and Power* (New York: Little, Brown, 2015); Joshua B. Freeman, *American Empire: The Rise of a Global Power, the Democratic Revolution at Home, 1945–2000* (New York: Penguin Books, 2012); William C. Berman, *America's Right Turn: From Nixon to Clinton*, 2nd. ed. (Baltimore, Md.: Johns Hopkins University Press, 1998); Romain D. Huret, *American Tax Resisters* (Cambridge, Mass.: Harvard University Press, 2014); James T. Patterson, *The Eve of Destruction: How 1965 Transformed America* (New York: Basic Books, 2012). For more on what the Johnson administration was doing in Vietnam before the election, see Mitchell Lerner, "Vietnam and the 1964 Election: A Defense of Lyndon Johnson," *Presidential Studies Quarterly* 25 (Fall 1995): 751–766; Larry Berman, *Planning A Tragedy: The Americanization of the War in Vietnam* (New York: W.W. Norton, 1982); Philip Jenkins, *Decade of Nightmares: The End of the Sixties and the Making of Eighties America* (New York: Oxford University Press, 2006).

INDEX

Numbers in italics represent pages with illustrations.

conservative-moderate split in the
Republican Party and, 56, 66, 99,
103
conservative Republicans and, 9, 61
Goldwater, his campaign, and, 5, 9,
60, 61, 82, 93, 95, 96, 160–161,
169, 178, 184–185, 189, 190
JFK and, 30, 38, 39–40
JFK's reelection campaign and, 42–43,
44, 62
Lady Bird Johnson and the 1964
campaign, 186
LBJ and the 1964 campaign, 122–123,
187
LBJ as vice president and, 40–41, 44
LBJ's pursuit of as president, 3, 10–11,
110–114, 119–121
legacy of the 1964 election and
Goldwater's southern strategy,
202–205
Mississippi Freedom Democratic Party
controversy, 129–136
protests at the Republican National
Convention, 97, 98
Republican Party uncertainty about,
60
Rockefeller and, 58–59, 66
southern Democrats and, 113–114, 117,
118, 119–120
Civil Rights Act (1964)
ethnic voters and, 155
Goldwater and, 96, 123, 160, 184, 189
impact on the Democratic Party, 3
impact on voting in the 1964 election,
203–204, 205
Lady Bird Johnson, views of, 186
LBJ and preservation of, 135
LBJ and the passage of, 10, 119–122
LBJ attacks Goldwater for opposing,
185
LBJ on in the 1964 New Orleans
speech, 187
Republican views on, 9, 120–121
used to compare LBJ to Hitler, 178
Wallace and, 117
Claremont Eagle, 73
Clay, Lucius, 21

Clifford, Clark, 125, 126–127, 152, 163, 164
Clinton, Hillary Rodham, 185
Coleman, J. D. Stetson, 61
collectivism versus individualism, 9, 105,
204
Committee to Support Moderate
Republicans, 195
Congress
Civil Rights Act of 1964 in, 110,
112–113, 114, 119–121
down-ballot races in 1964, 11, 82, 99,
135, 164, 194–196, 197, 205
Eisenhower's relations with, 14, 16–21,
22, 25–26
JFK's relations with, 10, 29, 30, 31, 32,
37–38, 39, 40, 42, 43
LBJ's relations with during the
presidency, 111–112, 114, 119–121,
161
productivity of the Eighty-Ninth
Congress, 205–206
Congress of Racial Equality (CORE), 97,
113, 129, 133, 154
Connally, John, 44–45, 113, 135, 138, 158
Conscience of a Conservative, The
(Goldwater), 7, 26, 52, 65, 71
consensus liberalism
and civil rights, 120
contrasted with Sunbelt conservatism,
141
LBJ's 1964 campaign speech in New
Orleans, 187–189
LBJ's ending of the South and
beginning of the Sunbelt, 119
LBJ's frontlash strategy in the 1964
campaign and, 3–5
LBJ's pursuit of as president, 110, 112,
116
legacy of the 1964 election and, 200,
204–205, 207
conservative coalition, 31, 37, 38
conservatives/conservatism
civil rights and, 9, 61
Goldwater and Sunbelt conservatism,
2, 5, 81, 86
Goldwater and the Far Right, 56, 66,
67, 68

foreign policy issues, the 1964 campaign and, 6, 60, 73, 99, 108, 164–166, 202

Fortas, Abe, 152, 163

Fort Worth, 44, 45, 46

Friedman, Milton, 70

frontlash
  effects on the 1964 campaign, 142–143
  extremisms and, 142–143
  LBJ's 1964 campaign and, 3–5, 147–149, 153–157, 159, 161, 169, 171, 174, 195
  LBJ's view of, 147
  legacy of the 1964 election for LBJ and Democrats, 204–205, 207

fundraising, 44, 58, 145–146, 149–151, 194, 205

Gainey, Dan, 151

Galbraith, John Kenneth, 114, 126

Gallagher, Wes, 151

Gallup Poll, 13, 94, 163

Garbo, Greta, 86

Gem Motel, 133

gender, 100–101, 185–187

General Electric, 150

Germond, Jack W., 201–202

Gimbels, 150

Goldenson, Leonard, 151

Goldman, Eric, 138, 146, 158

Goldwater, Barry M.
  anti-politician persona, 52, 54
  Civil Rights Act of 1964 and, 96, 123, 160, 184, 189
  The Conscience of a Conservative, 7, 26, 52, 65, 71
  early political career, 52
  Eisenhower and, 18
  on Eisenhower's modern Republicanism, 25, 52
  family background and the myth of rugged individualism, 51–52
  on the JFK-LBJ ticket in 1960, 35
  JFK's views of, 43
  life and views in the early 1950s, 18–19
  midterm elections of 1958 and, 51

presidential election of 1960 and, 5, 26, 27–28

Goldwater, Barry M., in 1964 campaign/ election
  active campaigning, 159
  backlash and, 102, 122, 142–143, 147, 153, 154, 156, 166, 167, 169, 180
  book publications and, 172–173
  California primary, 72, 80, 82–83, 85–87, 88–89, 90–91, 92
  campaign organization, 158–159
  civil rights, campaign, and, 5, 9, 60, 61, 82, 93, 95, 96, 160–161, 169, 178, 184–185, 189, 190
  competing views of the Sunbelt and, 7–8
  congressional races and, 194
  conservative advisors and supporters, 7, 66–69, 70–71
  conservative-moderate split in the Republicans and, 51, 53, 54, 56, 62–63, 66, 80, 99, 103
  crime as an issue in, 60, 122, 185
  delegate strategy, 80–82, 93
  Democratic views of as unfit to be president, 166–167
  Eisenhower and, 107, 178
  election results, 196–197, 216–220
  foreign policy issues and, 6, 73, 99, 108, 164–166, 202
  formal entry into, 69–70
  fundraising and, 58, 150–151, 194
  George Wallace and, 82, 98–99, 179
  Goldwater manifesto, 52, 54
  grassroots draft movement, 7, 55–58, 63, 64–65, 67, 69, 70
  Hershey meeting and, 157–158, 159, 160, 161
  impact of the Kennedy assassination on, 68–69
  indecision about entry into, 54–55, 59, 63–65, 69
  instinctual style of political operation, 54
  interviewed by Walter Cronkite in 1963, 67–68
  issue of extremism and, 159–160

New York riots, 122

New York Times, 4, 5, 40, 44, 52, 58, 65, 127, 140, 149, 172, 199

Niemeyer, Gerhart, 70

Nixon, Richard
Billy Graham and, 191
conservative-moderate split in the Republicans and, 54, 56
as Eisenhower's 1956 vice-presidential running mate, 23
failed gubernatorial bid in 1962, 29, 62
Goldwater and, 52, 60, 93–94
on Goldwater's Republican acceptance speech, 106–107
Hershey meeting of August 1964 and, 157, 161
on ideology and the political parties in the 1950s, 14
New Hampshire primary of 1964 and, 77
Oregon primary of 1964 and, 82, 83, 84, 85
presidential campaign of 1964 and, 10, 42, 59, 72, 76
presidential election of 1960 and, 26–27, 28, 29, 32, 35, 36, 51, 150
Republican National Convention of 1964 and, 105

None Dare Call It Treason (Stormer), 71, 172, 173

nonvoters, 154

North American Aviation, 144

North Atlantic Treaty Organization (NATO), 73, 98, 165

Novak, Robert
on Goldwater identity in 1964, 8
on Lawrence O'Brien and LBJ's 1964 campaign, 169
on LBJ and the Great Society slogan, 116
on LBJ's "Anti-Campaign," 163
on LBJ's Great Society consensus message, 207
on LBJ's mastery of Congress in 1964, 194

nuclear weapons
depicted in popular culture, 180–181
Goldwater's statements on, 10, 73, 164–166
television advertising during the 1964 campaign and, 174–177

O'Brien, Lawrence
on book publications during the 1964 campaign, 173
on "Daisy Ad," 176
Democratic congressional races in 1964 and, 195
on Eighty-Ninth Congress, 205
in LBJ's 1964 campaign, 147, 163, 169, 182
on LBJ's choice of running mate in 1964, 126
LBJ's concerns about loyalty, 137
on LBJ's relations with RFK, 139–140

O'Donnell, Kenneth, 124, 133, 137, 163

O'Donnell, Peter, 60–61, 70, 74, 81

Ohio, 102, 104, 122, 179, 181

Old Guard Republicans, 7, 15, 16, 18, 20, 21, 23, 25, 29, 93

Olin Foundation, 202

Opinion Research, 104

Oregon Republican primary, 10, 63, 77, 78, 82, 83–85, 87, 90, 93

Oswald, Lee Harvey, 46, 69

Other America, The (Harrington), 42

Paley, William S., 151

Pell, Claiborne, 125

Percy, Charles H., 195

Peter, Paul, and Mary, 139

Peterson, Elly, 64

Petticoat Junction (television program), 178

Peyton Place (television program), 178

Point of Order, 74

politics of race
conservative-moderate split in the Republicans and, 56, 66
Goldwater's 1964 campaign and, 9, 108, 160–161, 182–185, 189

Eisenhower's concerns about Nixon
and, 23
Goldwater and, 5, 26, 27–28
impact on the 1964 presidential
election, 29, 42–43
impact on the political parties, 36–37
JFK and, 32–34, 35–37
LBJ and, 32–35
party identification and, 13–14
President's Club, 149
press
coverage of LBJ during the 1964
campaign, 144–145, 152–153
endorsements of Goldwater in the
1964 campaign, 152
endorsements of LBJ in the 1964
campaign, 146, 149, 151–152
on Goldwater's 1964 campaign
organization, 158
John Chancellor's arrest at the
Republican National Convention,
103
LBJ's rejection of RFK as a running
mate and, 127
LBJ's use of in the 1964 campaign,
177
responses to Goldwater's nomination
at the Republican National
Convention, 107–108
See also news media
Price, Robert, 84
Protestants, 190

race riots
fears that rioting would disrupt the
Democratic National Convention,
129, 136
George Wallace and the 1964 riot in
Maryland, 119
LBJ on the Birmingham riots, 41
New York riot and the LBJ-Goldwater
joint response to, 122–123
in Philadelphia, 185
racism
backlash and the 1964 campaign, 156
(see also backlash)
Goldwater's southern strategy and

campaigning in the South, 9, 56,
60–61, 68, 160, 179–180, 182–185
Goldwater's takeover of the
Republican National Committee
and, 64
legacy of the 1964 election and
Goldwater's southern strategy,
202–205
Mississippi Freedom Democratic Party
seating controversy, 129–130, 131
Republican National Convention of
1964 and, 101
See also politics of race
Rand, Ayn, 70–71, 201
Randolph, A. Philip, 97
Random House, 172
Rauh, Joseph, 119, 130, 131, 133, 135
Rayburn, Sam, 19, 21, 31, 32, 34, 139, 188
Ready, Jack, 46
Reagan, Ronald, 5–6, 87, 150, 190,
192–194
Reedy, George
advice to LBJ about the press, 152
Bobby Baker scandal and, 144
"Daisy Ad" and, 176
on "Five O'clock Club," 163
LBJ's belief that there was press
"bigotry" against southerners, 3
LBJ's campaign strategy, 168
LBJ's indecision about entering the
1964 race and, 137
on LBJ's resentment toward the
Democratic National Committee,
206, 207
on LBJ's response to the 1964 election
results, 204
Rehnquist, William, 189
religion, 1964 presidential campaign and,
189–191, 198
Republican Businessmen for Johnson,
149
Republican National Committee, 22, 26,
55, 64, 82, 105, 173
Republican National Convention (1956),
23
Republican National Convention (1960),
27–28

results by state, 209–212
Texas, 81
Republican Senate Campaign Committee, 52, 55
Republican state conventions, 81
Reuther, Walter, 133, 135, 150, 194
Rhodes, Jim, 102
Richard and Helen DeVos Foundation, 202
Ripon Society, 203
Roberts, Juanita, 130
Robinson, Jackie, 66, 92–93, 97, 101
Roche, Charles, 42–43
Rockefeller, Margaretta Murphy "Happy," 62–63, 81, 83, 90–92, 113
Rockefeller, Nelson A.
   attacks on Goldwater, 66, 75
   California primary and, 85, 86, 87–88, 89–92
   civil rights and, 58–59, 66
   conservative-moderate split in the Republicans and, 51, 53, 54, 56, 62–63, 66, 103
   endorsement of Scranton, 96–97
   entry into the 1964 campaign, 58–59
   familiarity with Democrats, 59
   on Goldwater's Republican acceptance speech, 106
   Goldwater's response to the 1964 election results and, 197–198
   gubernatorial election of 1962 and, 62
   Happy Rockefeller and, 62–63, 81, 83, 90–92, 113
   Hershey meeting of August 1964 and, 157, 158
   Jackie Robinson and, 66, 92–93
   midterm elections of 1958 and, 51
   New Hampshire primary and, 73, 75, 76, 77
   New Jersey primary and, 81
   Oregon primary and, 78, 82, 83–85
   outreach to Goldwater, 60
   political evolution of, 58–59
   presidential election of 1960 and, 26, 27
   refusal to back Goldwater in the 1964 campaign, 148

Republican National Convention of 1964 and, 99, 100, 103
   Texas primary and, 81
   views of Goldwater's southern strategy, 61
Rockefeller, Winthrop, 179
Romney, George
   gubernatorial election of 1962 and, 62
   gubernatorial election of 1964 and, 195
   Hershey meeting of August 1964 and, 157
   as a moderate Republican, 54
   potential matchup against JFK in 1964, 42
   refusal to back Goldwater in the 1964 campaign, 148
   Republican National Convention of 1964 and, 100, 103
   Republican opposition to Goldwater and, 95
Roosevelt, Eleanor, 59, 139, 186
Roosevelt, Franklin, Jr., 180
Roosevelt, Franklin Delano, 4, 7, 11, 12, 13, 15, 35, 49, 79, 141, 148, 165, 188, 194, 196
Roosevelt, Theodore, 92
Rovere, Richard, 8, 182–184
Rowe, James, Jr., 127, 163
Rusher, William, 5, 50–51, 63, 86
Russell, Richard, 138

San Antonio, 44, 45
Sanders, Carl, 134, 135
San Francisco Giants, 150
Saturday Evening Post, 66, 152
Scammon, Richard M., 42, 155
Schlafly, Phyllis, 7, 50, 71, 72, 90, 172
Schlesinger, Arthur M., Jr., 48, 112, 116–117, 126, 141, 159, 199
Scott, Hugh, 95, 99, 104, 195
Scranton, William
   entry into the 1964 campaign, 65–66, 72, 88, 113
   Goldwater blames defeat in 1964 on, 197–198
   gubernatorial election of 1962 and, 62

politics of race and the 1964
campaign, 9
source of the backlash and the
frontlash, 142
See also South
Synon, John, 82

Taber, John, 16
Taft, Charles P., 195
Taft, Robert, Jr., 195
Taft, Robert A., 2, 16, 17, 64, 72, 92, 102,
195
Taft, William Howard, 35
Taft Republicans. *See* Old Guard
Republicans
Tampa, 44
taxation, 51, 56, 65, 66, 67, 73, 114, 116,
120, 146, 147, 169, 192–193, 194
tax resistance, 193
Tea Party, 203
television advertising, 84, 86, 87, 143,
165, 173–178, 190
television news
controversy over the reporting of the
1964 election results, 196
coverage of Goldwater and the 1964
campaign, 90, 102
coverage of LBJ and the 1964
campaign, 152–153
Democratic National Convention and,
130, 135, 136
Face the Nation (television news show),
152
Issues and Answers (television news
show), 166
Lady Bird Special and, 186
Meet the Press (television news show),
73, 95, 114, 152, 154
Rockefeller and, 103
Scranton and, 94
Texan Looks at Lyndon, A (Haley), 172, 173
Texas
attitudes toward Robert F. Kennedy in,
124–125
congressional races in 1964, 195, 201
Goldwater campaign in, 97, 108, 178,
195

JFK's reelection campaign and
assassination, 43–46
LBJ's concerns about losing, 134–135,
137
minority voter registration in, 43
political party identification in, 15, 16,
34, 91, 114–115
Republican 1964 primary, 81
Thomas, Albert, 47
Thornberry, Homer, 47
"Through a Looking Glass Darkly"
(political pamphlet), 166
Thurmond, Strom, 182, 203
Time, 54, 144–145
"Time for Choosing, A" (Reagan speech),
150, 194
Tower, John, 61
TRB. *See* Strout, Richard L.
Truman, Harry S., 4, 17, 141, 180, 184,
188
Tucker, Mr. and Mrs. Robert, 131
Tunure, Pamela, 47

Udall, Stewart, 148, 180
United Auto Workers (UAW), 125, 160
United Press International, 196
Urban League, 68

Valenti, Jack
JFK's assassination and, 45, 47, 48
on LBJ as a legislator, 114
LBJ's 1964 campaign strategy and,
162, 163–164
on LBJ's relations with JFK, 41
news media coverage of the 1964
campaign and, 152
press endorsements of LBJ in the
1964 campaign and, 151–152
reports reactions to LBJ's New Orleans
speech, 188
on RFK being considered for the vice
presidency, 124
selection of a vice-presidential
running mate and GOP support
for LBJ, 146
Valtman, Edmund S., 53
Vanderbilt, Cornelius, 166–167

Van Dyk, Ted, 125, 126, 128
Veterans of Foreign Wars (VFW), 172
Vietnam War, 148, 164, 165–166,
    206
Viguerie, Richard, 150, 194, 202
Virginia, 11, 16, 42, 82, 186, 203
Voting Rights Act (1965), 9, 204,
    206

Waldorf-Astoria, 150
Wallace, George C., 82, 98–99, 110,
    117–119, 179
Wall Street Journal, 52, 190
Walt Disney, 150
Warren, Earl, 21, 67
Washington Post, 127, 198
Washington Star, 189, 191
Wayne, John, 87, 178, 190
Welch, Robert, 66, 71
Welsh, Matthew E., 118, 154
West Virginia, 43, 154
Where I Stand (Goldwater), 172
White, F. Clifton
    John Chancellor's arrest at the
        Republican National Convention
        and, 103
    draft Goldwater movement and,
        57–58, 64, 69
    Goldwater conservatism and, 7
    Goldwater's California primary and,
        86, 88
    in Goldwater's campaign organization,
        158
    Goldwater's nomination at the
        Republican National Convention
        and, 64, 93, 104
White, Theodore H.
    on 1964 campaign and Goldwater's
        foreign policy statements, 165
    on Camelot as nickname for the
        Kennedy presidency, 139
    on differences in personality between
        LBJ and Goldwater, 7–8
    on heartland Republicans as
        "primitives," 51
    on LBJ's 1964 campaign organization,
        162
    on LBJ's campaign personae, 8
    on LBJ's Democratic acceptance
        speech, 140–141
    on LBJ's failure to build the
        Democratic Party following the
        1964 election, 207
    on LBJ's southern style of
        speechmaking, 188–189
    on maximizing visibility on television
        news, 153
    on personal attacks against LBJ
        during the 1964 campaign, 143,
        144
    on Rockefeller, 74
    on similarities between LBJ and
        Humphrey, 125
White Citizens' Council, 82
white ethnic voters, 117, *153*, 154–155,
    156–157
white resentment. *See* politics of
    resentment
white supremacy
    1964 election and Goldwater's
        southern strategy, 95, 203
    Goldwater's 1964 campaign in the
        South and, 183–185
Wicker, Tom, 5, 40, 44, 46, 47–48
Wilkins, Roger, 184
Wilkins, Roy, 160
Willkie, Wendell, 51
Wilson, Woodrow, 35, 151, 165
Wirtz, Willard, 140–141, 162
Wisconsin, 102, 182
Wisconsin Democratic primary, 117
women
    Democratic National Convention,
        138–139, 140
    Democratic women and the Lady Bird
        Special, 11, 185–187
    Goldwater campaign, 57, 86, 108, 177,
        184, 185
    Goldwater supporters, 92, 185
Women's Federation, 64

YAF, 10, 57, 64, 67, 150
Yai Bi Ken (Goldwater campaign plane),
    159